Wines and Spirits

A COMPLETE BUYING GUIDE

Books by William E. Massee

WINES AND SPIRITS
A Complete Buying Guide

WINE HANDBOOK

WINES OF FRANCE
(*in collaboration with Alexis Lichine*)

THE ART OF COMFORT

A COMPLETE BUYING GUIDE

BY WILLIAM E. MASSEE

DRAWINGS BY DOROTHY IVENS

McGRAW-HILL BOOK COMPANY, INC. NEW YORK TORONTO LONDON

For Dorothy

ᴖᘓ ᘜᴖ

Acknowledgments

More than five thousand people have helped in the writing of this book over the past decade, with information, advice, or encouragement, not to say criticism. The aim has been to present the essence of this material and the good will of the people who supplied it. The best help, of course, came from the pulling of many corks, and the conversations that followed. Let a September afternoon in Arthur Devletian's office at the Institut National des Appellations d'Origine on the Champs Élysées stand for all the rest, and may the health we drank to the makers of good wine be for all those who work to supply the world with fine bottles of all kinds. A representative few are listed here.

S. & J. Aaron, of New York
Dr. M. Amerine, of California
J. Bavard, of Puligny-Montrachet
F. Bartholomew, of New York
James Beard, of New York
Baron LeRoy de Boiseaumarié,
  of Châteauneuf-du-Pape
R. Cobb, of Oporto
Marc Brédif, of Vouvray
F. Burka, of Washington
Dr. Bürklin-Wolf, of Wachenheim
J. Daniel, of Napa
Kenneth Dean, of New York
A. Devletian, of Paris
J. & B. Domecq, of Jerez
M. Dreyfus, of New York
J. Drouhin, of Beaune
Abbé Dubaquié, of Bordeaux
René Engel, of Vosne-Romanée
C. Forman, of Philadelphia
C. Fournier, of Hammondsport

Henri Gouges,
  of Nuits-Saint-Georges
O. Goulet, of Santa Clara
Louis Gros, of Vosne-Romanée
R. Haas, of New York
François Hine, of Jarnac
M. Jaboulet-Vercherre,
  of Hermitage
Sybil Jacobsen, of New York
A. Lichine, of New York
L. Martini, of Napa
May Massee, of New York
Fürst P. von Metternich,
  of Johannisberg
A. Millman, of Washington
J. Monnot, of Puligny-Montrachet
Duc de Montesquiou-Fezensac,
  of Auch
R. and P. Mondavi
G. Moreau, of Chablis
M. Pestel, of Paris
C. Ramonet,
  of Chassagne-Montrachet

ACKNOWLEDGMENTS

T. & P. Sandeman, of London

F. Schoonmaker, of New York

M. Servin, of Chablis

A. Tchelistcheff, of Napa

P. Wagner, of Baltimore

S. Weller, of Bordeaux

H. & W. Wente, of Livermore

F. Wildman, of New York

G. Taylor, of Hammondsport

Vintages

Vintages get more concern than they warrant, perhaps because it's easy to remember a few years and hard to remember a lot of vineyards. One needs to know the year a wine was made just to be sure that the wine is of the right age for drinking—not too old in the case of white table wines and fruity reds like Beaujolais, for instance, and not too young for the great Burgundy and Bordeaux reds. A chart of the drinking span for various wines and vintages can be useful, but even that can be too general.

As a rule of thumb, great red wines from Bordeaux, Burgundy, and the Rhône need at least six years to become drinkable in good years, but don't reach their primes until eight or ten. Great white wines from the above regions and from the Rhine are ready to drink three years after the vintage, generally past their primes at eight, although the sweet whites can last longer.

As a second rule of thumb, First Growths are generally ready to drink before the greatest vineyards, say four years for the reds, and two for the whites, in a good year.

A good year is generally considered to be one in which the great vineyards produce great wines and good vineyards produce good wines. This occurs three or four times a decade.

A great year is considered to be when great vineyards produce outstanding wines, many good vineyards produce almost-great wines, and ordinary vineyards produce wines that are better than usual. Great years occur two or three times a decade.

But this isn't as straightforward as it sounds, because wines of a great vintage tend to be high in alcohol, which can throw a wine out of balance unless great skill and some luck is involved in its making. What's more, winemakers often use the word "great" to indicate large quantities, or a year when many vineyards produced exceptional wines, not just a handful. What's more, weather varies so in the great districts, that some vineyards may produce outstanding wines, while other equally good vineyards will produce ordinary wines.

If one had another thumb, it might be sensible to say that the wise buyer gets good and ordinary wines when the vintage is called great, and buys wine from the great vineyards in years rated as good or normal. Normal is a euphemism for ordinary.

The most sensible approach to the matter of vintages is to ignore
them, buying the best vineyards you can afford of the most recent
vintages on the market, and laying them down until they are ready for
drinking. Most good shops will store wines for no charge, or very little.
There's not much point in listing vintages much older than the previous
decade, because they are not available on the market, or are outrageously
expensive. As a matter of history, some past great vintages have been
1928 and '29, 1934 and '37, 1945, '47, and '49. All the dry whites from
these years are gone by now, and most of the sweet whites, as well. All
the pink wines are gone, all the lesser reds, and all but the greatest
Burgundies, the classed growths of Bordeaux, and the Rhône reds from
Côte Rôtie and Hermitage.

Vintages are often rated on a scale of 20, region by region, but it
should be borne in mind that exceptionally fine wines are often produced in poor years, and the other way around, so that a particular
rating for any vintage must be considered an average.

20,19	Many very great wines, many great wines
18,17	Many great wines, some very great
16,15	Some great wines, many very good
14,13	Many good wines, some very good
12,11	Good wines, some very fair
10,9	Many fair wines, some poor
8,7	Some fair wines, many poor
6,5	Poor wines

Below five, vintners wring their hands; they are pretty miserable if the
score is below 12, because the fair wines are sold in bulk, for blending,
and only wines rated as good are worth bottling with district or township names on the label.

A vintage rated as twenty usually means that even good vineyards
produce outstanding wines, while one rated at nineteen would indicate
that the very great wines might not be quite so numerous, and that good
vineyards produced exceptional wines, but these might possess some
tendency to be quick-maturing, or hard, or slightly out of balance in
some way. Or the differentiation might simply indicate that there were
not as many very great wines as one would hope for in such a great year.

Another big point is that many wines of a good year may develop
into greatness as they mature. Ratings are set soon after the vintage,
and are usually optimistic, but when the vintage is hard and slow to
mature, or the quantity is small, ratings are apt to be low. In any case,
the popular tendency is to focus attention on the great vintages, so that

a wise buyer can drink gloriously of vintages rated between twelve and sixteen, getting fine wines at low prices that are quickly ready to drink.

To avoid complications, it is practical to ignore vintages entirely. The following breakdown serves best to illustrate how wines can vary in the great wine regions, and is not an absolute guide to fine bottles, by any means.

BORDEAUX REDS

1952   Many great wines, particularly in St. Emilion and Pomerol, slow to mature and beautifully balanced. The good wines are ready to drink, but the great wines will not be ready much before 1962. 17/20

1953   Many very great wines, particularly in the Médoc, but soft and quick-to-mature, so that many are past their prime by now. At their fruity, round, and balanced best, they were rated 19/20, but only the greatest will live beyond 1962.

1954   Some good but thin wines in Graves, rated after the vintage at 10/20 or so, but now past their primes.

1955   Some very great wines and many great ones, particularly in the Médoc. Quick-to-mature and very well-balanced, all but the best are beginning to fade. Lack the elegance of the '53s. 17/20

1956   A disastrous frost ruined many vines, but some fair, hard wines were produced. 11/20

1957   A very good vintage, but very small in quantity, the wines are exceedingly slow to mature, and while good wines are now ready to drink, the few exceptional bottles from the great châteaux may not round out until 1965 or later. 16/20

1958   Light wines, fast-maturing, the small quantity is now ready to drink. 12/20

1959   The year of the century, particularly in Graves and the Médoc, the wines are exceptionally full, rich, and distinguished. High in alcohol, these wines were difficult to handle, and there were some misfortunes. St. Emilions and Pomerols suffered somewhat from volatile acidity. Most of the wines from good châteaux will not be ready to drink until 1964, the very great wines not for another two or three years. 19/20

1960   Many very good wines in Médoc and Graves, but heavy summer rains accounted for irregular quality, particularly in St. Emilion and Pomerol. The wines have a tendency to be light, but those who picked promptly and vintaged rapidly often made full, soft

wines. The lightest wines will begin to be ready for drinking in
1964. 16/20

BORDEAUX WHITES

1952   Sauternes and Barsac produced some great wines, rich and high
in alcohol but not fruity. 15/20 The Graves whites are past their
primes.

1953   Many great, full, and distinctive wines in Sauternes, some good
Barsacs, that will continue to be drinkable until 1963 or so. 17/20
Graves whites are past their primes.

1955   Many good wines, but Sauternes and Barsacs were not particularly rich or sweet, and the Graves, now past their primes, were
hard. 15/20

1957   A very small yield, but some fine Sauternes and Barsacs, now
fading. Graves are past their primes. 12/20

1958   Some fair whites, dry and light in Graves, not rich in Sauternes
and Barsac, now ready to drink, but fading quickly. 13/20

1959   A fabulous year. Rich, full, beautifully balanced Sauternes and
Barsac, now just becoming ready to drink. The Graves are full
and fruity, and also ready. 20/20

1960   Some excellent, light wines. 15/20

BURGUNDY CÔTE D'OR REDS

1952   Many great, beautifully balanced wines that were slow to mature,
and are long-lived. 16/20

1953   Many very great wines, fruity and with great finesse, but quick
to mature. Even the greatest ones are apt to be past their primes
by the end of 1962. 19/20

1955   Many great wines, but quick to mature. Like the '53s, many of
the greatest will be past their primes by 1964. The Côte de
Beaune suffered from hail, cutting quantity. 17/20

1957   Many big, full wines, some great, but short-lived, so that even
the sturdiest wines are now ready to drink. High in price because
of the small vintages of fine wines in previous years. 17/20

1958   A poor year. 11/20

1959   A fabulous year. Big, full, beautifully balanced wines, when well-
made, with great elegance and slowly developing bouquet. The
good wines are becoming ready to drink, but the great wines will
not mature until 1964. 20/20

1960 Many good wines, but light and quick to mature, so that many of them will be drinkable by 1963. 14/20

BURGUNDY WHITES

1952 Fantastically great whites, now almost all drunk up, and past their primes. 20/20 originally.

1953 Great wines, but soft, and now gone. 17/20 originally.

1955 Another great year, the Cortons, Meursaults, and Montrachets are full and fruity, and are just now passing their primes, and should be drunk up before 1963. 17/20

1957 A small vintage of very good wines that should be drunk up before 1963. Practically no Chablis was made because of a May frost. 16/20

1958 Some good but light whites were made, particularly those of Southern Burgundy. Good buys if low in price, they should be drunk promptly. 11/20

1959 Many very great wines, full and fruity, but the high alcohol made vinification difficult, and some producers made poor wines. The Pouilly-Fuissés and Macons were ready to drink in 1961, and the Cortons, Meursaults and Montrachets will come into their primes beginning in 1962. 19/20

1960 The whites are much better than the reds, some very good light wines having been produced, ready for drinking in the spring of 1962. 14/20

SOUTHERN BURGUNDY

The Southern Burgundies, including the red Beaujolais, Maconnais and Chalonnais vintages, as well as the whites of Pouilly-Fuissé and Macon, taste best when drunk young, as soon as they are bottled, or within two or three years of the vintage. The whites sometimes last for five years, but are better younger.

1959 Some good wines were made, now mostly past their primes.

1960 Enormous quantities of exceptionally light wines.

RHÔNE

1952 Reds are still very great, full, rich wines. 18/20

1954 Some excellent reds and whites, now rare. 15/20

1955 Very great wines, full sturdy reds and whites now at their peaks. The rosés are gone. 18/20

1957   Very fine wines, small quantity, now rare. 17/20

1958   Many very good reds and whites, full and fruity, but the rosés are past their primes. 15/20

1959   The grapes suffered from too much summer heat. 8/20

1960   Very fruity rosés now coming on the market. 17/20 As for the reds and whites, full and well-balanced, with a good bouquet, and perhaps equal to 1952. The whites will be ready to drink by 1963, perhaps the excellent Châteauneuf-du-Pape will be ready the following year. 17/20

LOIRE

Both the whites and reds mature quickly, and are past their primes after three or four years, although the sweet wines of Vouvray and Saumur often live for seven or eight years, and longer.

1958   Small quantities but some good, dry wines. 12/20

1959   Absolutely fabulous wines all along the Loire, despite early reports of poor vintages in Muscadet. These wines will continue to be magnificent through 1962, and offer a superb chance to taste a variety of wines that rarely rise to such peaks of excellence altogether. 20/20

1960   An enormous quantity of wine of generally excellent quality, very good in Sancerre, Pouilly-Fumé, and the nearby districts, with exceptional quality for the reds and rosés of the central districts, some good whites from Vouvray, Anjou and Saumur, and excellent whites in quantity from Muscadet. 16/20

ALSACE

1959   A very great vintage, the best in recent memory, producing full, well-balanced wines. They are at their peaks now. 20/20

1960   Some April frosts limited the quantity in Bas-Rhin, although a substantial vintage of light, flowery wines was made. Now ready. 16/20

CHAMPAGNE

1952   A very great year, wines of superlative balance and breed, likely to remain at their peaks until 1965. 19/20

1953   A great year, wines being extremely full and fast to develop, probably past prime by 1965. 17/20

1955 Very great wines, fruity and full-bodied, with a fine balance of properties that will keep them at their peaks past 1967. 18/20

1956 Disastrously small yield of poor wines. 7/20

1957 Some fine wines, but a disastrous freeze cut production. Light, acid, and quick-maturing, the wines were used mostly for blends. 12/20

1958 Another poor year, not much better than 1957. Small production. 12/20

1959 The year of the century, full, fruity, superbly balanced wines of great breed that will last through the decade. 20/20

1960 A vintage above normal in quantity, producing wines light in alcohol and body, with some delicacy, much of which will be used in non-vintage blends, balancing the much fuller 1959s to produce *cuvées* of excellent quality. 14/20

RHINE & MOSELLE

1953 A few Spätlesen and Auslesen of this great vintage will stay at their peaks until 1965. 18/20

1954 Practically no wines were made.

1955 Some fine light and flowery Moselles, now past their primes. 14/20

1956 A very poor year. 6/20

1957 A small vintage that produced some good flowery Rheingaus and a few Moselles. 12/20

1958 Some good wines from all the districts, generally light and short-lived, past their primes by 1964. 14/20

1959 A very great year, surpassing 1953 and often equal to and even surpassing the 1949s. Many Spätlesen and Auslesen, full and fruity wines of great power and breed, even the ripest of which are now on the market. Well-balanced, the best of them will last to the end of the decade and beyond. 19/20

1960 Many good wines, but with a tendency to lightness. 16/20

RED WINE VINTAGES

VINTAGE	RATING	1962	'63	'64	'65	'66	'67
B O R D E A U X							
45	20						
47	20						
49	18						
52	17						
53	18						
55	17						
57	16						
58	12						
59	19						
60	16						
B U R G U N D Y							
(Côte d'Or)							
45	20						
47	19						
49	18						
52	16						
53	19						
55	17						
57	17						
58	11						
59	20						
60	14						
R H Ô N E							
45	20						
47	18						
49	16						
50	14						
52	18						
54	15						
55	18						
57	17						
58	15						
59	8						
60	17						

KEY: . . . . First growth wines ready to drink.   20, 19 – Many very great wines
      Great wines not ready.   18, 17 – Many great wines
——— Wines at their best.   16, 15 – Many good wines
      Great wines ready.
------ First growth wines passing their primes.
      Great wines begin to decline.

WHITE WINE VINTAGES

VINTAGE	RATING	1962	'63	'64	'65	'66	'67
BORDEAUX							
53	17						
55	15						
58	13						
59	20						
60	15						
BURGUNDY							
55	17						
57	16						
58	11						
59	19						
60	14						
RHÔNE							
55	18						
57	17						
58	15						
59	8						
60	17						
RHINE							
57	12						
58	14						
59	19						
60	16						
MOSELLE							
57	12						
58	14						
59	19						
60	16						
CHAMPAGNE							
49	16						
50	14						
52	19						
53	17						
55	18						
57	12						
58	12						
59	20						
60	14						

NOTES ON VINEYARD LISTS

Usually there are minor differences between wines from vineyards placed next to each other in the lists. Outstanding vineyards are set in capitals, or head the list. Items read across from left to right, rather than up and down. Where there are many secondary vineyards, they generally appear in alphabetical order.

When wines are preceded by the word "Château" or the name or a town, this is indicated by indention.

Table of Contents

Wines and Spirits

A COMPLETE BUYING GUIDE

VOUVRAY · ALSACE · WHITE BURGUNDY · CHAMPAGNE NATURE

ANJOU · WHITE BORDEAUX · CHAMPAGNE

WINES OF EUROPE

RED BORDEAUX • MOSELLE • LONDON DOCK • HOCK • ALL • RED BURGUNDY • SHERRY • PURPOSE

The World of Wines

The world is full of wines, hundreds of them, good ones, great ones —more than ever before in history. But, for many people, the wonders of a good wine are a mystery—until after the first sip. Nothing but a sip will make clear what all the fussing is about.

The first taste of a good wine is discovery and excitement, like new love, the first snow of winter, the first glimpse of the ocean. Pictures flash through your mind—a backyard before anyone is up, a bed of moss under a tree, warm shadows in an attic, an armful of leaves. Scents come to mind—a piece of dusty velvet, a berry patch, a wheel of cheese, vegetables piled in a market, a child's flower pressed in a book. Old-fashioned memories, homely and sentimental, good and pleasing, amusing and full of delight. The light shimmers on the wine in the glass, throwing its gleam on the cloth. Dark bottles, bright wines, laughter, and remembering: a wonder that can happen again and again. It's good to be alive.

In the wine districts, where one is always welcome to taste the wines, a grower will lead you to his cellar, a handful of stemmed glasses in one hand, a *pipette* in the other. The pipette is a slightly bent glass tube over a foot long and about an inch in diameter, tapering to a point at one end, with a thumbhole at the other.

1

Removing the bung in the top of the cask, the vintner plunges the pipette into the opening, covers the thumbhole, and brings up the tube filled with wine. He dribbles a couple of ounces into your glass, stopping the flow by covering the thumbhole. Because he robs the cask of a little wine, the vintner calls the pipette a thief. You steal a taste.

Your mouth is filled with an acid, biting wetness. A new white wine has a green taste reminiscent of dandelions and the smell of silage being ground; a new red wine has a bitter taste and a fruity smell, like an orchard. There's a hard core of sharpness in both—like touching the tongue to metal—but this strong taste is different, something unique. When the wine is still in cask it isn't ready to drink. The elements haven't come into balance, haven't composed themselves.

You can taste all the separate parts of a new wine still in its cask. There is wateriness, which will become lightness in body later on. You taste the acid in the wine, which will become the fresh and lively part of the taste in the months to come. The tannin—like the taste of a grape stem—will lose its harsh bitterness with the years. There will be a yeasty quality that will disappear, and the fruitiness of the grape, and you can taste the alcohol.

Because you can easily discern the various parts of the wine, you can imagine how it will taste when all these come together. If the wine is very watery and acid, it will never develop; if there is too much tannin, the wine will never soften and round out. But if these qualities are balanced with fruitiness and a certain smooth fullness that comes from the oils and alcohols in the wine, you can sense the way the wine is going to be. It is easier, in fact, to judge the wine when it is green than when it is mature. Just before it is to be bottled, wine tastes like wine, but the great ones still taste harsh and strong, not the way they will taste after a year or two in bottle. A wine expert may have tasted a wine in cask several times, and in the bottle over a period of years, as it develops, reaches maturity, and slowly declines. No wonder he can recognize it, for the wine has become an old friend.

White wines are easier to judge than reds because they are simpler; there is less to them. You move on to another cask from the same vineyard, and the wine will taste different. This one may be marked by a chalk, initials or numbers, indicating that it has already been purchased—by a restaurant in Brussels, by a Swiss hotel, by a London wine merchant or an American retailer. Two years from now, you may order a bottle in Chicago or in Rio, and suddenly you are back in a winecellar, standing beside a cask, shivering in the cold dampness, spitting the wine out on the tamped earth, feeling a cold dribble down your chin.

The first taste of a green wine is unexpected, and is lost in confusion if you go on to try the wines in a hundred different casks in the course of a day. But the first sip of a good wine that has been bottled is even more confusing, not only because the tastes have come together, but also because the sample sends pictures racing through your mind, and because the sensation is such pleasure.

Once the wine has come together, "fallen bright" is the winemakers' term, there is nothing unpleasant or overpowering in the taste; it is not a collection of tastes any more, but a thing in itself, unique, a continuation of the smell, but more intense, more of the same. After you swallow, the essence remains—the aftertaste. A good wine is the same in the beginning, the middle, and the end, but each part is a different version of the same thing. Suddenly you realize that a poor wine may have a wonderful smell, but if the taste is less than the smell, the wine will be disappointing. And if the aftertaste isn't a continuation of what has gone before, or if it is missing, the wine is incomplete. All that in a single sip! A good wine is not disappointing.

People are curious about wines, and their first question is always "What is a good wine?" The answer is in the bottle; words won't do. It is hard to believe that a good wine is simply one that is good to drink, and that a poor wine is one that is incomplete and disappointing, unpleasant and unsatisfying.

People are hesitant about wines because they are afraid they won't be able to tell good from bad. After the first taste of a good wine, the uncertainties are unimportant because the pleasures are so satisfying. There are bound to be bad bottles (wine makes you realistic); a bad bottle now and then is part of the price for finding good ones (wine makes you tolerant, hopeful, and eager).

After tasting a good wine, it is easy to understand how wines can vary. The smell can be light or full, fresh and fruity or deeply mature and winy, simple or complex, delicate or rich, penetrating or soft. The taste can vary, as can the aftertaste, in endless combinations, which change in force as you sip. Also, the wine itself varies as it is open to the air.

The taste of a good wine comes from its volatile parts, released as the alcohol in the wine evaporates. Wine tastes best in large glasses that allow air to get at the wine. A wine glass is mostly chimney, so that its smell collects above the wine, and so that the glass can be swirled to get more air to the wine. To get plenty of air to the wine in his mouth, a wine expert on a buying tour through the vineyards will whistle in. One whistles in by sipping a teaspoonful of wine, pursing the lips, and sucking in air so that the wine is bounced around in the mouth. Some people think the sound is revolting at first, and are afraid of choking, so they whistle in daintily, trying not to make too much noise, trying not to dribble, sure the wine will go down the wrong way. Others smack rapidly, avoiding the issue. After a time or two, whistling in is fun, and the most reticent take to it with abandon, if only because they can taste so much more.

The taste buds are concentrated around the gums and around the tip and the base of the tongue. Children have more sensitive taste buds than grown-ups, which is why they like plain foods. In the early teens, we begin to lose the use of a few taste buds each year, which is why older people tend to lose their appetites and eat less. Nobody knows much about the chemistry of taste, but the sweet and sour taste buds seem to require more satisfying in the young; adults like to satisfy the salt and bitter taste buds. Salt and sweet buds are concentrated on the tip of the tongue, sour on the sides, and bitter at the base, but parts of the tongue taste these in combination. The muscle senses (such as those that make you grimace when you suck a lemon) and the sense of touch (which registers rough or smooth) and those senses that register biting sensations and hot and cold—all these become involved. And you can't taste anything unless you can smell it at the same time. It's a wonder that all these senses can be involved to register a single, complex taste.

Taste is not only the most complex of our sensory responses. When tasting, the other senses dim: the eyes seem to go out of focus and the ears stop hearing as one swallows. This focus of attention was once essential to life, perhaps enabling primitive man to reject instantly those eatables that would make him sick or poison him. When self-preservation was no longer involved, attention seemed to become directed at merely pleasing the sense of taste. But there is no doubt that nearly everybody has a fine tasting equipment that can make distinctions with great subtlety, just as our eyes note the different tones in a green wall dappled with shade and sunlight. Nobody has trouble recognizing a good steak, and it is even easier to taste a good wine, because there is more to taste, thanks to the alcohol.

Of course the mind gets in the way, as it is apt to do when we try to use our senses simply. Some people are uneasy in the presence of the new and strange. Their first reaction to the unknown is apt to be "I don't like it." This is a child's defensiveness, but grown-ups are apt to call it criticism. Good and great wines have gained their fame because people have been agreeing about them for centuries. A good wine isn't good just because *we* say it is, but because generations have said so. Liking or disliking is beside the point. In tasting wines, then, recognition of their qualities is more important than personal judgment. Too many wine drinkers are criticizers, not recognizers. A wine may be strange, at first, new or counter to past taste experiences, but there is more pleasure in the tasting when one suspends judgment. You may prefer some good wines to others, or you may not enjoy certain wines because you haven't tasted enough of them. In any case, tasting is the thing.

When people taste a good wine for the first time, they struggle to find words to express what the wine tastes like to them. Most of us fall back on the analogy or simile. Wine writing is full of descriptions that say a wine is like velvet, or raspberries, or truffles, and a wine may remind us of these things. Of course, your raspberries may be my blackberries, and we won't understand each other exactly. It is odd that there aren't good words to describe tastes specifically, but people do wonders in getting across their feelings without words. You will notice, for instance, that four people will empty a bottle of good wine quickly and be surprised when it's all gone. If they are drinking an ordinary wine, there will be heeltaps in the glasses, and a couple of inches left in the bottle. With a poor wine, there will be a lot left in most glasses, and perhaps the bottle will be half full. Glasses, not words, are needed for wine.

A wine language exists, however, and it often sounds silly. Refined words—and rough ones—have been given new meanings. These are generally quite specific, although they are meant to describe sometimes extremely elusive sensations. Many of them sound arbitrary or opinionated; generally, they are not. Here is the classic definition of a great wine, for instance: it is characteristic of the grape and region from which it comes; it is consistently the same, year after year, and it is long-lived. The first two limitations sound logical, but the third makes one wonder. Yet long life is the outstanding quality of a great wine, which is a living thing that continues to develop in the bottle.

Once a wine is made, its smell is described as an *aroma*, which means the first smell of the wine as a bottle is opened. The smell of young wine is fresh and fruity; after contact with the air for a time, the various alcohols in the wine take on slightly varying smells, and this collection is called the *original bouquet*. While the wine is in the cask, the original bouquet develops with the developing wine. When the wine is bottled, certain changes occur in the bouquet after a time; this is called *acquired bouquet*. The fresh and fruity qualities that developed into the original bouquet are changed into more subtle smells. These take years to develop, and a wine that is good, but not great, will not live long enough to develop these secondary qualities.

Acquired bouquet, however, is one characteristic of a great wine, the development that comes with long life, a quality that depends on the balance of all the elements that go to make up a wine. A quality described as *finesse* also takes years to develop. In short, long life is an essential quality of great wine, the phrase standing for finesse, balance, and a well-developed acquired bouquet, as well as other qualities.

By extension, a great wine region is one that produces many great wines. Seven are generally recognized. France boasts three: the Bordeaux region and its five great districts; the four districts of Burgundy; and Champagne. The German region of the Rhine and its tributaries is divided into five great districts. Hungary's Tokay region, Spain's Jerez region, and Portugal's Port region are the other three. In addition to their great wines, each region produces a multitude of good wines, ones that don't live long.

The great regions may produce great wines three or four times a decade, and a host of good wines perhaps every other year. The great vineyards in the great regions are planted in what are called noble vines, grape varieties that produce small quantities of wine, shy bearers generally planted at the northern extremity of their growing ranges. Such vines tend to produce ordinary wines when planted in warmer areas. It is this matching of the grape with the soil and the climate that produces great wines.

Good wine regions may produce some great wines in exceptional years when the weather is perfect, but such regions are more apt to produce a wide range of good wines seven or eight times a decade. Southern Burgundy and the Loire and Rhône valleys are the outstanding good wine regions of France. Franconia in Germany; the Piedmont region in Italy; the Rioja region of Spain; and the Napa, Sonoma, and Santa Clara valleys in California are examples of other good wine regions, and there are many more. Grapes that are hardier and more abundant bearers than the noble vines are generally planted in the good vineyard regions; the level of excellence that can be reached does not warrant the planting of the noble vines.

In any vineyard district, local experts will tell you that the way to find out about the wonders of wines is to start with wines from their district. Taste a variety of the lesser wines, they say, working your way up the scale. Some people suggest starting with the red table wines, because there are so many to choose from, drinking them with various foods. Others suggest the dry white wines, perhaps because they taste best chilled and chilled drinks are familiar and pleasing, or because there are fewer white wines and they vary widely in taste. If one likes Manhattans or Old Fashioneds, sweet wines are often suggested as starters, because the kind of taste will be familiar; but for those who like Martinis or Scotch and water, dry wines are recommended. But any really good wine will be pleasing.

There are more things to taste in a red wine than a white; consequently people seem to recognize the essence of wine more quickly when they begin with red table wines, which are those that contain less than 14 per cent alcohol and which taste best with foods. Wines without pronounced sweetness, the dry red and white wines, are good to begin with, because people have a tendency to notice sweetness at once, ignoring the other tastes in the wine. And young wines are better than old ones, because young wines are fresh and full and simple in taste, more direct and intense in their appeal than old wines with subtle qualities and overtones. Part of the pleasure in drinking old wines is finding in them what you know is supposed to be there, and this stems mostly from familiarity.

A hearty red Burgundy may be the best wine of all to start with; most reach maturity in five years, and these wines are full of taste. They go with, and bring out, the flavors of all kinds of roasts and grilled meats and fowl. Many of the red wines of Bordeaux take ten years or longer to reach maturity; an inexperienced buyer may choose a fine Bordeaux that isn't ready to drink and be disappointed when he tastes it.

The pleasures of wines come with familiarity, and the quickest way to become familiar with wines is to taste one against another. Many people find a few wines they like and refuse to try others, thus confining themselves to a small area of enjoyment. The endless variations in wines make them continually interesting and exciting. When buying in a wine district, an expert tastes many wines, and he has a fine time distinguishing one wine from another. Wines can be enjoyed at meals in the same way, by serving different wines from the same district. The French call this game *la musique des vins*, the melody of one wine contrasting with, or complementing, another. A bottle serves four people twice, but for small groups half-bottles offer a variety without the need for drinking a great deal.

A wine expert is considered a man with a good memory of the wines he drinks. But memory isn't needed in order to be a good winetaster. It is necessary only to recognize what one is tasting. Special wine words help in this recognition.

This special language is a kind of jargon, and while the definitions may be obscure, the meaning comes clear when one tastes what the words attempt to define. The poetic language of wine we can ignore, except to point out that there is always a strong inclination to personify wines, particularly to describe them as if they were various sorts and shapes of girls.

Most wine words are French, many are hard to translate, and all of them are supposed to be specific. Bear in mind, though, that part of the fun is finding one's own words. Wines are meant to be drunk, of course, but they are also meant to be talked about, and when you find yourself playing the music of the wines one day, you will be surprised to find that the conversation can be as pleasing as the contents of your glass. Wine sharpens the wit, and quite properly belongs with women and song.

⋞ᢒ *WINE WORDS*

Acerbe An acerbe wine is sharp to the taste, acid and thin.

Acid, acidity A taste of freshness characteristic of young wines. A wine lacking in acidity will taste watery and insipid, and will have little character. Lack of sweetness in taste, although the wine can be flowery or fruity. Definitely *not* sour, for a sour wine is a poor wine.

Aroma Distinctive fragrance given off by the wine after it has been exposed to the air.

Balance Said of a wine whose qualities are poised and equal, in balance.

Body Degree of wateriness. Wine light in body may taste watery or thin; it will be easy to swallow. A wine full in body will taste very "winy" and one prefers to sip it.

Bouchonné Wine that tastes of the cork is said to be *bouchonné*, or corky, and is unfit to drink. For this reason, one smells the cork when it is drawn; if the cork smells of wine, the wine is not corky.

Bouquet The collection of smells deriving from the volatiles in the wine. *Original bouquet* is the smell from the grape and action of fermentation; *acquired bouquet* is the further development as a result of the wine's life in bottle.

Bouqueté Wine that has a great deal of bouquet as its outstanding characteristic is said to be *bouqueté*.

Breed Wine of fine quality, distinguished of its kind, is said to have breed, or to be a wine of breeding.

Complet A wine that has rounded out, that lacks nothing.

Corsé A full-bodied wine, one that has much tannin, is *corsé*— strong in character.

Délicat Light, fine, soft, but not weak.

Doux Sweet. VDN means *vins doux naturel*, a term for unfortified natural sweet wines over 14 per cent in alcohol.

Elégant Distinctive, not heavy, well-balanced.

Etoffé Ample, full.

Fat, fatness Big and soft, much bouquet and little body.

Finesse A wine of finesse is delicate, rather than sharply pronounced, in taste; extremely excellent in its development; distinctively elegant, finely balanced.

Floweriness A characteristic of the original bouquet of wine, the smell or taste of the grape that comes from its oils; light in character, like the smell of flowers.

Franc de goût Straightforward, simple in taste. Without subtlety; clean or direct.

Fruit, fruitiness A pronounced taste or smell of the grape; full in character.

Fraîcheur A quality of a wine that tastes of freshness, or greenness; floweriness and lightness, with agreeable and definite acidity.

Full A full wine is big in taste or bouquet, rather than small; not light or watery.

Généreux A big wine, with a characteristic of fullness or richness.

Goût de cave An unpleasant taste in the wine, reminiscent of a damp cellar; a heavy, deadening taste.

Goût de terroir The often pleasing taste of the soil on which the vines grow. When pronounced, it is unpleasant—a taste of clay or mud.

Légèreté Lightness. No heaviness.

Maché Taste in a wine so full that one seems able to chew it. Such a wine coats the tongue, like spinach, and is so big that it fills the mouth.

Madérizé A white wine that has rusted, or oxidized, named after the taste of the fortified wines from Madeira, in which it is desired. A white table wine that has maderized is undrinkable.

Moelleux A word usually applied to the slightly sparkling wines of the Loire, meaning a slightly creamy or foamy taste in the mouth.

Mordant A characteristic of big, penetrating wines; an almost biting or stinging sensation, pleasant to the tongue, imparted to wines by substantial amounts of acidity.

Nerveux Strong and intense; vigorous, sinewy, virile. A big, full wine, without softness.

Oeil de perdrix A term for the color of a pink wine, pale as the eye of a partridge.

Parfumé Perfumed, characterized by freshness and fullness.

Racé A *racé* wine is true to type to an exceptional degree, with a character of strength; distinctive, similar to breed.

Robé A particularly large, full, and enveloping bouquet, characteristic of the greatest wines.

Sec Not sweet; a positive characteristic in light wines, meaning absence of sugar; such a "dry" wine may taste flowery or fruity, with a kind of light sweetness.

Seché Too dry; dried out; characteristic of wines that are too acid, and too light in tannin or alcohol.

Sève Sappiness, a pleasing quality of smoothness imparted by the glycerine that develops from grape oils during fermentation. Great wines need this quality to keep them from tasting thin. This oily characteristic gives a sensation of slight sweetness, or roundness, to a wine.

Souplesse The English word is suppleness, and this trait is often combined with *sève*. Such a wine is soft, its qualities combining smoothly.

Soyeux Silky, without harshness or bitterness.

Suave Smooth and full, with delicacy.

Tendre No harshness or sharpness; soft without being flabby or excessively light.

Velouté Velvety to the taste, full and rich.

NOTE. These attempts to give some sense to the subtle meanings of these words are merely suggestive; once you taste the various qualities in wines, you can easily expand the definitions to suit yourself. There is no way to set down the exclamations, the shrugs and gestures and facial expressions that most truly express the delight in wines. These are re-created by us all, while we are drinking, in an attempt to communicate with those who are enjoying the wine with us. All knowing is in the drinking.

Bordeaux

Bordeaux has been shipping wines from its surrounding vineyards for centuries, a river of wine as wide as the Garonne, along whose west bank the city lies. This port of a quarter of a million wine-lovers is sixty miles upstream from the Atlantic, and its life centers on the Quai des Chartrons, just below the town square, where most of the major shipping firms have their warehouses.

Of all the world's great wines, those from Bordeaux are the easiest to identify. The best are bottled and clearly labeled by the owners at the vineyards from which they come. The labeling system began a half-dozen generations ago, and is called *château-bottling*. There may not be an actual château at the vineyard, but the word sounds nice and is assurance of authenticity. Such wines are identified on the label by the phrase *mis en bouteille au château*. The system

13

worked so well in establishing the reputation of Bordeaux that all other great table-wine regions have copied it, more accurately describing this bottling by the owner at the vineyard as *estate-bottling*.

Ratings by quality of the wines in the steep-shouldered bottles were begun in the eighteenth century, and reached a certain peak in 1855, when the wines of the Médoc and Sauternes districts were classified for a Paris fair according to their market prices. This worked fine for Médoc and Sauternes, but not for Graves, St. Emilion, and Pomerol, the other great Bordeaux districts that were not rated.

Centuries ago, all the wine of Bordeaux was called *Graves*, the ancient name for the particularly gravelly type of soil that gives Bordeaux its distinction. In 1855, the wines of Médoc were still called *Graves du Médoc*, and the classification was an attempt to establish the Médoc vineyards in their own right. The Médoc owners were pretty well agreed on the comparative ratings of their vineyards, largely based on price. This was not true of St. Emilion and Pomerol; demand for these wines was not great, prices were not high, and each owner insisted his vineyard was best, so they were not included in the ratings.

The 1855 classification was too specific. The vineyards were divided into five numbered *crus classés*, or Classed Growths. Later, seven vineyards that had been omitted were classed as Exceptional Growths, and more than two hundred other Médoc vineyards were classified into *bourgeois supérieur*, *bourgeois*, *artisan*, and *paysan* growths.

Only Château Margaux, Château Latour, and Château Lafite in the Médoc were classed as *Premiers Crus*, or First Growths, although the Graves vineyard of Château Haut Brion was listed with them because it was too outstanding to be left out. No such consideration was extended to the châteaux of Ausone or Cheval Blanc in St. Emilion, or of Pétrus in Pomerol, which were ignored. Château Mouton in the Médoc, which frequently commands the highest prices of all in Bordeaux, was classified as a Second Growth, thus inspiring its motto: *Premier ne puis,*
Second ne daigne,
Mouton suis.

Together, these eight outstanding red-wine vineyards would fit nicely into the eight hundred forty acres of Central Park. In a good year, they may produce a total of seventy thousand cases of red wines. All sixty of the classified growths of the Médoc produce well under five hundred thousand cases, even in a good year.

These *crus classés* produce top-notch wines, but many of them are not in demand, simply because they are rated as Third, Fourth, or Fifth Growths. The old classification is still admired because most of the ratings are accurate, even though some half-dozen of the vineyards listed in 1855 are no longer producing, and many of those listed have improved during the past century. The great fault of the 1855 classification was that it did not include the best vineyards in Graves, St. Emilion, and Pomerol—a mistake that is being corrected by French law, so that all the top vineyards in these districts will have official ratings.

During the English occupation of ancient Gascony, which lasted for three centuries and ended in 1451, many of the red and white wines were mixed together to make a pinkish wine called *clairette*. The English called it "claret," and the name is still used in England for all the Bordeaux red wines, a fact that irritates the Bordelais until they reflect upon the fact that England is still the largest buyer of Bordeaux.

Bordeaux had no fame in France until the 1600s. The French court thought the wines were terrible; whenever one of the courtiers got out of hand, the king banished him to Bordeaux. This happened to Richelieu, who had annoyed Louis XIII. Friends tricked him into drinking the wines by substituting a Bordeaux for his favorite Burgundy. When he returned to the court he touted the wines, and their fame began. Today, Bordeaux is considered the world's greatest wine district because it produces more great wines than any other, as well as hundreds of good ones.

The solid citizens of Bordeaux don't take this fame for granted. The wines are listed on an exchange and are bought and sold by brokers while the wine is still in barrel at the châteaux. Brokers guarantee the condition and authenticity of a wine, selling casks to the shippers for blending into regional wines, or selling the wines bottled at the châteaux to buyers from all over the world. Prices are established by quality, supply and demand, and are generally a good reflection of value. A wine simply labeled *Bordeaux* may be sold for little more than a dollar a bottle. Wines with district names, like Médoc, will be higher. Those from a town in a district, like St. Julien, will fetch a still higher price, and château-bottlings will

cost most of all—invariably over two dollars a bottle, and up. Prices given here and elsewhere in this book are those prevailing in New York City.

The wines of Bordeaux may be the most readily available of all fine wines, but they are the wines one has to wait for the longest. The First Growths and the best of the Second Growths of a good year may take a decade to mature and those of a great year, such as 1959, 1955, 1953, 1952, 1947, or 1945, may take twice as long. Most of them are drunk before they are ready.

The wines come on the market when they are only two or three years old, but even those of châteaux of little fame require another year or two before they mature. They are worth waiting for. The Bordeaux whites mature much faster than the reds; the reds of St. Emilion and Pomerol and Graves mature faster than those of the Médoc. Many of these, and the Third, Fourth, and Fifth Classed Growths of the Médoc are the wines of Bordeaux to buy when you want to taste recent vintages, because many are ready to drink five or six years after the vintage. Regional wines, identified with district or township names, are ready to drink almost as soon as they are bottled.

❧ ❧

The Médoc

The greatest of all the Bordeaux districts is the Médoc, which begins just north of the city and runs down the estuary to the sea. On the ocean side are the dunes and pine trees of Les Landes, and on the river side are the vineyards. The best of them are in a thirty-five-mile stretch near Bordeaux, called *Haut-Médoc*, and the prefix carries such authority that many other districts add *Haut* to their names to increase their own prestige in the minds of buyers.

The vineyard road runs through farm country and villages, now and then in sight of the river, with an occasional vineyard on the slightly rolling land. But not until the Garonne joins the Dordogne to become the Gironde do the truly great vineyards begin, near the town of Margaux. Its greatest vineyard names the town and township.

❧ MARGAUX AND ITS NEIGHBORS

Château Margaux is owned by one of the important shippers of Bordeaux, Fernand Ginestet, a former president of the Bordeaux Wine Shippers Syndicate. Its nearly two hundred vineyard acres were badly mismanaged before the war, when Ginestet began buying the property, a task that took fifteen years. It took more years to rebuild the vineyards, and in 1947 the finest wine of all Bordeaux was made here.

The château has a porch modeled after the Parthenon, which is pictured on the label, but even this is dominated by the enormous *chai*, or storehouse, where the new wine is kept. Rows of casks cover the floor, and whitewashed walls and columns rise high above them, giving the feeling of a cathedral nave. This main *chai* is entered through a long wing, open on one side, which contains the winepresses, the destemming machines (called *égrappoirs*), the crushers (*fouloirs*), and the fermenting vats, which are twice as broad as a man is tall and twice as high. At harvest time, there may

MARGAUX AND ITS NEIGHBORS

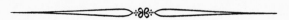

PREMIER GRAND CRU CLASSÉ
Château MARGAUX 1 *

* * *

CRUS CLASSÉS

Château

Brane-Cantenac 2 §
Lascombes 2
Rauzan-Gassies 2
Cantenac-Brown 3 §
Ferrière 3 †
d'Issan 3 † §
La Lagune 3 † §
Marquis d'Alesme-Becker 3 †
Marquis-de-Terme 4
Le Prieuré 4 §
Dauzac 5 §

Angludet E
Chasse-Spleen E
Villegorge E

Château

Durfort-Vivens 2 †
Rausan-Ségla 2
Boyd-Cantenac 3 §
Desmirail 3 †
Giscours 3 † §
Kirwan 3 † §
Malescot-Saint-Exupéry 3
Palmer 3 §
Pouget 4 §
Cantemerle 5 §
Le Tertre 5 §

Bel-Air-Marquis-d'Aligre E
Poujeaux-Thiel E

---

* Numbers indicate ratings according to 1855 classification. E stands for *Cru Exceptionnel*, a vineyard rated right after the classed growths.

† Production less than 2,000 cases a year, consequently rarely found on the market, and usually high-priced.

§ Vineyard in a neighboring township, producing similar wines.

be two hundred vineyard workers loading the ox-drawn carts. The grapes are dumped into an *égrappoir*, then are crushed and run into the vats (*cuves*), where they will ferment for as long as fourteen days, when the wine is pressed and drawn off into casks that are lined up in the big *chai*.

Fermentation begins almost at once, yeasts converting the sugar in the grapes into alcohol and carbonic-acid gas. The yeasts look like powder on the skin of the grapes—you can rub off the film with your finger—and the wine begins to bubble as they work, throwing up from the bottom of the vat the pulp and skins and bits of stem that remain after the destemming operation. These form a solid mass on the top of the wine, called the *cap*; this must be broken up and punched down periodically. When there is a lot of sugar in the wine, the cap will rise high in the vat, and the vintners say that the wine is wearing its cap on the side of its head.

Nobody understands much about fermentation, but the vintners know that if the temperature rises too high a poor wine will be made, and if the fermentation takes too long the wine may never mature. Today, the wine is allowed to ferment rapidly, and the process is sometimes over in three days. The wine picks up its color, as well as oils, from the skins, while tannin is obtained mostly from the stems. Tannin is one of the substances that permit the wine to live a long time, helping to hold together the substances of the wine until they mature. Château Margaux makes perhaps fifteen hundred cases of fine red wine in a good year.

Another thousand cases or so of dry white wine are sold as *Pavillon Blanc* because it is not thought good enough to bear the château label. To make the white wines, the grapes are pressed as soon as the stems have been removed. The white wines thus do not pick up the substances needed for color, long life, and big body as red wines do, and they do not live as long or have the other taste qualities possessed by reds. But white wines are ready to drink within a year or so after the vintage, reach their prime almost as soon as they are bottled, and are usually gone after seven years or so.

The other vineyards in the township of Margaux—and those in the neighboring townships of Cantenac, Macau, Labarde, Ludon, Arsac and Moulis—follow pretty much the same classic procedures for making wines, as do other wine districts around the world. The soil, the grape, and the climate make the differences in the wines.

The noble vine for the red wines of Margaux and the other Bordeaux clarets is the *Cabernet Sauvignon*. This grape sets the character of red Bordeaux, imparting long life, body, and a fruity, smooth quality to the wine called *sève*; somewhere between 60 and 70 per cent of vineyard space is customarily given over to it. Varieties called *Merlot* provide *souplesse*, richness, and the *Cabernet Franc* supplies bouquet. These varieties each account for somewhere between 10 and 20 per cent of the vineyard space. There are usually small quantities of Petit Verdot, Malbec and Carmenère planted, which give alcoholic strength, volume and richness to the wine. All these grapes are related, being of the V*itis vinifera* species of vine, the vine to make wines, the same group that provides all the great wine grapes of the world.

There are many Classed Growths around Margaux, and all of them have much in common. Nobody knows why Margaux stands above its neighbors. Perhaps it is some slight difference in soil or exposure to the sun. But it is an easy matter to taste the difference and detect the distinctive characteristics of the other wines. Just above Margaux, the gravelly soil has a larger percentage of sand, and the wines have a different character. Like all the wonders in wine, this too can be tasted in the glass.

Grouped around Château Margaux scarcely a mile away are the township vineyards classed as Second and Third Growths. South is Palmer, and (going clockwise around the town) then Durfort, Rausan-Ségla, Rauzan-Gassies, Marquis de Terme, Lamescot-St. Exupéry, Marquis-d'Alesme-Becker and Lascombes. Desmirail, a Third Growth, is now part of Château Margaux. Interspersed are lesser vineyards and others no longer in production. Like those of Margaux, the wines have a tendency to be big and full of taste. Most of the wines from the vintages of the 40s are now ready to drink, although Margaux will go on improving, the 1945 reaching its prime in the mid-60s, while the 1947 will be ready at the decade's turn. A Château Margaux may need twenty years or longer to mature in a great year, and the vineyards around it may need six or eight, even in a year that is rated merely good.

Château Margaux is famous for its finesse, exceptional balance and development, without heaviness or coarseness of any kind. When the season is hot, Margaux is outstanding, but in cool years this great finesse is slow in developing.

⋙ *ST. JULIEN*

For fifteen miles above Margaux, the road runs through vineyard country, then swings down to the river and the town of St. Julien, once a busy landing stage for ships seeking Médoc wines and still the name most familiar to the buyer of regional clarets. Its most famous wine is Château Beychevelle, so the town has tacked the name onto its own; but the best wines come from the châteaux of Léoville Las Cases and Léoville Poyferré, two of the vineyards classed in 1855 as Second Growths.

Beychevelle boasts a handsome court with a great pine tree spreading its branches in the center. The vineyards overlook the river. Whenever the name comes up, the Bordelais are sure to tell you that it derives from the shout of the sailors, *"Baissez les voiles,"* a ship's sails being dropped in salute as it passed this residence of a former Grand Admiral of France. The wind was taken out of Beychevelle's sails, certainly, when it was classified as a Fourth Growth in 1855, although the wines now sell at the prices of a Second Growth. A good year for Bordeaux is a great year for Beychevelle, the Bordelais are fond of saying—a remark that is made to distinguish several wines of Bordeaux that become big, soft, and round; Château Haut Brion and other top Graves reds are examples. The best of the recent Beychevelles is 1953. Like Margaux, Beychevelle is acclaimed for its finesse and bouquet, but these qualities are distinguished only when its wines are over 12 per cent in alcohol; in poor years the wines are thin.

All the best vineyards of St. Julien are within a mile or so of Beychevelle, just below or west of the town, on each side of the road. The two best share a single château, Léoville, and the vineyards vie with each other for top rank. In the 20s, Poyferré produced the better wines, big and full and round, repeating its supremacy in 1943, 1945, and 1959. Its twin, Las Cases, outdid it in 1947, 1948, and 1949, to slip back again in 1952, 1953, and 1955, because of the many young vines in the vineyard. Vines need a good four years before they begin to bear properly and are at their best when they are about twenty. Vineyard land needs long rest periods—ten years or more—to produce its best. Rotation planting has been introduced, so that while part is always resting and part is always planted in young vines, other sections will be in full bearing. At Las Cases, for instance, half of its three hundred acres were resting during the 50s. Las Cases is due to improve in the next decade and give Poyferré real competition. Frost and hail, however, upset all prognostications, because a single frost can wipe out a vineyard for half a decade.

There is a third vineyard entitled to be called Léoville, because it was once part of the original domain—the Second Growth of Léoville-Barton. Its wine is not château-bottled; nor are the wines of Kirwan, a Third Growth, or those of the Fifth Growth Château Pontet Canet, the largest Classed Growth in the Médoc, producing more than fifteen thousand cases in a good year. It is also one of the best known, owned by the excellent shipping firm of Cruse, which bottles the wines in Bordeaux. Various members of the Cruse family also own, among others, Château Rausan-Ségla and Château

S T .   J U L I E N
A N D   I T S   N E I G H B O R S

CRUS CLASSÉS

Château	Château
Ducru-Beaucaillou 2 *	Gruaud-Larose 2
Léoville-Barton 2	Léoville-Las-Cases 2
Léoville-Poyferré 2	Lagrange 3
Langoa 3	Beychevelle 4
Branaire-Ducru 4	Saint-Pierre-Bontemps 4
Saint-Pierre-Sevaistre 4	Talbot 4
La Tour Carnet 4 §	Belgrave 5 §
Camensac 5 §	Moulin-Riche E

* Numbers indicate ratings according to 1855 classification. E stands for *Cru Exceptionnel*, a vineyard rated right after the classed growths.
§ Vineyard in a neighboring township, producing similar wines.

d'Issan, the latter a magnificent medieval structure surrounded by a moat. The wines are château-bottled.

Most of the wine of St. Julien, and most of the wines from all the Bordeaux region for that matter, go to Bordeaux for bottling as regionals by shippers. The brokers, called *couriers* because they used to accompany buyers to the vineyards and protect them from highwaymen, call on the shippers with samples of the wines they have to sell. The shippers set aside regular hours to see the *couriers*, at which time they accept samples in what look like small medicine bottles, taste the wines, run tests on them, and decide whether to buy. If the shipper buys, the wine is brought in cask to the shipper's storage warehouses in Bordeaux, where it is blended with other wines, a practice called *coupage*. Wines are balanced against each other to achieve the desired blend of wines from a district or from wines of different years. The practice is disparagingly called *la grande cuisine*, but there is merit in it. When a wine that is too light is blended with one that is too heavy, the result may be a better wine than either of those that went into the blend. These regionals, labeled with township or district names, should be reasonable in price, well-balanced, and pleasant to drink. They often taste better than many of the minor château-bottlings.

The *crus classés* of St. Julien are often excellent values because they are not so well known as the Classed Growths from the other Médoc townships. They are particularly good values in great years, when the famous growths command high prices.

ᐳᔟ *PAUILLAC*

A few hundred yards north of St. Julien, and bordering Léoville Las Cases, is Château Latour. It is in the township of Pauillac, which boasts more fine vineyards than any other Médoc commune. Latour has no château, only a vine-covered water tower, but its wines need no architectural glorification. Over fifty Bordeaux châteaux have added *Latour* to their names, but the similarity ends there.

The wines of Château Latour, classed as a First Growth in 1855, are perhaps the longest-lived of the world's red wines, and they take the longest to mature. Always big and full, they have a quality the French call *maché*, meaning that the wine is so immense that you can chew it. In most Bordeaux vineyards, it is customary to bottle the wines after some thirty months in barrel, the third spring after the vintage. Latour generally waits until the fall—as did most of the other great châteaux until a decade ago. The brokers are anxious to get their hands on the wine to speed up the return on capital invested. Château owners approve of this, in principle, and try to bottle promptly. There is some danger in such prompt bottling, because flaws in a wine can be detected and corrected while the wine is in the cask; once the wine is in bottle, nothing can be done about it. Latour is so slow in maturing, however, that the Château waits as long as possible before bottling, and the world waits, too.

The château was burned during the French Revolution. The old tower, which looks like a chess rook and is now carved on the keystone of the arch that leads into the domain, appears on the label. The *chai* is a long, low stucco building, beautifully kept. Everything looks as impeccable as the wines taste: the plane trees neatly trimmed, the gravel roadways raked, the flower beds edged and weeded.

Latour produced the greatest wine of Bordeaux in 1929, which is just now becoming ready to drink, and which will continue to be magnificent for another decade or so. Every great year produces a magnificent Latour; the wines of 1934 and 1937 are just becoming drinkable, and will continue to improve through the 60s. The vineyard consists of a little over one hundred acres, and production averages somewhere around eight thousand cases a year. There is a market for ten times that much.

Between Latour and the town of Pauillac is a cluster of Second and Third Growths, all of which have long lives. The closest neighbors are Pichon Longueville and Pichon-Longueville-Comtesse-de-Lalande, the latter being the portion of the old vineyard that is owned and bottled by a syndicate of Bordeaux brokers.

Above Pauillac, the great wines take on exceptional softness and finesse, exemplified by Château Lafite and Château Mouton, each owned by branches of the Rothschild family. The châteaux are as handsome as the wines, and the cellars are the high points of a vineyard tour—Mouton especially. Sconces along the *chai* walls cast light on the rows of barrels; the cellars underneath are lit by wheels of small lights, illumined crowns that sparkle above the royal treasures.

In hot years, wines tend to develop excessive acidity, but a wine that is normally big and soft in a good year will be able to accept this excessive acid, simply taking longer to develop. The firm wines of Pauillac have a tendency to go out of balance in hot years, a fault minimized by fast vinification, according to vintners.

The wines of Lafite are usually the lightest of all the Bordeaux classed as First Growths in 1855. Many wine lovers prefer Lafite to all the other Bordeaux, because of this lightness and because of the magnificent bouquet the wine develops. Lafite was named long

P A U I L L A C

PREMIERS GRANDS CRUS CLASSÉS

Château
LAFITE 1 *

Château
LATOUR 1

MOUTON-ROTHSCHILD 2

* * *

CRUS CLASSÉS

Château
Pichon-Longueville 2

Duhart-Milon 4
Clerc-Milon-Mondon 5
Grand-Puy-Ducasse 5
Haut-Bages-Libéral 5
Lynch-Bages 5
Mouton-d'Armailhacq
(Baron-Philippe) 5
Pontet-Canet 5

Château
Pichon-Longueville-
Lalande 2

Batailley 5
Croizet-Bages 5
Grand-Puy-Lacoste 5
Haut-Batailley 5
Lynch-Moussas 5
Pédesclaux 5

La Couronne E

* Numbers indicate ratings according to 1855 classification. E stands for *Cru Exceptionnel*, a vineyard rated right after the classed growths.

before the time of the Caribbean pirate and probably originally meant height, for the château overlooks the surrounding country-side. Its 1934 was the best Bordeaux of the year. The '29s, '37s, '45s, and '49s are not far behind. The Lafites of 1934 and 1937 sold in 1961 in New York for $135 a case of twelve, compared to $75 for the Margaux and Latour '34s, and $68.50 for the 1937s. Prices for 1953s were less: Lafite, $60; Mouton, $57.50; Haut Brion, $53; Ausone, $49.50; Cheval Blanc, Latour, Margaux, and Pétrus were $39.50. 1952 Pétrus was $60; Ausone, $56; Latour, $55. Margaux and Mouton were $53; Lafite, $42.50, and Haut Brion, $39.50.

Like Lafite, Mouton is rated with the best in every great year, and there is still a dispute as to which excels in 1947: Mouton gets the most votes. For 1953, Lafite takes the honors. Mouton gen-erally tastes disappointing while in barrel and after first being bottled, but gradually grows and rounds into magnificence. Mouton matures slowly; the 1929, which is glorious today, is a perfect example. The great Mouton is not to be confused with the Fifth-Growth Mouton-d'Armailhacq, now called Mouton-Baron-Philippe, both of which are owned by Philippe de Rothschild.

The neighbors of Lafite and Mouton mature more quickly than the two greats. They also are distinguished by softness and finesse, but one can say that about all the classed growths of Haut-Médoc. Elegance and delicacy are what set the wines of Bordeaux apart. The very greats display these qualities more brilliantly, so out-standingly that such perfections are hard to believe, even when you are tasting them. They are the greatest red wines on earth, as everybody in Bordeaux will tell you, and the only people who are apt to argue the point are Burgundians, who have glories of their own to exclaim about. This is an argument to avoid, and there is an answer as classic as the wines, if not so satisfactory: "It's nice we have both." Such an answer stops talk and lets one get back to the wine, which is what most people want to do once they've tasted a great bottle.

◄§ ST. ESTÈPHE

Right above Château Lafite begins the cluster of vineyards in the township of St. Estèphe, the best of which are Cos d'Estournel, Montrose, and Calon-Ségur. The wines are bigger and fuller than the other Médocs, and Cos d'Estournel is considered one of the best Médoc wines produced in 1945. Being full of tannin, the wines stay hard for a long time.

The whole length of the Médoc looks peaceful and rich during the spring and summer, bountiful and gay during the vintage, but it is no paradise on earth, even though the wines can make it seem so. A hail or frost can destroy a vineyard overnight, and poor weather ruins many a vintage. A vintner thinks himself lucky if he gets four vintages a decade. Other years, he may make no wine at all, or wine so poor in quality or quantity it is fit only for *la grande cuisine*. Plague and pestilence are always close.

A hundred years ago, a powdery mildew appeared on the skin of the grapes. It was called *oidium*. It destroyed the fruit and there was only one good year in the decade of the 1850s—1858, the Year of the Comet. Many vineyards changed hands. Good grapes were so rare, the story goes, that those along the edge of the road were sprayed with copper sulphate to keep passers-by from picking them. At vintage time, it was noticed that these grapes were healthier than

S T .   E S T È P H E

CRUS CLASSÉS

Château	*Château*
Cos d'Estournel 2 *	Montrose 2
Calon Ségur 3	Rochet 4
Cos Labory 5	

* Numbers indicate ratings according to 1855 classification.

the others. Thus, by accident and from despair, the mildew was mastered. The story has a fine, false ring, but the fact is that sulphur did come into use about this time and that it does control mildew —and just about every other vile thing that is apt to attack the grapes.

Life continued its varied ways for a few years, until a zealous vineyardist decided to see how native American vines would do in French vineyards. Within a decade, nearly every European vineyard had been destroyed by a burrowing louse on the American roots, called the *phylloxera*. The American vines resisted the louse, but the noble vines and other varieties could not. The louse hit Bordeaux in 1875, working north. The only solution found was to graft the European vines to American roots, a tedious and expensive practice still being used today.

Some say that wines were better before the *phylloxera*, but wine experts disagree on this. Yield is a little larger, vine life is a little shorter, but the great vineyards and noble vines continue to produce magnificent wines, whenever the weather is right. The improved techniques of winemaking tend to outweigh any changes in the fruit and its maturing. Today, when given a chance, the minor vineyards of St. Estèphe can produce excellent wines and, in fine years, Cos d'Estournel and Calon-Ségur rank with the best. It is generally felt that Château Montrose is slightly overrated; it is sturdy and full but it lacks finesse. There's the same feeling about Château d'Issan, a Third Growth in Cantenac, below Margaux, but this may be due mostly to young vines in the vineyard. Generally, the *crus classés* of the Médoc are excellent buys, and when the most famous are too expensive there are many more to choose from.

◄§ ৡ►

St. Emilion and Pomerol

St. Emilion is across from Bordeaux, on a plateau overlooking the Dordogne. The road runs beside the winding stream for a while, then swings north up a narrowing valley banked by sloping vineyards to a scatter of old stone houses at the foot of a sheer bluff. This is half the town, and the other half is up on top. It is the loveliest wine town on earth.

The town church is in the lower section, a great cavern carved into the face of the bluff. The steeple is by itself, up above in a cobbled square it shares with a few shops and a restaurant whose windows and terraces look along the bluff to the vineyards. Fish from the river, meat and fowl from the pastures, and wines from the vineyards—over a hundred of them—are features of the menu, along with an unsweetened macaroon, which is a local speciality. Vines trained on wires make a dappled shade of the terrace, a delightful place to have lunch.

Down below, near the church entrance, is a cave where the hermit Saint Emilion lived and prayed. There's a wishing stone in the cave, and a pool into which girls throw hairpins. If a pair of pins falls in the form of a cross, the girl will be married within the year.

All around the town are arches, columns, and lengths of wall dating from the Middle Ages, when the town was a way station for pilgrims en route to the shrines of Spain. Here and there is a Romanesque cloister, or a flight of steps leading to a walled garden, all being used quite casually by the town's inhabitants—and not a uniformed guard or hands-off sign in sight, except at the shrine, where there's someone to sell you hairpins.

Vineyards surround the town, and the best of them are over toward Bordeaux, to the west. In 1955, just a hundred years after the Médoc classification, the official French control laws named two vineyards as Grand Growths, ten more as First Great Growths, and fifty more as Great Growths, the rest being classified as Principal Growths. Pomerol vineyards are due to be rated any year now, following the same pattern. Thus was settled, for a time, an argument that has been going on for centuries. Nobody has ever questioned the superiority of Ausone and Cheval Blanc, and nobody has really argued about the standing of the next ten vineyards, for they are the ones that command the highest prices year after year. Lesser vineyards argued and fought to avoid low classifications for fear these would affect prices. What happened, of course, was that the better vineyards became dearer, while the lower held their prices; the wines were made easier to buy, and more people are buying them.

These are some of the oldest vineyards in France and, here and there, the vines are planted in trenches dug out of the limestone and filled with earth a thousand years ago. The most famous vineyard is Ausone, named after the Roman poet Ausonius, who lived there. The vineyard consists of fewer than twenty acres, and produces less than two thousand cases a year. The wines often take twenty years to mature.

Nearby is the great vineyard of Château Cheval Blanc, which produced the best wine of Bordeaux in 1943 and 1948, and almost

ST . EMILION

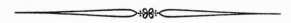

PREMIERS GRANDS CRUS CLASSÉS

Château   Château
   AUSONE   CHEVAL-BLANC

   Beauséjour (Duffau-Lagarosse) Figeac
   Beauséjour (Fagouet)   La Gaffelière-Naudes
   Belair   Magdelaine
   Canon   Pavie
   Clos Fourtet   Trottevieille

* * *

GRANDS CRUS CLASSÉS

Château

l'Angélus
Balestard-la-Tonnelle
Bellevue
Bergat
Cadet-Bon
Cadet-Piola
Canon-la-Gaffelière
Cap-de-Mourlin
Chapelle Madeleine
Chauvin
Clos la Madeleine
Corbin (Giraud)
Corbin-Michotte
Coutet
Croque-Michotte
Curé-Bon-la-Madeleine
Fonplégade
Fonroque
Franc-Mayne
Grand-Barrail-
   Lamarzelle-Figeac
Grand-Corbin-Despagne
Grand-Corbin-Pecresse
Grand-Mayne
Grand-Pontet
Grandes-Murailles
Guadet-St.-Julien
Clos des Jacobins
Jean-Faure
La Carte
La Clotte
La Clusière

Château

La Couspaude
La Dominique
La Marzelle
Domaine de Larmande
Larcis-Ducasse
Laroze
l'Arrosée
Lasserre
La Tour-Figeac
La Tour-du-Pin-Figeac
   (Bélivier) and (Moueix)
Le Chatelet
Le Couvent
Le Prieuré
Mauvezin
Moulin-du-Cadet
Pavie-Decesse
Pavie-Macquin
Pavillon Cadet
Petit-Faurie-de-Souchard
Petit-Faurie-de-Soutard
Ripeau
Saint-Georges-Côte-Pavie
Clos Saint-Martin
Sansonnet
Soutard
Tertre-Daugay
Trimoulet
Trois-Moulins
Troplong-Mondot
Villemaurine
Yon-Figeac

P O M E R O L

Château	*Château*
PÈTRUS	Vieux-Château-Certan
Certan	Clos l'Eglise
l'Evangile	Gazin
La Conseillante	Lafleur
Lafleur-Pètrus	Nenin
Petit-Village	Trotanoy
Beauregard	Certan-Marzelle
Clinet	Clos du Clocher
l'Eglise-Clinet	Domaine d'Eglise
Feytit-Clinet	Gombaude-Guillot
La Commanderie	Guillot
La Croix-de-Gay	La Croix
Latour-Pomerol	Lagrange
Plince	La Grave-Trigant-de-Boisset
Rouget	La Pointe
de Sales	Le Gay
	Vraie-Croix-de-Gay

Pomerol vineyards are not yet officially rated by the *Appellation Contrôlée*, but those listed here are the ones that command most consideration from the Bordeaux shippers. There are many others.

the best in 1945, when it was slightly outclassed by a Graves, Château Haut Brion. Like the other St. Emilions, Cheval Blanc is planted in the Cabernet Franc. It produces big, soft wines that are often called *gras*, or fat, meaning that they lack firmness and that kind of hardness and fullness that comes from acidity and tannin.

All the great vineyards are within a mile of town, and while they are called châteaux, most of the buildings are comfortable stone houses with high ceilings and big rooms, with views through tall windows of vineyards, valley, and plains beyond. The earth is thin and many of the cellars are carved out of the soft limestone. Some of these caves are quite large, and were used as storehouses and living quarters in the days of the pilgrimages.

Several other vineyards vie with the two leaders for attention, among them Clos Fourtet and Châteaux Belair, Canon, and Gaffelière-Naudes, three neighbors of Château Ausone.

Sharing the plateau with St. Emilion are the vineyards of its twin district, Pomerol. The greatest Pomerol is Pétrus, followed closely by its neighbor, Vieux-Château-Certan; by Château l'Evangile and Château La Conseillante, which is right across the road from St. Emilion's Cheval Blanc.

Wines of these two districts are the heaviest of the Bordeaux, with the Pomerols being fuller and fatter than the St. Emilions. The 1952s are better than the 1953s. These wines have less bouquet than those from the Médoc, according to the Bordeaux trade, and they mature faster. Even so, a great St. Emilion or Pomerol will take ten years or more to round out. The 1945s, as an example, are coming to maturity in the 60s. Many of the vineyards suffered in the 1956 frosts, and large sections had to be replanted, so that we will have to wait until the 60s for fine St. Emilion and Pomerols of recent vintage.

These wines are dubbed "the Burgundies of Bordeaux," and because of their full quality, many Bordeaux experts think that these are the clarets to get to know first, before going on to the more delicate and elegant Médocs and Graves. This is an over-refinement, of course, but because the St. Emilions and Pomerols are big and fruity, they taste best with very simple foods such as roasted and grilled meats—a turkey, or a steak, for example. Chicken and pork or veal roasts, to continue the distinction, might taste best with the Médoc and Graves red.

❧ ❦

Graves

The Graves district is the largest of Bordeaux, surrounding the town as well as the district of Sauternes, its vineyards extending into the suburbs. In the old days, the vineyards were a wreath about the medieval town, but when Graves became famous, in the 1700s, the city began to grow, crowding the vines that made its fame. Fortunately there was room for the city to stretch out along the river bank, where the soil was not suited for grapes, so now the tight old city is surrounded by broad, tree-shaded boulevards and squares stretching out to the waist-high vineyards.

Best of all, of course, is Château Haut Brion, once owned by Talleyrand, and now owned by American financier Clarence Dillon. It was classed as a First Growth in 1855. Bordeaux seems to have attracted the banking element, although—three hundred years ago—it was the English traders who came to establish warehouses, and in the early 1800s it was the Alsatian and other northern Europeans who came to see that the wines were being shipped expeditiously. The great names among the brokers and shippers reflect this blend of English, Dutch, German, and French heritage: Barton & Guestier, Calvet, Cruse, Delor, De Luze, Eschenauer, Ginestet, Johnston, Kressman, Lawton, Schroeder & Schyler, and Sichel & Fils.

Haut Brion is directly on the edge of town and produces not only a great red wine in its deep gravel vineyards but also a thousand cases of a fine dry white wine each year, made from the same grapes that produce the sweet Sauternes, half Semillon and half Sauvignon. This is sold as Château Haut Brion Blanc. Nobody knows why grapes a scant dozen miles away should produce sweet wines, but they do, which is why vintners insist that it is the soil that makes the wine. It would certainly seem so at Haut Brion, which produces exceptional wines in off years, and long-lived wines whenever the vintage is good. In hot years, the gravel is said to deflect the sun's heat, and in wet years the gravel permits the rain to drain away quickly. In great years, Haut Brion has the strength and balance needed for complete development, and its 1945 is said to be the finest of all clarets. More interesting to a wine-drinker, though, is the fact that the wines of Graves seem to develop after being opened, because of their big bouquet, where the wines of the Médoc seem to fall off slightly after being open for a time. An English saw, "Médoc with the meat, and Graves with the cheese," seems to bear this out.

Graves châteaux give one the feeling of wine aristocracy, just as do those in the Médoc, but because the district is so large and there are so many vineyards, occasionally one finds comfortable seventeenth- and eighteenth-century houses, like those of St. Emilion. The showplaces are magnificent, but even the great wines cannot sell for enough to support them. Many shippers and brokers have bought châteaux for dwellings or headquarters, so that the wine does not have to pay the whole cost of maintaining them. In some cases, syndicates have been formed, either to bring back a vineyard that has deteriorated or to guarantee a supply of a great wine. In the Médoc, one group of Americans bought Château Lascombes, receiving wine from each vintage as a dividend, and untold pleasure from visiting the château and tasting the old bottles in its cellars. The showplace of Graves is Château de la Brède, where Montesquieu wrote his *Spirit of the Laws*. It is a fairy-tale building surrounded by a moat, and while its wines are in the official lists, their quality is no longer of any interest.

The wines are the real ornaments of Graves, and Haut Brion is the prize. Its owner is fond of inviting people to lunch or dinner to taste a range of wines, sometimes as many as twenty. In front of each place will be six or eight glasses, and with each course three or four wines may be served, starting with the most recent bottling and going on back, past '49, '47, '45, and '42 through '37 and '34, beyond '29 and '28 and '26, perhaps all the way back to the classic 1906, or even the magnificent 1900 or 1899. In between will be bottles of the lesser vintages, some of which will be delights. At first, the sheer number of wines is overwhelming, and then comes the sudden realization that playing such a fantastic version of *la musique des vins* is a memorable event. Before you parade sixty years of great wines, each different, each exceptional in its own way. One of the delights in knowing about wines is that every once

GRAVES

GRAND CRU

Château HAUT-BRION

* * *

CRUS CLASSÉS

Château	Château
Bouscaut	Carbonnieux
Domaine de Chevalier	Fieuzel
Haut-Bailly	Latour-Haut-Brion
Malartic-Lagravrière	La Mission-Haut-Brion
Olivier	Pape Clément
Smith-Haut-Lafitte	La Tour Martillac

GRAVES WHITES

CRUS CLASSÉS

Château	Château
Bouscaut	Carbonnieux
Couhins	Domaine de Chevalier
Laville-Haut-Brion	Malartic-Lagravrière
Olivier	La Tour Martillac

in a while such a chance presents itself, because the wines are available, thanks to generations of winemakers.

Across the street from Haut Brion is La Mission Haut Brion; nearby are La Tour Haut Brion, Fanning La Fontaine, and Pape Clément. In the neighborhood are nine other vineyards officially classified as outstanding in 1953.

The white wines of Graves are perhaps the best known in the world. They are never very dry and they are never very sweet, and, perhaps because they are not pronouncedly one or the other, they are often disappointing to drink. In an effort to make them resemble the wines of Sauternes, which are good only when they are sweet, much sulphur is often used in Graves whites to kill all sorts of enemies of the wine. It is known to inhibit the action of bacteria and elements that can hurt the wine. Acetic acid, which turns a wine to vinegar, is checked by sulphur, as is the process of oxidation that causes a wine to rust. Graves whites have a tendency to oxidize, a development called *madérization* in French, because it causes the wine to take on the taste and character of a wine of Madeira. The taste is fine in Madeira, but terrible in Graves, and destroys the wine. With sulphur, the wine takes on a sweet taste which will hide flaws. The taste is precisely that of the smell of a burnt match, and it is easily identified.

Haut Brion is leading the way to producing very dry Graves and in encouraging the bringing out of the natural, soft, pleasing qualities of the wines, without the heavy use of sulphur. In the years to come, fine white Graves may be offered that are light, moderately dry, and full of perfume. Today, with few exceptions, the wines taste of sulphur.

A dozen miles south is the village of Léognan, boasting such vineyards as Haut-Bailly, Larrivet-Haut-Brion, the Domaine de Chevalier, and Carbonnieux. Carbonnieux, like many of the other Bordeaux vineyards, once belonged to the Church, and the local fathers made fortunes by selling the wines to Mohammedan Turkey, which prohibited alcohol. In a classic book on wines, published a century ago in England, a man named Charles Redding tells this story: "To mystify Mahomet was a worthy and holy work for the children of the Popish St. Bernet. So they exported their white wines, of which the limpidity was remarkable, as 'The mineral waters of Carbonnieux.'" The French comment on the story is always the same: "Better to sell wine as water than water as wine, which is what usually happens."

The official listings of the vineyards are making it easier to buy Graves, both reds and whites, just as the classification of St. Emilions has made its fine wines more readily obtainable. You are sure of a good bottle when you buy the best-rated growths.

꧁ ꧂

Sauternes and Its Neighbors

The wine of gold, one of the greatest sweet wines on earth, comes from a district barely half a dozen miles square, half an hour south of Bordeaux. Château d'Yquem has been in the family of the Marquis de Lur Saluces for a couple of centuries, and its fame is still older. The vineyards surround the complex of buildings that forms the domain, and are dominated by the towers and stone walls of the castle, from the terrace of which you can see the road, the river, and the lesser districts on the far shore. All around this queen of sweet white wines is a royal family of vineyards.

The grapes are picked late, after a mold, *Botrytis cinerea*, has worked to shrivel them. The French call it the *pourriture noble*, the noble rot, and only bunches that show the mold are picked for pressing. Vintages often continue into November; sometimes they go on until Christmas, the vineyards being gleaned for the mold-touched grapes several times. Yquem's more than two hundred acres produce less than ten thousand cases of wine, even in a great year. A generation ago, a wine called *crème de tête* was produced, made of the best barrels of the vintage, but it was later decided to sell all wines that were less than *crème de tête* to the shippers for bottling as regionals.

Two dozen top growths were singled out for special mention in 1855, and a long list of others was rated. Nearly one hundred thousand cases are produced by the top vineyards in a good year, and when the hundred-odd lesser Classed Growths are included, a third of a million cases are produced, which amounts to about a quarter of the total production of Sauternes and its neighbor, Barsac.

At Yquem, the wines may ferment for three weeks, and will remain in barrel for three years. At one time, all the wine-making equipment was silver-plated, but today glass and enameled copper and brass are used. Wine is never allowed to touch metal because it will pick up taste. Absolute and constant cleanliness is vital for winemaking, and while a stranger to a vintage may be surprised at the casual way grapes are handled, dumped, and shoveled into battered vats with shabby tools and rickety machinery, this equipment has been scrubbed and rinsed until it is immaculate. At the wealthiest domains, the *pressoirs* look like operating rooms or ships spruced up for an admiral's inspection, but cleanliness is vital in even the poorest and shabbiest winemaking quarters or the wine will go bad.

The soil is responsible for Sauternes and Barsac—men can only bring out what nature provides. Sauternes is fuller and richer than the wines of Barsac, but the good wines from both townships are always sweet. There is no such thing as a dry Sauternes or Barsac. You will occasionally see the phrase *Haut Sauternes* on a label, but this has no meaning, and is merely a way to convince the buyer that the Sauternes is very sweet, in much the way that *Haut-Médoc* is supposed to indicate a superior claret.

The usual planting in Sauternes and Barsac is 40 per cent Sauvignon, 55 per cent Semillon, and 5 per cent Muscadelle. The Semillon is a small bearer, but supplies the richness and finesse that makes the wines great. Some vineyards have tried to increase yield by increasing the Sauvignon planting, but this has been unsuccessful. At Château Climens in Barsac, which is the greatest white Bordeaux after Yquem, the vineyard is planted entirely in Semillon and the fermentation is allowed to continue for six or eight weeks.

Many of the vineyards produce outstanding wines. In 1929, Climens surpassed Yquem. Its neighbor is Coutet, whose vineyards are 65 per cent Semillon; the wine is lighter and drier than Climens. The driest of all the great Sauternes is considered to be Château Filhot, which is underclassed by the 1855 listings as a Second Growth. All the great wines of the two districts live for decades, protected from old age by their sweetness. Vintages follow the Graves pattern, but the grapes are susceptible to frost, and in cold years the wines fail to gain the desired sweetness.

Sweet wines are somewhat out of fashion today, and many people pass them by; but there is nothing quite so wonderful as a Sauternes with a sweet dessert—say a chocolate pudding or some other rich sweet that calls for luscious accompaniment. The wines are deceptively strong—very often as much as 14 per cent alcohol—and when they are lightly chilled they have the great ability of bringing out the taste of sweet foods, because the character of their own sweetness is so different and so completely satisfying. People are apt to want less of a sweet wine than a dry one, so that half-bottles are often enough for a small dinner party.

SAUTERNES
AND BARSAC

FIRST GREAT GROWTH
Château D'YQUEM

* * *

FIRST GROWTHS

Château	Château
Bayle (Guiraud)	Climens
Coutet	La Tour-Blanche
Peyraguey	Rabaud
Rieussec	de Suduiraut
Vigneau	

* * *

SECOND GROWTHS

Château	Château
d'Arche	Broustet
Caillou	Doisy
Filhot	Lamothe
de Malle	de Myrat
Nairac	Peixotte
Romer	Suau

The Classed Growths listed here were rated in the Bordeaux classification of 1855, and are recognized by the *Appellation Contrôlée*. There are many others in the communes of Sauternes, Barsac, Bommes, Fargues, and Preignac.

❧ ❧

Minor Wines of Bordeaux

The five great Bordeaux districts produce the great wines of Bordeaux, but there is a group of other districts that produces good wines and provides most of the tonnage needed for wines that are labeled simply *Bordeaux Rouge* or *Bordeaux Blanc*. Some of these names get on a label occasionally. Each district is carefully delimited by law, and only wines that meet minimum standards are permitted to use place names on a label.

Across the Dordogne from the Médoc are the districts of Bourg and Blaye, and around St. Emilion and Pomerol are townships that have the right to add one or the other name to their own, and the districts of Fronsac and Néac. In the tongue of land between Bordeaux and St. Emilion, called Entre-Deux-Mers, are the Premières Côtes de Bordeaux and Graves de Vayres. Just above Sauternes and Barsac is the district of Cérons, while across the river are Loupiac, Ste.-Croix-du-Mont, and St. Macaire. The wines are red, white, and *rosé*, dry and sweet, generally light and fresh when young, and in no way comparable to the rated growths from the great districts.

Slightly farther afield to the east stretch more vineyards, but these are not considered part of Bordeaux. The closest is Montravel, which produces second-rate red wines, and to the south are Bergerac and Monbazillac, whose wines are often drunk in France as a substitute for Sauternes. These wines are produced in quantity and are short-lived, but improved winemaking makes it possible to ship them abroad, and their low prices may give them some popularity in foreign markets. They taste best on the spot.

CRUS BOURGEOIS SUPÉRIEURS OF THE MÉDOC

CHÂTEAU	TOWN	CHÂTEAU	TOWN
de l'Abbé-Gorsse-		Cambon-la-Pelouse	Macau
de-Gorsse *	Margaux	Canteloup	St.-Estèphe
Abel-Laurent	Margaux	Capbern *	St.-Estèphe
Angludet *	Cantenac	Caronne-Ste.-Gemme	St.-Laurent
Anseillan	Pauillac	La Chesnaye-	
Antonic	Moulis	Ste.-Gemme	Cussac
d'Arche	Ludon	Citran-Clauzel	Avensan
d'Arsac	Arsac	Clarke	Listrac
Balogues-		Clauzet	St.-Estèphe
Haut-Bagès	Pauillac	La Closerie	Moulis
Barateau	St.-Laurent	du Colombier-	
Beaumont	Cussac	Monpelou	Pauillac
Beauséjour	St.-Estèphe	La Colonilla *	Margaux
Beau-Site	St.-Estèphe	Conseillant	Labarde
Cru Beau-Site-		Constant-Trois-	
Haut-Vignoble	St.-Estèphe	Moulins	Macau
Domaine de la		Corconnac	St.-Laurent
Bégorce-Zédé *	Soussans	La Couronne	Pauillac
Bellegrave	Pauillac	Cru Coutelin-Merville	St.-Estèphe
Bellevue-		Le Crock	St.-Estèphe
Cordeillan-Bagès	Pauillac	Cusseau	Macau
Cru Bibian-Darriet	Listrac	Daubos-Haut-Bagès	Pauillac
Biston-Briette	Moulis	Doumens	Margaux
Bontemps-Dubarry	St.-Julien	Dubignon-Talbot *	Margaux
Le Boscq	St.-Estèphe	Duplessis	Moulis
Bouqueyran	Moulis	Duroc-Milon	Pauillac

CHÂTEAU	TOWN	CHÂTEAU	TOWN
Dutruch-Grand-		La Houringue	Macau
Poujeaux *	Moulis	de Labégorce *	Margaux
Dutruch-Lambert *	Moulis	Ladouys	St.-Estèphe
d'Egmont	Ludon	Lafitte-Carcasset	St.-Estèphe
Fatin	St.-Estèphe	Lafon	Listrac
Felonneau	Macau	de Lamarque	Lamarque
Fonbadet	Pauillac	Lamothe	
Fonpetite	St.-Estèphe	de Bergeron	Cussac
Fonréaud	Listrac	de Lamouroux *	Margaux
Fontesteau	St.-Sauveur	Lancien-Brillette	Moulis
Fourcas-Dupré *	Listrac	Lanessan *	Cussac
Fourcas-Hostein *	Listrac	Lemoyne-Lafon-	
Fourcas-Laubaney	Listrac	Rochet	Ludon
Cru Robert		Lestage	Listrac
Franquet	Moulis	Larrieu-Terrefort-	
du Galan	St.-Laurent	Graves	Macau
Gironville	Macau	Cap-de-Haut	Lamarque
du Glana	St.-Julien	Gloria *	St.-Julien
Grand-Duroc-Milon	Pauillac	Grand St.-Julien *	St.-Julien
Grand-Duroc-		Lestage-Darquier-	
Pauillac	Pauillac	Grand-Poujeaux	Moulis
Grand-Village-		Leyssac	St.-Estèphe
Capbern	St.-Estèphe	Liversan	St.-Sauveur
Granins	Moulis	Ludon-Pomiès-	
Gressier-Grand-		Agassac	Ludon
Poujeaux *	Moulis	Mac-Carthy	St.-Estèphe
Guitignan	Moulis	Mac-Carthy-Moula	St.-Estèphe
La Gurgue	Margaux	Malécot	Pauillac
Haut-Bagès-Averous	Pauillac	Malescasse	Lamarque
Haut-Bagès-		de Marbuzet	St.-Estèphe
Drouillet	Moulis	Martinens	Cantenac
Haut Senot	Soussans	Maucaillou	Moulis
La Haye	St.-Estèphe	Maucamps	Macau
Houissant	St.-Estèphe	Mauvezin	Moulis

CHÂTEAU	TOWN	CHÂTEAU	TOWN
Clos de May	Macau	Poujeaux-Marly	Moulis
Meyney	St.-Estèphe	Priban	Macau
Meyre-Vieux-Clos	Avensan	Cru Ramages-	
Monbrison	Arsac	de-Batisse	St.-Sauveur
Monpelou	Pauillac	Reverdi	Lamarque
Montbrun *	Cantenac	Robert-Franquet	Moulis
Morin	Moulis	Cru Roche	St.-Estèphe
La Morère	St.-Estèphe	Romefort	Avensan
Moulin-à-Vent	Moulis	La Rose Capbern	St.-Estèphe
Moulin-Riche	St.-Julien	Rose-La-Biche	Macau
Moulis	Moulis	Rosemont *	Labarde
Nexon-Lemoyne	Ludon	de Ruat	Moulis
Les Ormes-de-Pez	St.-Estèphe	St.-Estèphe	St.-Estèphe
Paloumey	Ludon	Clos St.-Estèphe	St.-Estèphe
de Parempuyre		Saransot-Dupré	Listrac
(Cruse)	Parempuyre	Ségur	Parempuyre
de Parempuyre		Cru Ségur-Fillon	Parempuyre
(Durand-Dassier)	Parempuyre	Sémeillan	Listrac
Pauquet	Margaux	Sénéjac *	Le Pian
Paveil-de-Luze *	Soussans	Siran	Labarde
Peyrabon	St.-Sauveur	du Taillan	Le Taillan
de Peyrelebade	Listrac	du Testeron	Moulis
de Pez *	St.-Estèphe	La Tour-du-	
Phèlan-Ségur	St.-Estèphe	Haut-Vignoble	St.-Estèphe
Pibran	Pauillac	La Tour-de-Mons *	Soussans
Picard	St.-Estèphe	La Tour-Milon	Pauillac
Pierre-Bibian	Listrac	La Tour-de-Pez	St.-Estèphe
Plantier-Rose	St.-Estèphe	La Tour-Pibran	Pauillac
Pomeys	Moulis	Cru La Tour-	
Pomiès-Agassac	Ludon	des-Ternes	St.-Estèphe
Pomys	St.-Estèphe	des Trois-Moulins	Macau
Pontac-Lynch	Cantenac	Tronquoy-Lalande	St.-Estèphe
Poujeaux-Castaing	Moulis	Tujean	Blanquefort

* Outstanding vineyards marked with asterisk.

† Those châteaux not in italics produce 10,000 cases or more, annually. Others produce over 1000 cases, annually.

৺ SUMMARY

Considered to be the greatest of red wines in great years. Usually good buys in good years. Top vineyards generally produce wines of good quality even in poor years. A red Bordeaux is always the safe, conservative buy.

The top wines are so famous that they are always high in price, because the demand is so great. The First and Second Growths are wines that should be bought as soon as they come on the market, at which time they are usually at their lowest available prices. Such wines usually need ten years to mature.

Best buys in Bordeaux reds are the Classed Growths, including Exceptional Growths, Bourgeois Supérieur Growths. They should be château-bottled. The Third, Fourth, and Fifth Growths often cost half as much as First and Second Growths.

Wines not appearing on the official listings are dubious buys; they may be good or bad, but they are invariably overpriced. Exceptions to this rule are rare.

Regional wines (those labeled Haut Médoc, Médoc, Margaux, St. Julien, St. Estèphe, St. Emilion, Pomerol, or Graves) are generally well-made but overpriced.

The rated white wines of Graves and Sauternes are generally excellent. Unrated wines are generally poor. Regional whites are sometimes good, always overpriced.

The mere word, "Château," on a label means nothing, unless the wine is on the official lists. Only tasting will determine whether an unlisted wine is good, and worth the price.

Burgundy

The legendary wines of Burgundy—in short
supply for a thousand years and famous for
another thousand before that—come from
three groups of vineyards a hop, skip and
jump apart—Chablis, the Côte d'Or, and
southern Burgundy.

Chablis lies a hundred miles south of
Paris, the great white wines of the township
coming from a scant ninety acres of Great
Growths and some seven hundred acres of
First Growths that produce perhaps a hundred thousand cases in a fine year—and
practically nothing at all two or three years
in a decade, when frost hits.

Eighty miles to the south is Dijon, the
city from which the royal dukes once
reigned, and a dozen miles farther south is
the Golden Slope, a vineyard strip thirty
miles long that produces all the rest of the
great white and red Burgundies in its two

47

sections, the Côte de Nuits and the Côte de Beaune. There are some eight hundred acres of *Grands Crus* and some four thousand acres of *Premiers Crus* in the Côte d'Or, producing perhaps seven hundred thousand cases in a fine year. Another five thousand acres, bearing Côte d'Or vineyard names, produce an additional three quarters of a million cases of good wines, comparable to the lesser growths of Bordeaux.

Southern Burgundy begins just south of the Golden Slope, three hilly districts famous for their annual flood of good wines—Chalonnais, Mâconnais, and Beaujolais. There's never enough to go round.

Only in the past couple of decades has it been possible to buy a wine bearing the name of one of the fabulous vineyards with any assurance that you were getting what you paid for. In the Middle Ages, the great wines were reserved for royalty. Pope Gregory XI gave a cardinal's hat to the man astute enough to send him thirty casks of Clos Vougeot. Burgundians still claim that less than half the wine was genuine. Burgundy's last duke, Charles the Bold, prohibited the import of foreign wines in an effort to control adulteration, and even Charlemagne attempted to control the practice. When the vineyards passed into the hands of the people after the Revolution, demand grew so great that merchants devised a new way to cash in on famous vineyard names.

All the great vineyards of the Golden Slope lie in that curve where the hill meets the flatland. Out in the plains and high on the hill, the vineyards—usually planted in the ordinary Gamay grape, not the noble Pinot—produce ordinary wines. Each town added the name of its most famous vineyard to its own, so that wines from the whole township could go to market bearing a great name—Gevrey became Gevrey-Chambertin, Morey became Morey-St.-Denis, and so on. Nobody was supposed to be the wiser. But in the 1930s, owners of the great vineyards, both nobles and farmers, began setting up the French government's *Appellations d'Origine* laws, which today limit and define every great Burgundy vineyard and those of most of the other French regions. The *Appellation Contrôlée* laws are an assurance of authenticity for the great wines of France.

Burgundy comes in bottles that have sloping shoulders and look broad and burly beside the slimmer, high-shouldered Bordeaux bottles; the phrases on the labels identify what's inside. The al-

coholic content, yield per acre, grape varieties, the method of pruning, vine care, and winemaking are all specified.

The *Grands Crus* of the Côte d'Or must be at least 11.5 per cent
alcohol for reds, 12 per cent for whites. (These are also expressed
in degrees, interchangeably.) The *Premiers Crus* must be 11 degrees
for reds and 11.5 degrees for whites; those bearing simply the name
of the town are half a degree less. Wines bearing town names, the
vineyard name, or the phrase *Premiers Crus* are limited to a yield
of 35 hectoliters per hectare (a hectoliter is 26.4 American gallons
and a hectare just under 2.5 acres). There are about 2.4 gallons in
a case of twelve bottles, so the yield is about 150 cases per acre.
Great Growths are limited to a yield of 30 hectos per hectare, about
132 cases per acre. In southern Burgundy, yields running up to 50
hectos are permitted. All this is summed up on the label with the
phrase *Appellation Contrôlée,* the best wines bearing a vineyard
name.

Since the 1930s, more than a million vineyard deeds throughout
France have been examined, but a scant ten thousand have been
approved for classification.

The French say *"Respectez les crus"* when they talk of Burgundies, meaning that you look for the vineyard name on the label
when you want a good wine.

Wine shippers came into their own after the Revolution; they
still provide most of the world's Burgundies, buying wines from the
vineyard owners and buying bits of the famous vineyards whenever
they get the chance. There is a temptation, of course, to stretch
the great wines, and shippers have been known to sell hundreds of
cases of a famous wine when they owned only enough of the genuine product to fill a few bottles. Fines are stiff, but temptation is
strong; many *négociants* have made fortunes by blending. There
are honest shippers, and some of the best are listed ahead of the
vineyard listings in towns where they have holdings.

Unlike Bordeaux, Burgundy vineyards are divided among different owners. In some of the great vineyards, a man may own a section scarcely the size of a tennis court.

In the past decade, there has been a great increase in the number of vineyard owners who bottle their own wines and market them directly, rather than sell to the shippers.

This practice, called estate-bottling, is patterned after the Bordeaux château-bottling system, and is a further guarantee of authenticity. Such wines always bear the name of the grower, followed by the word *propriétaire, vigneron, viticulteur,* or *récoltant* on the label. There is invariably an additional phrase on the label to identify these estate-bottlings, generally one of the following:

> *Mis en bouteilles par le propriétaire*
> *Mis en bouteilles au Domaine*
> *Mise de la propriété*
> *Mise à la propriété*
> *Mis au Domain*
> *Mise du Domaine*

All these phrases mean that the wine was bottled by the grower or at the estate. The last phrase means the wine may not actually have been bottled right at the estate, but that it is from the grower.

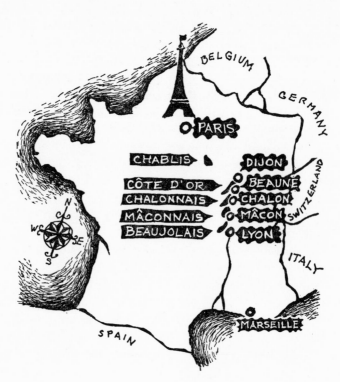

Several misleading statements meant to imply estate-bottling are used by opportunistic shippers. A favorite is *Mise en bouteilles dans mes caves,* which means "Bottled in my cellars"; this has no meaning, of course, because all wines are bottled in cellars. A still more specious phrase that attempts to cash in on the Bordeaux nomenclature as well is *Mise en bouteilles au Château.* There are no châteaux in Burgundy, at least in the Bordeaux sense, and the phrase is meaningless and misleading. Shippers buy vineyards so they can put the word *propriétaire* on their labels, hiding the fact that they are *négociants,* but French law makes a point of insisting that the title can only be used with wines from the proprietor of a vineyard. A shipper who owns vineyards in one town but ships from another must put the word *négociant* on the label. He may try to get around this by listing on all his wines the fact that he is a *Propriétaire à Nuits St. Georges* or some other township. *The important point to check is that the man whose name is on the bottle is the actual producer of the wine in the bottle, not a proprietor somewhere else.* It is wise to inspect with care any bottle that contains the word *négociant* on the label, to make sure that it is a bottle from one of the many good shippers, not from the swarm of poor ones.

The control laws make it easy to buy Burgundies in spite of the nomenclature, if only because of the care with which the vineyards have been rated. As vineyards improve, their ratings are elevated on the basis of a series of tastings by local experts, who, before passing judgment, consider the original bouquet, acquired bouquet and body of the wine, along with chemical analyses for alcohol, sugar, acid, tannin, tartrates, glycerine, and other elements. A Burgundy with a high rating has earned its rank.

The wines that warrant such fantastic attention and meticulous definition are legally defined as Great Growths, generally cost over three dollars a bottle in New York City, and are the most sought-after of all the world's great wines.

These eight hundred-odd acres of Great Growths correspond in area to the Great Growths of Bordeaux, and produce just about the same amount of wines. Altogether, the châteaux of Pétrus, Ausone, Cheval Blanc, Yquem, Haut Brion, Lafite, Latour, Margaux and Mouton may produce seventy-five thousand cases of wine in a good

BURGUNDIES DEFINED AS GRANDS CRUS

---◦❀◦---

CHABLIS (90 *acres*)

Bougros
Les Preuses
Vaudésir

Grenouilles
Valmur
Les Clos
Blanchots

* * *

CÔTE DE NUITS (620 *acres*)

Chambertin
Chambertin-Clos de Bèze
Latricières-Chambertin
Mazoyères-Chambertin
Charmes-Chambertin
Mazis-Chambertin
Griotte-Chambertin
Ruchottes-Chambertin
Chapelle-Chambertin
Clos de la Roche
Clos Saint-Denis

Bonnes Mares
Clos de Tart
Musigny
Clos de Vougeot
Echézeaux
Grands-Echézeaux
Romanée-Conti
Romanée-St.-Vivant
La Romanée
La-Tâche
Richebourg

* * *

CÔTE DE BEAUNE (100 *acres*)

Corton
Corton Charlemagne
Charlemagne
Montrachet

Bâtard-Montrachet
Chevalier-Montrachet
Bienvenues-
    Bâtard-Montrachet
Criots-Bâtard-Montrachet

year, most of which is offered on the market. In Burgundy, many sections of the great growths are in private hands, and portions of the production are held off the market; perhaps not fifty thousand cases of these wines are available in a good year.

Many of the First Growths are unknown, and may cost two dollars or less. Importers hesitate to bring them in because so many people still buy by fame, unaware that many of the First Growths are underpriced. To simplify buying, all the *Premiers Crus* of Burgundy are listed, town by town, so that they may be recognized when they come on the market.

It is not the soil alone that makes a great wine; it is also the weather and the vineyard exposure to the sun. Because the vineyards are on a slope, they get the full force of the sun, and because the Golden Slope angles slightly to the east, they get early-morning sun to dry the dew. Those in the southern half, in the Côte de Beaune, face slightly more to the east, getting additional sun, which has a tendency to make the wines fatter and softer. Noonday glare hits the soil at an angle, so that the grapes do not get too much heat. Long, warm days without intense heat or cold are needed to bring the grapes to a slow perfection. For such reasons, Burgundy vineyards are called *climats*, for the climate is as important as the soil.

Frosts are a danger in Burgundy, particularly in Chablis and the Côte d'Or. Winds from the east or north, blowing from the Alps and across the Burgundian plain, can freeze those parts of vineyards that are exposed or that face eastward. For this reason, many Burgundians own small portions of different vineyards rather than large sections of one, the idea being that frost or hail may strike one section and miss another completely. This is precisely what happens, and is one reason why vintage classifications of Burgundy are inadequate. Because the vineyards are broken up, and each man makes his wine in his own way, there are further variations in the quality of the wines, even those from one particular vineyard.

◆◊◆

Chablis

A trip to Burgundy usually starts in Paris, and the wine buyer drives down during the winter. A few tourists on the way to the Riviera may turn off the Route Nationale for a summer day in Dijon, but there are few great bottles to be bought in the restaurants, one vineyard looks like another, and the Côte d'Azur seems more inviting. It is the Parisian who enjoys Burgundy, driving down in May when the vines are in flower, or at vintage time, to watch and help with the picking. And the most knowing of Parisians drive down to Chablis for Sunday lunch.

Chablis is a slate-roofed village in a great amphitheater of a valley, across the hills from Auxerre. On the edge of the town square is the Hôtel de l'Etoile, which makes a point of serving dishes cooked with Chablis: a roast pork basted with the wine, or a chicken from Bresse; ham or veal from Burgundian farms; a fish poached in Chablis from the tiny river, appropriately called Le Serein, that meanders past the town. Dessert is a soufflé served in an orange. All the recipes are yours for the asking, printed on bits of colored paper. And the wine is from the surrounding vineyards— cool, green-gold, glinting Chablis.

After lunch, you step out into the square and look over the dark slate roofs of the town to the deep green of the vineyards that produce one of the most famous wines on earth. Across the river to the north is the oyster-shaped hillside draped in the vines of the seven vineyards that produce all the Chablis entitled to be called *Grand Crû*, ninety acres in all. Flanking it are the seven hundred-odd acres that produce the wines of the *Premiers Crûs*, about a quarter of which are resting; and on around the horizon are the vineyards that produce wines that can be called simply Chablis or Petit Chablis. These last account for a quarter of a million cases, most of which is sold in France. But the vineyards are so exposed and so far to the north that hail and frost often cut the yield in half. In 1953, nearly the entire vintage was destroyed by spring frosts; almost half the vintage was ruined in 1955 and again in 1957. In 1960 no wine was made. Some of the younger men have given up in disgust and gone off to make their livings elsewhere.

Growers own small portions of the various vineyards, producing a *feuillette* from one section, a *quartaut* from another. The first holds perhaps 175 bottles of wine, the second holds half that.

Chablis is the wine for oysters. It is also the driest of all the great table wines in the world, a perfect balance of fresh, sharp taste combined with a full and satisfying bigness that is the perfect foil

C H A B L I S

GRANDS CRUS (*about 90 acres*)

BLANCHOTS	*LES PREUSES*
BOUGROS	*VALMUR*
LES CLOS	*VAUDÉSIR*
GRENOUILLES	

* * *

PREMIERS CRUS (*about 700 acres*)

Beauroy	*Mont de Milieu*
Beugnon	*Montée de Tonnerre*
Butteaux	*Montmain*
Châpelot	*Pied d'Aloup*
Châtain	*Séchet*
Côte de Fontenay	*Troeme*
Côte de Léchet	*Vaillon*
Fourchaume	*Vaucoupin*
Les Forêts	*Vaulorent*
Les Lys	*Vaupinent*
Melinots	*Vosgros and Vogiras*

for simply cooked fish and sea food, for such cheeses as Camembert and Brie, and for all kinds of ham and pork dishes. Experts talk about its gunflint taste, reminiscent of the smell of sparked flint, a taste imparted by the kind of chalky clay—called Kimmiridgian clay—that sets the vineyard soils apart. This is the same kind of soil found in the Champagne vineyards, which begin fifty miles to the north, and something in the taste of Chablis links it to the wines of Champagne, as well as to the other white wines of Burgundy to the south—the Montrachets, the Cortons, the Meursaults, and the southern Burgundies of Pouilly Fuissé. All are produced from the same grape, the Pinot Chardonnay, called *Beaunois* in Chablis and in Pouilly Fuissé. But the wines are different, varying with the change in soil.

In spite of the control laws, there are many fake Chablis bottles on the market. Dishonest shippers stretch their small stocks of genuine Chablis with white wines from the Rhône and from Algeria. The worst offenders are apprehended regularly and pay stiff fines, but if they have managed to sell a few hundred cases of fake Chablis before they are caught, the fine is worth it.

The best shipper in Chablis is J. Moreau et Fils, who sell nothing but the wines of Chablis, and are proud to own two acres in the vineyards of Les Clos and two in Valmur, both *Grand Crûs*, and twelve acres of the First Growth, Vaillon, as well as numerous holdings in vineyards that are entitled to be called simply "Chablis."

There are many fine growers who bottle their own wines for market. One of the best is Marcel Servin, who owns seven acres of vineyard, divided among Bougros, Les Preuses, Blanchots, and Vaillon—a substantial holding. Pushing him hard are men like Michel and Vocoret, Jules Merat, Robert Monin, B. Fevre and more than seventy other growers. Such names are the ones to look for on a bottle of Chablis.

❦ ❧

The Côte de Nuits

A professional wine buyer, who is always short of good red Burgundies, may ignore Chablis when he drives down from Paris and head straight for Dijon, stopping only long enough at Saulieu to have lunch if he made an early start—dinner if a late one—but stopping on the way to phone ahead for a reservation at Alexandre Dumaine's Hôtel de la Côte d'Or. One of the three greatest restaurants in France, it has the best collection of Burgundies on earth. If Dumaine knows far enough ahead of time, he will prepare one of those fabulous French dishes that take a day or so to get ready—an incredible chicken steamed over the French stew called *pot au feu,* or something equally unbelievable created from the veal or beef from Charolles to the south, or game, or a *pâté en croûte,* or something evolved out of fish or sea food. With the first courses he will serve you a young Beaujolais or a slightly older wine from the Côte de Beaune, but with the masterpiece he will serve a great bottle from the Côte de Nuits, a wine that will be at least five or six years old, and perhaps two or three times that. Three hours later, a glazed but contented wine buyer will hoist himself into his car and drive the thirty miles to the Hôtel de la Cloche in Dijon. After a good night's sleep, he'll be ready for an early start the next morning, to taste in the cellars of the Côte de Nuits.

In the old days, the vineyards around Dijon produced popular wines, but when transportation improved, nothing would do but the great wines a dozen miles to the south. The Dijon vineyards were replanted in Gamay grapes after *phylloxera* destroyed them in the 1870s, and these are now used mostly for making pleasant *rosé* wines, production of which centers around the little town of Marsannay. Not far away, at Chenôve, is Grosse Margot, the world's largest winepress, named after a bawdy medieval Marguerite, who presided over the vintage bacchanalia, joining in the fun. The reward for her prowess is her nickname, Big Maggie, for the largest winepress in the world.

The great vineyards of the Côte de Nuits begin at the little town of Fixin and run south for a dozen miles to a stone quarry below the town of Nuits-St. Georges.

There are vineyards everywhere one looks, but all the great ones stretch along a single broken slope, an expanse sometimes hardly two hundred yards wide, where the flatland meets the hill. All the great vineyards are planted in the Pinot grape: the Pinot Noir for the red wines; the Pinot Blanc, also called the Pinot Chardonnay, for the whites. These are related grape varieties. Over the centuries slight mutations in the vines have occurred, and experts say that differences in the vines can be noted from vineyard to vineyard. These variations help account for the incredible variety of the wines. Burgundy is not one wine but many, similar but distinctive, and the wines get progressively lighter and softer as you travel south.

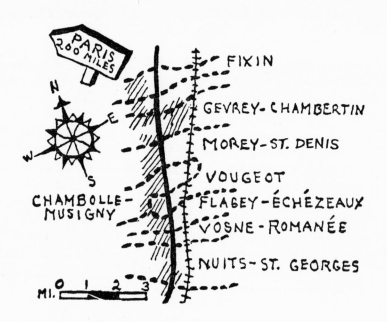

⊷§ *FIXIN*

Fixin is back off the main road, and the tourist guides note it because there is a Napoleonic museum above the town, at the end of a long avenue of pines. Much more interesting than the Bonapartist influence is an old church built in the days when William was conquering England. Nearby is a roofed pool where the local wives do their laundry.

It is a town the French call *culterreux*. Politely translated, this means "backward"; literally translated, the word means "backside in the ground," the implication being that the local residents have not made the complete transition from vegetable to animal. The farmers—*paysans* is the French word that we translate as "peasants" —wear *sabots* on their feet and olive corduroys on their backs, the wooden clogs and coarse cloth still signifying the primitive countryman.

The best vineyards are Clos de la Perrière and Clos du Chapitre, both slightly less than a dozen acres in extent. They are unofficially called *têtes de cuvées*, or head vats, it being the custom in every Burgundy town so to designate outstanding vineyards regardless of official ratings.

Pierre Gelin, an owner of Clos du Chapître, is one of the fine winemakers of Burgundy. When you taste his wines, he will hand you a *tastevin* to use. A *taste* is a silver saucer the size of a small ashtray, perhaps an inch deep and three inches across, with a loop on the brim by which it can be held. The traditional tasting-cup of Burgundy, it is dimpled and ridged on the inside to catch the light, and so that the wine can be seen at various depths, its color being an excellent way to judge its quality. The wine should be absolutely clear and brilliant. In Fixin, it should be an extremely dark, rich ruby.

Two of the owners of Clos de la Perrière are Jehan-Joliet and Bellote. They will tell you that *clos* is an old French word meaning "walled enclosure," and as you travel down the Golden Slope, you will see that many of the vineyards are walled, with stone arches or gateways in the walls, leading to the vines. These are built by the

F I X I N

PREMIERS CRUS (about 50 acres)

Les Arvelets	Clos de la Perrière
Aux Cheusots	*Les Hervelets*
Clos du Chapître *	*Les Meix-Bas*

* Those vineyards which are set in roman are traditionally classed *têtes de cuvées*.

different owners of the vineyards to mark their sections, and there is usually a plaque on each with the owner's name and address.

Like most red Burgundies, the wines of Fixin spend at least two years in barrel and need at least another two or three years to reach maturity. They are often at their peak at seven or eight years old, but many of them will continue improving for a decade, still being drinkable twenty or thirty years after the vintage.

◆ GEVREY-CHAMBERTIN

Gevrey is a pleasant village of solid stone houses back off the National Highway, and it is here that the *Route des Grands Crus* begins, a winding dirt road that passes by all the great vineyards of the Côte de Nuits. It is almost unknown to tourists, but familiar to every wine buyer in the world who has any knowledge of Burgundies, for he drives along it every year or so, checking for frost damage, for vineyard sections that are resting, for sections that are planted in young vines and thus make poor wines, for sections that are poorly tended. The vineyard name on a wine label is not enough, for wine is a product of man as well as of nature.

But one has to start with the soil, and there are 215 acres of the best in Gevrey entitled to bear the name of Chambertin. The first vineyard was named in the year 630, when the Duke of Burgundy gave some vineyard land to the Abbey of Bèze. The abbey imme-

GEVREY - CHAMBERTIN

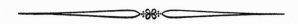

GRANDS CRUS *(about 215 acres)*

LE CHAMBERTIN

CHAMBERTIN-CLOS DE BÈZE

CHAPELLE-CHAMBERTIN

CHARMES-CHAMBERTIN

GRIOTTE-CHAMBERTIN

LATRICIÈRES-CHAMBERTIN

MAZIS-CHAMBERTIN (OR MAZYS)

MAZOYÈRES-CHAMBERTIN

RUCHOTTES-CHAMBERTIN

* * *

PREMIERS CRUS *(about 175 acres)*

Bel-Air	*Ergots*
Champeaux	*Estournelles*
Championnets	*Le Fonteny*
Cherbaudes	*Gazetiers*
Clos du Chapître *	*Les Gémeaux*
Clos-Prieur *	*Les Goulots*
Le Clos Saint-Jacques	*Issarts*
Au Closeau	*Lavaut*
Combe-aux-Moines	*La Perrière*
Aux Combottes	*Petite-Chapelle*
Les Corbeaux	*Poissenot*
Craipillot	*Les Veroilles*

* Only a part of these vineyards are officially rated, the wines being identified on the label by the phrase *premier cru*.

diately walled the thirty-seven acres in order to thwart grape-stealers. Twenty generations later, sometime in the thirteenth century, the neighboring field, or *champ*, was planted by a peasant named Bertin. In later years, the lands surrounding these two were planted in vines; today they are divided into eight vineyards. All of them are called Chambertin, and all are classed as Grands Crus. In Burgundy, Chambertin is called *Le Grand Seigneur*—the biggest and fullest of the great Burgundies—because of its deep color (called *robe*), its immense bouquet, great intensity and the strength and power of its taste.

Up behind the town are the two vineyards of Clos St. Jacques and Les Veroilles, the latter owned entirely by the Domain Deschamps. The local people feel that these should be classed with the vineyards that are allowed to be called Chambertin. These two are near the little town of Brochon, a name that rarely appears on a label because its best wines are permitted to go to market as Gevrey-Chambertin.

Among the finest producers of Chambertin is Armand Rousseau, one of those who first led the trend to estate-bottling. This was a brave move, because the shippers boycotted the estate-bottlers in the beginning. The early pioneers were in a bad way in poor years: when the wines weren't good enough to be bottled under the vineyard names, angry shippers refused to buy them for their blends. Many growers, consequently, estate-bottle only part of their production in order to placate the shippers.

Other vineyard owners in addition to Rousseau who have parcels in Le Chambertin or Clos de Bèze as well as in other vineyards, are Camus, Damoy, Drouhin-Laroze, the Domains of Marion and Trapet, Deschamps, General Rebourseau, and Jaboulet-Vercherre. Three of Burgundy's best shippers—Joseph Drouhin, Louis Latour, and J. H. Remy—also own sections; another shipper, the Comte de Moucheron, has holdings in Clos St. Jacques. Many of these owners also have holdings in the other eight Chambertin vineyards, along with such growers as Pierre Gelin, J. Coquard, Belorgey, and Veuve Tortochot.

Because of the fame of Chambertin, many of the First Growths of Gevrey are ignored; when these are available they are excellent buys, often a dollar less a bottle than Chambertin.

✇ MOREY-ST. DENIS

A hundred yards down the vineyard road from Chambertin, just over the town line, is the first *Grand Cru* of Morey, Clos de la Roche. One of the world's great winemakers, Henri Ponsot, owns portions of it, along with several of the Chambertin proprietors. Ponsot consistently produces outstanding wines from his section, bottles that rank with the greatest.

The little commune boasts nearly forty acres of Great Growths, divided among Clos de la Roche, which has eleven acres, the five acres of Clos St. Denis, the seventeen of Clos de Tart, and five of Bonnes Mares, the rest of this last vineyard being in the next town down the line, Chambolle. Most of these wines are big and full, sometimes taking a decade or longer to reach maturity; the exception is Clos St. Denis, which is invariably light. The vineyard gets a lot of sun because of its slope, and its wines are more like those from vineyards farther to the south. The wines of Morey are almost unknown because, until the control laws were passed, they went to market as Chambolle or Gevrey, or simply with their vineyard names. Having no fame, many of them were sold to shippers, who used them to perk up their blends. Today, they are excellent buys under their own names.

Often enough, a good vintage will be sandwiched between two great ones, and its wines will be ignored. Such a vintage was 1948, which came between the incredible '47s and the magnificent '49s. Such vintages are called *intermediate years*, and because they are ignored in the rush to greatness they are invariably underpriced. Precisely the same thing happens to vineyards—they are over-shadowed by their neighbors. The vineyards of Morey are such intermediates, as are those of Fixin. For generations the wines have been underpriced in much the way many third and fourth growths of Bordeaux have been undervalued. They are still among the most reasonable of the great wines on the market, and while their reputation and the demand is slowly increasing, they will continue to be bargains for a few years longer, as will the many excellent Burgundies that are classed as First Growths.

Among the owners of Morey vineyards, in addition to Ponsot, are Mommesin, Cosson, Bertrand-Sigaud, Coquard, Groffier, Jacquot,

Lignier, Marchand, Moine, H. Remy, Rameau, Rousseau, Seguin, Tortochot, and Ory. Some white wine is produced in the lesser vineyards.

MOREY-ST.-DENIS

GRANDS CRUS (*about 40 acres*)

BONNES-MARES CLOS DE TART
CLOS DE LA ROCHE CLOS SAINT-DENIS

* * *

PREMIERS CRUS (*about 250 acres*)

Les Bouchots ———	*Les Faconnières*
Calouères	*Les Fremières*
Chabiots	*Les Froichots*
Les Chaffots	*Les Genevrières*
Aux Charmes	*Les Gruenchers*
Les Charrières	*Maison-Brûlée*
Les Chénevery *	*Meix-Rentiers*
Le Clos Baulet	*Les Millandes*
Clos Bussière	*Les Mochamps*
Clos de Lambrays	*Monts-Luisants*
Le Clos des Ormes	*La Riotte*
Le Clos-Sorbés	*Les Ruchots*
Côte Rôtie	*Les Sorbés*

The vineyards which are set in roman command higher prices than the others.
* Only a part of this vineyard is officially rated, the wines being identified on the label by the phrase *premier cru*.

⤳ CHAMBOLLE-MUSIGNY

The vineyard road is just downhill from Bonnes Mares, the last great vineyard on the particular slope that begins with the Chambertin vineyards. The hill extends to the village of Chambolle, at the base of the Golden Slope's biggest little mountain. Pines and beeches climb the steeps above the town, forming a dark and eerie backdrop where one can imagine a medieval opera might be played, all about trolls and mountain kings and enchanted princesses.

Legend and superstition must have been born in Chambolle. Perhaps it was here that an early vintner devised the idea of burying a toad under each vine to ward off frost and hail, a practice that continued until the turn of the century. Somewhere in the neighborhood, the idea that women were dangerous to wines, vines, and vineyards may have also begun. To this day, French women are not welcomed in a winecellar—foreign females are, when escorted—and many vintners still quote the old saying that pregnant women can make the wines go sour. At one time, pregnant women were prohibited from entering vineyards, and if one worked undiscovered during the harvest, the whole vintage was supposed to go bad. On the other hand, pruning vines has always been considered woman's work; she is supposed to provide wonderful meals for harvest hands, and if she conceives during vintage time, it's a sign of a good year. The phases of the moon, as well as those of women, were once important to vintners: a red moon, for instance, was considered a good omen when new vines were being planted.

Vintners have every reason to be superstitious, because nobody really knows why one wine should be good, while another from an adjoining vineyard is indifferent. The mysteries of fermentation must be somehow involved, as well. The most recent discovery is that the second fermentation that occurs early in the spring, called the *malo-lactic fermentation,* is as important to a wine as the original action of the yeasts on the sugar in the grape. Up to a decade ago, many vintners bottled before the slow malo-lactic was complete and the wines often began to work in the bottle. The result was that many wines were thought of as not being able to travel; these wines are shipped without trouble today, and more and more of them will become available in the years to come.

CHAMBOLLE –
MUSIGNY

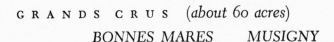

G R A N D S C R U S (*about 60 acres*)
BONNES MARES   MUSIGNY

* * *

P R E M I E R S C R U S (*about 140 acres*)

Les Amoureuses	*Derrière-la-Grange*
Les Baudes	*Les Fousselottes*
Aux Beaux-Bruns	*Les Fuées*
Les Borniques	*Les Groseilles*
Les Charmes	*Les Gruenchers*
Les Chatelots	*Les Hauts-Doix*
Aux Combottes	*Les Lavrottes*
Les Combottes	*Les Noirot*
Les Cras *	*Les Plantes*
	Les Sentiers

Those vineyards which are set in roman command higher prices than the others.
   * Only a part of this vineyard is officially rated, the wines being identified on the label by the phrase *premier cru*.

The stage set at Chambolle is the best place to get the feel of Burgundy. Just south of town, the high slope makes a sudden drop of more than a hundred feet; spread below are the rest of the vineyards of the Slope of Nights. On the right are the twenty-five acres of Les Musigny and Petits Musigny, which go to market as Le Musigny and which are light, delicate, full of perfume, and possessed of that quality the French call *race*, breeding. These are thought of as feminine wines: it is only proper that one of Musigny's neighbors be called Les Amoureuses, women in love.

The Comte de Voguë is the largest owner; others are Adrien & Roblot, Clair-Dau, Hudelot, Groffier, and the Domains of Prieur and Mugnier.

✒️ CLOS DE VOUGEOT

The Golden Slope takes four giant steps down from the heights of Chambolle to the walled expanse of Clos de Vougeot, the largest of the great Burgundy vineyards. Its 127 acres extend to the main road leading to Beaune, and the wall along it is broken with a series of ornate gateways built by the owners of these lower sections.

This vineyard, like so many others in wine lands all over Europe, was first planted by monks. The custom in the twelfth century was for bands of monks to move out from the religious centers and set up their own communities. The group that chose the swampy lands where the river Vouge emerges from the slope came from Cluny. They decided to call themselves Cistercians, after the reeds that choked the spot. They adopted the motto *The Cross and the Plow* and immediately put all the local residents to work draining the land. They probably borrowed vines for their vineyards from the Tart nuns and Bèze monks up the hill. The wines quickly became famous. It is still the custom for French troops to salute the vineyard whenever they pass as a mark of respect.

The castle took a couple of hundred years to build and the story goes that the monk who did the original plans was so pleased with his design that he signed them before showing them to his abbot. The abbot was so displeased with this show of pride that he turned the plans over to another monk—who botched them—then ordered the architect to build the castle and include all the flaws. The architect died of shame on the spot.

Today, all that remains of the monastery is the castle, the press house, and the wall around it. The wall alone took a century to build. The handsome turreted building encloses a great court and a press house, all of which have been restored since World War Two. It is the property of the Chevaliers du Tastevin, a promotional organization that raised the rebuilding funds by popular subscription. Every other month they hold a dinner in the press house, wearing their red robes and monkish hats, singing old Burgundian drinking songs and downing toasts to the Burgundies pouring into their cups. The organization is a colorful sort of Chamber of Commerce for Burgundy, and—among other things—the Chevaliers have sponsored an annual festival for the vineyards near Dijon, en-

V O U G E O T

GRAND CRU *(about 127 acres)*

CLOS DE VOUGEOT

* * *

PREMIERS CRUS *(about 30 acres)*

Le Clos Blanc   Clos de la Perrière
Le Clos Blanc de Vougeot (*white*)   Les Cras *
                                       Les Petits-Vougeot

* Only a part of this vineyard is officially rated, the wines being identified on the label by the phrase *premier cru.*

couraging the vintners around Marsannay to produce a pleasant pink wine that is now shipped all over the world. They also market under their own label a series of wines which have a wide distribution.

For a time during the nineteenth century, Clos de Vougeot was a single domain, but today there are more than fifty owners. The wines vary widely, but are generally big and flowery, and are supposed to have a scent of violets. However this may be, the best sections are in the top third of the vineyard and were once reserved for royal gifts. The choicest section is said to be the corner nearest Chambolle, which is called Les Musigny de Clos Vougeot, owned by grower Louis Gros. All the wines command high prices because of their fame, including those from a separate small five-acre vineyard just outside the walls that produces a white wine of good quality. Most of this is owned by L'Héritier-Guyot, who is a maker of cassis in Dijon. Cassis is the currant syrup used in Vermouth Cassis, and for Burgundy's greatest hangover remedy, *rince cochon.* Rinsed pig is made by putting an ounce of cassis in a highball glass, then filling the glass with white Burgundy. It tastes good even when you don't have a hangover.

Owning a section of the Clos is a mark of distinction in Burgundy, for shipper and grower alike. Nobody owns much, but the larger owners are J. Morin, with fourteen acres, and Veuve Noellat and Champy Père & Fils, with five acres each.

✍§ *FLAGEY-ECHÉZEAUX*

The vineyards just behind the walls of Clos de Vougeot are in the township of Flagey by a tour de force of mapmaking that would do credit to the wildest American gerrymander. They produce some of the finest wines in Burgundy, reasonable in price and easy to buy because they are sold under the vineyard name of Echézeaux.

Flagey is way across the tracks, out in the Gamay vineyards of the plain. The Echézeaux plantings are joined to the rest of Flagey by a narrow strip of land along the southern side of Clos Vougeot. The vineyards give the town any luster it may have—and the *Appellation d'Origine* has dulled even this, because the wines are allowed to go to market as Vosne-Romanée, the township just to the south.

These are intermediate wines, overshadowed by the neighboring Romanées and Vougeot, but they are big wines, famous for their balance, and they often spend a decade developing.

The vineyard of Grands Echézeaux is on the left along the *Route des Grands Crus*, backing against the wall of the Clos. This Great Growth is twenty-three acres in extent, and owners are the Domaine de la Romanée-Conti, a writer and wine authority named René Engel, Louis Gros, Mongeard-Mugneret, Groffier, Jayer-Marius, and L. Gouroux, among others. All these also own sections in the vineyards across the way, wines from which are marketed as Echézeaux.

There are ten Great Growths on the right of the vineyard road. They extend over some eighty acres, and can go to market as Vosne-Romanée according to the *Appellation Contrôlée*. The vineyard control laws not only take into account the actual properties of the vineyards and its wines, but also the traditions and customs that have become part of the vineyards. In this case, custom provides a single name for a group of vineyards, greatly simplifying buying— a practice that might well be extended to other townships, both in Burgundy and in other vineyard districts. But such changes would flout tradition elsewhere, and so the multiplicity of names goes on.

F L A G E Y – E C H É Z E A U X

GRANDS CRUS (*23 acres*)
LES GRANDS ECHÉZEAUX

* * *

E C H É Z E A U X (*80-plus acres*) *

Champs Traversins	*Les Loachausses*
Clos-Saint Denis	*Les Poulailliers*
Les Cruots or *Vignes Blanches*	*Les Quartiers-de-Nuits*
Les Echézeaux-de-Dessus	*Les Rouges-du-Bas*
En Orveaux	*Les Treux*

* These ten vineyards of Flagey-Echézeaux go to market as Les Echézeaux and are classed *Grands Crus* by the *Appellation d'Origine* laws.

Other owners in those vineyards whose wines are called simply Echézeaux are J. and R. Bossu, Confuron, and Mugneret-Gibourg.

Here again the wines mark a transition, combining the big and sturdy qualities of Clos Vougeot wines with the breed and balance and full bouquet of the Romanées. The resulting taste is similar to that of Bonnes Mares and the other wines of Morey-St. Denis, which are also intermediate wines. Maybe these wines are unfamiliar because they are not famous, or because they are distinctive in their own way and unlike their neighbors, or because they combine the outstanding characteristics of the famous wines on either side. There seems to be less temptation to tamper with wines that are not famous, which may account for the continuing magnificence of these through the years.

But there is no real justification for their lack of fame. Echézeaux wines continue to be among the best bargains in Burgundies and, like the other intermediates of the Côte de Nuits, they consistently outclass the more expensive wines from the Côte de Beaune, the southern half of the Golden Slope. In case they are ever so famous as to be marketed under their vineyard names, see listing above.

⌘§ VOSNE–ROMANÉE

The greatest wines of Burgundy come from scarcely sixty acres of vineyard in the commune of Vosne-Romanée. Only the two great vineyards of Chambertin, the best wines of Clos Vougeot, and those of Musigny can match the incredible balance achieved by the Grands Crus of Vosne, and none can match La Romanée-Conti for *"sa couleur brillante et veloutée, son parfum et son feu charment tous les sens."* Its charming fire can bring the dead to life, said the prospectus for the sale of the vineyard after the Revolution, adding that all this wonder may be partly achieved because the vineyard is higher in the west than in the east, presenting its breast to the first rays of the sun, thus gaining for it *"les impulsions de la plus douce chaleur."* The recipient of this softest heat measures four and a half acres.

The owner of this fabulous vineyard is the Domaine de la Romanée-Conti de Vilaine et Chambon. The Domaine takes its name from its greatest vineyard, but owns all fourteen acres of La Tâche, as well as portions of Richebourg, the fullest of the wines, and parts of Grands Echézeaux and Echézeaux.

The Domaine is responsible for much more than its own great wines, because M. de Vilaine, the present owner, was the man who introduced estate-bottling to Burgundy. Estate-bottlings are available today from every Grand Cru and every great winemaker thanks to the example set by the Domaine.

La Romanée-Conti takes its second name from the Prince who was diplomatic chief for Louis XV and bought it to spite Madame de Pompadour, who wanted to own the finest vineyard property in France. It has changed hands only nine times since the thirteenth century, the last being in 1869, when the ancestors of the present owner paid what would be today something like $25,000 an acre for it.

The vineyards of the Domaine are perhaps the most meticulously cared for of any on earth. The caretakers of the property for M. de Vilaine, called *régisseurs* in French, have devoted their lives to the vineyards. Old methods are clung to. For fifty years after other growers had begun grafting their stocks, the Domaine clung to the old vines; not until 1946, when yield had fallen off greatly, were grafted stocks planted in the vineyards.

Nothing repays such attention, of course, as well as these greatest of Burgundy vineyards. The finesse and strength of the great wines often take ten years to develop, and they may still be perfection after twenty years or longer in bottle. Today there are two small cellars behind the larger cellar for new wines under the Domaine buildings in Vosne. In them are all the bottles that are left of the great vintages; a few of them go back to the last century. From time to time, a few bottles are sent out into the world, and when this happens, it is a rewarding thing to be a friend of the man who receives them.

The corks used by the Domaine are always stamped with the vineyard and vintage, a practice now followed by most of the world's great winemakers. And it is a very long cork. Good corks are expensive, the best coming from Spain and Portugal. A long cork is protection for the wine, guarding it through its long life. Through the cork, say the vintners, wines breathe the slight quantity of air that permits them to continue to develop. When a vintner uses a long cork, it is an indication that he thinks the wine is good and will live a long time.

Vosne is blessed with fine winemakers. In addition to the Domaine, others include Lamarche—who owns all three acres of La Grande Rue as well as sections in other vineyards—Matrot, Marey-Monge, Louis Gros, Charles Noellat, and Arnoux. Louis Latour is considered the best shipper owning property in the commune; another shipper, Liger-Belair, owns all of the two-acre vineyard of La Romanée. Many of the vineyards classed as First Growths are in good years on a par with the Great Growths to the north.

Many Burgundies suffer from lightness in poor years. The wines of Vosne are no exception, and are *chaptalized*. Three generations ago, a man named Chaptal discovered that you could add sugar to the fermenting grape *moût*, or must, and this would be changed into alcohol during the fermentation. The practice is permitted when the must is light in natural sugar, and the amount that may be added is decided by inspectors of the *Appellation d'Origine*. Some experts feel that Burgundians are too eager to chaptalize their wines, desiring the higher degree of alcohol, which makes a wine taste big and full at the expense of delicacy and balance. The best vineyards produce wines that are over 12 degrees of alcohol, even in ordinary years, and often reach 14 degrees, which is the legal

V O S N E – R O M A N É E

GRANDS CRUS *(about 54 acres)*

RICHEBOURG   ROMANÉE-CONTI
LA ROMANÉE   ROMANÉE-ST. VIVANT
                              LA TACHE

* * *

PREMIERS CRUS *(about 100 acres)*

Les Beaux Monts   La Grande Rue
Aux Brûlées   Aux Malconsorts
Les Chaumes   Les Petits Monts
Le Clos de Réas   Les Reignots
Les Gaudichots   Les Suchots

maximum for table wines. In exceptional years, 15 degrees are not unknown, although such tremendous amounts of sugar cause trouble during fermentation.

Some experts feel that chaptalizing makes a wine that is heavy and without distinction. Others claim that they can actually taste the crystalline flavor of sugar in a chaptalized wine, but this is probably imagination. The slight tinge of sweetness that is often noted in a dry Burgundy or Bordeaux is more apt to be glycerine. This is one of the oils that develop naturally during a normal fermentation, imparting smoothness to a young wine, which is in turn transmuted to softness and velvet as the wine ages. The wines of Vosne and the other great wines of the Golden Slope develop good amounts of glycerine, and this may be what gives a slightly sweet taste to a great Burgundy, especially when it is drunk before it reaches maturity. The glycerine can be noticed in the wine on the sides of your glass, as it holds back the run of drops to the pool in the bottom. They are called the *tears* of wine. A thin wine clings hardly at all to the sides of the glass, and shows no tears.

Whatever its evils, chaptalization is nearly universal in Burgundy. It is permitted by law and makes possible the production of full wines in poor years. In good years, many of the better producers forgo the practice, the tendency being to avoid manipulating the wines as much as possible.

Some feel that the wines of the Domaine are overchaptalized. Much experimentation with chaptalization is taking place today, as well as with all details of winemaking. Here and there, an ancient technique is modified slightly, and gradually the vintner's knowledge is extended. Basically, of course, he must have a sense about wines and what is happening to them, but science helps him, letting him focus on things that are still beyond measure and beyond words—for instance, that moment when fermentation is complete and the wine must be drawn off the lees and put in barrel. Only a skilled winemaker can decide, and he is as important to the wine as the vineyard and the noble vine that produces the grape.

◄§ NUITS-ST. GEORGES

Nuits is the metropolis of the slope it names, a thriving town of a couple of thousand people that straddles the main road and a shallow stream that almost dries up in summer. The township is the largest of the slope, and more wines come from it than any other, but none of them are classified as *Grands Crus*. This may be why the *Route des Grands Crus* ends on the rise above the stream and joins a road that leads down to the town.

Nuits is a town of shippers, few of whom own vineyard sections of any distinction, but who thrive on growers who do. After the wines have fermented, the barrels are trundled to the cellars of the shippers, where they mature and are bottled and otherwise prepared for market. Much of the preparation consists of "balancing" the wines, a practice called *la grande cuisine*. The "cooking" consists of blending big wines with small ones, acid ones with fat ones. As one wag has put it, the shippers of Nuits have done more for the *Appellation Contrôlée* than any other group, the fines they pay supporting the inspection teams of the *Appellation*. There are others who deny this vigorously, claiming that the Beaune shippers contribute much more in fines, if only because there are more of them. More tolerant observers are quick to note that the shippers offer large quantities of good wines, year after year, at not unreasonable prices, and while the labels on the bottles may leave something to be desired when accuracy is considered, many of them are brilliant examples of typography.

The shippers of Nuits can claim fame for one thing, however—sparkling Burgundy, one of the most popular sparkling wines the world has ever known. The market for it was greatly expanded during the 1930s, when the shippers had trouble selling their poorer wines and hit upon the idea of adding bubbles. Burgundians have been jealous of the Champagne producers to the north ever since the days of Louis XIV, whose physician persuaded him to try the sparkling wine of Champagne, the district from which the good doctor came. Champagne became the rage at court, grievously affecting the sale of Burgundy. The shippers of Nuits finally devised a way of getting their own back. The fact that sparkling Burgundy is invariably made from mediocre wines, and that no sparkling wine of distinction is made from red wines because they are too heavy and full of taste, has had no effect on its popularity. Sparkling Burgundy is rarely available in France, having been invented for the export market, where it has found eager customers because it is usually a little cheaper than Champagne.

Perhaps the most illustrious citizen of Nuits-St. George (although not the most popular) is Henri Gouges, the vice-president of the Comité National du Vins Fins de France, and one of the members of the Appellations Committee, which is charged with the task of prosecuting cases of wine fraud. He has spent his life fighting frauds, and is one of the men most responsible for winning the passage of sensible control laws. He is also an owner in several vineyards, among them being Les St. Georges, which is still the best in the township and which produces the biggest wines.

All the wines of the commune are noted for bigness, and because they possess much tannin they develop slowly and live a long time. They are very full to the taste—*juicy* is a word frequently applied to them—and the French say they are *mordant*, so full that one seems able to bite and chew them.

There is some feeling that these wines of Nuits are underrated, and that several of them deserve to be classed as Great Growths, particularly those that are neighbors of Les St. Georges, such as Les Vaucrains, Les Cailles, and Les Porrets. Those from the north, near the town line of Vosne, are also well thought of, particularly Aux Boudots, Aux Cras, and Aux Murgers. All these are rated as First Growths, however, along with more than thirty others. Nuits St. Georges has more First-Growth vineyards than any other town in Burgundy.

Prémeaux is the southernmost town of the Côte de Nuits that produces wines of distinction. Because they are so similar to those of Nuits, they are marketed as Nuits-St. Georges.

Some white wines are produced. They are generally wines that are big and full, but, like those from Chambolle-Musigny and Clos de Vougeot, quantity is small.

In addition to Gouges, other growers include Besancenot-Granane, J. Confuron, Gessaume-Bourgeois, Grivot, Guy, E. Michelet, Misserey-Rollet, and Morizot-Pelletier. General Gouachon owns all of the vineyard of Clos des Corvées, and Domaine Mugnier owns all of the Clos de la Maréchale in Prémeaux, and Henri Gouges owns Les Porrets vineyard. The Hospices de Nuits owns portions of several vineyards, and all of Les Didiers, which is next to Les St. Georges. A substantial portion of the hospital's income comes from sale of wines from its vineyards; many of the properties were originally donated to the hospital.

N U I T S – S T . G E O R G E S

P R E M I E R S   C R U S (*about 335 acres*)

Aux Argillats *	*Perrière-Noblet* *
Les Argillats *	*Les Porrets*
Aux Baudots	*Les Poulettes*
Les Cailles	*Les Procès*
Les Chaboeufs	*Les Pruliers*
Aux Chaignots	*La Richemone*
En la Chaîne-Corteau *	*La Roncière*
Aux Champs-Perdrix *	*Aux Rousselots*
Aux Cras	*Rue-de-Chaux*
Aux Crots *	Les St. Georges
Aux Damodes *	*Aux Thorey* *
Les Hauts-Pruliers *	*Les Vallerots* *
Aux Murgers	Les Vaucrains
La Perrière	*Aux Vignes-Rondes*

P R É M E A U X

P R E M I E R S   C R U S (*about 130 acres*)

Clos Arlots	*Clos des Grandes Vignes*
Clos de la Maréchale	*Le Clos Saint-Marc*
Clos des Argillières	*Les Corvées-Paget*
Clos des Corvées	Les Didiers
Clos des Forêts	*Aux Perdrix*

Those vineyards which are set in roman command higher prices than the others.
  * Only a part of the vineyard is officially rated, the better wine being identified on the label by the phrase *premier cru.*

◆◦§◦◆

The Côte de Beaune

The southern half of the Golden Slope begins with the vineyards called Corton and continues fifteen miles to Montrachet—which produces the greatest dry white wine in the world. In between these two *Grands Crus* are ten townships that produce a flood of soft red and big white wines that vary widely but form a family because all of them come from this single extensive slope and from the Pinot grape, either Noir or Chardonnay. Once these wines were all called Beaune, but now the town and vineyard names appear on the label to identify some of the most satisfying wines on earth. They are generally ready for drinking two or three years after the vintage, reaching their prime when five years old and usually gone when ten. Their life is short, but it is glorious.

People come from all over the world to the wine auction held in Beaune every November. The wines are from vineyards up and down the Beaune Slope, owned by the Hospices de Beaune, and the prices not only support the Hospices but also establish a general level for other Burgundies of the vintage.

The first auction took place a hundred years ago, although the first hospital was founded four centuries before that by Louis XI's tax collector, Nicolas Rollin. There are really two hospitals— l'Hôtel-Dieu takes care of patients from the vicinity who cannot afford to pay, and the Hospice de la Charité takes care of the old and young, fifty of the first and sixty orphans. The holdings consist of about a hundred acres of vines, and the entire cost of the hospital is paid for by the wines. A good year for Burgundy, then, is a good year for the ancient and the orphaned and the ill, and will even benefit the as-yet unborn, for a charity maternity wing is soon to be built. The vineyards take care of their own, as well as the thousands over the world who love Burgundies.

In the old days, the Dukes of Burgundy gave their vineyards to the Church, perhaps to insure salvation, and today's owners give vineyard parcels to the Hospices, perhaps for the same reason. It is a mark of distinction to own a cask from the Hospices. Quality varies widely from one parcel to another; prices are invariably high. Because the wines are bought in cask, there is a chance that they may not be bottled properly. The auctions are held in the court of the Hospices, bidding for each cask continuing until a candle burns down to a mark—all a fascinating procedure. The wines are sold under the name of the donor of the vineyard, not by a vineyard name, and the outstanding *cuvées*—a word that generally means "vat," or "vatting," but in this case means "lot"—are these red wines:

Cuvée	*Cuvée*
Nicolas Rollin	*Dr. Peste*
Charlotte Dumay	*Dames Hospitalières*
Guigone de Salins	*Clos des Avaux*
Brunet	*Huges et Louis Betault*
Rousseau-Deslandes	*Estienne*
Dames de la Charité	*Billardet*
Fornet	*Fouquerand*
Arthur Girard	*Boillot*
Blondeau	*Général Muteau*

The best *cuvée* is generally considered to be that of Nicolas Rollin, and it is often the highest-priced Burgundy. The Hospices also own some white-wine vineyards in Meursault, among which are:

Cuvée	*Cuvée*
Baudot	*de Bahèzre de Lanlay*
Albert Grivault	*Goureau*
Jehan Humblot	*Loppin*

The red wines of the Beaune Slope should always be less expensive than those from the Côte de Nuits, because they do not reach the same heights of development, nor live as long. The exception is Corton, which experts rank with wines of Chambertin and Vosne-Romanée.

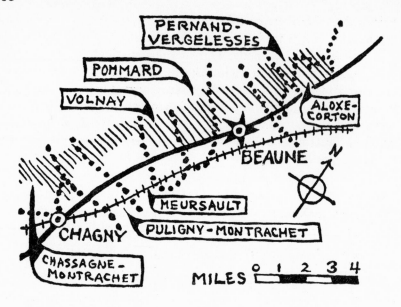

The wines of Beaune are particularly easy to drink, tasting fine with simply cooked meats, fowl, and wild game; also with sauce dishes and those with delicate flavors. They are wines to swallow rather than sip, wines that fill the mouth. They are also perhaps the most satisfactory wines to serve at a dinner party where the food may be elaborate. Good wines like those from the Côte de Beaune are made for good food and good company.

∝§ ALOXE CORTON AND ITS NEIGHBORS

People fall in love with wines. The happiest are those who love all good wines, but many are not promiscuous and find contentment with a single mistress. Voltaire was such a man. "Your wine has become a necessity to me. I give a very good Beaujolais to my guests from Geneva; but, in secret, I drink your Corton," he wrote to the owner of the Beaune Slope's greatest red wine.

Burgundies attract ardent admirers, perhaps because they are the fullest and most generous of all the world's great wines. But this may be simply because most vineyards have several owners, a group of swains hopelessly adoring, to praise their beauties. Most often, the first great wine you taste is the one you love the most. Fortunate the man is who falls in love with Corton.

The vineyards slope down to the village of Aloxe. Backed on the north by a wooded knoll, they curve around the height, reaching to the tiny hamlet of Pernand-Vergelesses, on its farther side. The Pernand wines are so similar that some are sold as Corton. Down on the highway is the village of Ladoix-Serigny, and from vineyards adjoining those of Aloxe are produced wines that can also be marketed as Corton.

But the glory of Aloxe is Le Corton, the greatest red wine of the Côte de Beaune, a perfect balance of fire and light. This wine matures faster than most of the Great Growths of the Côte de Nuits. It is often ready to drink when five years old. Its mature life is ten years or more, longer than the others of the Beaune Slope. The owners of the largest sections are Louis Latour, the prince of Burgundy shippers, and the Prince de Mérode, whose wines are marketed by another of Burgundy's great shippers, Joseph Drouhin. Few of the smaller owners estate-bottle their wines. As elsewhere along the Côte d'Or, the name *Corton* supplants the name of the township on the label.

Other vineyards near Corton are permitted to add the famous name to their own. Among them is Les Bressandes, the principal owner being Yard; others include Jaboulet-Vercherre and the Prince de Mérode. Clos du Roi, principally owned by Baron Thénard and the Prince de Mérode, is similarly entitled to use Corton on its label; the vineyard was once a pond originally filled in and planted by Charles the Bold, Burgundy's last Duke, from whom it passed to the French crown. Sections of several other vineyards are entitled to add Corton-Charlemagne or Corton to their names, depending on whether they produce white or red wines; any of the three names on a label is assurance of a superior wine, and the First Growths of the township are excellent values. Under the trade name Corton-Grancey, Louis Latour markets a good wine that is a blend of wines from his First Growth holdings.

Charlemagne was a vineyard owner here, and his name is added to the one that produces a great white wine that is big and full and said to hold the smell of cinnamon in its bouquet. Such detection of spice, fruit, and other scents in a wine is often fanciful. When a wine is so identified, what is meant, of course, is that there is a hint

A L O X E – C O R T O N

GRANDS CRUS *(about 330 acres)*

CORTON †
CORTON-CHARLEMAGNE
CHARLEMAGNE

Les Bressandes *	Les Maréchaudes *
En Charlemagne *	Les Meix *
Les Chaumes *	Les Meix-Lallemand *
Les Chaumes de la Voirosse	En Pauland *
Le Clos du Roi *	Les Perrières
Les Combes *	Les Pougets *
Le Corton *	Les Renardes *
Les Fiètres	Le Roguet et Corton
Les Grèves	La Vigne-au-Saint *
Les Languettes *	Les Vergennes

* * *

PREMIERS CRUS *(about 65 acres)*

Les Chaillots *	Les Meix *
Les Fournières	En Pauland *
Les Guérets	Les Valozières *
Les Maréchaudes *	Les Vercots

* Only a part of these vineyards are officially rated, the better wines being identified on the label by the phrase *grand cru* or *premier cru*.

† All the red wines from the listed vineyards go to market as CORTON.

L A D O I X - S E R I G N Y

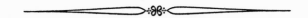

P R E M I E R S   C R U S *(about 25 acres)*

La Coutière

Les Grandes-Lolières

La Maréchaude

Les Petites-Lolières

La Toppe au Vert

P E R N A N D - V E R G E L E S S E S

P R E M I E R S   C R U S *(about 150 acres)*

Les Basses-Vergelesses

En Caradeux *

Creux-de-la-Net *

Les Fichots

Iles-des-Vergelesses

The vineyard which is set in roman is traditionally classed *tête de cuvées.*

* Only a part of these vineyards are officially rated, the better wines being identified on the label by the phrase *premier cru.*

of a smell or taste reminiscent of these things. Corton Charlemagne tastes like Corton Charlemagne, for example, not like a big, dry wine with cinnamon in it, not like a Chablis with a steely taste replacing the Chablis gunflint. The wine is distinctive, and when you taste it, you know it is a white Burgundy, because there is the characteristic taste of the Pinot Chardonnay grape in all white Burgundies, and you know it is Corton Charlemagne simply because it is not Chablis, or Musigny Blanc, or Meursault, or Montrachet. The wines are as like, or unlike, as children in a family.

Production of Corton Charlemagne is small, and likely to become smaller. The vineyard is as steep as those in Chablis. In both places, mud washed down by rains must be carried up again on the backs of men and placed around the vines, a job too difficult for animals and machines. Old vintners complain bitterly that tending such vineyards is also too difficult for the younger generation, who prefer easier ways of making a living. Louis Latour and Louis Jadot own large sections of the vineyard, and other sections are owned by such excellent growers as Cornu, Duc, Jaffelin-Rollin, Naudin, Page, Pialat, and Rapet.

Two of the best wine lots auctioned by the Hospices de Beaune each year, Cuvée Charlotte Dumay and Cuvée Dr. Peste, are produced on five vineyard sections in Aloxe Corton.

⤞ BEAUNE AND SAVIGNY-LES-BEAUNE

All Burgundies were once known as Beaune, even in Roman days, when the walled town was a stopover for travelers. Wines from other vineyards and townships along the Golden Slope have crowded to the top of the lists in the past thousand years, but the town of some 10,000 continues to be the capital of the world's most famous wine region. The ancient walls are used as wine vaults by some of the shippers. A Roman quarry provides magnificent storage for the wines of the excellent shipper Joseph Drouhin, and there are great cellars under many of the town houses, where the owners live atop their treasures and crow about the greatness of their wines.

Buyers from all over the world come to stay at the Hôtel de la Poste or the France et Terminus, but you can't buy a great bottle in either one. You do even more poorly in the pleasant restaurants of the town, which occasionally rate a star in the *Guide Michelin*, that annual guide to good cooking which continues to be the finest published. In fact, it's impossible to buy a fine Burgundy in any restaurant along the Golden Slope, perhaps on the theory that buyers will taste so many mediocre wines in the restaurants they will be overwhelmed by the wonders in the cellars, and pay the asking price. Nobody does, of course, for haggling with growers and shippers is as much a part of wine-buying as is tasting the wines in the cellars. But there is probably no better example of hope that springs eternal than the hope that leaps in the breast of a Burgundy shipper at the sight of a buyer.

Beaune is a wealthy town and a pleasant one, dominated by the Hospices, whose handsome cobbled court is framed, high overhead, by the steeply pitched roofs of the enclosing buildings, the diamond shapes of the black, green, and yellow slates forming patterns that were adapted from the Flemish and have become typical of Burgundy.

The most curious thing about Beaune is its phone book, a thin catalogue filled with the names of hundreds of wine shippers, many of them oddly similar. There are many more names than numbers, for a single shipper may export wines under a dozen different names, thus being able to offer his wares exclusively to a number of importers in the same country, under different labels. Printing of labels is a flourishing business in Beaune, and many of them, quite inappropriately called *étiquettes* in French, are as fancy as they are fanciful. Burgundy has been called the land of fraud, and it isn't hard to imagine those shippers who practice the *grande cuisine* gathering together after a busy day of blending wines to think up new firm names and phrases that will steer the innocent buyer away from the fine shippers and the estate-bottlers.

Good buyers like to taste in the morning, or late in the afternoon, because it is hard to taste with discrimination after a meal, when thirst and hunger have been satisfied. Certain foods will make any wine taste good, and a wineseller is delighted when he can persuade you to have a cup of bouillon. He will tell you there is no better way to clear the palate, but actually the broth gives your stomach an alkaline tone, making you both hungry and thirsty for almost anything. A small steak or some simple food will then make

B E A U N E

PREMIERS CRUS *(about 750 acres)*

Les Aigrots	*Les Epenottes* *
Les Avaux	Les Fèves
Le Bas des Teurons	Les Grèves
Les Blanches-Fleurs *	Les Marconnets
Les Boucherottes	*La Mignotte*
Les Bressandes	*Montée-Rouge* *
Les Cent-Vignes	*Les Montremenots* *
Champs-Pimont	*Les Perrières*
Les Chouacheux	*Pertuisots*
Le Clos de la Mousse	*Les Reversées*
Le Clos des Mouches	*Les Seurey*
Clos-du-Roi *	*Les Sizies*
Aux Coucherias *	*Sur les Grèves*
Aux Cras	*Les Theurons*
A l'Ecu	*Tiélandry*
En Genêt	*Les Toussaints*
En l'Orme	*Les Vignes-Franches*

Those vineyards which are set in roman are traditionally classed *têtes de cuvées*.
 * Only a part of these vineyards are officially rated, the better wines being identified on the label by the phrase *premier cru*.

S A V I G N Y – L E S – B E A U N E

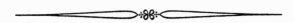

P R E M I E R S   C R U S *(about 400 acres)*

Basses-Vergelesses *
Bataillière *
Les Charnières
Aux Clous *
Dominodes *
Aux Fourneaux *
Aux Grands-Liards *
Aux Gravains
Aux Guettes *
Les Hauts-Jarrons
Les Hauts-Marconnets

Les Jarrons *
Les Lavières *
Les Marconnets *
Les Narbantons
Petits-Godeaux *
Aux Petits-Liards *
Les Peuillets *
Redrescuts *
Les Rouvrettes *
Aux Serpentières *
Les Talmettes
Aux Vergelesses

Those vineyards which are set in roman are traditionally classed *têtes de cuvées*.
* Only a part of these vineyards are officially rated, the better wines being identified on the label by the phrase *premier cru*.

a Gamay from the plain taste like a slope wine, and with a little cheese to follow, you will almost believe you are drinking Chambertin. As one buyer puts it: "Beware of a Burgundian bearing bouillon. He's trying to make you buy a bad Beaune."

The township of Beaune is the largest in the Côte d'Or, and the best wines of the commune are on the slopes north of the town, Les Grèves and Les Fèves, Les Bressandes and Les Marconnets. This last is on the line between Beaune and Savigny-les-Beaune, a hamlet on the banks of a tiny stream at the foot of the peak of Corton. Many of the Savigny vineyards are a continuation of those of the Pernand slope, and are also called Vergelesses. Their full southern exposure makes their vintages taste more like the soft wines of Beaune. In all, there are some twenty-five hundred acres of classified growths in the two communes. Most of the wine is red, possessed of finesse and elegance, and the wines become fuller in body and softer with age as you go south. On the southern town line that borders on Pommard is the vineyard of Clos des Mouches, from part of which is produced a white wine that is shipped by Joseph Drouhin. Some of the wines of Grèves go to market as Beaune-Grèves de l'Enfant Jésus.

Only the wines of Beaune township can go to market as Côte de Beaune, according to the *Appellation Contrôlée*. They must possess at least 10.5 degrees of alcohol if red, 11 if white. When the vineyard name appears on the bottle, they must possess an additional half degree. The same extra alcohol is needed if the wine bears the phrase *Premier Cru;* if this is not accompanied by a vineyard name, it is an indication that the wine in the bottle is a blend of wines, supposedly from various First-Growth vineyard holdings within the township. The way out of all this confusion, of course, is to look only for Côte d'Or Burgundies that have a vineyard name on the label, and to remember that the best of these will also have the name of the grower who made the wine, and bottled it himself.

The phrase *Côte de Beaune-Villages* is used when the red wines come from one of the other communes along the slope. According to the *Appellation Contrôlée*, the wines must be made from the Pinot grape, when the name of a town of the Golden Slope appears on a label. When Gamay and Pinot Noir wines are blended together, the wine is called *passe-tout-grains*. When Pinot Chardonnay and the white wines from the inferior Aligoté grape are blended, the wine is called *Aligoté*. Both are usually marketed simply as Burgundy.

In addition to Joseph Drouhin and Louis Latour, some other owners of vineyards in the Beaune commune are Carimontran, F. Clerget, H. Darviot, Goud de Beaupuis, J. Guillemard, and Martin-Bourgeot, plus the shipping firms of Bouchard Père et Fils, Champy Père et Fils, and Chanson Père et Fils.

⋙ POMMARD

The red wines of Pommard came to be known in the seventeenth century, when French Protestants who had fled to find religious freedom rhapsodized about the loveliness they had left behind. It wasn't only the wine. The village of Pommard on a summer day is cool and full of shade, the green of trees and ivy against the yellow split stone of the walls and buildings, the sun bright on the dusty cobbles. A small river runs in its walled bed beside the road, stone bridges arching across. The air is full of the rustle of leaves, the run of water, the creak of a wheel. It must have been painful to leave.

Vineyards surround the town—fairly large ones, many a dozen acres or more—and the town is a stone jewel set in this bed of greenery. The wines seem to call up the centuries before the Revolution, when life here was slow and close to the land. The wine is soft and sunlit, generous and full, a wine for romance and low laughter. The Pommards are the first hint of the warm south in the wines of Burgundy, and they deserve their fame.

Because Pommards became so popular, they were stretched and blended by shippers during the nineteenth century, but in recent years many growers have taken to estate-bottling their wines, and it is now possible to buy many excellent ones. The best of all is Rugiens, followed by Épenots, which is somewhat softer and rounder. All the Pommards have a big bouquet, reaching their peak four or five years after the vintage, and often lasting for ten years or more. This is the pattern for all the red wines of the Côte de Beaune.

The wines fill your mouth when you drink them, but they are so soft that you find yourself taking two or three swallows at a

POMMARD

PREMIERS CRUS *(about 330 acres)*

Les Argillières	*Les Croix-Noires*
Les Arvelets	*Derrière-Saint-Jean*
Les Bertins	Les Épenots
Les Boucherottes	*Les Fremiers*
La Chanière *	*Les Jarollières*
Les Chanlins-Bas *	Les Petits-Épenots *
Les Chaponières	*Les Pézerolles*
Les Charmots	*La Platière* *
Le Clos Blanc	*Les Poutures*
Clos de la Commaraine	*La Refène*
Clos du Verger	Les Rugiens-Bas
Le Clos Micot	Les Rugiens-Hauts *
Les Combes-Dessus *	*Les Saucilles*

Those wines which are set in roman are traditionally classed *têtes de cuvées.*

* Only a part of these vineyards are officially rated, the better wines being identified on the label by the phrase *premier cru.*

time, not sipping them as you do the bigger Burgundies from the Côte de Nuits. Two people have no trouble at all drinking a bottle with dinner; the French call such wines *facile à boire,* although the phrase is usually applied to wines of the south.

Growers include such men and firms as Comte Armand, Cavin, de Chavigny and de Lavoreille, F. Clerget, Clerget-Buffet, Mme. de Courcel, M. Drouhin, Domaine Gaunoux, Faivre, B. Gonnet, Goud de Beaupuis, Grivot, J. Guillemard, Jaboulet-Vercherre, Lochardet, L. Michelot, Domaine Lejeune, M. Parent, Poirier, and Pothier-Rieusset.

❧ VOLNAY, MONTHÉLIE, AND AUXEY-DURESSES

The long stretch of vineyards that begins north of Beaune continues unbroken through Volnay, the land rising slowly here as the slope curves west to the villages of Monthélie and Auxey-Duresses. The wines are soft and round, but their particular distinction is their bouquet and light, clear elegance. If Pommard is the wine for love and laughter, Volnay is for dalliance, the distinction perhaps being one of duration as well as intensity, because Volnays do not live quite so long as the Pommards. Even the Romans sensed this, and an old Latin saw becomes in French, "*On ne peut être gai sans boire du Volnay.*"

However essential to gaiety, Volnays are delightful to drink, and they are wines of which one is not apt to tire. The name comes from that of the Roman goddess of hidden springs and is applied to the wine not so much because one keeps finding new wonders in its depths as because there are many springs under the town and its vineyards.

On a rise behind the village is the domain of the Marquis d'Angerville, a young man who believes that adding sugar to the fermenting must destroys the balance of all Burgundies, not only the light ones of the Côte de Beaune. His ideas on the process of chaptalization are gaining support among other estate-bottlers, and the practice is slowly coming into disrepute. The father of the present Marquis was one of the leaders in the fight for French vineyard control laws, as well as for estate-bottling, and he is one of the group of men we can thank whenever we taste a fine Burgundy. Each generation can boast a few such men in every great wine-producing region, and they are the ones who keep alive the long tradition of great wine.

Volnay's greatest vineyard is Les Caillerets, but there are many others, among them Les Champans, Les Fremiets, and Santenots.

The demand for fine Burgundies is increasing, and many that were not formerly exported are now finding their way to market. Among these are the wines of Monthélie, generally lighter than Volnays, and much lower in price because they are not well known. The same is true of wines from Auxey-Duresses, one of the best of which is the red wine sold at auction by the Hospices de Beaune under the name Cuvée Boillot. Both townships produce red and white wines.

In addition to the Marquis d'Angerville are such growers and shippers as H. Bitouzet, H. Boillot, Bouchard Père et Fils, Bouley-Duchemin, F. Buffet, R. Caillot, de Chavigny and de Lavoreille, Clerget-Buffet, P. Emonin, Mme. François, Veuve Fabregoule, Malivernet, J. Prieur, R. de la Planche, H. Rossignol, Thévenot, and M. Voillot.

V O L N A Y

PREMIERS   CRUS   *(about 325 acres)*

Les Angles	Les Cras
Les Aussy *	*Fremiets*
La Barre or *Clos-de-la-Barre*	*Les Lurets* *
Bousse d'Or	*Les Mitans*
Les Brouillards *	*En l'Ormeau*
En Caillerets	Les Petures
Caillerets-Dessus	*Les Pitures-Dessus*
Carelle-Dessous *	*Pointe d'Angles*
Carelle-sous-la-Chapelle	*Robardelle* *
En Champans	*Ronceret*
Chanlin *	Les Santenots
En Chevret	*Taille-Pieds*
Le Clos-des-Chênes *	*En Verseuil*
Le-Clos-des-Ducs	*Village-de-Volnay* *

Those vineyards which are set in roman are traditionally classed *têtes de cuvées*.
   * Only a part of these vineyards are officially rated, therefore the best wines bear the phrase *premier cru* on the label.

M O N T H É L I E

P R E M I E R S   C R U S   *(about 65 acres)*

Le Cas Rougeot	*Le Meix Bataille*
Les Champs Fulliot	*Les Riottes*
Le Château Gaillard	*Sur La Velle*
Le Clos Gauthey	*La Taupine*
Duresse *	*Les Vignes Rondes*

* Only a part of this vineyard is officially rated, therefore the best wines bear the phrase *premier cru* on the label.

A U X E Y - D U R E S S E S

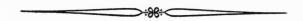

P R E M I E R S   C R U S   *(about 90 acres)*

Les Bas des Duresses	*Les Duresses*
Les Bretterins	*Les Ecusseaux **
La Chapelle	*Les Grands Champs*
Clos du Val	*Reugne*

* Only a part of this vineyard is officially rated, therefore the best wines bear the phrase *premier cru* on the label.

❧ MEURSAULT

Meursault has been cause for controversy ever since the Côte de Dijon ceased to produce great Burgundies. It is stated in French doggerel:

> La Bourgogne a trois côtes ou je ne suis qu'un sot,
> Côte de Nuits, de Beaune, et Côte de Meursault.

Fool or not, there are several good reasons for giving the slope a new name because the land flattens out and the character of the wine changes. What's more, all the great wines from Meursault to the end of the Golden Slope, near Santenay, are white wines. The name *Meursault* comes from the fact that a mouse can jump from the red vineyards to the white without a running start.

A small stream, named after the town, trickles down to the plain and the village straggles along its bank. The vineyards adjoining Volnay produce red wines which go to market as Volnay. The best of these is Santenots; some of this vineyard is planted in Pinot Chardonnay, and these white wines are marketed as Meursault. Les Cras and Les Petures are two other red-wine vineyards.

The vineyards south of the village produce big, soft white wines. They all have a special savor, a sunlit quality that reminds one of a haystack in the sun, or of straw. It is a taste as distinctive and unforgettable as the flinty taste of Chablis, and wineacres say it is the first hint of maderization. It is not, being much closer to a taste of the soil—a *gôut de terroir*—which is often found in wines, and which can be a drawback.

Oxidation is particularly common in dry white wines that are too old, turning the wine dark yellow and then brown. Because of this tendency toward maderization, Meursaults have a short life, rarely being drinkable after ten years in the bottle, and at their prime from two to six or seven years after the vintage.

The town has its own hospital, which was founded in the twelfth century, but some of its best vineyards are owned by the Hospices de Beaune, which auction the *cuvées* of Baudot, Goureau, Albert Grivault, Jehan Humblot, Bahèzre de Lanlay, and Loppin. The town also boasts a fine restaurant called Le Chevreuil, which means roebuck, where small wines from the local vineyards can be drunk with such specialities as local ham, snails, or rabbit stew. These would taste even better with a great Meursault such as a Les Perrières, which is the outstanding vineyard in the commune. Part of the wine from this vineyard goes to market as Clos des Perrières, a section that is considered the best, owned by Mme. Grivault.

Southwest of town is the hamlet of Blagny, a cluster of houses not large enough to be a commune in its own right, whose wines go to market as Meursault.

In addition to Mme. Grivault, growers and shippers include Ampeau, Battault-Rieusset, F. Boillot, Boillot-Buthiau, Boillot-Beorget, Boulard, Bouzereau-Bachelet, Bruey-Mouchaux, Cauvert-Monnot, Chouet, Coche-Vincent, Grosyeux-Polet, Hanauer-Latour, E. Jobard, P. Jobard, Jobard-Morey, Domaine Lafon, Latour-Boissard, Leger-Charton, Lochardet, J. Matrot, Michelot-Morey, Michelot-Rocault, Michelot-Truchot, J. Monnier, R. Monnier, Monnot-Meney, Comtesse Montlivault, E. Morey, R. Morey, Morey-Porcheret, Comte de Moucheron, Nouveau-Desandre, etc., etc.

M E U R S A U L T

PREMIERS CRUS (*about 275 acres*)

Les Bouchères	*Aux Perrières*
Les Caillerets	Les Perrières
Les Charmes *	*Les Petures Blancs*
Clos de la Perrière	*La Pièce sous le Bois*
Les Cras	*Le Poruzot* *
Les Genevrières *	*Les Santenots Blancs*
La Goutte d'Or	Les Santenots du Milieu
La Jennelotte	*Sous le Dos d'Ane* *

Those vineyards which are set in roman are traditionally classed as *têtes de cuvées*.

* Only a part of these vineyards are officially rated, therefore the best wines bear the phrase *premier cru* on the label.

This list gives a good indication of what happens in Burgundy: father divides his holdings among his sons and daughters, who marry the children of other vintners, whose children marry children of still other vintners, all of whom receive a portion of vineyard as a dowry. Or maybe they don't. Probably when the names and holdings get too complicated, they sell. All this must be handled through the local notary. His grasp is noticeable not only in vine-yard country but everywhere in France, and it is he who advises timid widows and youthful scions what to do about their property. The tangle has been getting more complex with every generation. In a way, it's a wonder that anything at all comes out of France, let alone the wines of Burgundy, where a man may produce less than fifty cases of wine each year from his few vines in a precious vineyard.

The red wines of Mersault are traditionally marketed as Volnays. The best of them are:

Les Santenots
Les Cras
Les Petures

⋙ PULIGNY AND MONTRACHET

The greatest dry white wine on earth comes from the vineyard of Le Montrachet, ten acres of which are in the township of Puligny, with another nine in the neighboring commune of Chassagne. In all, the dozen owners of this vineyard produce less than a thousand cases of wine each year, scarcely half of which gets on the market. The owners keep the rest for themselves and their friends. Dumas once said that Montrachet should be drunk kneeling, with the head bared, a feeling shared by those who have the chance to taste it.

Several neighboring vineyards are also classed as *Grands Crus*, and are allowed to add Montrachet to their names, just as can the neighbors of Chambertin, at the other end of the Golden Slope. Just above Le Montrachet are the fifteen acres of Chevalier-Montrachet. On its northern edge is Le Cailleret, once called Les Demoiselles, and some three acres of this is marketed as Chevalier-Montrachet. Just below are the twenty-three acres of Bâtard-

P U L I G N Y – M O N T R A C H E T

GRANDS CRUS *(about 60 acres)*

LE MONTRACHET
BÂTARD-MONTRACHET
BIENVENUES-BÂTARD-MONTRACHET
CHEVALIER-MONTRACHET
CRIOTS-BÂTARD-MONTRACHET

*   *   *

PREMIERS CRUS *(about 155 acres)*

Le Cailleret	Les Folatières *
Les Chalumeaux	La Garenne
Le Champ-Canet	Hameau de Blagny
Clavoillons	Les Pucelles
Les Combettes	Les Referts
	Sous-le-Puits

S A I N T – A U B I N

PREMIERS CRUS *(about 165 acres)*

Champlot	Les Murgers des Dents de Chien
La Chântenière	En Remilly
Les Combes	Sur Gamay
Les Frionnes	Sur le Sentier du Clou

* Only a part of this vineyard is officially rated, therefore the best wines bear the phrase *premier cru* on the label.

Montrachet, flanked on the north by Bienvenues-Bâtard-Montrachet, and on the south by Criots-Bâtard-Montrachet, both of which add another eight acres or so that can attach Montrachet to their own vineyard name. All in all, there are scarcely seventy acres of Great Growths producing the great white wines, divided among more than three dozen owners. When buying these wines, one must look for the name of the grower on the label.

The Marquis de Laguiche owns the largest part of Le Montrachet, almost five acres. Baron Thénard owns four acres, Bouchard Père et Fils two and a half. Ten others, including Duvergey and the Comte de Moucheron, own scarcely an acre each.

Puligny is a village on the edge of the vineyards, with the houses of the *vignerons* huddled around the placid town square. *Vigneron* is the French word for vine-grower, and, often enough, an owner will hire a *vigneron* to tend the vineyard and make the wine, in exchange for half the vintage. This system of sharecropping is called *mie-fruit*, or half-crop. Only the finest winemakers are employed to tend the great vineyards, so that the *vigneron*'s name will appear on the bottle as a guarantee of authenticity. Julien Monnot, perhaps the greatest winemaker of Burgundy, is the vintner for Countess Lafon's parcel of Le Montrachet; P. Mathey is vintner for Dr. Blanchet; J. Bavard is vintner for Mme. de Chauvigné. All three ship to the United States.

Wines from the neighboring commune of Saint Aubin are marketed as Puligny-Montrachet.

◄§ CHASSAGNE–MONTRACHET AND SANTENAY

The Paris-Riviera highway swings down from the Burgundy hills to cut through the Chassagne vineyards, and that part of Montrachet lying in the township comes right up to the edge of the road. This is about as close as the tourist is apt to get to the great Burgundy vineyards, and before he knows it, he will be in the town of Chagny, which boasts of one of the best country restaurants in Burgundy, the owner of which is wise enough to stock a few bottles of the red and white wines of Chassagne.

The pride of Chassagne, in addition to those sections of the Montrachet vineyards that lie across the town line, are the red wines from Clos St. Jean and Les Boudriottes and the white wines of Morgeot and Les Ruchottes. Substantial sections of all these vineyards are owned by the Ramonet brothers, who are admired all along the Golden Slope for their magnificent winemaking. They have cellars throughout the village, their own not being large enough to contain all the wine they make.

The Ramonets have a genius for winemaking, an instinct for knowing what to do with their wines, and precisely when to do it. They are also daring winemakers, willing to risk their vintage for a few extra days of sun if they feel the weather will hold, willing

CHASSAGNE – MONTRACHET

GRANDS CRUS *(about 40 acres)*

    LE MONTRACHET

    BÂTARD-MONTRACHET

    CRIOTS-BÂTARD-MONTRACHET

* * *

PREMIERS CRUS *(about 300 acres)*

La Boudriotte	*Les Macherelles*
Les Brussonnes	*La Maltroie*
En Cailleret	Morgeot (white) *
Les Champs-Gain	*La Romanée*
Les Chenevottes	*Les Grandes Ruchottes* (white)
Clos Saint-Jean *	*Les Vergers*

Those First Growths which are set in roman are traditionally classed *têtes de cuvées.*

* Only a part of this vineyard is officially rated, therefore the best wines bear the phrase *premier cru* on the label.

SANTENAY AND ITS NEIGHBORS

PREMIERS CRUS *(about 400 acres)*

Beauregard *	*La Comme* *
Beaurepaire	Les Gravières *
Clos de Tavannes *	*Le Maladière* *
	Le Passe-Temps
Les Maranges	
	La Boutière
	Le Clos des Rois

The vineyard which is set in roman is traditionally classed *tête de cuvées.*

* Only a part of these vineyards are officially rated, therefore the best wines bear phrase *premier cru* on the label.

to pick early if the weather is apt to break, depending on their skill to make a good wine even when sugar content is low.

Their *succès-fou* was in 1947, when the wine fermenting in the vats showed that the alcohol might be over 16 degrees. They filled their vats only half full, but even then they threatened to foam over. At one point, to prolong the fermentation, the Ramonets greased the insides of the vats so that the rising cap of solid matter that is formed would not get a purchase on the vat sides. The resulting wine was glorious in a year when many vintners made poor wines because they were unable to handle the tremendous amount of alcohol.

The Ramonets and the other winemakers grumble about the official classifications of their vineyards, feeling that Les Ruchottes, at least, ought to be a Great Growth because its white wines often surpass those of Bâtard-Montrachet. Their claims are being reviewed by the *Appellation Contrôlée*, with others all along the Golden Slope, and there is an excellent chance that many of the wines now classified as First Growths will one day go to market as *Grands Crus*. This will raise their prices, of course, pleasing growers, if not buyers.

The Golden Slope ends with the vineyards of Santenay, just south of Montrachet. The commune produces both red and white wines, lighter and less distinguished than those from Chassagne, and generally rated on a par with those of Monthélie and Auxey-Duresses. Just across the town line to the south are the vineyards called Maranges, spread across several communes, and these occasionally produce good red wines, as does Le Clos des Rois and La Boutière. But the great wines of Burgundy end with Chassagne, giving way to the good wines from the larger vineyards and townships of southern Burgundy.

◆§ ३◆

Southern Burgundy

As if unable to believe that the Golden Slope is really at an end, the *vignerons* south of Chassagne, in the Côte Chalonnaise, continue to plant the noble Pinot in their vineyards, in the hope that wines from the townships of Rully and Mercurey, Givry and Montagny, will equal those of the Côte d'Or. The surprise is that those from the first two communes do, and their First Growths have been classed by the *Appellation Contrôlée*.

◆§ CÔTE CHALONNAISE

The light red wines of Mercurey and Rully taste best when drunk young. When the name of the vineyard appears on the bottle the wine must contain at a minimum 11 degrees of alcohol, with the whites possessing 11.5, the same percentages as those for the First Growths of the Côte de Beaune.

The reds of Givry are lighter than those of Mercurey, somewhat fruitier than those of Rully; the Givry whites and the whites of Montagny are best described as *bons vins du pays*. Good country wines, from the French viewpoint, are those that taste fine when drunk young, are fresh and pleasing, light and fruity, better balanced than *vins de carafe* drawn straight from the cask. They are *facile à boire* and they taste better when cool, or slightly chilled.

None of the vineyards of Givry or Montagny have been officially rated *Premiers Crus*, but the wines of these communes can carry this phrase if they possess the extra half-degree of alcohol above the minimum. As this is usually the case, most wines of the Chalonnaise go to market with the phrase on the label. Like those of Monthélie, Santenay, and Auxey-Duresses, they should be drunk when less than three years old.

C H A L O N N A I S E

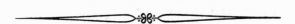

R U L L Y :   P R E M I E R S   C R U S

La Bressande	*Meix-Caillat*
Champ Clou	*Mont-Palais*
Chapitre	*Moulesne*
Cloux	*Les Pierres*
Ecloseaux	*Pillot*
La Fosse	*Préau*
Grésigny	*Raboursay*
Margotey	*La Renarde*
Marisson	*Vauvry*

* * *

M E R C U R E Y :   P R E M I E R S   C R U S

Clos des Fourneaux	*Clos du Roi*
Clos des Montaigus	*Clos Marcilly*
Clos Voyen or *Les Voyens*	

↝ CÔTE MACONNAISE

The vineyards of Mâcon lie west of that handsome town on the banks of the Saône, on the slopes of a broad valley over which towers a bulging mount that looks rather like Gibraltar. From them come the wonderful white wines of Pouilly-Fuissé, made from the great Pinot Chardonnay, the vine that produces all the great white Burgundies.

The wines of Pouilly-Fuissé have a hardness and freshness that make them similar to those of Chablis, north of the Golden Slope, and, like Chablis, they taste best with oysters and all sorts of fish and sea food, ham, and pork.

A decade or so ago these were considered merely *bons vins du pays*, but improved methods of filtering have raised them in the eyes of buyers.

Pouilly-Fuissé is produced in five communes: Fuissé, Pouilly, Solutré, Vergisson, and Chaintré. When the vineyard name is put on the label, the wines must possess 12 degrees alcohol. Without the vineyard name, the wines must have 11 per cent alcohol. Production is limited to about two hundred cases an acre, and the number of vines, or feet, per acre is limited to four thousand. The great vineyards of the Côte d'Or are limited to a third less production, and wines from First Growths and those simply bearing commune names are allowed only slightly more. Production of every great vineyard is controlled to preserve quality, to discourage the crowding of vines in precious soils and to prevent the planting of heavily bearing vines in choice *climats*.

This limiting of production occasionally results in a buyer's bonus in Pouilly-Fuissé, because in good years the vineyards exceed their quotas. This *excès de production* is sold as Vin Blanc Chardonnay under the name of the grower and can be bought for less than two dollars a bottle; exactly the same wine costs nearly three dollars when it is estate-bottled. This is not the same as Mâcon Blanc or Pinot-Chardonnay-Mâcon, however, which are generally blends of wines from various vineyards not entitled to be called Pouilly-Fuissé.

Two townships with separate *appellations* are Pouilly-Loché and Pouilly-Vinzelles, whose wines are only required to be 11 per cent alcohol and do not generally have the big body and depth of Pouilly-Fuissé.

Some of the best growers are E. Laneyrie, J. Burrier, M. Dondin, and Joseph Drouhin.

M A C O N N A I S E

Vineyard names one is apt to find on a label are:

F U I S S É
Beauregard
Chatenay
Le Clos
Clos Gaillard
Menetrières
Les Prales
Les Vignes Blanches

S O L U T R É
Champ Roux
Les Chataigners
Les Crayes
La Frerie
Rousselaine
Le Vigneray

P O U I L L Y
Les Bouthières
Les Chailloux
Au Clos
Aux Coreaux
Les Cours
Aux Morlays

V E R G I S S O N
Les Charmes
Les Crays
En France
La Maréchaude

C H A I N T R É
Les Fournieaux
Aux Murs
Les Plessis
Les Verchères

◆§ BEAUJOLAIS

The glory of southern Burgundy, the delight of France, the best *bon vin* on earth is Beaujolais. It is made from the Gamay grape, which here makes glorious wines, even though it makes horrible ones farther north or farther south. Beaujolais is the good young wine *par excellence*, and settles forever the argument that great wines are the only ones that can be drunk with delight.

Eight townships produce the river of Beaujolais that flows to great restaurants all over the world. The lightest wines are produced in Juliénas; those of Saint Amour and Chénas are similar. Just to the south is Moulin à Vent, its vaneless windmill now a national monument, whose vineyards produce perhaps the fullest Beaujolais. Bordering the vineyards of the windmill are those of Fleurie, the fruitiest of all Beaujolais; below them are the Chiroubles vineyards, from which comes probably the most popular Beaujolais in France. Morgon is next, the longest-lived of the Beaujolais. Below Morgon is Brouilly, whose wines are full and fruity, with Côte de Brouilly in its center, where some Pinot grapes are permitted.

But distinctions here are minor. All produce Beaujolais, and if a commune or vineyard name is placed on the label, the wine must contain 11 degrees of alcohol. The wines can be drunk six months after the vintage and reach their height shortly after, certainly before they are two years old; many are long past their prime at five years old, even from great years. The wines of Beaujolais are meant to be drunk young and often; they represent the opposite end of the tremendous range of Burgundies that begins with Chambertin and goes through every variation there is in wine, until the light, fresh, fruity Beaujolais is reached from the vineyards at the southern end of the fabulous world of Burgundy.

◆§ SUMMARY

Intermediate wines, those overshadowed by their famous neighbors, are generally good Burgundy buys. Those of Fixin and Morey-St. Denis are examples, as are many of the wines from First-Growth vineyards in the famous townships such as Chambolle-Musigny and Nuits-St. Georges.

Nuits-St. Georges has more vineyards than any other in the Côte de Nuits; consequently quantities are large so that prices tend to be reasonable.

Côte de Beaune wines are less expensive than those of the Côte de Nuits because its larger vineyards produce greater quantities of wine, and also because the wines mature faster and can be sold before costs of storing become a large factor in the price.

Estate-bottled wines, those bottled by the vineyard owners, are generally better in quality than wines bottled by shippers, and worth the slight premium.

Wines of Santenay, Monthélie, Savigny-les-Beaune, and Auxey-Duresses, generally lighter and more quickly maturing than the other wines of the Côte de Beaune, are lower in price.

The red wines of Chassagne-Montrachet are not well known but are of excellent quality.

Beaujolais should be drunk before it is three years old and is best when under two.

No vineyard name is needed to insure good wines from Beaujolais, Pouilly-Fuissé, Givry, Rully, or Mercurey.

Red Burgundies taste best served cool, the bottle having been opened a couple of hours before it is to be poured. White Burgundies taste best chilled.

The Rhône

In the olden days there was a noble who had two daughters. One had golden hair and a smile that dimmed the sun; the other's locks were glossy and dark as a freshly peeled chestnut, and she was the quiet one. The father loved them both equally and lived with them in his castle, which was surrounded by a glorious sun-filled vineyard high above the banks of the Rhône. But one cold winter, as the wines were falling bright, he felt the weight of his years upon him, heavy as a cart full of grapes, and as the wines cleared decided to make his peace with the world. He did so by willing half his vineyard to one daughter, half to the other; then he died. The blonde ripened early, had a blazing love affair with a prince who was lost on a crusade, and quickly faded; the brunette ripened slowly into a passionate woman who was the lifelong joy of the king she married.

Today, good red wines of the Côte Rôtie are quite different, like the king's daughters: those from the Côte Blonde are soft and light, fading quickly once they have reached their peak; those from the Côte Brune are plain and undistinguished when young, but round into rich, full wines.

Every vineyard has its story, sometimes two or three, pointing up some characteristic of its wines. The stories are often better than the wines; some of the smallest are touted by the tallest tales. But in the French regions of good wines, if there's a yarn worth spinning, there's a wine worth drinking; nowhere more so than in the districts near the rivers of the Rhône, the Loire, and the portion of the upper Rhine that borders Alsace.

Rhône vineyards begin below Lyons, and there are three clusters of them along the river near the towns of Vienne, Valence, and Avignon. In between, along the steep slopes and hill ranges flanking the majestic river, are more vineyards, producing the full and fruity wines called Côtes du Rhône, generally the best of the regional wines of France.

Vienne is half an hour's drive below Lyons, once a Roman garrison; one turns to the right off the main road, drives past a shaft that looks like a small, latter-day obelisk, and parks before a whitewashed brick wall. Through its gate is a grassy garden bordered with ramblers and backed by a wide terrace shaded with sycamores, and a rambling house. This is Fernand Point's Pyramide, now run by his widow, and still one of the great restaurants. Sitting under the leafy trees, one is served a hot slice of pâté in a flaky crust, foie gras from the Massif Central, quenelles with a crayfish sauce, fish from the Rhône or the cold mountain streams of the Savoie, chicken from Bresse, Charollais beef, fruits and vegetables from the artists who grow them in the surrounding countryside. Each morning, the chefs select the most perfect cauliflowers, the whitest endive, the tenderest, greenest miniature peas, the most orange carrots, tiny artichokes whose leaves are stiff with freshness, lettuce and celery of unmatched crispness, pears and plums and peaches and strawberries of unbelievable juiciness, melons, crisp apples, the most crumbly of cheeses—and the most runny—each in its season, brought to market at the moment of perfection. Food is prepared in that greatest tradition of French cooking, which brings out the essences of each in the simplest or best way. (Fernand Point once said it took a great cook to fry an egg perfectly. First, of course,

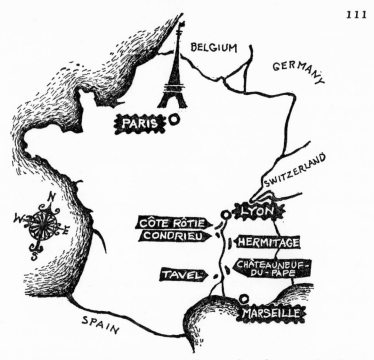

you must find the perfect egg, and the perfect butter, the finest pepper and the perfect pan, over just the right heat. . . .)

After such food, people smile and then laugh. Talk quickens and brightens; women glow and become more feminine, men are more attentive. The wine sparkles in the glass, each swallow tasting better, matching the taste of the food, bringing out its flavors. A wine you sip, a great wine of Burgundy or Bordeaux, is not what you want here, unless perhaps with the subtle foie gras, or the quenelles, or the chicken with a cream sauce. But even then you want to take swallows of a wine—a big white Montrachet would be fine. Better yet would be less majestic wines, simpler and fruitier in taste, like the white wines from Condrieu and Château Grillet, or the reds from Côte Rôtie, vineyards just across the Rhône from Vienne; these have always been the most favored wines at La Pyramide, served with the simplest dishes and the first courses, followed perhaps by a great Burgundy or Bordeaux if you are having a particularly delicate dish.

The Rhône is considered a district of good rather than great wines because so many of them go to market as simple Côtes du Rhône, but half a dozen of them are truly great; three of these come from the district of Côte Rôtie and its neighbors.

✍ CÔTE RÔTIE

The Roasted Slope is a single hillside of steeply terraced vineyards that looks from the road like a series of stone walls, the tall vines propped on tripods of poles so that the grapes are held high to catch the hot sun. The entire slope, both Brune and Blonde, is a scant two miles long, rarely more than a hundred yards wide, with a production of not much more than ten thousand cases a year. The informing vine is the Syrah, which produces heavy and ordinary wines outside the Rhône Valley. The Syrah must occupy 80 per cent of the vineyard space, according to the control laws, the other 20 per cent consisting of several different varieties that impart lightness and softness to the otherwise big wines.

The wines mature in cask, often for five years and more, taking that long to throw off excess tannin and tartrates. Many of the wines are not ready to drink until a dozen years after the vintage. Those from the southern half, the Côte Blonde, are ready first, sometimes drinkable after a mere half-dozen years; those from the Côte Brune continue to develop slowly, lasting for thirty years and more. Both have a distinct scent and taste, reminding many people of raspberries.

The wines are stored above ground in great stone warehouses filled with the casks of many vintages. But the most curious thing

CÔTE RÔTIE

CÔTE BRUNE	CÔTE BLONDE
La Brocarde	Le Clos
Fontgent	Grande Plantée
Le Moulin	La Garelle
Pavillon Rouge	La Grosse Roche
La Pommière	Balaiyat
Tharamont-de-Gron	Le Mollard
La Turque	

about these dark storage vaults is that the walls and ceilings, the casks, and even the black earth floors are covered with a white mold, like a sprinkling of fine snow; as you walk between the barrels, your footprints stand out black on the soft earth. When mold forms, it is a sign of even temperature in the vaults, vital to the proper maturing of great table wines.

Acreage of the Roasted Slope is about the same as that of Clos Vougeot, about 125 acres. The largest owner is Vidal-Fleury; others are Bonnefond, Cachet, Chapoutier, Dervieux, and Pouzet. Many of the small plots have vineyard names that occasionally appear on a bottle.

⊷ CONDRIEU AND CHÂTEAU GRILLET

Of course there is white wine to go with the red of Côte Rôtie—from two tiny districts just to the south. Condrieu has less than twenty acres and that many owners, producing from the Viognier grape, in a good year, about two thousand cases of a wine with a pale golden cast, marked by a distinct but not unpleasing earth taste. But the best of all is Château Grillet, a white wine that is one of the rarest in France: its fewer than three acres planted in Viognier produce fewer than two hundred cases of wine in a good year. The entire vineyard is owned by Henri Neyret-Cachet. The wine is extremely dry, with a bouquet less than that of Condrieu, but with no *goût de terroir*, and a body fuller than a Pouilly-Fuissé. It is one of the finest white wines of France, with an extremely dry aftertaste, or *finish*.

⊷ HERMITAGE

The Brune and Blonde reds of Côte Rôtie may be considered the greatest of the Rhônes in France, but in England, long affection awards the palm to the wine of Hermitage, twenty miles to the south, just above Valence. The great vineyard hill rises above the village of Tain, its some 350 acres divided among more than sixty owners. Nearly two thirds of the some thirty thousand cases produced each year is red wine, and still more comes from Crozes-

Hermitage, which lies behind Hermitage, and which produces a lesser wine. The vineyards are divided into *quartiers*, and it is the Hermitage practice to blend the wines from one *quartier* with those of another. Consequently, while some vineyards stand out, most Hermitage goes to market under the district name. This does not mean that the wine is inferior, for Hermitage is one of the most distinctive wines in the world, full, strong, and incredibly long-lived, with great vinosity even when old, and showing fine breed after two or three decades or more.

The white Hermitage is the sturdiest of the world's dry white wines, often taking two or three years before it is ready to drink, and frequently not reaching maturity for five or six years. Many great vintages live for twenty years, and because of their big, full taste, the wines bring out all the flavors of spicy dishes or such salty ones as those made with ham. One of the largest owners markets his white Hermitage under the name of Chanté-Alouette, which is also the name of the vineyard; the wine is produced from several different *quartiers*, however, and the firm of Chapoutier now uses it as a trade name.

The informing vine for the white Hermitages is the Marsanne, although a small percentage of the vineyards are planted in the Rousanne vine. Like the Syrah, these vines were supposed to have been brought back from the East by crusaders, but they must have arrived much earlier. The planting of the Syrah, at least, was made compulsory by the Emperor Probus in the third century, when he lifted the prohibition against planting vines in Gaul. This prohibition had been instituted in A.D. 89 by Domitian, the last of the twelve Caesars, and completely disrupted Gallic winemaking. Not until the establishment of the monkish orders in the days of the Holy Roman Empire did modern winemaking really begin.

Hermitage gets its name, naturally enough, because a hermit established himself on the vineyard site. Several different hermits seem to have done so, in fact, for the various stories are conflicting. The most fanciful of them has to do with wine:

A crusader, desiring to retire as a hermit from the cruelty of the world, built a stone hut on the top of a mountain overlooking the Rhône. When his abode was finished, he determined to plant a vineyard on the rocky soil. Consequently, he broke the stones into

H E R M I T A G E

REDS	WHITES
Les Bressards	*Beaume*
La Croix	*Chanté-Alouette*
Les Deognières	*La Chapelle*
Les Greffieux	*Maison-Blanche*
Gros-des-Vignes	
L'Hermite	
L'Homme	
Le Méal	
Les Murêts	
La Pierelle	

pebbles and planted vines, but they failed to flourish. This particular hermit was kind to animals, in compensation for the cruelty of other men, and one stormy night he gave shelter to all the beasts of the field. An angel observing this shed a tear which fell on one of the vines, and at once it began to grow, as did the others planted by the hermit, and thus began the story of the wines called Hermitage.

It is only fair to state that this same story of heavenly tears is told about other vineyards all along the Rhône and through Provence.

ST.–PÉRAY AND CORNAS

St.-Péray produces a white wine, part of which is made into *vin mousseux*, sparkling wine, and Cornas produces small red wines, equally uninteresting.

≈§ CHÂTEAUNEUF-DU-PAPE

Down near Avignon is the seat of the French popes, and the vineyards of Châteauneuf-du-Pape and Tavel. Châteauneuf-du-Pape
was the first wine to come under the control of the *Appéllation
d'Origine* laws, thanks to the efforts of Baron Le Roy de Boiseaumarié, one of the pioneers of the vineyard classifications. The wines
carry the highest alcoholic requirement of any in France, 12.5 per
cent, and are made from a variety of grapes. Production varies
widely, averaging perhaps half a million gallons of red wines per
year, plus a few thousand gallons of firm and not unpleasant white
wines. The red wines are soft and full, ready to drink after three
years, fading after another year or two. They are good wines, although they rarely approach those of Hermitage or the Côte
Rôtie. Good producers, in addition to Baron Le Roy, are the wine
cooperative, Brotte-Armenier, Brunel, Chapoutier, Jouffron, and
Ponson, among many others.

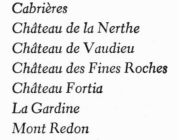

CHÂTEAUNEUF-
DU-PAPE

Cabrières
Château de la Nerthe
Château de Vaudieu
Château des Fines Roches
Château Fortia
La Gardine
Mont Redon
Saint Patrice

◄§ TAVEL

Tavel is the greatest *rosé* of France, truly pink without an orange cast, with a full taste and good body. It is high in alcohol and is made from the Grenache grape which produces good pink wines wherever it is grown. The color comes from the skins which are left for a time with the grape juice. The wine is bottled promptly after fermentation, and should be drunk within a year or so. Well chilled, it is pleasant to drink with light lunches and casserole dishes, but goes well with most foods, particularly the sort that are served with white wines.

◄§ SUMMARY

Vintages are relatively unimportant along the Rhône because there is enough sun to ripen the grapes in most years even when there is not enough to produce large quantities of wine. In vintages when early frosts have harmed the grapes in Burgundy or Bordeaux, the Rhônes often produce outstanding wines, for example in 1954, when both quality and quantity were high. In the 1950s, every year but 1951 produced excellent wines; among the best are the '52s, '53s, '56s, and '57s. In 1959, the Rhône vineyards produced good wines, except in Châteauneuf-du-Pape and Tavel, where early rains rotted the grapes. The Rhônes are wines to look for when one is seeking a good wine at a low price, or a great wine at a reasonable one. They are invariably superior to minor growths of the two great districts, and they often match the classed wines, when compared dollar for dollar. A good rule when in a restaurant whose cellar is unfamiliar is: Buy a Rhône. You could do a great deal worse.

 The Loire

The Loire begins in southern France, high in the Massif Central, flowing north for nearly two hundred miles, then making a great sweep west in its meander to the sea. The vale of the Loire, the smile of France, begins in the sweep, and so do the best vineyards. This is Berry, the glory of *vieille France*, with its cathedral city of Bourges. Here, it is said, the nightingale first sang.

Long ago, the nightingale was sad and silent because it had only one eye to see the beauties of the Loire. A worm, taking pity on the bird, lent her one of his eyes, saying that two eyes were scarcely enough to see the beauties of the vale, but only one was needed to dig in its soil. All night, the bird sang, but when the worm asked for his eye, the nightingale refused, and fell asleep under a vine. Now it was the vine's turn to take pity on the worm, and a tendril crept out to the nightingale's throat, wrapping

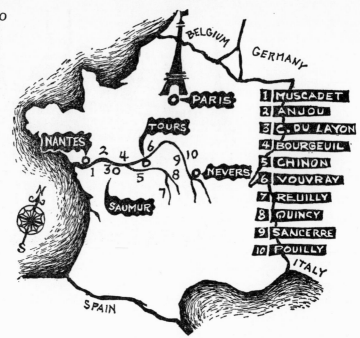

around once, twice. . . . Choking, the nightingale thought the worm
had caught her, so she struggled loose and flew to the highest tree.
Safely there, she swore that she would never sleep again. And that
is why a worm has only one eye, and why the vine grows and grows
in the valley of the Loire, and why the sleepless nightingale sings.

The vine grows everywhere in this garden of France, and each
district produces distinctive vintages. There are two pairs of districts near Bourges. Pouilly and Sancerre are on opposite banks of
the river; Quincy and Reuilly are on the rolling hills above the
valley. All produce light, dry white wines. The river curves past
Orléans and Blois—near which the praline was invented, which
tastes best with Vouvray or one of the other sweet or sparkling wines
from the vineyards of the Touraine. Near Tours are the only red
wine districts of the Loire, Chinon and Bourgeuil. Below Tours is
Saumur, then the white- and pink-wine district of Anjou, and
toward the mouth of the river, near Nantes, are the white-wine
vineyards of Muscadet. Most of the wines taste best when one is
touring the château country, but thanks to improved wine-making
practice, each district produces a few wines sturdy enough to be
exported. The vineyards of the Loire are on a line with those of
Burgundy's Côte d'Or, but the grapes in the best vineyards are

mostly those from Bordeaux. Here, the wines are light in alcohol, flowery and fresh. They taste best when only a year or two old, consumed sitting on a terrace having cold salmon, brook trout, or a luncheon casserole. One sip, and it's almost as if you were in the valley on a summer day, ambling through history at Azay-le-Rideau, or Rochambeau, or Chambord. The smile of France is in your glass.

◄§ POUILLY-FUMÉ

The best dry white wine of the Loire, and the favorite of Marie Antoinette, is Pouilly-Fumé. Sometimes it is called Blanc Fumé de Pouilly; it is always made from the Sauvignon grape of Sauternes and Graves. Here, the noble vine is called Blanc Fumé—some say because the vineyards are often shrouded with morning mists, some because the chalky soil gives the vines a smoky, dusty look; perhaps, though, because the wine has a flinty taste. There is also a taste of the soil in this wine, not unpleasant when light, and Pouilly-Fumé reminds one of its fuller Burgundy neighbor, Chablis, or another wine (with which it is sometimes confused), Pouilly-Fuissé.

The name is important because wines that bear only the name of the district, Pouilly-sur-Loire, are made from a table grape, the Chasselas, and need be only 9.5 per cent alcohol. The much better Pouilly-Fumés must be 11 per cent. They usually cost more, and all are made from the Sauvignon grape. When the wine is too heavy in alcohol, around 13 per cent, it loses the light, springlike freshness that is its most pleasing quality. The best known of the Pouilly-Fumés is Château du Nozet, the popularity of which in England and the United States has influenced other growers to put vineyard names on their labels. Here are some one is apt to see:

P O U I L L Y - F U M É

Les Berthiers	*Les Cassiers*
Boisgibaude	*Château du Nozet*
Le Bouchot	*Les Girarmes*
	Le Soumard

◆§ SANCERRE

Across the Loire in Sancerre is the best view in all of Berry, and a sometimes-best wine from the vineyard of Chavignol, which is the only vineyard name apt to be found on a bottle of Sancerre. All wines entitled to the district name must come from the Sauvignon grape and contain 10.5 per cent alcohol. Unless frosts strike in the spring, Sancerre and the other Loire districts produce wines a degree or two above the legal minimum; when the wine is low in alcohol, it tastes acid and watery, without bouquet or finesse, and is not entitled to the *appellation*. The Sancerre vineyards generally face more to the east than those of Pouilly, thereby getting less of the afternoon sun, and are not so apt to become heavy in alcohol, thus losing the lightness and fresh bouquet that make these wines distinctive. There are twenty-five hundred acres of vineyards in Sancerre, slightly more than in Pouilly-sur-Loire, and the wines are usually marketed as Sancerre.

◆§ QUINCY

West of Bourges on a high tableland above the valley is another pair of districts that produce dry white wines from the Sauvignon grape, Quincy and Reuilly. It is said that many of the five hundred acres in Quincy were planted by Cistercians from the nearby Benedictine monastery in Beauvais. The soil is sandy here, with a chalky undersoil, which brings out in the wine a special and almost spicy bouquet. Most of the wine used to go to Paris and Belgium, but since the war producers have taken to filtering it more carefully so that it can be shipped abroad. It had just begun to gain admirers in the United States when the vineyards were nearly destroyed by frosts in the spring of 1956, a catastrophe that also decimated the other nearby districts and most of the other Loire vineyards. Such happenings are more discouraging in good districts than in great ones; a man has to work as hard to produce a wine that would sell for two dollars in New York as he would to make one costing twice as much. The fact that he can produce more per acre means only

that he must sell more. But the best producers replanted in the
hope that buyers who prefer not to pay the premium for scarce
Chablis, and who want a lighter wine than Pouilly-Fuissé, will be
attracted to the light, dry whites of Berry. Some of them have taken
to estate-bottling their wines, but the name of the vineyard is not
very important here, unlike the situation in Burgundy.

✑ REUILLY

Reuilly vineyards lie south of Quincy, and the wines are similar.
There were a thousand acres entitled to the *appellation* before the
1956 freeze, but today there are only half as many. The wines are
similar to those of Quincy, but with a bouquet more like the wines
of Sancerre. These, too, must possess 10.5 degrees of alcohol and
be made from the Sauvignon. Good filtering and winemaking are
important here, not vineyard names. In the sixteenth and seventeenth centuries, the whites of Reuilly were regularly classed as
the best of Berry but are out of fashion today. Foreign wine-buyers
tend to buy the lesser wines from the great districts, depending on
the name of Burgundy or Bordeaux to help sell the wines. It is only
when minor wines from the great districts rise in price, or when
a new "item" is desired to intrigue new customers, that buyers
begin searching the *bons vins* districts for good wines. The growing world market for wines will send buyers sniffing through
Reuilly, and in the 1960s they will doubtless be discovered all over
again.

✑ VOUVRAY AND MONTLOUIS

Tours is the capital city of the Loire, and nearby vineyards produce
the most famous of the valley's wines, the still and sparkling white
Vouvrays.

Vouvray vineyards stretch along the top of a steep slope on
the far side of the Loire, up from Tours. Houses line the river
road, the backs of many of them running into the chalky cliffs.
Some are mere façades, like those of a Western U.S. frontier town,
and many of the caves run hundreds of feet back into the slopes;

one literally lives under his vineyards. People have been here for thousands of years and their wines have been famous since the Middle Ages.

The informing vine in Vouvray is the Pineau de la Loire or Chenin Blanc, no relation to the Burgundy Pinots, and the white wines develop a creamy quality which the French call *moelleux*. This is coupled with the silky, crisp quality that sets Vouvrays apart, becoming more pronounced when alcoholic content is high. Rabelais dubbed them *vins de taffetas*. Vintners wait for the noble rot before picking, and the acohol sometimes goes as high as 15 per cent. The minimum for the still wines is 11 per cent, for the sparkling wines, only 9.5. Across the river is Vouvray's satellite, Montlouis, which produces half a million gallons to Vouvray's three quarters of a million in a good year, all of which is marketed as Vouvray.

The better the year, the sweeter the Vouvray. It is bottled within six months, right after the malo-lactic fermentation, and takes three or four years in bottle to reach maturity. It is best drunk young, but when the wine is very rich and full, it can live for twenty years, and bottles have been opened after sixty years and found to be good. When grape sugar is high, fermentation is a problem; it is the unconverted sugar that gives Vouvray its quality of sweetness and prickliness, this *moustille* or slight foaminess forming a kind of collar around the neck of the bottle, under the cork.

The still Vouvrays are always soft, and frequently slightly sparkling, or *pétillant*, a more pronounced version of this foamy quality. No wonder vintners long ago took advantage of this tendency to make sparkling wines, which are generally called *vins mousseux*. Sparkling Vouvrays should be reasonable in price, but these pleasant wines carry the same U.S. tax as does Champagne, so that they are only a dollar or two less than their more distinguished and celebrated relatives. They are excellent wines when you are not seeking that incredible dryness that can be found in Champagne. The Vouvrays are good with dishes that have a sweet savor, with desserts, and in all kinds of punches.

Vouvrays, both still and sparkling, go to market under the name of the vineyard or simply as Vouvray. Two of the better growers are M. Brédif and Mouzay-Mignot, along with such fine shippers as Monmousseau, and Ackerman-Laurence. Vineyards frequently take the name of a château or use the word *clos* to identify themselves. These include Château de Moncontour, Clos Paradis, Clos de la Tisserie, Clos Chevrier and Château de l'Étoile; there are many others.

৻৽ *CHINON*

Rabelais was born near Chinon, a town that crouches on the bank of a shallow river called the Vienne, a few miles downstream from Tours. A bluff, surmounted by the enormous tumbledown castle of Chinon, towers above the little town, which looks at night much the way it must have in the sixteenth century, when Rabelais roamed its dark and narrow cobbled streets. In Chinon, you can buy the wines from the surrounding vineyards and drink them with excellent local specialities in the town's only hotel, the Gargantua. All the dishes, including omelets and fried potatoes, carry some name from Rabelais' masterpiece. Active in the town is a local wine-promotion group, called Chantepleure, a cheerfully Rabelaisian concept of the effects of heavy drinking. While they sing-cry over a Gargantuan meal in the Hotel Gargantua, the merry boosters raise glasses designed especially for the wine of Chinon, and cry out, "*Toujours buvez, mourir jamais,*" words etched on the side of the glasses. After a few glasses, the wine seems to merit all the attention.

The wine is fresh and fruity and full of taste, light enough for drinking several swallows at a time. There's a definite taste of the grape in it, customarily called the taste of raspberries. There is also a definite aroma of the grape in the bouquet, which is customarily referred to as the smell of violets or truffles. This quality recalls the Rhône wines of the Côte Rôtie or Hermitage, or perhaps the Corton from Burgundy, which somebody once said tasted like bamboo. It's all from the grape, however, and the sandy soil. The grape is the Cabernet of Bordeaux. Chinon is nothing like a Bordeaux, of course, yet one can recognize the Cabernet character in much the way one notices a family resemblance when it's pointed out. Until a couple of years ago, nobody believed these wines could be shipped, the minimum legal alcohol being 9.5 per cent. The accepted rule of thumb was that a wine needed 11 degrees of alcohol to withstand the jouncing and temperature changes of an overseas journey. For the past couple of decades, people have been demanding great clarity in wines, and in an attempt to make them so, extremely efficient filters from Germany were introduced. At the same time, it was discovered that one reason wine went off in taste after bottling was that bottling took place before the slow winter (malo-lactic) fermentation was completed. By watching these two things, it was found that extremely light wines could be shipped, even those that matured quickly. Today, some of Chinon's annual production of three hundred thousand gallons is finding a market outside Europe. Rabelais would be delighted.

◄§ BOURGEUIL AND ST. NICHOLAS DE BOURGEUIL

Bourgeuil is across the river from Chinon, its vineyards along the north bank of the Loire, adjoining those of St. Nicholas de Bourgeuil, which produce better wines. Both of these have a slight edge over Chinon because they have more vinosity, being slightly more *corsé* and astringent, more of a *vin nerveux*—a fuller but drier wine, in short. St. Nicholas is the only commune with a controlled *appellation* in Touraine, producing half a million gallons in an average year, while Bourgeuil produces a million. The high plateau is four miles wide in places, and nearly twelve miles long, so that there's *plenty* of wine to go around. Like Chinon, the wines are bottled two years or so after the vintage and should be drunk before they are five years old.

◄§ JASNIÈRES AND COTEAUX DE TOURAINE

Jasnières is a white wine with a lovely name from a tiny district back from the river, north of Bourgeuil. In dry, hot years the wine has a light, fresh quality combined with a slight crispness, like the texture of a Vouvray. This takes three or four years to develop, and the wine falls off quickly after that. The grape is the same as that of Vouvray, the Chenin Blanc, but the weather is rarely hot enough to permit it to reach maturity; if it does not, the wines are hard and acid. Surrounding the better districts of Touraine are others whose wines are sold as Coteaux de Touraine. Most of these are white, some are dry, and a few are pink. Jasnières might be considered the best.

৺৯ *ANJOU*

The biggest district of the Loire, producing dry and sweet white wines as well as many reds and *rosés*, is Anjou. The best wines come from Saumur, from the Coteaux du Layon, and from the Coteaux de l'Aubance, all on the south side of the river. The sweet white wines of Saumur are heavier and fuller than the Vouvrays, either sparkling or still, and are made from the Chenin Blanc with an oc- casional small percentage of Sauvignon; some people prefer them to the Vouvrays. The Coteaux du Layon produces even sweeter wines, the best of which is Quart de Chaume, a wine that occasionally reaches 16 per cent in alcoholic content. The Coteaux de l'Aubance produces pleasant pink wines, and some whites that are drier than those from Layon.

There are nearly fifteen thousand wine producers in Anjou, many of them on the north side of the Loire, in the varied districts called Coteaux de la Loire and Coteaux du Loir. The best wines come from the commune of Savennières, which produces a white wine high in alcohol, often 13 per cent and often taking three years to mature. Among its best vineyards are Châteaux de Savennières, La Coulée de Serrant, and La Roche-aux-Moines—names that can be found on labels.

৺৯ *MUSCADET*

Muscadet is a big district that extends almost to the mouth of the river, and into Brittany. It also surrounds Nantes, and its wines were once drunk all over the world—as Chablis. With control laws, it can now go to market under its own name, and while the price is low, the wine, when well made, is excellent—dry, light, and good with sea food. Its name comes from the grape variety, and André

Simon has described its taste as having a "squeeze of lemon" sharpness. He also notes that it was at one time made into something called Nancy brandy, which is smuggled into England whenever there's a war on.

Muscadet is the only wine with an *appellation* in Brittany, which is perhaps why they make such a big thing of it. Every time a vine is planted, for example, a bottle of wine must be drunk, and three drops must be sprinkled on the stem and root. In some places the vines can be planted only in the wax of the moon; in others, only the wane will do. For good luck the Bretons sprinkle a few drops of wine on every section of new road that's built, and they believe that the way to make a hen hatch is to have her placed upon her eggs by a drunkard. Brittany may have only one wine, but it makes the most of it.

Wine is part of life in the Loire, and here as elsewhere there are as many stories as there are wines. One has to do with a town drunk.

There was once a small village that laughed at the one man among them who liked the juice of the grape too much. Early one spring a storm of hail began to fall. To save his vines, the man tore off his clothes to cover as many as he could. Children on their way to school laughed and told their parents; and when the man's wife heard the tale, she determined to stop her husband's drinking once and for all. That night, after he was asleep, she put a jug of water beside his bed.

At dawn, the *vigneron* sensed something was wrong. He sat up in bed, looked, saw the water, and died of shock. They buried him, and at once a vine began growing on his grave, bearing grapes both red and white. When the grapes ripened, they dropped tears on his headstone. The strong aroma of the juice drew birds from the whole countryside, who pecked at the grapes, then fell swooning around his grave. Soon the whole village reeled with drunkenness, and even grandmothers did foolish things.

To this day, whenever the villagers are cruel to one another, the ghost of the *vigneron* walks the streets, and his breath even makes the mayor act silly. There are some who say that he is simply looking for the water jug, to tip it over. Whenever a jug is spilled in the village, whatever may be in it, it is always rinsed out with wine, so that the ghost of the *vigneron* will not make one look foolish. The wine, of course, is from the Loire, which never makes one foolish.

Alsace and Other Bons Vins

Thirst-quenching draughts are produced from the Rhine to the Pyrenees. Much of every vintage is carafe wine that goes straight from barrel to pitcher, but the best of the *bons vins* get into bottle, some of them get to Paris, and a few are shipped abroad. Some of the most interesting ones come from small districts. None of them are great, or even fine, but many of them are good to drink.

The best vineyards of Alsace begin back from the Rhine plain at Colmar and extend twenty miles north to the town of *Sélestat*. These are the vineyards of what the French call *Haut-Rhin*, and while there are others extending all the way up to Strasbourg and to the German border and still more to the south of Colmar, the vineyards near the fairy-tale towns of Ammerschwir, Mittelwihr, Kientzheim, Kaysersberg, Riquewihr,

129

Ribeauvillé and Bergheim produce the best wines. The towns were battered during the last war, but the vineyards were the first things restored, and today each town has a substantial cooperative winery through which many of the growers market their wines.

The great valley that stretches to the Rhine was once a lake and is now a sea of wheat and hops and orchards edged with vineyards. The grapes are trained high in Alsace, and the vines are Sylvaner, Traminer, Gewürz-Traminer, and Riesling, with some Pinot Blanc and Pinot Gris, called Tokay here, because the Alsatians thought it came from Hungary. Alsace remains without an *Appellation d'Origine* law, which is one reason why its best wines and vineyards are not ranked with the best of the Loire and the Rhône.

The Riesling grape in Alsace produces a good, light, flowery wine. Slightly spicier and less dry wines are made from the Gewürz-Traminer, which means "spicy Traminer." They are a strain of the crisp and flavorsome regular Traminers. Both produce the floweriest wines of France. The best-known of Alsatian wines comes from the Sylvaner, which is usually planted in lesser vineyards toward the plain and above Sélestat. The Alsatian vintners are not apt to cause the owners of great German vineyards to lose sleep nights, for though German grapes are used, differences in soil and climate bring out differences in the wines. Sometimes, a blending is made of wines from the better varieties, and it is marketed as *Edelzwicker*. Blends from Sylvaner and the lesser grapes are marketed as *Zwicker*. The Pinot Gris of Alsace is a popular pink wine, but almost all of it is brought in from outside the district for bottling; the acreage of red wine grapes in Alsace is very small. Vineyard names rarely appear on a label since the wines are blended so that they can be sold cheaply. Some of the growers estate-bottle their wines, but these are much higher in price than the general run, and the market for them is small. The wines are best when drunk young, from two to not more than five years after the vintage, and the best recent year was 1959, with 1957, in general, very good. The wines mature in great oval oak casks, two hundred and more years old, many decorated on the ends with carvings of vineyard scenes. It is the custom in Alsace to taste from small, straight-sided glasses, and to swallow the green wines, which means that your sips are small and wary, since the wines still in cask produce astonishing gastric effects among the incautious.

✑ THE JURA

South of Alsace, in the mountains across the plain from Burgundy, are the four small districts of the Jura. Pasteur carried out his researches on fermentation here a hundred years ago, the first major discoveries about winemaking that had been made for centuries. What started him on his discoveries was the fact that many wines were going bad during shipment. He found that wines could be heated and thus kept from turning, and pasteurization became standard practice with ordinary wines whenever they were out of balance. The heating destroyed freshness in the wine, stabilizing it at a low level, but kept it from spoiling. Pasteur's most important discovery was that fermentation was caused by bacteria, and this led to later discoveries about yeasts and their actions.

Arbois produces pleasant white wines, and *rosé* wines that rank with the best from Tavel. Both are fresh and pleasing, best when only a year or two old.

Château Chalon is the district just south of Arbois and produces the only wine in France where maderization produces a good wine, called *vin jaune*. A film of yeast forms on the wine so that it continues to develop in contact with the air. The wine is deeply golden, and tastes something like an old Fino Sherry. *Vin de paille* is also made here, following the ancient custom of spreading grapes on grass mats after picking so that they lose some of their moisture. These straw wines have a sweet, distinctive taste, and they can live for decades.

The best white wines of the Jura come from the little district of L'Étoile, where sparkling wines and yellow wines are also made. Much of the wine is marketed simply as Côtes du Jura, and this is rarely shipped out of the country.

✑ THE SAVOIE

The mountainous country to the east of Burgundy is famous for its farm produce and its *poulets de Bresse*, but it should also be famous for the excellence of its inexpensive wines. One of the best wine shops in New York imports a sparkling wine from the Savoy that sells for less than four dollars, making it the best sparkling-wine buy in the country. The wine is dry and hard, but sound and pleasing, and these characteristics are those of the other wines from the ski-country vineyards.

Up on the south shores of Lake Geneva is the tiny district of Crépy, and a little farther down the Rhône is Seyssel, both of which produce pleasant white wines. From Die and Bellegarde, in the hills below Hermitage and Valence, comes a wine called Clairette. These are true country wines of France, rarely getting out of the districts, let alone out of the country.

✒ PROVENCE AND THE RIVIERA

The wines of Provence are mostly white and pink, and the four best districts are La Palette, near Aix; Cassis, near Marseilles, Bandol, a few miles farther east along the coast; and Bellet, near Nice. Off the coast near Bandol is the island of Porquerolles, where one of the best *rosés* is made. The white, pink and red wines from these districts are drunk along the Mediterranean, although some of the *rosé* from Cassis is occasionally exported. A score of small vineyards producing pink wines outside these districts have also been classified. None of the *rosés* approach the Tavels, but they all taste pleasant on the Riviera. So does the *rosé* from Corsica, full and alcoholic; some of it, called *Patrimoniaux*, gets to the mainland.

Castel Roubine
Château de Selle
Clos Cigonne
    du Relais
Domaine de l'Aumérade
    de la Clapière
    de la Grande-Loube
    du Jas-d'Esclans
    des Moulières
    du Noyer
    de Saint-Martin
    de la Source

Château de Sainte Roseline
Clos de la Bastide-Verte
Mireille
Coteau du Perrage
Domaine de Brégançon
    de la Croix
    du Galoupet
    de Mauvanne
    de Minuty
    de Rimauresq
    de Saint-Maur

These vineyards are classed by the *Appellation Contrôlée*. There are many others.

THE PYRENEES AND THE MIDI

The white wines of the Pyrenees are Jurançon, Gaillac, and Blanquette de Limoux. The last is sparkling and small; Gaillac is sweet and small; and Jurançon, the best of the lot, is sweet and spicy and aged four years in wood, which destroys any freshness it might have.

There are a number of wine districts along the Mediterranean, extending from the Spanish border to the Midi, but the wines are best tasted while passing through the regions. Banyuls produces sweet wines that are called *vins doux liquoreux* or *vins doux naturels* (VDN), of little interest wherever sherry is obtainable. Neighboring districts produce similar wines, among them Rousillon, Minervois, Rivesaltes, Agly, Maury, the Muscat de Frontignan and Clairette du Languedoc.

The Midi produces enormous quantities of wines which are sold by alcoholic percentage, wines of *onze pour cent* costing little more than those at 10 or 10.5 per cent. The vineyards were vastly expanded at the time of the *phylloxera* panic in the great vineyards and have been overproducing ever since. These are coarse and heavy wines, and tank trucks roll north daily to the blending vats of shippers in more famous districts. Some pleasant big red wines are good enough to be protected by control laws, among them those of Corbières, Saint-George, and Costières du Gard. Like all the red wines of the Midi and many other full red wines from better districts, a brownish tinge can be seen on the edge of the glass when the wine gets old. This is called onionskin, *pelure d'oignon*, and is invariably the sign of an old wine.

~§ ALGERIA

Algerian vineyards on the mountains and in the plains were planted at the time of the *phylloxera* scare. Today, there are nearly a million African acres under vine, producing four hundred million gallons a year. Most of it goes to France and some of it is excellent.

The wines sometimes reach 16 per cent alcohol in the mountains, and are characterized by great fullness, tannin, and glycerine. Those of Oran, near Mascara and Tlemçen, are among the fullest of the red wines; those from Médéa are exceptionally fruity; and those from Miliana are noted for full bouquet. Both of the last named develop remarkably after a couple of years in cask and a couple more in bottle. All of them seem particularly pleasant when fresh, yet none appear capable of developing that lightness of balance which is a mark of a great wine. White and pink wines are made in many of the districts as fortified wines. Most of these are used for blending and sold to shippers in famous districts. The vineyards are irrigated and the winemaking is on an enormous scale.

Not much information is available on the best Algerian wines because little attempt has been made to market the outstanding wines, but reds from Coteaux de l'Harrach and the Domaine de La Trappe de Staoüeli near Algiers, the white and pink wines from Bouira, and the red wines of Monts du Tessalah in Oran are good.

Wines carrying a seal on the label with the initials VDQS—*Vins Délimités de Qualité Supérieur*—are apt to be better than most.

Morocco produces some twenty-five million gallons of wines each year near Casablanca, Marrakesh, and Meknès, but none of this is being exported at present.

Champagne and Sparkling Wines

Champagne is full of fun. There's the country girl come to the city, who can dance or paint or act like an angel, but the cruel streets are dark and rainy. She clutches her thin coat around her shivering, girlish figure with its hint of curves, stumbles back when the restaurant door bursts open to reveal bright lights and laughter inside—alas, not for her. And then she meets the worldly man who has seen too much. Strangely touched by her haunting quality of innocent freshness, he orders Champagne, and as she lifts the glass, she crinkles her nose. "Oh, it tickles!" she cries. After a glass or two, she throws caution to the winds, and a little later she is famous and wiser. It's a lovely story. Champagne made Garbo laugh; Anna Held bathed in it. No ship can be launched without Champagne dripping down its prow, no wedding is complete without it, no New Year's Eve, no anniversary.

All Champagne worth the name comes from about twenty thousand acres of Marne vineyards eighty miles west of Paris, and some believe that Paris is Paris because it is so near this source of supply. Every country makes wine with bubbles, but none comes close to Champagne. The wines from its chalky vineyards are transmuted into an incomparable unity that is matched nowhere else. Champagne was made to sparkle as a child is born to grow.

The vintage begins late in September, when the growers bring their grapes to the *vendangeoirs*, presshouses maintained by the great firms, where the grapes are weighed, priced, and then pressed. A committee of growers sets a price, the shipping firms set a lower one, and the two committees argue out an agreement. Each vineyard has its rating. The best, *hors classe* vineyards, are rated 100 per cent and command the full price agreed on. *Première Catégorie* vineyards get from 90 to 98 per cent of the agreed price. The second and third categories get perhaps a fifth or a quarter less than the *hors classe* vineyards.

Vineyards stretch along the Marne, on each side of the little towns of Ay and Epernay, those around the first town being in the highest category. Across the river to the north is the mountain of Reims; the city is out in the plains beyond, but the towns with their top-rated vineyards circle around the mountain like so many jewels on a necklace: Louvois, Bouzy, Ambonnay, Mailly, Verzenay, Beaumont and Sillery. All these are planted in varieties of Burgundy's red grape, the Pinot Noir.

To the south are vineyards planted in the white Pinot and Chardonnay, on a long slope called the *Côte des Blancs*. Champagne is usually a blend of wines from all three districts, but some extremely delicate Champagne is made only from white grapes, and this is called *Blanc de Blancs*. It is usually sold as *Champagne de Cru* under the name of the town. The towns with vineyards in the top category are Cramant and Avize; Mesnil is also well known.

The juice is taken to the fermenting vats of the large firms, most of them located in Ay, Epernay, and Reims, although there are small firms, cooperatives, and branches of the large firms in several of the towns. Cane sugar dissolved in wine is added to the juice before fermentation, so that all the resulting wines will contain 12 per cent alcohol. The wines are blended and bottled in the spring, a light dosage of sugar syrup and yeast culture being added, which will be transformed into bubbles. Champagne is rarely made from the 100-per-cent vineyards only, the standard practice being to blend the wines of one category with those of another—this being called a *cuvée*, or vatting. The aim of each firm is to preserve the same character of their *cuvées* from year to year, and when nonvintage Champagnes are made, the current vintage will be balanced with wines from other years. As nearly all Champagnes are blended, vintage Champagnes can be considered an extravagance, and there is no doubt that the nonvintage Champagnes from the best houses are superior to the vintage Champagnes of firms with lesser concern for quality.

The slightest off-taste is increased by the sparkle; great care is therefore taken not to bruise the grapes. Only a first light pressing, somewhat more than half the juice, goes into a fine *cuvée*. The rest is made into lesser sparkling wines and ordinary wine.

The first-press wine is promptly removed from the vats after the first fermentation. The second spring fermentation takes place in cask. When the wine is completely fermented out, it is fined, which means that it is filtered to remove unwanted solid matter, blended with other wines from its district (*l'assemblage*), fined, blended with wines from other districts (*la coupage*), fined a third time, then bottled with its dosage of sugar and yeast, and finally stored for three years or longer. Each spring, fall, and winter—when the vine flowers, when the vintage takes place, and when the second fermentation begins—the wine in the bottles also ferments. The cellars are at a constant temperature, somewhere between 60° and 65° Fahrenheit, varying scarcely a degree from one season to the next, but whenever a change takes place in the vineyard or the fermenting vats, the wine in the bottle also begins to work. Nobody knows why; perhaps it has to do with the equinox or the moon, but this fermentation in the bottle, slow and steady, is what makes Champagne.

Four years after the vintage, the scant ounce of sugar that was added has been changed into alcohol and carbonic-acid gas by the action of the yeasts. The wine is clear, but there is a sediment in the bottle. A line of whitewash, to mark the position of the sediment, is put on the thumbhole at the base of the bottle, called the *punt*, and the bottle is put in the *pupitre*. These pulpits are slanting racks with holes in them for the neck of the bottle. The object is to move the sediment to the neck of the bottle by giving the bottle a little twist one day, and an upward tilt the next, actions called the *remuage*. A good *remueur* can shake as many as thirty thousand bottles in a day. After six weeks or so, the bottle is almost standing on its neck, the sediment resting against the bottom of the cork.

Disgorging the sediment is done by pulling the cork so that the gas shoots out the deposit, then the bottle is filled and corked again before the wine or gas escapes. A good *dégorgeur* does this in a couple of seconds: the cork flies into a hood, the deposit shoots out, and the bottle is set on the corking machine, all in a single movement. In the process, he manages to let some of the clear wine fall on his thumb, which he smells and tastes, making sure that the wine is in good condition. If it is not, he sets the bottle aside. The corking machine has two bottles suspended above it, one containing sugar syrup, here called *liqueur d'expédition*, the other containing wine of the same *cuvée*, and these automatically refill the bottle that has been disgorged. Some firms freeze the neck of the bottle, so that the sediment flies out in a plug of ice, but many firms still consider this newfangled, and not the way to treat Champagne.

The dosage of sugar syrup varies. *Brut* is driest of all, less than 1.5 per cent by volume. *Extra Sec* contains up to 3 per cent sugar; *Sec* contains as much as 4 per cent; and *Demi-Sec* contains up to 8 per cent, or a couple of tablespoonfuls. The pride of the Champagne firms is their *Brut*, because there is very little sugar in the wine under which to hide defects. Most people really prefer *Extra Sec* or *Sec*, however, because *Brut* is quite austere.

Some firms use .5 per cent of sugar for their *Brut*, but rarely make a completely dry Champagne. If no sugar at all is used, the wine is puckery, almost parching the mouth, and splendidly refreshing. The old roués used to like it for seduction, because it made a girl thirsty and eager for more—but it is hard to come by these days, and expensive. *Extra Dry* and *Sec* serve very well. Few firms make sweet Champagne, called *Doux*, because so many cheap sparkling wines are sweet, masking their flaws with the sugar.

The development of the cork made Champagne possible, and this is attributed to Dom Pérignon, who was a cellarmaster at the monastery of Hautvilliers at the turn of the seventeenth century. Before his time, bottles were stoppered with a wad of cloth, a drop of oil being poured on the surface of the wine to keep out bacteria.

Dom Pérignon is also credited with the invention of sparkling wines, although they had been known for centuries. His monastery owned much vineyard land, and he had the chance to experiment with many wines, greatly improving the winemaking techniques. His cork made practical the use of bottles, and even though he didn't invent Champagne, his cork started a revolution.

Champagne is expensive today for three reasons: scarcity, taxes, and cost of making. The Pinots grow at their farthest limit in the chalky vineyards of Champagne, the yield is small, and frost and freeze often cut it more. Scarcely two out of three years can be expected to produce a normal crop. The usual yield is somewhere between three and three and a half million cases, often higher. Sometimes there is none. There are more than eleven thousand growers in the district, but fewer than a hundred fifty own more than a dozen acres. What adds most to the cost of Champagne is the outrageous taxes on the bubbles. A table wine carries a thirteen-cent U.S. federal tax, but a bottle of Champagne with the same amount of alcohol carries a tax of $1.65, plus local taxes. Someday there may be sensible tax laws on Champagne, but until there are, try to forget that every time you drink a glass of bubbly Uncle Sam takes a quarter for the privilege.

A bottle goes through more than a hundred hands before it is shipped, and the work is skilled. Even the attaching of the metal cap on the cork demands a sense of touch, because if the cork is tamped down too hard the wire muzzle will not hold properly, and the bubbles will be lost. Considering the care needed, it is remarkable that so many bottles reach their destination to open with a satisfying pop. Perhaps one bottle in a hundred will be flat.

Although the pop is satisfying, it is not considered proper in Champagne itself, where all good corks are removed silently. The muzzle is carefully unwired and the cork is gently loosened by pushing against its bulge with the thumbs. The pop may be improper, but it is a salute to joy unrestrained. The pop is part of the pleasure.

Champagne is at its best when it is not chilled too much, fifteen minutes in a bucket of ice and water being about right. You can speed up the cooling by adding salt to the water, which makes the ice melt faster. If the bucket isn't tall enough, and few of them are, the bottle should be upended for a few minutes, so that all the wine will be cooled. Quick chilling is bad for all wines, the shock throwing them out of balance. A refrigerator can do as good a job as an ice bucket if the bottles are placed in the warmest section. If the refrigerator is too cold, the bottle can be wrapped in a damp towel before it is set inside. The towel slows the chilling so that the process may take an hour. The custom of wrapping a towel around the bottle originated so that waiters wouldn't drip on fussy patrons. The best practice is to dry the bottle, then rest it on one's palm, fingers spread on the underside, thumb in punt and label on top, pouring carefully without touching the neck of the bottle to the glass, twisting deftly at the finish so that the last drop is caught on the bottle's rim. This takes practice, but it's the proper way to pour Champagne.

Champagne glasses are much more important than pouring technique. Everybody should be offended if the wine is served in the shallow, sloshing *coupes* that used to be the fashion. They are supposed to have been modeled after the right breast of Helen of Troy. There is some question as to whether the glasses go back that far, and even more doubt that Helen ever stayed still long enough to have her breast sculped. Her glasses, in any case, dissipate the bubbles, which are the reason for Champagne in the first place. A good Champagne glass is narrow, coming to a point in the bottom of the bowl so that the bubbles have a starting place from which to begin their rise. The glass should be tall, so that its upper half acts as a chimney, collecting the bouquet and the popping bubbles, which tickle the nose as part of the fun.

You can tell a good Champagne by the bubbles, called the *bead*. The smaller the bead, the better the Champagne. A wine with a small bead produces a particularly light and tingling sensation that is the essence of Champagne. A bond, formed between the gas of the second fermentation and the wine, slows down effervescence, and makes a remarkable difference to the taste.

The top vintages in recent years have been 1947 (now disappearing from the market), 1949, 1952, 1953, 1955, and 1959. The outstanding recent vintage is 1959. The 1952, which tops the '47s and often matches the '55s, is rated ahead of the quickly maturing 1953, which is slightly better than 1949. Many of the vines were frozen in 1956 and 1957, but there were some excellent '57 *cuvées*, and 1958 will prove to be a good year. Unless the bottles have been well stored, the 1947 vintage is now apt to be a disappointment. Champagne can be drunk a year after its final corking, although it reaches a peak seven or ten years after the vintage, and may continue to hold up for another five years or so, but loses its freshness.

Each Champagne house blends wines to bring out the best in its particular stocks, carefully balancing the wines in each *cuvée*, following a pattern that may go back for a century or more. Each drinker has his preference—some like full wines with much bouquet, others wines that are extremely light; both sorts will be distinguished by balance and delicacy, and that quality called *breed*. Among those firms whose wines are noted for fullness and bouquet are Krug, Bollinger, Perrier-Jouet, the Dom Pérignon of Moët & Chandon, and Château Salon (a small firm of great reputation that specializes in Blanc de Blancs). Among those noted for delicacy are Veuve Clicquot, Mumm's Cordon Rouge, Charles Heidsieck and Piper Heidsieck.

A fine Champagne should have body and roundness coupled with elegance, delicacy, and breed. *Champagne des Crus*, those Blancs de Blancs that bear the name of the town from which they come, are distinguished as being "complete." *Complet* is the French wine term that means the wine is perfectly developed, lacking nothing. The word is applied to wines from the vineyards around Ay, which are also generally classed as *fin, corsé*, and *racé*, and its wines add softness to a *cuvée*. Cramant is called the "Ay of the Côte des Blancs," its wines distinguished by being *corsé* and *complet*. Those of Avize are said to be *fin, racé*, and *élégant*, while those of Mesnil are slightly less so. The distinctions seem slight, but the characteristics emphasized give some idea of what Champagne is supposed to be when it is at its best. It is a wine of great character, not famous for its bubbles alone.

The largest Champagne firms produce wines of high quality because they have a reputation to maintain. Largest of all is Moët & Chandon, which may produce three million bottles in a good year; its finest Champagne is Dom Pérignon, made only in fine years and in small quantities. Those firms producing more than a million bottles a year are: Mercier, Pommery & Greno, Veuve Clicquot, Mumm, Heidsieck Dry Monopole, and Taittinger, which has absorbed Irroy, a famous name in the English market. Those producing just under a million bottles are: Ayala, Charles Heidsieck, Piper Heidsieck, and Castellan. Bollinger, Perrier-Jouet, and Pol Roger produce perhaps half a million bottles in a good year, while Krug, Besserat de Bellefon, Louis Roederer, Lanson, Duminy, and Goulet produce perhaps a quarter of a million each. The rest produce less than twenty thousand cases a year, and Château Salon produces about two thousand.

Of these, the United States buys two hundred fifty thousand cases a year.

Champagne has been a truly French wine since A.D. 496, when Clovis, the first king of the Franks, was crowned at Reims. French kings were crowned there from then on. In those days, the wine was red. First Bordeaux and then Burgundy became a part of the kingdom, seizing the market until Dom Pérignon showed the growers of Champagne how to make light, pink wines from black grapes.

Nobody knew it at the time, but the big news of 1659 was that Dom Pérignon renounced the world to join the Benedictines at the abbey near Épernay. His winemaking genius led the way to better wines from the district, by blending, the first fine wines to be so made. By the time another century had rolled around, Champagne was on its way. For a time, pink Champagne was the vogue, and a fine Champagne *rosé* is being made today in Mailly by the cooperative of the *vignerons*, as well as by other producers in the district. There is even some red Champagne produced at Aubigny, but this has never found a real market. A partially sparkling wine, *Crémant*, is made, which carries the same tax as a fully sparkling one. Still white wines of excellent quality, called *Champagne Nature*, and some still reds, are produced but rarely exported.

Champagne gets linked with fashion, as well as fame and fortune. In a recent whirl with that heedless dame, swizzle sticks appeared; the idea was to twirl the stick in one's bubbly to make it frothy and get all those bubbles right out of there. For a while, fashionable shops in all the gay cities sold folding gold or silver swizzle sticks, and the gaudier ones were studded with jewels. Night clubs still supply wooden ones, but usually their wines are so bad it doesn't make much difference what you do to the bubbles. The fad has pretty much disappeared by now.

Champagne is wonderful for breakfast, particularly with scrambled eggs and bacon, or even without them. It's a fine wine to drink in the afternoon, or before dinner. The wine tastes good with meals, particularly festive ones that call for a turkey or a ham or other roasts and grilled foods. It's good with fish and sea food and luncheon salads, and it's wonderful with sandwiches. Very good after dinner; excellent just before retiring. Some people keep splits in the refrigerator, to open whenever the mood hits them, but a couple has no trouble finishing a bottle, or even two. A *Magnum*, the double bottle, is the right size for dinner parties of four, and large bottles are particularly suited to Champagne; wines mature more slowly in big bottles. Champagne used to come in larger sizes, but the waste was so great if the cork was poor that this is pretty much a thing of the past. *Jeroboams* hold four bottles of wine, *Rehoboams* hold six, the *Methuselah* holds eight, the *Salmanazar* holds twelve, the *Balthazar* holds sixteen, and the *Nebuchadnezzar* holds twenty bottles of wine, or four gallons eight ounces. These are rarely seen these days, because they aren't practical. They were big, though.

Every Champagne *étiquette*, or label, is registered with a control board and identified by numbers which indicate the *cuvée* and the year. A pair of letters precedes the number, and this identifies the producer: CM stands for *Cooperative de Manipulation*, which means that the wine is produced by a cooperative cellar and bottling operation from wines produced by the members. RM indicates the wine is made and bottled by the vineyard owner himself, an estate-bottling. NM indicates that the label is a major mark of a Champagne house, a *Négociant-Manipulant*, that buys wine and does its own handling and bottling. MA indicates a secondary mark of a Champagne house, or a Champagne from a house that does not do its own bottling. All genuine Champagne will have the word inscribed on both the label and the cork, and all must be bottle-fermented.

⊷ ⊶

Sparkling Wines

All sparkling wines would be Champagne if they could. Failing that, they steal its name. Even so, many of them are good, and while every district makes sparkling wines, a few of them stand out. The sweet wines from the Loire—Vouvray and Saumur—the Asti Spumante of Italy, and the dry wines from New York and California have found American customers, and even sparkling Burgundy has had some success.

If the wine is bottled before the second fermentation, some carbonic-acid gas is apt to be formed, and many sweet wines have a tendency to show a bead. In France, such slightly sparkling wines are called *pétillant;* the German word is *spritzig,* and the Italians call them *frizzante.* German wines, particularly Moselles, have a tendency in this direction, and so do the wines of the Loire. Many fresh young red wines develop a slight sparkle in late winter—out of sheer exuberance, perhaps. In most wines, it is a pleasant quality, but if the wine is poorly made an unpleasing odor develops.

Not all sparkling wines are bottle-fermented according to the *Méthode Champénoise.* Many cheap sparkling wines have carbon dioxide added to them under pressure. This is called the impregnation method, and the bubbles quickly disappear when the bottle is opened. Another way, called the Charmat process, is to put the wines in a closed tank during the second fermentation. The wine is filtered and bottled under pressure, so that none of the carbonic-acid gas escapes. The bubbles formed in such wines are coarse and also disappear quickly.

⊷ FRANCE

Every district produces sparkling wines, but the good ones come from Vouvray and Saumur. They are naturally sweeter than Champagnes, are made in the same way, and are pleasant as dessert wines with melons and cakes that aren't too sweet. Because of the tax, they are too expensive in the United States, costing almost as much as Champagne.

Burgundy got into the sparkling-wine business because of the success of Champagne. The center of the trade was once Nuits-St.-Georges, but now Beaune and Rully and Savigny boast establishments. The wines are solely for export. Some are pleasant, particularly the white wines of Rully. Second-rate wines and second pressings are used to make red Sparkling Burgundies, and none have any distinction, except the color, which is cheerful. The high tax makes it a poor value in the States, as it does for all sparkling wines except Champagne.

The good Bordeaux shipping firm of M. Nathaniel Johnston makes a sparkling wine in which part of the production of Château Ducru-Beaucaillou is used. It is called *Royal Médoc Mousseux*, the last word being the term for sparkling wines in French.

Some of the wines of Savoy, the Rhône, and other regions are made into sparkling wines, but unless the price is well under that for Champagne they are not often worth trying.

GERMANY

Germany makes an enormous amount of sparkling wine, more than a million and a half cases each year, called *Sekt* or *Schaumwein*. The Champagne method is used for some, but tank fermentation is the rule. They are very popular and inexpensive—in Germany. One type, called *Perlwein*, is bottled at low pressure, scarcely more bubbly than the still-fermenting and cloudy *Federweisser* that is drunk after the vintage. Even red wines are made to sparkle, and so are various fruit wines—the bubbles add sprightliness to the drinks.

ITALY

Asti Spumante is the most famous sparkling wine of Italy, but almost every district produces its own *Spumante*, or at least a *Frizzante*, which is the Italian term for *pétillant* wines, among them the Prosecco of Venetia, the shimmering Gragnano produced near Capri, some Lacrima Christi, and several of the wines of the Piedmont, which are often called *amabile* when they show a tendency to effervesce. They are wines to taste out of curiosity, or in Italy, where taxes do not make them cost almost as much as Champagne.

◄§ PORTUGAL AND SPAIN

A Portuguese *rosé*, Lancer's, is the only sparkling wine from the Iberian peninsula generally available in the United States. It comes in tall earthenware bottles. Several good sparkling wines are made in both Portugal and Spain, but taxes make them too expensive for the American market.

◄§ AMERICAN SPARKLING WINES

Nearly a million bottles of sparkling wine are made in this country each year, in New York, Ohio, and California. Most of the quality wines come from New York state, produced by Gold Seal, Great Western, and Taylor, for the most part, while Meier's and Bellows produce most of the sparkling wine in Ohio. On the coast, Korbel and Almadén produce excellent sparkling wines. All these are bottle-fermented. Many of the producers of standard wines produce large quantities of sparkling wines by the tank method, and they can be pleasant to drink, although taxes make them exorbitant in price.

◄§ SUMMARY

Champagnes are generally blended from wines of similar qualities but different characteristics, and one year is balanced with another to produce nonvintage Champagnes, which are usually best buys.

Vintage Champagnes, generally excellent, command a high premium that is warranted by the rarity of the wines, not by the superiority in quality over nonvintage Champagnes.

The driest Champagne produced by a house is called *Brut*. These are wines that command a premium for their dryness, too dry for most tastes, and for serving with most foods except salty ones like caviar and smoked meats and fish. Champagnes labeled *Extra Sec* and *Sec* are next in dryness, usually possess some flowery characteristics, and are the ones generally preferred with food and for celebration. The sweet Champagnes, labeled *Doux* are the cheapest on the market, hiding taste flaws under sweetness, and are the ones to use for punches.

Champagnes are too expensive because of the outrageous U.S. federal tax on the bubbles, and yet the Champagnes are the only sparkling wines truly worth the price. Other sparkling wines worth considering are produced mostly in France, and include sparkling Vouvray and Saumur, and occasional wines from the Savoie. The level of excellence of other European sparkling wines rarely warrants the payment of the excessive tax; New York and California sparkling wines are to be preferred.

ermany

All the great wines of Germany are white, made from Riesling grapes in vineyards along the Rhine and its tributaries. The vineyards begin almost at the river's rise in the Swiss Alps, but the Rhineland's four great districts are in Germany: just above Alsace are the Rheinpfalz and the Rhein-hessen; the Rheingau slopes rise above the westward crook of the river below the city of Mainz; and farther downstream is the district of the Moselle, named for the river whose waters join the Rhine at Coblenz.

Good wines also come from two districts on rivers that join the Rhine at either end of the Rheingau. *Steinwein* comes from the Franconia vineyards along the Main, which flows west to meet the Rhine near Mainz, and there are some fine vineyards along the Nahe, which flows north to join the Rhine opposite Rüdesheim. A few great wines,

151

called *Spitzenweine*, or peak wines, come from the Moselle tributaries of the Saar and the Ruwer, and a few good wines originate in
the Black Forest vineyards across from Alsace.

The best vineyards produce perhaps four million cases of excellent wines in a good year from scarcely 18,000 acres. Total
production is perhaps sixty million gallons in a good year, produced from less than 150,000 acres by more than 150,000 growers—a drop in the bucket compared to France's two million
gallons from three million acres under vine. In the good German
vineyards, or *lagen*, yield is less than 500 gallons an acre; 225 cases
would be a good yield in a good year.

The confusing thing about German wines is that each owner
of a fine vineyard will try to produce in a good year not one wine,
but two, a dry and a sweet. And in great years, they try for three or
more.

But what's still more confusing is that the dry wine isn't simply
dry, but flowery or fruity, and the sweet wine isn't simply sweet, but
ripe and luscious without being heavy or syrupy. It's not the dryness
you note first in the dry wines, but freshness and floweriness and
balance. It's not the sweetness you note first in the sweet wines, but
elegance and richness. And all of them will have the distinctive
flowery taste of the Riesling, while the other German grapes, the
Sylvaner and Traminers, will have similar flowery characteristics,
but to a lesser degree.

Contrariness seems to be involved in the making of all great
wines. Cold climates produce wines that tend to be hard and acid,
so it seems sheer mulishness on the part of the Rhine growers to
try to produce sweet wines. But nowhere else can such wines be
made. Even in the less-than-great vineyard wines, and in the
blended district wines, there is the desire to bring out the flowery
taste. Many of these are sweetened lightly, to mask acidity and to
make them taste more like the wines from the great vineyards.
Such sugared wines are bottled under the name of the township
or district. Many of them are surprisingly good. But the natural
wines, bearing a vineyard name on the label, are the ones that are a
delight to drink and a joy to praise.

Naturwein, dry and flowery, is made when the Ice Saints are kind.
Particularly *die Kalte Sophie*. Cold Sophie is the last of the *Eis-
Heiligen*, and her day is the fifteenth of May. She is preceded by

three other ice saints, all male, and it is the belief that if these days pass without a frost, there will follow a hundred days of good weather. With less, the winemaker must add sugar to the juice to build up the wine's alcoholic content.

When the good weather holds, the vintner will wait to pick his best grapes until the noble rot, called here the *edelfäule*, sets in. Such a wine will be bottled separately, and the label will identify it as a *Spätlese*, wine from the late picking. It will be fruitier than a Naturwein, with a more flowery bouquet, and those from the best vineyards may be somewhat sweet. To make such wines of any quality, the grower will need 120 days of good weather, and this occurs perhaps three times a decade.

In particularly good years, the vintner may find that a number of his grapes may be especially ripe, and that the *edelfäule* may have touched a good number of bunches. In this case, the grower will set aside these exceptional bunches, making them separately into wine. It will be called *Auslese* on the label, meaning selection. Generally somewhat sweet, an Auslese tastes best with sweet or spicy foods and with desserts.

In great years, some of the great vineyards will produce grapes heavily touched with the *edelfäule*, and the vintner will select individual berries from these bunches, making a wine that will be labeled *Beerenauslese*, berry selection. Sometimes the grapes will have shriveled, looking like so many raisins, and if a separate wine is made from these, it will be labeled *Trockenbeerenauslese*, or dried-berry selection. Both wines are incredibly sweet, the very essence of the Riesling, and even a large vineyard may produce only a barrel or two, once or twice a decade. Such wines can live for twenty years or more, costing upwards of $20 a bottle, being more a *tour de force* than simply commercial endeavor, a way of showing what the vineyard can produce.

All the wines, Naturwein, Spätlese, Auslese, Beerenauslese, and Trockenbeerenauslese, are bottled the spring after the vintage, although some of the sweetest may rest a little longer in the cask. The driest of them are ready to drink after a few months in bottle; even the Auslesen reach their prime within two years, and are generally past it after five. Ten years is generally the outside limit for an Auslese, even when it has been well kept, away from vibration and sudden temperature changes.

The most unusual of the German wines may be the sweet wines, but the ones drunk most often are those that are not too sweet. The Germans are most apt to drink them in the afternoon or evening, not necessarily with meals, when they often prefer beer. But the wines, well chilled, are wonderful with fish and sea food, with hams and spicy dishes and cold cuts. They are easy to drink, and there's scarcely a better thirst-quencher than the *Spritzer*, half Rhenish and half soda, which tastes best when both wine and soda are chilled, and served without ice cubes.

The owners of the best vineyards estate-bottle their wines. They are joined together in an organization called the *Verband Deutscher Naturwein-Versteigerer*, with separate groups in each district. Their wines carry the phrase, *Original-Abfüllung*, original bottling, a guarantee that the wine has been bottled by the grower; *Kellerabfüllung, Kellerabzug*, and *Schlossabzug* all mean the same thing. The vineyard name may be identified on the label by *Wachstum, Gewächs, Eigengewächs*, or *Creszenz*, each of which signifies that the wine is natural, unsugared, and from a specific vineyard.

These estate-bottled wines are carefully labeled, bearing the name of the township, followed by the name of the vineyard, and the vintage. Often enough, every cask—called *fass* or *fuder*—will be bottled separately, and the wine will carry that cask number to identify it. Prices are generally set at a series of wine auctions, different *fuder* bringing different prices. Often enough, the best wines will be marked as *Kabinett*, to indicate superiority, while others will be marked *feine, feinste*, or *hochfeinste*—fine, finest, or high-finest; all of these wines command premium prices.

Selling wines by cask and trying to make the various Auslesen have their drawbacks. The grower may put the juice from his best grapes in particular *fuder*, putting his poorest lot in another; these will command widely varied prices at the auction, but when they are bottled they will appear under precisely the same label. The only difference will be the *fuder* number, so that a buyer will have no way of knowing which is the better wine unless he has a list of auction prices. One wine with a famous name may be magnificent, another from a different cask may be mediocre. At the same time, if too many choice berries are reserved for Auslesen wines, the other wines will be made from less perfect grapes so that those marketed as Naturwein or Spätlese under the name of the vineyard and grower may be quite ordinary.

There is a tendency today to make fewer Auslesen, partly because they are so expensive, partly because the other wines suffer from the removal of the best grapes. The practice of blending one cask with another, so that only one or two wines will be made from a vineyard's vintage, not half a dozen, is becoming more common. Auslesen are sensible buys only when they come from the best vineyards in good years. Naturweine and Spätlesen are good buys when one is looking for fine German wines at reasonable prices.

The great hills behind the Rhineland vineyards protect them from the chill winds of the north, giving the country a southern aspect, full of orchards and flowers and farmland. This was the outpost of the Holy Roman Empire, and it is today the outpost of the vine—to the north is Schnapps country and beer country. But here, on a latitude with Labrador, the quick-ripening Riesling, and its lesser cousins the Sylvaner and Traminer, can flourish.

The Benedictines, particularly the Cistercian order, planted most of the vineyards, as they did in so many other parts of Europe. The Church still owns many vineyards, although most of them were long ago confiscated by the state, which is the largest vineyard owner. And it is the Church that is credited with the discovery of the secret of great Rhine wines. Many years ago, the abbot in charge of a vineyard had to wait for permission from his bishop to harvest. When vintage time arrived, an abbot sent to his bishop for the needed order, but the messenger was waylaid by robbers and killed. A second messenger was sent, and he was done away with. The third got through. A month too late, wailed the abbot, looking at his rotting, shriveled grapes, but he ordered the harvest anyway. The wine was golden, ripe as a maiden of seventeen summers and sweet as first love. Ever since, the winemakers of the Rhineland have tried to repeat the miracle. Who can say that they are wrong?

The vintage of the century was 1949. Most of it is gone today, as are the wines of 1952 and 1953. What's left of 1953 are ripe and beautifully balanced. The vineyards were damaged by frost in 1955, almost destroyed in 1956, and frozen again in 1957. The year 1958 was plentiful, but is generally high in price because of the poor years that went before. And then came 1959, bringing a new vintage of the century, even better than '49.

᪲᪲

Rheinpfalz

The Pfalz begins at the French border, but all its great vineyards are in the Mittel-Hardt, thirty miles inside Germany. A vineyard road, the Weinstrasse, runs from the border and up into the Rheinhessen, connecting the colorful vineyard towns and winding through thirty-five thousand acres of vineyards, a tenth of which produce fine wines. Most people take the *autobahn* at Strasbourg, hurrying up the east side of the Rhine to Heidelberg, and miss it all.

The great vineyards lie along a five-mile slope, twenty-five hundred acres of Riesling grapes, flanked on each side by some good vineyards planted mostly in Sylvaner, and fronted by the great flatland vineyards that stretch to the Rhine and produce what the Germans call *Schoppenwein*, a carafe wine like the cheap ones of the Midi, marked by a heavy soil taste called *Bodengeschmack*. The great wines are less known than the other famous wines of Germany, perhaps partly because they are surrounded by such oceans of ordinary wine. This is Germany's largest district and produces most of Germany's red wines, as well as whites. The district was once a Roman outpost, ruled through its Counts Palatine, whose main job seems to have been supplying the empire with wines, and the district is still known as the Palatinate.

Because these are the southernmost of the great German vineyards, the grapes ripen quickly, so the wines are good buys in years when sunshine is scanty.

As elsewhere in Germany, the vineyards are broken up among many owners, but the directory of estate-bottlers lists the most important. The largest landholders in the Pfalz, whose names are assurance of quality, are:

Reichsrat v. Buhl—200 acres

Dr. Bürklin-Wolf—165 acres

*Geheimer Rat Dr. v. Basser-
    mann-Jordan—90 acres*

Dr. Deinhard—65 acres

Wilhelm Spindler—45 acres

Dr. med. Jos. Pioth—37 acres

*Georg Siben Erben *—30 acres*

Hch. Koch-Herzog Erben—27
  acres
Dietz-Matti—22 acres
Josef Biffar—20 acres
Jos. Reinhardt II—20 acres
Jul. Ferd. Kimich—20 acres
Ferd. Heinemann—12 acres

Dr. Kern—12 acres
Heinrich Spindler—12 acres
A. Tiemann—12 acres
Herbert Giessen Erben—10
  acres
Geo. Mosbacher—10 acres

* Erben means heirs.

These holdings consist of parcels in various towns and vineyards, most of which are on the great slope. Each of the important towns of the Pfalz, and those in the other districts, operate at least one cooperative, called a *Winzerverein* or *Winzergenossenschaft*, made up of owners of small parcels who send their wines to market under a single label.

⌃§ *RUPPERTSBERG AND KÖNIGSBACH*

The great slope begins just south of Ruppertsberg, a homely village that lies out on the plain. Königsbach lies above the slope, and both claim about a hundred acres of the great soil. The wines are noted for full body and bouquet.

R U P P E R T S B E R G   A N D
K Ö N I G S B A C H

———————⊃∗❀∗⊂———————

Ruppertsberger	*Ruppertsberger*
Reiterpfad	*Speiss*
Kreuz	*Hoheburg*
Quelle	*Gaisböhl*
Achtmorgen	*Diedel*
Goldschmied	*Grund*
Gutgeistl	*Hausbrunnen*
Hofstück	*Kaft*
Kieselberg	*Königsbacherweg*
Linsenbusch	*Mandelacker*
Mühlweg	*Nussbein*
Schlossberg	*Stückelpfad*
Weinbach	*Weisslich*

* * *

Königsbacher	*Königsbacher*
Bender	*Falbert*
Harle	*Idig*
Ölberg	*Rolandsberg*
Satz	

◄§ DEIDESHEIM

This is one of the handsomest towns of the Rhineland, and the
home of most of the great wine producers, including Bassermann-
Jordan, whose father was the outstanding authority on German
wines, and Reichsrat von Buhl, who owns more great vineyards than
anybody else in Germany—about two hundred acres. The town is
full of gardens and orchards, and the old houses are made of red
sandstone the color of the soil. There are some five hundred acres
of great Riesling vineyards surrounding it, producing, with Forst, the
greatest wines of the Palatinate. There are two excellent cooperatives in the town.

D E I D E S H E I M *

Deidesheimer
　Hohenmorgen
　Kieselberg
　Grainhübel

Deidesheimer
　Leinhöhle
　Kränzler
　Reiss

Anweinchen
Buschweg
Dopp
Erdner
Forster Strasse or *Strasse*
Gemminger
Gutenberg
Hainschleid
Hassert
Herrgottsacker

Breitenerde
Deidesheimerweg
Eides
Fleckinger
Geheu
Grain
Hahnenböhl
Haide
Hayern
Hofstück

* Some of the Deidesheim vineyards extend into Forst, and those portions go to
market as Forsters.

Deidesheimer	Deidesheimer
Höhe	Hunger
Kaft	Kalkofen
Katharinenbild	Katzenstuhl
Kehr	Kieselberg
Kirchberg	Klostergarten
Langenböhl	Langenmorgen
Letten	Linsenbusch
Martenweg	Maushöhle
Mühle	Neuberg
Neunmorgen	Östrichweg
Petershöhle	Rennpfad
Schafböhl	Schloss
Schnepfenflug	Steingasse
Tal	Taleck
Tiergarten	Vogelgesang
Waldberg	Walshöhlen
	Weinbach

⋅⧸ FORST

The tiny village of Forst is surrounded by its vines, the slope pushing out here toward the river plain. The wines from the Pfalz slope are considered the finest, having a full bouquet and extraordinary balance. Two of its best vineyards are in the town itself and are among the top three or four most valuable vineyards in Germany: Jesuitengarten is owned entirely by Dr. Bassermann-Jordan, and Kirchenstück is owned by several proprietors. Reichsrat von Buhl owns nearly a seventh of the some 350 acres of Riesling vineyards in Forst.

There are quarries of black basalt near the town, and local experts claim that chips of the rock give the wine its special elegance. At any rate, stones from the quarries are placed around the vines in all four of the towns that claim the slope. Some years ago, vineyards on northern slopes were moved to southern slopes, in one of the most anxious earth-moving projects on record, but everybody agrees that the change made the wines still greater. The Beerenauslesen and Trockenbeerenauslesen frequently command ten or twelve dollars a bottle even before they leave the producers' cellars.

F O R S T *

Forster	*Forster*
Kirchenstück	*Jesuitengarten*
Ungeheuer	*Kranich*
Ziegler	*Langenacker*
Alser	*Berg* or *Altenberg*
Boländer	*Deidesheimerweg*
Elster	*Fleckinger*
Forster Strasse or *Strasse*	*Freundstück*
Geibel	*Gerling*
Hahnenböhl	*Hellholz*
Knobloch	*Langenböhl*
Langenmorgen	*Langkammert*
Linsenstück	*Mariengarten*
Mäuerle	*Mühlweg*
Musenhang	*Myrrhe*
Neuberg	*Neunmorgen*
Pechstein	*Pfeifer*
Satz	*Schnepfenflug*
Sechsmorgen	*Sperb*
Spitzmorgen	*Stift*
Süsskopf	*Trift*
Wachenheimer	*Walshöhle*
Weissling	

* Some of the Forst vineyards extend into Deidesheim, and such portions are marketed as Deidesheimers.

◄§ *WACHENHEIM AND BAD DÜRKHEIM*

The slope ends above Wachenheim, which boasts some two hundred acres producing great wines noted for their fullness and *finesse*. Dr. Bürklin-Wolf, who owns portions of many of the best vineyards and who lives in the town, is also president of the German Association of Estate-Bottlers and one of the leaders of the German wine trade. Some of the other towns above Wachenheim have slopes planted in Riesling, and good wines come from Bad Dürkheim, which is the business center for wines of the Pfalz as well as a spa, and from the vineyards of Ungstein and Kallstadt.

W A C H E N H E I M *

Wachenheimer	*Wachenheimer*
Gerümpel	*Bächel*
Goldbächel	*Luginsland*
Altenburg	*Böhlig*
Dreispitz	*Gerichtspfad*
Hägel	*Hellholz*
Höhe	*Kaspari*
Katzenloch	*Langenbächel*
Neuberg	*Neustück*
Odinstal	*Rechbächel*
Rennacker	*Riedbrunnen*
Schenkenböhl	*Schlossberg*
Süsskopf	*Wolfdarm*

* Some Wachenheim vineyards extend into Forst, and those portions go to market as Forsters.

BAD DÜRKHEIM

Dürkheimer
  Michelsberg

  Abtsfrohnhof
  Forst
  Hochmess
  Schenkenböhl

Dürkheimer
  Spielberg

  Feuerberg
  Hochbenn
  Rittergarten
  Vigilienberg

Rheinhessen

The Hessian vineyards begin near Worms and extend all the way to Mainz, but less than three thousand of the more than thirty thousand acres of vines in Hesse produce top wines, most of the rest of it going to market as *Liebfraumilch*.

Liebfraumilch, the Milk of the Blessed Virgin, once named only the wines from the twenty-five acres of the *Liebfrauenstift*, a vineyard that surrounds the Church of Our Lady in Worms. The original vineyard still produces pleasant wines, its three owners marketing them as *Liebfrauenstiftwein*. Today, Liebfraumilch is only a regional name, the wines varying widely with each producer.

The Hessian wines are soft and full of fruit. The leading producers are the German state, whose headquarters is in Mainz, with a branch called *Staatsweingut* in each of the principal towns. There are cooperatives in each of the towns, and a wine school that calls itself the *Landes-Lehr-und-Versuchanstalt*, with holdings in the town of Oppenheim and elsewhere. The wines are shipped in slim brown bottles like those of the Rheingau and Nahe. Those of the Pfalz and the Moselle are in green bottles. None of the bottles seem big enough for the long names that have to go on the labels.

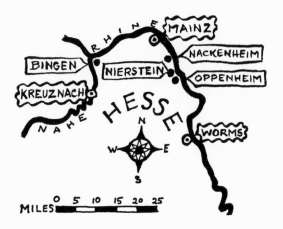

⥽ OPPENHEIM AND DIENHEIM

The town of Oppenheim sits above its vineyards, facing across the farmland of the plain to the Rhine and looking south to its vineyard slope, which runs into that of Dienheim. Between them, the two towns have perhaps three hundred acres planted in Rieslings, the best of which are in Oppenheim. In addition to the town itself, the wine school and the State Domain, other producers include Carl Koch Erben and Weingut Reinhold Senfter. The wines are noted for being soft and full, with great fruitiness in fine years.

OPPENHEIM AND DIENHEIM

Oppenheimer
  Kreuz
  Sackträger

Oppenheimer
  Herrenberg
  Goldberg

  Krötenbrunnen
  Steig

  Riesekahr
  Zuckerberg

* * *

Dienheimer
  Goldberg

Dienheimer
  Krötenbrunnen

  Ebenbreit
  Gumben
  Tafelstein

  Gulden Morgen
  Rosswiese

ᴥᢢ NIERSTEIN

Nierstein is the most famous township of the Rheinhessen, producing wines of finesse and breed. All its finest vineyards are on two terraced slopes, the *Rheinfront*, which faces the river, and the Tal, which turns to the south. These are among the peak wines, Spitzenweine, and some of the greatest rank with the greatest wines of Germany. The town vineyards produce more wine than any other in the Rheinhessen, well over 350,000 gallons a year, mostly from the Sylvaner grape, which here makes very good wines. Perhaps thirty thousand cases a year are Riesling, and bear a vineyard name. Major producers are the State Domain, the Wine School, Freiherr Heyl zu Herrnsheim, Franz Karl Schmitt, Reinhold Senfter, and the cooperative, plus several small producers.

NIERSTEIN

Niersteiner
　Rehbach
　Auflangen
　Orbel

　Brudersberg
　Fockenberg
　Galgenberg
　Heiligenbaum
　Kehr
　Ölberg
　Pettental
　Schnappenberg
　Streng

Niersteiner
　Glöck
　Hipping
　Flächenhahl

　Floss
　Fuchsloch
　Gutes Domtal
　Hölle
　Kranzberg
　Paterberg
　Rohr
　Spiegelberg
　Tal
　Weissenberg

✑ NACKENHEIM

Nackenheim produces the finest of Hessian wines, most of it coming from not much more than eighty terraced acres of the Rothenberg, or red hill. The soil is the color of brick, and the wines are outstanding for their finesse, full bouquet, and breed. There are more than one hundred and fifty acres planted in Sylvaner; these wines are rated as being the best that are produced from this grape, a sort of Beaujolais of white wines. The State Domain, Gunderloch-Lang, and Gunderloch-Usinger are the leading producers. The State Domain also has holdings in Bodenheim, the only other town of the Rheinhessen that produces wines of distinction; another important Bodenheim producer is the estate of Colonel Liebrecht.

N A C K E N H E I M

Nackenheimer
   Engelsberg
   Langer Tag
   Rheinhahl
   Stiel

Nackenheimer
   Fenchelberg
   Platte
   Rothenberg

BINGEN

The town that produces most of Germany's corkscrews stretches along the Rhine, looking across to the Rheingau, and backed by a great red hill called the Scharlachberg. The fine vineyards are on the far side of the hill, facing away from Bingen and to the south.

Those facing the Rhine produce wines that are not so distinguished, and are supposed to be noted for a smoky taste that comes from the engines of the trains that run along the river. The corkscrews made in Bingen are called pencils, because there's a story about the Bishop of Mainz, who called a meeting of his Bingen clergy. In the course of the discussion, he asked for a pencil, but when the priests fished in their cassocks for stubs, they came out with corkscrews instead.

Practically suburbs of the town are Büdesheim and Kempten, the names of both of which are preceded on the labels by that of Bingen, and which share the Scarlet Hill. The wines are big and full. The top producers are the State Domain, Villa Sachsen, and P. Ohler; the most important vineyards include:

BINGEN

Binger
   Eisel or Eiselberg
   Ohligberg
   Rosengarten
   Schwärtzerchen

Binger
   Mainzerweg
   Rochusberg
   Schlossberg

Binger-Büdesheimer
   Scharlachberg
   Häusling
   Schnakenberg
   Steinkautsweg

Binger-Kempter
   Hinterhäuser
   Kirchberg
   Pfarrgarten
   Schnack

Binger-Kempter
   Kapellenberg
   Langenberg
   Rheinberg
   Wolfskaut

❦

Nahe

The wines of Nahe were popular in the United States just before the First World War, but they are almost unknown today, and few exporters have taken the risk of introducing them again. The wines are like the best of the Rheinhessen.

The first important town, just up the Nahe from Bingen, is Bad Kreuznach, which is the home of most of the top producers, as well as of the Seitz-Werke, manufacturer of the Seitz filters that have been instrumental in improving winemaking all over the world. The firm has also developed filters that can remove microscopic particles, but they are not desirable for wine, the feeling being that too much filtering will remove the character of the wine along with the impurities. The best wines come from Kreuznach, Münster, Niederhaus, Norheim, Roxheim, and Schloss Böckelheim, this last being an area that was established just before the First World War by the State Domain, the leading producer and developer of the Nahe vineyards. The wines may eventually reappear on the American market and should be worth watching for. Another wine district is in the making in the steep and twisting valley of the Nahe.

BAD KREUZNACH

Kreuznacher	*Kreuznacher*
Hinkelstein	*Kahlenberg*
Kröttenpfuhl	*Narrenkappe*

BAD MÜNSTER

Münsterer Pittersberg   Münsterer Dautenpflänzer

NIEDERHAUS

Niederhauser   Niederhauser
  Hermannshöhle   Pfingstweide
  Hermannsberg   Steyer

NORHEIM

Norheimer   Norheimer
  Kafels   Götzenfels
  Kirschheck   Hinterfels

R O X H E I M

Roxheimer Huttenberg   Roxheimer Hollenpfad

S C H L O S S
B Ö C K E L H E I M

Böckelheimer   Böckelheimer
Kupfergrube   Königsfels
Kupferberg   Königsberg

⊷§ ৡ⊷

Rheingau

The greatest wines of Germany come from a range of hills that looks down on the Rhine as it bends westward around Mainz, sweeping slightly southward for more than a dozen miles, then veering north again after passing the racewater at Rüdesheim. The vineyards produce the most graceful wines on earth.

Along the northern bank there are a string of towns that lend their names to the wines and, among the hillside vines, a few villages with names that have a hard and medieval sound. Those of the great vineyards sound like a chant: Sonnenberg, Gehrn, Baikern, Gräfenberg, Marcobrunnen, Steinberg, Schönhell, Schloss Vollrads, Schloss Johannisberg, Rothenberg, Mäuerchen, Rüdesheimer Berg. The Rheingau is Weingau, say the Germans, wine like Lieder, rich and full and haunting, the essence of the Rhine, the vintage, and the vine.

After the vintage, the vineyard owner gives a feast for the harvesters and before the dancing begins, the Kallermeister presents to the host the last grape plucked from the vineyard, a token of the wines to come. The more raisinous the grape, the happier the banqueters, but nobody can really tell about the wines until the long fermentation is complete. Just before the auctions, there is a final tasting, to choose the wines to be offered.

The cellars are huge and deep, and many of the old casks are still used, some of them enormous, standing as high as a man, their faces carved with garlands, grapes, and vineyard scenes by men who drank the wines over a hundred years ago. Some of the wines may stay in barrel five or six years, but prompt bottling is the rule, usually within eighteen months. Here and there in the cellar are small casks for the *Auslesen,* and one goes from one to another, tasting. Occasionally, wine in one of the casks will go *bloop-bloop,* then subside into silence, suddenly to *bloop* again unexpectedly. After the first violent fermentation has subsided and the wine is put in casks, a cellar is full of wonderful sounds. Each cask has its own

special noise and rhythm, some going *bup-bup-bup* for minutes, then changing to *bop-bop*, *bop-bop*, only to vary again a few moments later. On days when the wine is working vigorously, the cellar is a setting for a kind of audible pyrotechnics. This may be the reason people usually come out of a cellar smiling and blinking at the sudden brightness, like people leaving a matinee.

When fermentation is ended, the wines develop quickly, those from the eastern end of the Rheingau—from Hochheim, Eltville, and Rauenthal—becoming full and soft and fruity; those from Erbach, Hattenheim, Vollrads, and Johannisberg developing the finesse and elegance which is their mark; and those from the western end—from Geisenheim and Rüdesheim—becoming full and rich and ripe.

Ripeness is a term that has particular meaning for the Rheingau. It is fruitiness with a difference—a sappy, rich taste that does not come entirely from sweetness—an extension and concentration of the floweriness inherent in all wines made from the Riesling, developed into a bouquet one can taste. There's a juicy, succulent quality in it. The finish, or aftertaste, is more than an echo of the wine; it is almost a rebound, a second sustained taste after one has swallowed. Liquid sunshine, the wines have been called, and bottled gold.

The natural wines and the Spätlesen, and even some of the Auslesen, are usually ready to drink as soon as they are bottled, within two years; most of them begin to fall off after five. Only a few may be drinkable after a decade. Even the Beerenauslesen have usually reached their prime five years after the vintage, no matter how long they may continue to live.

As in other German districts, the great proprietors—called *Weinbaubesitzeren*—usually have holdings in various townships. The exceptions are Fürst von Metternich, who owns all of Schloss Johannisberg, and Graf Matuschka-Greiffenclau, who owns all of Schloss Vollrads. The largest owner of vineyards is the State Domain, the *Staatsweingüter*, which has all sixty acres of the great Steinberg in Hattenheim and maintains five separate establishments to handle the wine from its three hundred acres of outstanding vineyards. Many of the *winzeren*, growers who own only a few parcels, sell their wines through cooperatives they have formed. Here is a list of the largest landholders with vineyards in several townships:

Verwaltung der Staatsweingüter	300 *acres*
Graf von Schönborn-Wiesentheid	82 *acres*
Administration Schloss Reinhartshausen	75 *acres*
Gräfl. Eltz	65 *acres*
Freiherrl. Langwerth von Simmern	58 *acres*
Jul. Wegeler Erben	50 *acres*
Krayer Erben	32 *acres*
Dr. R. Weil	32 *acres*
Freiherrn von Ritter zu Groenesteyn	31 *acres*
Dr. Jul. Mühlens-Berna	11 *acres*
	736

There are about six thousand acres of vineyards in the Rheingau, some two thirds of which are in production; not much more than half produce superior wines.

◄§ *HOCHHEIM*

Hochheim gives its name, or the first syllable, at any rate, to all the wines of the Rheingau, at least so far as the British are concerned. The growers have never objected to this typical English simplification of the unpronounceable, because they send so much hock to Britain. Over a century ago, the canny Hochheimers named one of their secondary vineyards after Queen Victoria on the occasion of her visit there. This may have helped the sale of the wine, but most British still prefer their hocks from the vineyards to the west.

Hochheim isn't on the Rhine at all. It's back up the Main, nearly a dozen miles east of the Rheingau. Its vineyards aren't even on a slope, its five hundred acres being situated on slightly rolling land in the midst of orchards and truck gardens. Most of the wines are ordinary, with a slight earth taste, called *Bodenton*. The Deanery and the Churchpiece, or Domdechaney and Kirchenstück, are considered the two best vineyards, and there are several others. The State Domain, the city of Frankfurt, Graf von Schönborn, Domdechant Werner, and Aschrott all have important holdings there. There are two cooperatives and a number of growers with small holdings.

In hot years, the wines have a tendency to be heavy, losing their finesse. Contrarily, in years that are less than great, the best vineyards produce fruity wines of real distinction, with good bouquet.

H O C H H E I M

Hochheimer	*Hochheimer*
Domdechaney	*Kirchenstück*
Daubhaus	*Hofmeister*
Hölle	*Neuberg*
Rauchloch	*Sommerheil*
Stein	*Stielweg*
Wiener	

◆§ *ELTVILLE*

Eltville is the biggest wine town on the Rhine because so many firms have headquarters there, among them the State Domain. It is also the center of the German sparkling-wine trade, the various firms buying up wines not good enough to bear a vineyard label, blending and carbonating them, and calling them *sekt*. Some firms even go to the trouble of fermenting in bottle, but the result is not worth the extra time, trouble, or cost.

Eltville has more vineyards than any other town of the Rheingau, some eighteen hundred acres, the best on a single great hill over four hundred acres in extent. Yet the wines are almost unknown outside Germany, and are consequently low in price. They are drier than most Rheingaus, therefore more pleasing to many, with greater distinction than those from Hochheim, and with more bouquet. They are excellent buys.

The State Domain, Schloss Eltz, Langwerth von Simmern, Jakob Fischer Erben, the Hesse-Nassau wine school, the Stadtpfarrgut, R. C. Belz, Franz Boltendahl, and Dr. R. Weil are the principal owners listed by the national association of producers, and there are several good *winzeren*.

E L T V I L L E

Eltviller
   Sonnenberg
   Freienborn
   Klümbchen
   Rheinberg
   Taubenberg

Eltviller
   Langenstück
   Kalbsflicht
   Mönchhanach
   Sandgrub

◄§ RAUENTHAL

The Rauenthalers command the highest prices at the wine auctions, yet they are almost unknown outside Germany. The two finest vineyards are Gehrn and Baiken, the latter being the most precious vineyard soil in Germany. The wines are distinguished by their fruitiness, perfect balance, and that indescribable quality of ripeness, a tang or spiciness that is called *würzig* in German.

There are fewer than three hundred acres of great Rauenthal vineyards, the principal owners being the State Domain, Langwerth von Simmern, Graf Eltz, and a cooperative. Several growers own small parcels. The two nearby towns of Martinsthall and Walluf produce some fine wines in good years, little known and low in price.

RAUENTHAL

Rauenthaler	*Rauenthaler*
Baiken	*Gehrn*
Herberg	*Pfaffenberg*
Rothenberg	*Wieshell*
Wülfen	

◄§ ERBACH AND KIEDRICH

Erbach is just downstream from Eltville, and its greatest vineyard is the Marcobrunnen, the fountain mark, sometimes spelled with a *k*. The name comes from a fountain that marks the boundary between Erbach and Hattenheim. The wine has the great fruitiness of all the distinguished Rheingaus, along with perfect balance and a full bouquet, but it stands out because of its breed, an ability to mature perfectly without any coarseness or overdevelopment. They generally go to market without the town name on the bottle, the vineyard name only being used to identify the famous wine.

The principal owners of Marcobrunn, in addition to the State Domain, are Schloss Reinhartshausen, Langwerth von Simmern, Graf von Schönborn-Wiesentheid, Max Ritter und Edler von Oetinger, and Kolhaas.

The other wines of Erbach are harder, taking longer to mature. They have less fruitiness than the Marcobrunners.

Wines very like those of Erbach, of great character and breed in good years, come from the vineyards of Kiedrich, up in the hills. The two best vineyards are Gräfenberg and Wasserrose, and the principal owners are Graf Eltz, Dr. Weil, Freiherrn von Ritter zu Groensteyn, and, of course, the Staatsweingut. There are several good small producers. Both towns have about three hundred acres in vines.

E R B A C H

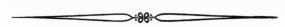

Marcobrunnen (*Erbacher Markobrunn*)

Erbacher	Erbacher
Siegelsberg	Steinmorgen
Bachhell	Brühl
Herrnberg	Hohenrain
Kahlig	Rheinhell
Langenwingert	

K I E D R I C H

Kiedricher	Kiedricher
Gräfenberg	Wasserrose
Sandgrub	Turmberg

✑ *HATTENHEIM*

Wines of great finesse come from Hattenheim, which looks like the setting for a German folk opera, or a musical revolving around a crown prince and a village maid who is really a queen in disguise. There are flowers in the window boxes, cobbles in the streets, girls leaning out of dormers, and a wide green pasture before the town, sloping down to the Rhine.

Two of the best vineyards—Wisselbrunner and Nussbrunnen— are extensions of the Marcobrunnen. The wines are more delicate and more quickly ready to drink.

Up behind the town is Kloster Eberbach, a monastery built by the Cistercians in the twelfth century, and here many of the wine auctions are held each spring and fall. Much of the wine of the State Domain is stored here in the vaulted cellars. The Cistercians also built a hillside vineyard, which they walled in, as they did at Clos de Vougeot. The vineyard is the Steinberg, one of the greatest in the Rheingau, and produces wines as lordly as the name. They have great power, tremendous body, and big bouquet. They are supreme in great years, needing much sun. In poor years, they are

H A T T E N H E I M

Steinberger

Hattenheimer	Hattenheimer
Wisselbrunner	Nussbrunnen
Mannberg	Engelmannsberg
Bergweg	Hassel
Heiligenberg	Kilb
Pfaffenberg	Schützenhaus
Stabel	Tillmetz

often hard. The entire vineyard of some sixty acres is the property of the State Domain. The town name is not used on its wine label.

The most important owners of the some four hundred acres in Hattenheim are Graf von Schönborn-Wiesentheid, Langwerth von Simmern, Schloss Reinhartshausen, the Pfarrgut, a foundation called Georg Müller-Stiftung, the town itself, and the State Domain.

HALLGARTEN AND ÖSTRICH

Just west of Kloster Eberbach are the vineyards and village of Hallgarten. Like their Steinberg neighbor, the Hallgarteners excel in great years, being very full in body and somewhat dry. In poor years, they are out of balance and too light in alcohol. Down toward the river is the town of Östrich, which has more than 700 acres of vineyards but few famous sites. The wines are said to be like those of Hallgarten, but softer. Prince Löwenstein, Karl Franz Engelmann, and three wine cooperatives are the principal producers from the more than 350 acres of Hallgarten vineyards.

HALLGARTEN

Hallgartener	*Hallgartener*
Schönhell	*Mehrhölzchen*
Deutelsberg	*Hendelberg*

ÖSTRICH

Östricher	*Östricher*
Lenchen	*Hölle*
Doosberg	*Eiserberg*
Eiserweg	*Mühlberg*
St. Nikolaus	

◄§ WINKEL

Winkel is a town down on the river, but its great vineyards are up in the hills, near Schloss Vollrads, its greatest vineyard. Vollrads is eighty acres, the largest single vineyard owned by an individual in the Rheingau—the family of Matuschka-Grieffenclau.

Graf Matuschka, the president of the German Wine Producers' Association, is active in the wine trade and a leader, by example, of the best traditions in German winemaking. A special identifying system has been developed for his full, ripe wines. Natural wines are sold as Schloss Vollrads and bear a green capsule over the mouth of the bottle. Specially selected wines carry the word *Schlossabzug* on the label and have a red capsule. No wines are bottled as Spätlese, but those that are richer are marked *Kabinett* on the label and bear a green capsule with a gold stripe. Auslese wines have a pink capsule, and whenever Beerenauslese or Trockenbeerenauslese is made, these have white capsules. Price, of course, gives an equally good idea of quality, but the capsules make for easy identification, if one knows the code.

Schloss Vollrads has great distinction and is one of the half-dozen greatest vineyards of Germany. Its neighboring vineyards are not far behind. Other producers, in addition to Graf Matuschka, are Kommerzienrat Krayer Erben, Von Brentano, Geromont and Jakob Hamm, as well as several small producers.

W I N K E L

Schloss Vollrads

Winkeler	*Winkeler*
Jesuitengarten	*Hasensprung*
Ansbach	*Dachsberg*
Honigberg	*Klaus*
Kreutzgarten	*Oberberg*

↝§ JOHANNISBERG

The most famous wine of Germany is Schloss Johannisberg. The castle itself is on a plateau above the vineyard, and from its terrace one can look down over the rows of vines, like so many neat rows of hedges, cut here and there by rills that carry water to the vines and let excess water drain off. Beyond is the Rhine, barges and excursion steamers working upstream or racing down toward the Binger Loch, the hole of Bingen—a great swirl of water that once endangered every passing craft.

This panorama you see from the terrace is pictured on the labels, but reversed, as if one were standing on the far side of the river, looking across to the vineyard and the schloss. It's a view that doesn't exist in actuality—artistic license working so that the Rhine, the vine, and the schloss make a pleasing composition on a label four inches high. It is similar, though, to the view that Charlemagne might have had, for the too-often-told legend is that he looked across the Rhine one spring, and ordered that a vineyard be planted where the slope was bare. Some say it was Schloss Johannisberg, others claim that it was the Berg of Rüdesheim. In any event, many of the vineyards go back that far, and a Benedictine monastery was built on the present site during the eleventh century.

The wine is so famous that the Riesling grape is known as the Johannisberger in Switzerland and in the United States. The vineyard became the property of William of Orange when the crown seized all church estates at the turn of the eighteenth century, and it became the property of Prince Metternich as a reward for his brilliant diplomacy at the Congress of Vienna in 1814. There was a string attached; the Austrian emperor demanded a tenth of the annual production. The present prince still pays the tithe, but in money, not in wine, to the Hapsburg heirs.

Fürst Metternich lives at the schloss, but there is a century-old tradition that the vineyard be managed by an expert winemaker, the present one being Christian Labonte. His signature appears on the label, and it is he who is responsible for the introduction of some revolutionary techniques of winemaking: the use of glass-lined tanks for storing wine, new filtering equipment developed by

Seitz across the river, and a new grape-pressing machine that consists of a slitted stainless-steel cylinder through which the juice oozes when an inner plastic sleeve is blown up. Traditionalists are perhaps most shocked by the sprinkling system for the vineyards that is used during dry spells. But the wine is still great, an aristocrat of the Rheingau, a light and poised balance of fruitiness, body, and bouquet, a classic example of a wine with breed.

Colored capsules differentiate the various wines. A red capsule marks the Naturwein, while a green one is used to identify the wine from late-picked grapes, which may or may not be marked Spätlese; Auslesen are always identified with a pink capsule. The labels display the Metternich crest; the picture label appears on Kabinett wines and uses orange capsules for natural wine, white for wines made from late-picked grapes, pale blue for Auslesen, and gold for Beerenauslesen and Trockenbeerenauslesen.

There are some two hundred acres in the township, in addition to the sixty-five of Schloss Johannisberg; the leading producers are Krayer Erben, G. H. von Mumm, Geromont, and Graf von Schönborn-Wiesentheid. These wines, too, are distinguished by great finesse and breed.

J O H A N N I S B E R G

Schloss Johannisberger

Johannisberger Klaus	Johannisberger Erntebringer
Klauser Berg Klauser Garten	Klauser Steinacker

✤§ *GEISENHEIM*

This pleasant town produces fine wines in good years and magnificent wines in great vintages, but its vineyards, on a slope consisting of nearly 500 acres, are not very well known. These are intermediate wines, dimmed by the brilliance of Schloss Johannisberg on one side and the Rüdesheimer Berg on the other, but they offer some of the finest values of any of the Rheingaus, marked by fine balance and great finesse.

One of the finest wine schools in existence is in Geisenheim, and connected with it is a research institute. The school owns extensive vineyards in the town, and other producers are Krayer Erben, Josef Bergeff Erben, Weingut Rebhof, Freiherr von Zwierlein Erben, Zobus Erben, and Graf von Schönborn-Wiesentheid.

G E I S E N H E I M

Geisenheimer	*Geisenheimer*
Rothenberg	*Mäuerchen*
Altbaum	*Hohenrech*
Katzenloch	*Kilsberg*
Kläuserweg	*Lickerstein*
Morschberg	*Rosengarten*
Schlossgarten	

✥ *RÜDESHEIM*

The biggest, fullest, ripest wines of the Rheingau come from Rüdesheim, because no great vineyard slope receives so much sun as does the Berg. The sun can be a disadvantage in great years, throwing these wines out of balance, but they are invariably outstanding in good and fair vintages. The wines are rich and golden, often heavier in alcohol than wines from other vineyards, but in dry years the wine lacks fruit. The experiments in sprinkling at Schloss Johannisberg are watched by the Rüdesheim producers, but the steep vineyard, terraced every few feet, would make any watering system expensive.

Rüdesheim is the tourist town of the Rheingau, crowded toward the river by the looming Berg. A ferry runs across to Bingen and a cable railway carries visitors to the top of the Niederwald, high above the surrounding countryside. From here you can see the entire Rheingau, and the famous ruined castles on the crests of the many hills, some constructed during Victoria's day to add a romantic touch to the countryside. Far below is the Berg, and the other vineyards of Rüdesheim, more than 650 acres of them, several of which outdo those of the famous Berg when the vintages are extraordinary.

Principal owners, although no holdings are very large, include Freiherrn von Ritter zu Groensteyn, Graf von Schönborn-Wiesentheid, Jul. Wegeler Erben, Fritz Rücker Erben, and Julius Espenschied, and of course, the Staatsweingut Rüdesheim, the State Domain. Here, particularly, are many producers with small holdings who bottle their own wines.

R Ü D E S H E I M

Rüdesheimer Berg
   Rottland
   Burgweg
   Hellpfad
   Lay
   Mühlstein
   Paares
   Roseneck
   Schlossberg
   Zollhaus

Rüdesheimer Berg
   Bronnen
   Bischofsberg
   Hinterhaus
   Klosterkiesel

~§ ฿~

Mosel

Bacchus loves the hillsides, says Vergil, but the poet had no idea
how much because he never saw the Mosel. Driving upstream from
the cathedral town of Koblenz, vineyards are on each side of the
meandering river, and then the hills begin to rise, the road twists
with the river, and suddenly the clifflike vineyards seem to become
giant steps, with high retaining walls every few feet and stairways
or ladders connecting some of the plots.

All the great wines come from the Mittel-Mosel, which begins
with the great loop in the river near Traben-Trarbach—half on one
side, half on the other—and extends past Piesport. If the Mosel
could be straightened out, there would be perhaps twenty miles of
vineyards all the way to Trier, and more on the Saar and Ruwer,
which join the Mosel near the city. Each vine is tied to its own
stake, flat slates carefully placed around its roots to hold the sun
heat and reflect its rays on the vines. It's almost as if wines are
made here just to show it can be done.

You couldn't ask for lovelier country in which to work, and perhaps vineyards were planted here just because it is so beautiful.
Nothing else will grow on the *bergen,* and there is little flat land
along the river to develop into farm, orchard, or pasture. The people
of the Mosel manage, however, because in spring the slopes not
planted in vines are white with apple blossoms. Few people have
much money in the Mosel, but fewer still are poor.

Der Mosel is the German name for the region that produces the
most astonishing range of wines, from light and dry to full and
rich. But the wines were called Mosella by the Romans, and most
of the rest of the world persists in calling these German wines by
the French *Moselle.*

In some years, *Eiswein* is produced. The grapes freeze on the
vine, and when these are pressed lightly only the most syrupy juice
is released, to produce exceptionally light, sweet wines. A few were
made by Johann Joseph Prüm in Wehlen in 1949, and in 1950

Schloss Johannisberg made a single cask. These rarely come on the market.

In poor years, the lesser vineyards of the Mosel produce *Drei-männerwein*, and this is all too often obtainable. A three-man wine is one that is so small and acid that it takes two men to hold the third while he steels himself to take a sip. None of these wines is bottled, but sold to the blenders to become *Tischwein*, table wine, pitchers of which are drunk in every small café or restaurant as a substitute for beer.

Trier is the big city of the Mosel; it was the birthplace of Karl Marx, who left as soon as he could, perhaps because nobody there was much interested in his ideas. A bishop who resided there in the old days had interests closer to home, and one of them was wine-drinking. "Whosoever, after drinking his ten or twelve bottles, retains his senses sufficiently to support his tottering neighbor . . . let him take his share quietly and be thankful for his talent. . . . It is but seldom that our kind Creator extends to anyone the grace to be able to drink safely sixteen bottles, of which privilege he hath held me, the meanest of his servants, worthy." Bottles were smaller in the sixteenth century.

The wines of the Mosel are the lightest of the world's great wines, scarcely more than 10 or 11 degrees in alcohol, and often less. The wines are best drunk young, before they are five years old, and the drier ones are best when around two. They are as spectacular as the countryside—light, fresh, flowery, and dry, with great finesse, developing a delicate fruitiness in great years and in the wines touched with the *edelfäule*. They are perfect wines to drink with smoked salmon, ham, or turkey, with spicy foods, with fish and sea food and all kinds of delicatessen. The Auslesen taste fine with foods that have a sweet savor and with dishes that have some sweetness, but perhaps they taste best of all by themselves well chilled on a hot summer afternoon.

There are over twenty thousand acres of vineyard along the Mosel and its tributaries, but of the ten million gallons normally produced, less than half is of good quality or better. Vineyard names are extremely important in the Mosel, because the Riesling cannot ripen to full maturity unless the vineyards face full south.

The list of the wine producers' association contains forty-two landowners, but there are hundreds more. The *Staatsweingut* has

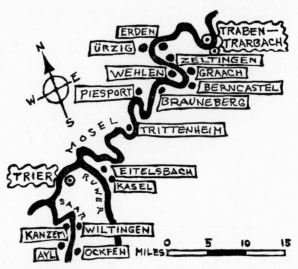

large holdings in the Saar, but others own the best vineyards of the Mittel-Mosel, the most extensive holdings belonging to various branches of the Prüm family—Joh. Jos. Prüm, S. A. Prüm Erben, Peter Prüm, and the heirs of Bergweiler-Prüm.

Some of the most important landholders are institutions. The *Vereinigte Hospitien* is a foundation that maintains a home and hospital, as well as seventy-five acres of vineyard. The *Bischöfliches Priesterseminar* is a Catholic school with seventy acres, while a refectory, the *Bischöfliches Konvikt*, has fifty acres. The cathedral in Trier, *Hohe Domkirche*, has thirty-three acres, as do Bernkastel's church, the *Pfarrkirche St. Michael*, a Bernkastel hospital called the *St. Nikolaus Hospital*, and a school called the *Friedrich Wilhelm Gymnasium*.

Vintages follow the Rhineland pattern but, as in the Rheingau, frosts can upset all the generalities. The 1955 and 1953 vintages were outstanding, the first being light and the second being full and well-balanced, with great finesse. The vintages of 1952 and 1950 both produced good wines, and although the '49s were magnificent, all these are gone now except for the Auslesen. The 1956 and '57 vintages are to be forgotten, the vines having been frozen out in the spring, but the '58s are excellent wines, although there aren't many of them because so many vines were destroyed the preceding year. Those of 1959 are the wines of the century. Many of the '60s are good.

⤜§ ERDEN, ÜRZIG, AND THEIR NEIGHBORS

The first outstanding wines of the Mittel-Mosel come from the vineyards of Erden, which are on the steepest slopes of all. The wines are full and fruity and well balanced, with great depth. Principal owners in the nearly two hundred acres of vineyard are the Bischöfliches Priesterseminar, various members of the Berres family, and Robert Eymael. Several others bottle their own wines but are not members of the producers' association, which merely means that they prefer to sell their wines independently.

Ürzig vineyards adjoin those of Erden, but are on a separate declivity, the soil of which is reddish in color. This soil contains iron and imparts a spicy taste to the wine in good years that makes it easy to identify. The wine is often *spritzig*, which brings out its spiciness, and is lighter than its neighbors. Because the hundred

ERDEN AND ÜRZIG

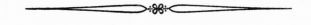

Erdener	*Erdener*
Busslay	*Filiusberg*
Herrenberg	*Herzlay*
Himmelreich	*Hödlay*
Kammer	*Kaufmannsberg*
Prälat	*Treppchen*

* * *

Ürziger	*Ürziger*
Hofberg	*Kranklay*
Würzgarten	*Schwarzlay*

acres of vineyards are so hard to tend, the wines are expensive.
Many of the families who own vineyards in Erden also own sections
here.

Back down the Mosel are some vineyards that produce pleasant,
light, flowery wines, particularly those of Traben-Trarbach and
Enkirch, but much better known are those of Crov and Zell. Most
of the wines of Crov go to market as *Nacktarsch*, which means
"bare bum" in German, and on the label there is a drawing of a
boy being spanked. A black cat on the label identifies *Zeller
Schwarze Katz*, which comes from the vineyards around Zell, in
the Unter-Mosel. Both of these light wines are known more because of their labels than by what's in the bottles.

~§ ZELTINGEN

There are nearly five hundred acres of vineyard on the great hillside that looms above Zeltingen, making it the largest producer of
the Mittel-Mosel. Slate outcroppings are broken up, and the pieces
are set around the vines, giving such wines a special taste. Vineyards that are particularly slaty often add the suffix-*lay* (slate) to
the name of the vineyard. Because the wine is so well known, vineyard names are especially important. Those bearing only the name
of the town are often excellent, although apt to be overpriced. The
great wines are varied, Sonnenuhr being fruity and rounded, Schlossberg big and full, Himmelreich full and elegant, Steinmauer intense, Stephenslay light, and Kirchenpfad noted for balance.
Generally, the wines are soft and full. J. J. Prüm, R. J. Berres,
Ehses-Berres, Franz Merrem, and the old family of Freiherr von
Schorlemer are top producers.

ZELTINGER

Zeltinger	Zeltinger
Himmelreich	Rotlay
Kirchenpfads	Steinmauer
Schlossberg	Stephenslay
Sonnenuhr	

WEHLEN

The best wines of Wehlen command the highest prices of any of the Mosels. They are famous for their ripeness, balance, and great breed. Their fame and excellence is due to the vigorous efforts of the Prüms, who have large holdings in the two hundred vineyard acres—including spicy Sonnenuhr, the greatest of all.

W E H L E N

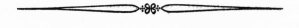

Wehlener	*Wehlener*
Sonnenuhr	Lay
Nonnenberg	Rosenberg
Klosterlay	
Wertspitz	Feinter

ᵉᵍ GRAACH

Some of the best-balanced, floweriest, loveliest wines of the Mosel come from Graach, whose nearly 250 acres of vineyard are just upriver from Zeltingen. One of Graach's greatest wines goes to market as Josephshofer, without the town name, the entire vineyard being the property of the Kesselstatt family, whose wines have been famous for decades. Winemakers here are various Prüms, Dr. Weins Erben (who are related to the Prüms), the estate of Dr. Thanisch (an owner of Bernkastler Doktor), the Bergweiler family, as well as the St. Nikolaus Hospital, the Pfarrkirche St. Michael, and the Friedrich Wilhelm Gymnasium.

G R A A C H

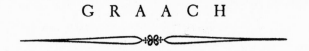

Josephshofer

Graacher	*Graacher*
Himmelreich	*Domprobst*
Abtsberg	*Bistum*
Goldwingert	*Heiligenhaus*
Homberg	*Kirchlay*
Lilienpfad	*Münzlay*
Stablay	

◆§ BERNKASTEL AND KUES

Bernkastel is the tourist center of the Mosel and the possessor of its famous wine, Bernkasteler Doktor. A fourteenth-century archbishop of Trier, lying on a sickbed, is said to have named the wine. No medicine was any help to him; then one day a farmer came to the prelate's quarters with a small cask of wine from his vineyard. After a few glasses, the archbishop sat up and began singing the praises of the doctor of Bernkastel, the wine that did what all the medicines and physicians had failed to do. The estate of Dr. Thanisch is the principal owner of the vineyard, but sections are also held by Deinhard and Lauerberg. The wine continues to be outstanding, but there are other vineyards in the township, and in Graach and Wehlen, that produce wines of equal distinction. Its fame is due as much to the fact that the name sticks in one's head as it is to the excellence of the wine. There are more than four hundred acres of vineyard in the town and its twin village across the river, and a surprising number of them are good.

Mosels can be pleasant medicine, but they are also the wines for sunny days and starry nights. Perhaps they taste best of all on the first Sunday in September in the town square of Bernkastel, when the fountain in the center of the square gushes *Moselwein* to celebrate the new vintage, and the eyes of the village girls sparkle as brightly as the wine. Proprietors include the St. Nikolaus Hospital, the Pfarrkirche St. Michael, Johann Joseph Prüm, and many others.

B E R N K A S T E L

Bernkasteler	Bernkasteler
Altenwald	Badstube Held
Bratenhöfchen	Lay
Doktor (und Graben)	Pfalzgraben
Pfaffenberg	Schlossberg
Rosenberg	Theuernkauf
Schwanen	Kueser Weissenstein

✒ BRAUNEBERG

This town takes its name from the great hill that rises above it, and produces wines that are extremely full and fragrant, similar to the Zeltingers, but with a pleasing *bodenton*, or taste of the soil. Principal owners of the hundred acres of vineyards are the St. Nikolaus Hospital, Ferdinand Haag, and a cooperative. Similar but lesser wines come from nearby Lieser, and these go to market as Lieserer Niederberg or Lieserer Schlossberg.

B R A U N E B E R G

Brauneberger	*Brauneberger*
Bürgerslay	*Falkenberg*
Hasenläufer	*Juffer*
Lay	*Sonnenuhr*

✎§ *PIESPORT AND ITS NEIGHBORS*

The gold drops from Piesport's most famous vineyard are produced on a great natural amphitheater that curves above the town. The famous *Goldtröpfchen* has dimmed the glory of several other fine vineyards among the hundred-plus acres planted in vines, whose wines are usually more reasonable in price because they are not so famous. The wines are fragrant and flowery, typical of the Mittel-Mosel, with much finesse. The Vereinigte Hospitien, the Bischöfliches Konvikt, the Vereinigte Pfarrgut (the holding of the local church), and the Kesselstatt family are among the principal owners.

All the way up the river to Trier are other towns: Wintrich, Dhron, Neumagen, and Trittenheim. Wines are fresh and light, rarely reaching the fullness and distinction of those from the better vineyards, but they are lower in price, and when drunk young are extremely pleasant. There are vineyards in Trier itself, and these, too, are pleasant to drink. The best of them come from the nearby town of Avelsbach, which is considered part of the Trier district. They are very light and dry, exceedingly good to drink if you like the dry, hard wines produced by the Riesling when it does not get much sun. The State Domain and the Cathedral of Trier are the most important producers.

PIESPORT

Piesporter	Piesporter
Falkenberg	Goldtröpfchen
Gräfenberg	Güntherslay
Lay	Pichter
Schubertslay	Taubengarten
Treppchen	Bildchen

❦

The Saar

The Ruwer enters the Mosel just below Trier, the Saar enters it upstream from the cathedral town. Along both rivers are a host of vineyards, producing some of the lightest, driest wines made of the Riesling grape. Only in great years, when the sun beats long and hot on the vineyards, do the wines reach balanced maturity. Spring comes late and winter comes soon in the two valleys. In the time between, hard and steely wines are usually produced.

The best-known wine town in the Saar is Wiltingen and its greatest vineyard is the Scharzhofberg, owned by the Müller family. The wines go to market under the name of the vineyard, not that of the town. Along the river are Kanzem, Wawern, Schoden, Oberemmel, Niedermennig, Ayl, Ockfen, Saarburg, and Serrig, the wines getting progressively lighter. Many of the Mosel owners have vineyards in the townships. Apollinar Joseph Koch, Van Volxem, Le Gallais, Adolf Reinhart, Gebert, Geltz, and Max Keller all have important holdings, and there is a cooperative in Ayl.

WILTINGER

Scharzhofberg	*Kupp*	*Gottesfuss*
Scharzberg	*Rosenberg*	*Klosterberg*

KANZEMER

Sonnenberg	*Altenberg*	*Berg*

OBEREMMELER

Hütte	*Agritiusberg*	*Junkerberg*

NIEDERMENNIGER

Sonnenberg	*Euchariusberg*

AYLER

Kupp	*Herrenberg*	*Neuberg*

OCKFENER
 Bockstein   Geisberg   Herrenberg

SAARBURGER
 Rausch   Antoniusbrunnen   Leyenkaul

SERRIGER
 Schloss Saarfelser Schlossberg
 Schloss Saarfelser Vogelsang

&§&~

The Ruwer

The wines of the Ruwer, the lightest of all the world's fine wines, are called *Sonnenfeuer, Sternengold, Kuhlen Mondlichtstein*—sunfire, stargold, cool moonshine. They are strange wines, almost weird, so light they seem ghosts of Rhine wines from centuries past— wines to be drunk on the moon, or on a ship far at sea, or on a mountaintop. They are also perfectly good in more normal surroundings, too, but they seem more at home when the mood or place is exotic.

All in all, there are some five hundred acres of vineyards, but only a few of the wines are exported. The Carthusian monastery in Eitelsbach has given its name to several vineyards, the wine going to market as Karthäuserhofberger, usually with a tiny label around the bottle neck, as if to offset the length of its name. There are also the Herrenberg vineyard of Maximin-Grünhaus, the Nie schen, Taubenberg, and Hitzlay vineyards of Kasel. Up behind Kasel is the estate of Schloss Marienlay, whose wines are well known.

Like so many German wines, those of the Ruwer seem to be *tours de force*. At one end of the scale are the Trockenbeerenauslesen of the Rheingau, and at the other end are the fantastic light wines of the Ruwer. In between are the hundreds of great wines produced by the Riesling in the Rhineland. Nowhere else is such a tremendous variety of wines produced from a single noble vine.

❧ ❧

Franconia and the Minor Wines of Germany

When the wines fall bright after the first of the year, the time has come for *Fasching*, the German festival before the coming of Lent. Houses are decorated with great sheets of paper to disguise the shapes of the rooms, small holes are cut for doorways, streamers are hung from the ceilings, and scenes of bacchanalia are painted on the paper—nymphs chasing satyrs, satyrs chasing nymphs, and practically anything else that comes into the heads of the artists. *Fasching* begins on Friday and continues without stopping through Sunday night. The revelers wear gay costumes, the briefer the better, and all strictures are supposed to be forgotten. New wine is drunk continuously. Even in these days, *Fasching* can become quite exciting.

With the coming of spring, great bowls of spiced wine are set out, in which *Waldmeister* (the herb woodruff) has been steeped, and the first wild strawberries are floated in the bowl. It is May-wine time and the season for frolic. In July, a punch is made with peaches, the *Pfirsichbowle*. One or two are sliced into a bowl and lightly sugared, then a cup or two of brandy is added, and a bottle or two of Rhenish. This is set aside to draw for an hour or so, preferably in the refrigerator, and just before serving, a bottle of carbonated *Perlwein* (sparkling Mosel) is added. Other fruits, fresh or canned, can be used. A version called *Kalte Ente* (cold duck) is made by pouring two bottles of Rhenish over a sliced lemon that has been sprinkled lightly with sugar. The lemon can be removed after fifteen minutes or so, half a cup of Curaçao is added, and then a bottle of sparkling wine.

And in the fall, after the vintage, the still-fermenting wine is drunk to celebrate the harvest; it is pale and cloudy and potent, and is called *Federweisser*, whitefeather.

Wine is part of German life, but part of celebration and good times, not so much involved with mealtimes as it is in the Mediterranean countries. Perhaps the most popular wine for good times is

Frankenwein, dry and flowery, from the Franconian vineyards along the Main.

This has come to be called *Steinwein* because the best of it comes from the Stein vineyard near Würzburg. It is shipped in the *bocksbeutel,* a round flask of green glass, that is supposed to have derived its name from its similarity in shape to the nether parts of a goat.

The wines are made from the Sylvaner grape and vary in quality from one large vineyard to another, from one producer to another. A cross between the Riesling and the Sylvaner, called Müller-Thurgau, is also planted in Main vineyards. There are other varieties grown here, none of them distinguished. Frankenwein can be good, but rarely is it more than that. The towns producing the best wines are considered to be Escherndorf, Iphofen, Randersacker, Rodelsee, and Würzburg. Large quantities are produced, so the wines should be reasonable in price, well under two dollars a bottle, which would be half or a quarter that of the great wines from the Rhineland.

Even Wiesbaden produces wine, unique because of the hot springs. It is a devilish wine. But the devil never comes to Wiesbaden. Long ago he came, to find out why so few people entered his realm from that wine-loving city. He presented himself at an inn and inquired of the innkeeper, who recognized him at once, innkeepers being what they are. "You look like the devil," said the innkeeper, "and the one thing that will save you is what preserves all of us, the wine of Wiesbaden, the mulled wine that wells from the ground. Now, five glasses a day is enough for any man, or ten, perhaps, or better yet, a score. But you look so devilish bad, you'll need fifty, at least, for seven days running. The wine that makes so many sound should not be refused to the devil himself. But if you do not complete the cure, you must leave and never return, for even the wine of Wiesbaden cannot help you." The devil began to drink, fifty glasses the first day, half a hundred the second. On noon of the third day, he asked for a rest, but the innkeeper held him to his cure. On the morning of the fourth day, the innkeeper handed the devil his due, the first glass of fifty. The devil stared and began to shudder, then with a shriek he ran screaming from the inn. That day, the mulled wine ceased to well from the ground, and ever since the vineyards have had to be tended as they are elsewhere. The devil has never been seen again, at least not in Wiesbaden, or so they say.

A great amount of wine comes from extensive vineyards on the east side of the Rhine, opposite Alsace, and there are wines from the vineyards around Lake Constance, called *Seewein*, and from Württemburg. The largest cask in all the world is the Heidelberg Tun, and there are vineyards around that student city and all through Baden. All of southern Germany is wine country where it is not farmland, orchard, forest, or town. Some of the wines are good, but they taste better on the spot. Most of them have an earth taste, or are too light in body, or not in balance. At their best, they compare with some of the Alsatian wines.

They say that once the very source of the Rhine produced wines. But no more. Where the Rhine rises was once a green alp, owned by a farmer. When he died, a rich neighbor went to the widow and said the alp was his because the farmer had pledged the peak as security for a small loan. A wicked magistrate confirmed the pledge, and as the widow wept, the neighbor rode up the green alp to inspect his new domain. But as he neared its peak, thunder boomed and rain fell, and the thieving neighbor swooned. He woke at dawn, to see the alp covered with ice. Many centuries of sun have failed to melt the ice, but a trickle is released, and this swells to become the Rhine, a symbol and a warning to all men who are tempted to cheat their neighbors.

Down the Rhine, below Rüdesheim, are the vineyards of the Mittel-Rhein, and in the town of Assmannshausen, the best red wines of Germany are produced from Burgundy's Pinot Noir. They are light and pleasant but not worth exporting.

There are hundreds of wines from Germany, made from many varieties of grapes. But the ones that are both good and great are those from the Riesling grape, produced in the Rhineland. The rest, except for the best of the Sylvaners and Traminers of the Rheinhessen, and the Pfalz and Franconia, are for local consumption.

SUMMARY

Estate-bottled wines, those with the name of the vineyard and grower on the label, are generally the best buys.

Wines produced from the Sylvaner and Gewürz-Traminer grape rarely warrant the estate-bottling premium, although the very best of these may carry the name of a vineyard and the grower.

Wines from Franconia, sold as Steinwein or Frankenwein, are rarely worth the estate-bottling premium and should be appreciably cheaper than those from a particular vineyard and grower in the great districts. Such blends of wines as those from the Rheinhessen, generally called Liebfraumilch, and those from the Mosel, generally called Moselblumchen, are usually of ordinary quality and should be low in price.

Wines from famous vineyards command a premium, and because neighboring but less famous vineyards are often almost peers of their great neighbors, their wines are best buys in good and great years. In ordinary years, when lesser vineyards produce mediocre wines, those from the famous vineyards are often exceptional in quality and fairly reasonable in price.

Fine estate-bottlings from the Rheingau and the Mosel command greater fame than their peers in the Rheinhessen and Rheinpfalz, these last two producing generally softer wines that may be somewhat lower in price and are often best buys in good and ordinary years.

In the Rheingau, wines from Rüdesheim are considered excellent buys in cool years and normal years because they receive a great deal of sun, but for the same reason they are considered poor buys in dry years.

Wines from the less-famous towns of the Mosel are good buys in years that are good or great, but poor buys in ordinary years.

Wines from the Saar and Ruwer are exceptional only in excellent years, being generally too dry and hard in years that rank as good or fair.

 *taly*

Vines grow all over Italy, in vineyards and in orchards, trained over terraces, slung between trees, propped on stakes, strung on wires, festooned against walls. Every farmer makes a cask or two for himself, selling the rest to the local winery. It's all very casual, and much of the wine is bad. But over a billion gallons are made every year—and much of it is good.

Here and there, a nobleman will bottle and ship his own wines, or a group of growers will form a cooperative to do the same, or an important winery will select the grapes from particular vineyards for special bottling. These can be excellent. But in most cases, what is exported is *vini tipici*, typical wines that have established their reputation as being true to type and to the district from which they come. On the label they are identified by the name of the grape or the

town, or both, and on the neck of the bottle will be the red government seal that identifies the wine as genuine and up to standard.
Most of these established wines are full and hearty, to go with the
hearty, well-seasoned dishes of Italy.

There are well over a hundred of these standard wines, some
of them not so standard that they don't vary from shipper to shipper
and vat to vat. Many of them are called *classico*, known for centuries, and the best of them are red. But each district produces
white wines, some dry and usually light in body, others sweet and
full, sometimes fortified, sometimes sparkling, and generally a
pleasure to drink. The red and white table wines rarely cost much
over two dollars a bottle, and many cost half that, just the wines
for everyday drinking. Vintages are not particularly important, and
while the dry white wines and many of the reds are ready to drink
within a year or so of vintage, and are often past their prime at six
or seven, some of the reds need four or five years to mature, and
the best may need two or three years longer.

★ WHITE

1 BAROLO
2 INFERNO
3 TEROLDEGO
4 BARDOLINO
★ 5 SOAVE
6 VALPOLICELLA
7 SANGIOVESE
8 CHIANTI
★ 9 VERDICCHIO
★ 10 ORVIETO
★ 11 FRASCATI
★ 12 CAPRI
13 CIRO
14 MARSALA
★ 15 VERNACCIA

◆§ PIEDMONT

The finest wines of Italy—half a dozen of the best—come from the Piedmont in the north. The finest of all comes from the district of Barolo. The wine is fruity and full, and often 14 per cent in alcohol. It resembles a Rhône, often needs eight years or so to round out, and has a big bouquet, lacking in most Italian wines. Barolo is the king of *vini per arrosto*, wines meant to go with roasts. The best Barolo is considered to be that shipped by the Opera Pia, a name which means pious works, works which were performed by the marchesa who was the last of her line, and whose efforts are carried on by a company formed at her death.

The Nebbiolo is the informing vine in Barolo. The grape produces several superior wines, full and big ones called *vini generoso*, the one almost comparable to Barolo coming from Barbaresco, a few miles away. Barbaresco is lighter, usually ready to drink in five years, and softer than its headier neighbor. It develops a brownish tinge with age, and is said to have the taste of almonds. Other Nebbiolo wines of excellence come from Gattinara and Carema. Other lighter wines of the Piedmont go to market under the name of the grape, and are usually better than *vini di pasto*, the ordinary table wines casually listed on the usual Italian menu. All are said to have a bouquet reminiscent of violets.

The Grignolino produces good light red wines in the Piedmont, at their best not far behind the Barolos. Other often good grape names you are apt to find on a label are Barbera, Freisa, Dolcetto, and Bonarda. The Freisa produces particularly fruity wines that are supposed to taste of raspberries and can be delicious. Wines from these grapes often taste better when they are cool, but like all red wines that are better when not too warm, sudden chilling has a tendency to make them taste flat, flabby or dead. The Romans used snow to cool wines, and liked their wine watered. Pliny talked about the immorality of drinking wine neat, but the wines in those days were much harsher and needed dilution.

Every district, the Piedmont not excepted, makes what the Italians call aromatic wines, usually from the Muscat grape, but also from the Brachetto and others. The process resembles that for making Sherry; while these fortified wines can be interesting, they

PIEDMONT

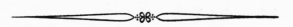

REDS	WHITES
Barbaresco	*Asti Spumante*
Barbera	*Caluso*
Barolo	*Cortese*
Carema	*Moscato d'Asti* or *Canelli*
Freisa	
Gattinara	
Grignolino	
Nebbiolo	

are rarely exported. Sweet wines from dried grapes, called *passito*, are also made, the best in Piedmont being called Caluso; it is rarely shipped.

The sparkling Asti Spumante is also made from the Muscat, in the vineyards around Asti. This is often sweet, even for Italian tastes, and sparkling wines from the Pinot Chardonnay grape, grown near Asti, are preferred. Some of the red wines are made into *spumante*, which means sparkling, while others are made into *frizzante*, which means slightly sparkling. They taste best in Italy. A good dry white wine, Cortese, has its adherents, but most of the wine from this grape goes into the making of vermouth, the manufacture of which centers in Turin, the wine capital of the Piedmont. Among the top producers of table wines, in addition to the Opera Pia, which is now called Vinclap, are Mirafiore, and Fontanafredda.

◆§ LOMBARDY AND LIGURIA

In Lombardy, grape names aren't used to identify the wines, but the best are made from the Nebbiolo. They are the fine reds from the valley called Valtellina. The terraced vineyards are in the province of Sondrio, in the alpine foothills near the Swiss border, and the full, fruity red wines go to market as Sassella, Grumello, Inferno, and Valgella. They take four years to mature. Negri is a

L O M B A R D Y   A N D
L I G U R I A

REDS	WHITES
Grumello	Cinque Terre
Inferno	Frecciarossa
Sassella	Valtellina Bianco
Valgella	Vermentino

famous producer. White wines, dry and light, are also made, marketed as Valtellina Bianco. Another white wine, Frecciarossa, comes from southern Lombardy. It is full in body, hard and heady, without great distinction. Sweet white wines and a very light red are marketed under the same name.

Over on the shores of Lake Garda are pleasant light red and *rosé* wines called Valtenesi and Chiaretto, Moniga and Riviera del Garda. A white wine to go with the lake fish is called Lugana.

The Italian Riviera, like the French Riviera, produces several pink wines in the steep and terraced vineyards above the wide blue sea, but the best known are the white wines from the Vermentino grape, and the red wine called *sweet water* after the town of Dolceacqua, both from vineyards near the French border. Down near Genoa, white wines come from the vineyards of Coronata and Polcevera. And near La Spezia are the vineyards that produce the Cinque Terre that has been the favorite of writers, from Pliny and Petrarch through Boccaccio to d'Annunzio. Unlike the others, it is a big and full white wine, often quite sweet. Some of the vineyards are so steep that the grapes are brought down to the water and loaded into boats for hauling to the presses.

✑ VENETIA

From Lake Garda in the west to the Yugoslavian border, there are vineyards on the slopes and along the rivers that produce some of the best white wines of Italy. Soave is the queen, dry and full, from the little town of Veneto, near Verona. Its companion is the light red Valpolicella, a wine of breed and bouquet. A lighter, less distin-

——————————————▷·※·◁——————————————

R E D S	W H I T E S
Bardolino	Prosecco
Caldaro	Soave
Santa Maddalena	Terlano
Valpolicella	Verdiso

guished red wine of the same type is Valpantena; Bardolino, from Lake Garda vineyards, is another. Among the leading shippers are Bertani, Bolla, and Fontonari. One of the most famous wines of Verona is the sweet Recioto, red or white, made from dried grapes on the outside of the bunches, which is popular in Italy but for no particularly good reason.

North of Venice are the dry Verdiso and the sweet and sparkling Prosecco, light and pleasant white wines to drink in the Piazza di San Marco. To the north, in the valley of the Adige, are the wines of the Tyrol, vineyards that once belonged to Austria. German grapes predominate, with a few French white vines here and there, and the best wine is Terlano, made up partly of Riesling and Traminer. Red wines are Caldaro, Santa Maddalena, Santa Giustina, and Meranese di Collina; light, fresh, with distinctive bouquets. A generally good *rosé*, or *rosato*, is called Lagarino. Many of these wines are shipped north, into Switzerland and Austria, others are drunk in Venice, Trieste, and Fiume, and very few find their way to other markets. The Italians think highly of the light red Marzemino and full red Teroldego, named for their grapes, and of the aromatic white Termeno, Italian for Traminer. Among the leading shippers are Kettmeir, Lageder Alois, Lechthaler, and Kupelwieser.

ᴇ§ EMILIA

Bologna, home of the sausage of the same name, is the capital of this area, and its citizens down thousands of gallons from the red Lambrusco and Sangiovese grapes, plus the white Albana. Vineyards are everywhere, thousands of acres, but none of them produce wines worth more than a mention, something to drink with spaghetti when nothing better is available.

≈§ TUSCANY

Chianti is the best known of Italian wines. The best Chiantis are shipped in ordinary wine bottles, not in the straw-covered flask called a *fiasco*. Those called *classico* are supposed to be the best, but towns like Rufina and Carmignano, outside the district which is allowed to put the word on the label, often produce better wines. Those called Brolio, after a nearby castle, are also good. Some Chiantis are meant to be drunk young. Others are allowed to pick up much tannin during fermentation and take years to develop. The first is very fruity, the second can be quite aristocratic. Chianti is made from a blend of grapes, mostly Sangiovese. The Chianti you'll find in the best Italian restaurants is the Riserva Ducale shipped by Barone Ricasoli, a well-balanced wine that takes four or five years to mature. Other leading shippers are Antinori, Melini, Ruffino, and Serristori.

Another dry red Tuscan wine is Montepulciano, once famous, now fair. A sweet red is the Aleatico di Portoferraio from Elba, named after its grape. Far better is the sweet white wine called Vino Santo, made in many districts but perhaps best here, supposed to be able to engender warmth between husband and wife, and to make grandpa feel twenty again. Most wines of body and fire are said to possess these qualities, and have been recommended for centuries as wines to "build the blood," whatever that means.

Some of the strangest wines in Italy are made from the Vernaccia grape and have a faintly bitter taste. The grape is grown in several parts of Italy, but the best wine is Tuscany's Vernaccia di San Gimignano. It's a good wine before dinner when it is well made, very light and distinctive.

T U S C A N Y

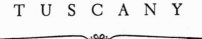

RED	WHITES
Chianti	*Aleatico*
	Vernaccia
	Vino Santo

▪§ MARCHE, UMBRIA, AND LATIUM

Over on the Adriatic is the light red wine called Rosso Piceno, and the white wine called Verdicchio, from Castelli di Jesi. Across the Apennines, nestled among the hill towns, are the vineyards producing Orvieto, best of the three. Orvieto is dry or fruity, depending on whether dried grapes are used, and one of the well-known white wines of Italy. Among the leading producers are Spolletti and Bigi. Just below Orvieto is the village of Montefiascone, the home of Est! Est!! Est!!!. This sweet and light white Muscatel gets its name from a Rome-bound German bishop. Unwilling to taste bad wine or to miss good ones, he sent a servant ahead instructed to mark *Est* on the walls of every inn that served good wine. By the time the servant reached Montefiascone, he was in transports and wrote the word three times on the inn wall. When the bishop arrived, he was so pleased with the wine he drank himself to death. As proof, the locals point to a tomb in the local church, which is said to be inscribed by the zealous servant, "*Est, est, est*. Because of too much Est, here Johannes Duc, my master, died."

But the most popular wines in the Roman area are those from Colli Albani, the Alban Hills, forming part of Castelli Romani. The villages name the wines of Albano, Frascati, Velletri, Marino, Ariccia, Genzano, Rocca di Papa, and those of nearby Bracciano. They have a strong, full taste that comes from the volcanic soil on which they are grown, and a golden color. They vary from dry to slightly sweet, and the favorite is Frascati, which was praised by Horace. Some red and sweet wines are made, none very good. The Cerasuolo from Abruzzi has some fame.

MARCHE, UMBRIA, AND LATIUM

➤⦂◀

WHITES

Colli Albani	*Orvieto*
Est! Est!! Est!!!	*Velletri*
Frascati or *Cannellino*	*Verdicchio*

✑ CAMPANIA

The Italians like to put pungent herbs and garlic with their fish and pasta dishes. Their white wines taste particularly good with these. They also add tomatoes to these dishes, and the reds, rough or light, can stand up to the love apple's acidity. The northern wines go best with the northern dishes, those from around Rome seem to taste best with the more heavily seasoned foods of the capital, and those from the south go best with the garlic accents of Neapolitan foods. Over the centuries, the foods have wedded the wines, nowhere more so than in Campania.

The white wine of Capri, pale, one of the driest, and made from Greco grapes, comes mostly from mainland vineyards around the Bay of Naples. It is much better when it comes from the romantic isle, and best of all when it comes from Ischia, the precipitous neighboring island. Less dry and not as good are Falerno, both white and red and the most famous wine of the ancient world, the red Gragnano, and Ravello. From the slopes of Vesuvius comes La-crima Cristi, red or white, somewhat dry, sometimes extremely fruity. The fruity wines are sometimes *frizzante,* and a government publication notes that "the surface of the wine has a constant gay shimmer" as the bubbles rise to the surface, something rarely noticed, at least in the first few glasses.

C A M P A N I A

REDS	WHITES
Falerno	*Capri*
Gragnano	*Ischia*
	Lacrima Cristi
	Vesuvio

⤳ THE SOUTH, SARDINIA, AND SICILY

Of the millions of gallons of wine that gush out of the south today, the best come from Lucanian vineyards around Vulture Mountain, a red wine made from the Aglianico grape, marketed as Aglianico del Vulture. Robust reds are Castel del Monte, Savuto, and Ciro di Calabria. Full whites are made from Malvasia and Moscato grapes, both sweet, and Greco di Gerace, which is said to smell faintly of orange blossoms and reach 17 per cent in alcohol.

Most of the red and white table wines of Italy, at least the best of them, are usually 11 to 13 per cent alcohol. When they are lighter, the wine often tastes watery, and when they are more powerful, the wines taste heavy. Sansevero and Torre Giulia are pleasant whites in between, while a similar red wine is San Stefano. The sweet wines tend to get heavier as you go south, and these dessert wines often maintain their balance. Such a wine is the Aleatico di Puglia, which has a tonic taste and an orange-red color.

But the best wines of the south come from Sicily, the home of Marsala, a wine invented by an Englishman named John Woodhouse in the last decades of the eighteenth century. Sherries and Ports were popular in England in the gouty days of George III, and Woodhouse tried to crack the market with a dark wine made from a blend of grapes, fortified with brandy, sweetened with boiled-down grape juice, and marketed under such initials as LP (London Particular), OP (Old Particular), and SOM (Superior Old Marsala). Coming from volcanic soil, the wine resembles Madeira, which is better. Many Marsalas are mixed with eggs and seasonings, then bottled and sold as a sort of ready-mixed punch.

Sweet wines from Malvasia grapes are produced on the Lipari islands of Salina and Stromboli, but others from the Muscat grape, planted in Zucco, Syracuse or Noto, and Pantelleria, are much more interesting. The wines are usually unfortified and golden yellow in color, averaging about 15 per cent alcohol. The exception is the Moscato di Pantelleria, which is dark brown.

A fairly dry white wine made from a blend of grapes is Corvo, which is golden and full and the most characteristic of the southern white wines. A white wine from the slopes of Mount Etna is similar. A full red is also made on Etna, and there's another called Faro, made in vineyards overlooking the Straits of Messina.

The most interesting wine of Sardinia is probably the Vernaccia del Campidano, with a bitter tang and a roundness that makes it a wonderful before-dinner wine; it can reach 18 per cent, it is said, without fortification. There's a lighter dry Vermentino from Gallura that is similar, a golden Nasco, Muscatels from Campidano and Tempio, a Malvasia, a couple of portlike wines from Giro and Monica, and a full red from Oliena that d'Annunzio called a wine of forgetfulness, Nepente di Oliena. All of these are wines to taste as you find them—out of curiosity, as contrast to the generally better wines made from nobler grapes, and as an indication of how wines can vary. The wines of Italy are for casual drinking. They have warmed the hearts of men for two thousand years, and the hearts of women, too.

S A R D I N I A A N D S I C I L Y

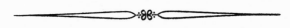

R E D S	W H I T E S
Giro di Sardegna	*Corvo*
Monica di Sardegna	*Greco*
Oliena	*Lipari*
Vulture	*Vernaccia*
	Zucco

Tokay and Other Wines

Thirsty travelers are forever discovering and rediscovering wines, wines that nobody else ever heard of, that the world forgets, that never get into bottles or never get shipped when they do; delicious draughts served at an inn near Zagreb, or drawn from a cask by an Austrian peasant, or poured from pitchers in an Ankara café. Wines are made wherever the vine can be made to bear, and the native vintage is always touted above foreign wines of greater fame in sturdy support of local endeavor.

In Europe, the vineyard country roughly follows the ancient boundary of the Holy Roman Empire, and many of the districts were planted so that Roman legions could be supplied with local wines. The line runs east from Flanders along the Rhine and the Danube, through Bavaria and Austria and Hungary to the Caucasus. There is some feeling that the line is moving southward because famous wines were once made north of Paris, but this shift may be temporary or even imaginary. The more celebrated districts are producing better and better wines, which naturally eclipse local wines that became well known simply because there was nothing else available.

৵§ LUXEMBOURG

The wines of Luxembourg, from vineyards along the upper Mosel, are frequently exported to enthusiasts, the best known coming from the townships of Wasserbillig, which means "cheap water," and Wormeldingen; other wine towns are Grevenmacher, Ehnen, Ahn, Machtum, Remich, Remerschen, Schengen, Wallerstein, and Wintringen. The best of these bear a government seal on the cork, a guarantee of authenticity, and they are bottled in green bottles like those used on the Mosel. The white wines often carry the name of the grape—Riesling, Traminer, Sylvaner. They are generally hard and dry with a pleasant crispness, but can't compare with their betters from the Mosel. Pink, red, and sparkling wines made in Luxembourg are strictly for local drinking.

৵§ SWITZERLAND

Swiss wines are low in price, excellently made, and widely available. The whites were the favorites of James Joyce, who liked his wines dry and hard, but even this hasn't been enough to make them popular.

The best wines come from the steep vineyards on the northern shores of Lake Neuchâtel and Lake Geneva, these last being in the canton of Vaud, with its three districts of La Côte, Lavaux, and Le Chablais. Others come from the canton of Valais, whose vineyards lie along the Rhône. Grapes are planted everywhere in Switzerland, generally Fendant for white wines. In the Upper Loire and Alsace, where it is called Chasselas, it produces wines that have a tendency to be flat and too light in acid. In Germany it is called Gutedel. The Riesling, which is called Johannisberger in Switzerland, is planted here and there, as are the Sylvaner, Traminer, Pinot

Chardonnay, and others. The Pinot Noir is used to make the best red wines.

The wines have a tendency to be slightly *pétillant* or *spritzig*, showing what the Swiss like to call "the star." This imparts a light and sprightly quality to the wine, prickly to the tongue, which can be seen on the sides of the glass as tiny bubbles that resemble those formed by soda water. The whites from Neuchâtel are particularly light and starry, but the best come from such La Côte villages as Féchy, Mont-sur-Rolle, Vinzel, and Luins, and such Lavaux towns as Lutry, Cully, Grandvaux, Riex, and Dezalay. These are closely followed by the slightly fuller wines from Valais.

The Swiss will tell you that their classic *fondue* must be made with Swiss white wine, preferably the Fendant of Valais. To make it, rub an earthenware casserole with a garlic clove, dumping in a pound and a half of grated Gruyère or Emmenthaler, or a mixture of both, along with half a bottle of Fendant. Set the casserole over a medium flame from a spirit lamp, using an asbestos pad if the flame is too hot, and then begin to stir. When the cheese begins to melt, sprinkle in a generous tablespoonful of potato flour or cornstarch, and then pour in two ounces of kirsch and stir some more. When the mixture is hot and creamy, add another dollop of kirsch, and dip into the casserole with torn bits of crusty bread speared on a fork. The Swiss prefer to dunk with their fingers, twisting deftly to break the strings of cheese that cling to the bread. If the *fondue* gets too stringy, add more kirsch. If one drops his bread into the casserole, he must buy another bottle of wine to drink with the rest of the *fondue*, or drink an extra glass himself.

Two fine red wines come from the districts of Cortaillod on Lake Neuchâtel, and from Dôle, near Sion in the Valais. The Dôle is the best, fruity as a Burgundy, but the Cortaillod is a little fuller. A fresh pink wine is made from the Pinot in the Rhine valley near Maienfeld, and there are a few others to be found here and there. Wine is made in every one of the twenty-two Swiss cantons, and even a straw wine, *vin fletri*, is made. There are the Pagan from Visp vineyards four thousand feet above sea level, the Glacier wines from the Sierre, white and hard because they are aged on the mountaintops, and more white wines from the Geneva district of Mandement, from Zurich and Ticino. Many of them are produced by co-operatives, but the more than twenty million gallons made each year are scarcely half enough for the Swiss, who, along with the Belgians, are the largest buyers of Burgundies. Every Swiss valley has its own wine—distinctive, delicious, and impeccably made— and in the great hotels are the best bottles from the greatest vineyards of France and Germany. Switzerland is a great place to drink wines.

◄§ AUSTRIA

On the country roads in Austria you will see a wreath stuck on a pole, an invitation to stop and taste *Heurige*, the farmers' white wine, straight from the cask. The new wine is hard and potent, and the best of it comes from Grinzing, now a Viennese suburb, where pitchers of it are served in the cafés. The finest white wines come from the vineyards around the town of Gumpoldskirchen, and from Klosterneuberg on the Danube. Both are wines with big bouquet, full of taste. Wines from the nearby towns are hard and powerful, and of little distinction. The best reds come from Voslau and are pleasant to drink in Vienna.

◄§ EASTERN EUROPE

Many once-Austrian vineyards now belong to satellite countries, those in Bohemia and Slovakia producing generally ordinary wines, those in Hungary and in northern Yugoslavia producing wines quite similar to those still called Austrian.

Yugoslavian viticulture has suffered under the present regime, and while all types of wine are made, the most popular are highly alcoholic sweet white wines, particularly those of Ptuj and Ljutom. A once-famous wine called Tigermilk is produced at Radgona, on the Hungarian border. The wines of Istria and the Dalmatian coast are popular locally, and the best white is said to come from Zilavka, in Herzegovina. Few are being exported.

Even less wine comes from Bulgaria, Romania, and the USSR, but vineyards extend across the Crimea into the Asian oases of Tashkent, Samarkand, and Bokhara. All kinds of vines are used, but the wines are generally sweet and fortified. The best are said to come from the Massandra vineyards near Yalta. A great deal of experimentation is going on throughout the wine-growing areas of southern Russia in an attempt to counteract the demand for vodka with inexpensive fortified and sparkling wines and to supply the home market with table wines. In a decade or so, production should be enormous, and some of the wines are certain to be good.

৵ HUNGARY

A miracle of nature produces Tokay, one of the greatest wines of the world, which is rarely drunk today—a wine that is the peer of the finest from Rheingau or Sauternes. Other districts of Hungary produce red and white wines that are often better than good, but it is Tokay that is the prince of eastern Europe, the only great wine produced east of the Rhine.

Tokaj is a village in northeastern Hungary, surrounded by a plateau of fewer than five thousand acres, from whose volcanic soil the Furmint grape draws the tonic iron that gives the wine its fiery taste.

The best sections were once owned by the crown, and this Imperial Tokay was reserved for royal gifts. The grapes are picked late, and those touched by the *edelfäule* are collected separately. The must often contains more than 30 per cent sugar, which often becomes 15 degrees of alcohol. In years when there are little or no overripe grapes, the wines are dry and perhaps 14 per cent alcohol, but when some of the grapes are dried and raisinized, the wines can be sweet. All these are marketed as *Tokaji Szamarodni,* and many of them live for twenty years and more.

The most famous of the Tokays is the *Aszu.* The dried grapes are picked separately and placed in *puttonyos,* baskets that hold about thirty pounds. As many as five baskets of these grapes are added to the fermenting must of regular wines, which are in thirty-gallon casks. The wine is identified on the label by the number of *puttonyos* that have been added, the more *puttonyos* the sweeter the wine. *Tokaji Aszu,* which is sometimes called *Ausbruch,* is round, full, and extremely satisfying, with none of the cloying, overpowering sweetness of many lesser sweet wines. Many live for a century or longer, and are invariably sold in half-bottles.

The rarest of all Tokays is the *Esczencia*, made by slightly crushing only the dried, overripe grapes, then collecting the juice that oozes from the small barrels in which the grapes have been placed. Only a few bottles of this wine can be made, even in great years. It is allowed to ferment exposed to the air, which may take months, and it rarely exceeds 8 per cent alcohol. *Esczencia* lives for centuries. It has an astonishing tonic effect. Because of this quality, Tokay has been called the old man's wine, and P. Morton Shand quotes the Englishman who said, "When childless families despair, when January is wedded to May, and when old men wish to be young, then Tokay is in request."

The taste of Tokay is particularly elusive and hard to describe, but it is generally likened to the aroma of freshly baked bread. This seems too homely a way of describing Tokay, but the bouquet of the wine suggests the same tantalizing, exciting aroma.

Tokays are at least ten years old before they go to market, spending three or four years in the cask. Some of them are blends of various vintages, but among the vintage Tokays on the market today is an 1876, a long-necked half-liter bottle selling in New York for about ten dollars.

Hungarian wines are marketed under the name of the district and the name of the grape, and among other white wines are Somlyoi Furmint, a pale yellow-green wine that is hard and distinctly aromatic, from the Somlyo district near Lake Balaton. Many of Hungary's best wines come from the vineyards around this long lake southwest of Budapest, the most important district being that of Badacsony, on its northern shore. The letter *i* means "from" when stuck onto the district name, so that *Badacsonyi Szurke-Barat* means a wine of that grape from Badacsony. The grape is also called *Auvergnac Gris* in France. The Keknyelu grape produces a similar wine that is full and somewhat sweet, with an aromatic fragrance reminiscent of freshly cut hay. Near Budapest are the full white golden wines made from the Ezerjo grape, which are usually slightly sweet, and the flowery wines of the Nezmely district, made from the Riesling.

Farther north is the district of Eger, where the Leanyka and Harzlevelu grapes produce white wines that are generally sweet and highly perfumed. Over toward the Austrian border is the Sopron district, where the sweet white Veltillin is produced. Eger also produces red wines, the most famous from the grape called Bikaver, which means "bull's blood," an indication of the deep ruby color of the full wine. Other reds come from Villany-Pecs, Nemes, and Szekszard, produced from the Kadarka grape, which is also planted in Eger. A lesser red wine from the Leanyka grape is made in the district of Kecskemet.

Only small quantities of the best-known wines are exported. One that is rarely found is the excellent sparkling wine called Gyongyos-Visonta, which has a great reputation in Hungary, as do the red and white table wines from the district. There are many other districts that produce good wines, but these are consumed at home, and many are probably shipped east. The few that come our way are proud examples of a long tradition, but there is some question whether they are the best available.

GREECE AND THE AEGEAN

In Homer's day, pitch was used to seal the jars in which wine was stored. This gave the wine an alien taste, which is reproduced today in the Greek white wines called Retsina, and red ones called Kokinelli. The wines are nothing much to start with, hard and acid, and the pitch makes the first sip taste like chilled turpentine.

Red and white wines without resin, from Dekeleia, Patras, and Achaia, are becoming more popular. The various Aegean islands produce celebrated but not exceptional wines. The sweet wine of Samos, beloved of Byron, the slightly drier wine from Santorin, and that from Crete (all made from the Muscat grape) are popular, and so is the sweet red wine from the Mavrodaphne grape. All are fortified. The red Commandaria created by the Knights Templar on Cyprus was famous five hundred years ago. The wine was flavored with herbs, sweetened, and fermented in earthenware jars, but it is of no interest today. All the wines have a warming, fiery quality supposed to be due to the volcanic soil.

ᴽ TURKEY

The best wines of Turkey are produced from native grapes and come from Anatolia and its districts of Ankara, Gaziantep, and Elazig. Still more wine is produced in Thrace, where Turkey joins Europe, but these are not as good as those from central and eastern Turkey. There has been great development in the past decade, and some of the wines are so good that they are beginning to find a market in northern Europe.

ᴽ PERSIA AND THE EAST

Wines first came from the East, and were spoken of thousands of years ago in the old Chinese and Indian tales. But Persia claims to be the birthplace of wine, citing the legend of the ancient King Jamshid's harem favorite, Gulnare, who devoured a plate of fermenting grapes in order to do away with herself because she had been cast aside. Her despair, not her vitality, disappeared, and the shah was so pleased with her discovery that he clasped her again to his bosom. This unlikely story is still repeated in Iran, and versions of it are told throughout the East. But Persia did give the western world the Shiraz grape, known in France as the Syrah, where it is made into the red wine of Hermitage. Pungent Shiraz, both red and white, is still made in Iran, the juice poured into large earthenware jugs to ferment, then bottled in long-necked, straw-covered flasks called *carabas*. This is probably the wine of Omar Khayyám. The most famous wine of Iran is that of Ispahan, but the best is said to come from Tabriz, near the Turkish border. The wines are often sweetened, scented, and fortified. None is exported, and expert opinion holds there is no reason why they should be.

There is the same disinterest in the few wines made in Kashmir and other parts of India. The old stories are full of wine, but contemporary Indians ignore wine, at least when they are in India.

Grapes were once planted in China, but the wines had such an adverse effect on the populace that the vineyards were destroyed by imperial order more than two thousand years ago. Even before that, the Chinese made a scented wine from rice, a practice that continues today. The best qualities are called *mandarin,* and are identified by the region from which they come. Mandarin was supposed to make one immortal, and was reserved for the emperor. A court official once stole some from his emperor, who ordered him put to death, but the minister was spared when he said that if the wine made him immortal, death was impossible, and if it did not, such a minor crime was not worth the penalty. These wines are only legends today, their secrets lost in the dregs of centuries, as are so many of the wines of the ancient world.

ᴈ§ ISRAEL

Vineyards were well developed by the Rothschild family before the First World War, but declined steadily, and have been reconstituted only in the past decade. The best vineyards are along the coast and in the Megiddo plain. An extensive variety of wines is produced, many of which are shipped to this country. Quality ranges from fair to good.

ᴈ§ EMPIRE WINES

The wines of South Africa and Australia are of little interest in the United States, because California does the same thing better. European vines were first brought to Cape Town three centuries ago, and they have been nurtured ever since, producing first a trickle, then a flood, of wines with famous European names. The same pattern was followed in Australia, starting about 1800. Both countries produce good standard wines today.

The only wine of South Africa to make a proud name for itself is that from Constantia, a full-bodied red wine, but the vineyards are rapidly being encroached upon by the Cape Town suburbs. Still fuller wines come from Paarl and Stellenbosch. All three are made from Bordeaux and Rhône valley grapes. South African white wines from European stocks mature too quickly, failing to develop needed acidity and those qualities that made for delicacy and bouquet. The same problem exists in Australia and elsewhere in the world where the climate is too mild.

In Australia, the vineyards cluster along the southern coast, along the Murray River which divides Victoria from New South Wales, on the slopes of the Mount Lofty ranges near Adelaide, around Melbourne, near Sydney, and on the west coast near Perth. Full red wines come from the Murray vineyards, while claret types come from Sydney and Perth vineyards, those from around Perth promising most. All mature rapidly.

Spain — Sherry and Other Wines

A certain look comes to the face of a winemaker when he presents for tasting a wine
he knows to be magnificent. He tries to keep
his face still and his eyes from twinkling, so
as not to deprive the taster of the surprise in
store, but pride and delight pull at the cor-
ners of his mouth as he watches for that first
instant of recognition. No matter how non-
committal the taster may wish to appear,
the marvel that has been made will wreck
his reserve, and he will feel the need to let
out a whoop, stamp his foot, slap the vintner
on the back. The vinter will try to look
modest, perhaps even shrugging as if it
didn't really matter. Then he, too, gives way.
It is a fine moment. This byplay takes place
in France and Germany, in Hungary and
Portugal. Particularly, it takes place in Spain,
in Jerez de la Frontera.

Jerez is a place of such celebration because some of all the great wines made there are always kept on hand. Sherry, like Port and Champagne, is a blend of wines. Blending is malpractice when great table wines that come from great vineyards are blended with inferior wines, so that distinctiveness is lost. Blending is an approved way of handling some table wines that can never be better than fair. Heavy is balanced with light, rough with smooth, hard and acid with soft and delicate. But the art of blending is essential to reach perfection when fortified wines —those that are between 14 and 21 per cent—are produced. Nowhere is this art more skilled than in Jerez.

Sherry is unique because its magnificence comes directly from the matching of wines from one vintage with closely similar wines from vintages that have gone before. This matching is done in the *solera* system, a word meaning foundation or base.

A solera is composed of tiers of Sherry butts, wines for shipment being drawn from the tier containing the oldest wines, small amounts from each butt. This is refilled from the second tier, which holds the next oldest wines, and the second is replenished from the third. Three tiers form a solera, generally, and the tier of youngest wines is usually "topped off" with wines from a younger solera or from a *criadera* (cradle), where new wines progress through a similar series of tiers.

In some soleras, wines may be two years passing from one tier to another, because no more than half the wine can be withdrawn from the oldest tier in any one year. Usually the draw is much less. In soleras of very old wines, the Sherry may be five years passing from tier to tier—or ten, or twenty. Once established, a solera is never emptied. The system came into being when the nineteenth century was beginning, and Jerzaños like to point out that in every withdrawal there will be an infinitesimal amount of the first wines placed in the solera. But the amount of such wines is not so important. The essential thing is that when Sherries are carefully matched, the young wines take on the character of the old wines, and are "educated" into being like their elders.

This is not the end of the matching. A shipped wine is usually composed from various soleras and carefully matched to the style of the preceding shipment. The custom during Victorian days was for the buyer to have his Sherry blended to his specifications. A firm may continue to supply dozens of styles that were established decades ago, as well as its own famous brands. *Style* is the word used to denote the character of a Sherry. Each firm has its own, based on stocks available and on what the winetasters, present and past, consider true to type or popular. It is the most complex, artful, and at the same time precise blending system in use, dependent on an enormous investment in wines. A single solera may consist of several hundred butts, and the wines from old soleras are priceless. The cost of starting a new solera would be almost prohibitive today. This matching is not something imposed on the wine, but has developed because of the essential nature of Sherry, which is to vary endlessly.

The Jerez district is just up the coast from Gibraltar, across the Guadalete River from Cádiz. Wines have come from its vineyards for twenty-five hundred years; the Greeks rounded the Pillars of Hercules expressly for them. The triangle of vineyards almost surrounds the city of Jerez, a town of over 100,000, running north to the Guadalquivir, west over rolling country to Sanlucar de Barrameda on the coast, and south to Puerto de Santa Maria, near the mouth of the Guadalete. There are scarcely twenty thousand acres in all, an area no larger than Manhattan Island. The soil is the chalkiest vineyard land on earth, called *albariza*, white in the glaring sun. The dark green vines are mostly Palomino, producing enormous bunches of golden, almost transparent grapes. In the clay soils called *barros* and sandy soils called *arenas* mostly Pedro Ximínez is planted, a vine said to have been brought from Germany by one Pieter Siemens; the wines are used for coloring and sweetening Sherries. There are small amounts of several other varieties, each imparting special qualities to the wines.

Some of the vineyards are owned by the famous firms, but many of them are in the hands of farmers, who begin the picking immediately after the feast of the Blessed Mother, September 8, when the first grapes are blessed on the cathedral steps and flocks of pigeons are released to carry the glad tidings of the vintage all over Spain. There is dancing in the streets; a queen is crowned; wine stands are everywhere. The next day, the first ripe bunches are carried to the courtyards of the farmhouses, where they are piled in mounds on round straw mats made of *esparto* grass. The grapes dry in the blazing sun for several hours and then are dumped into the *lagares*, wooden troughs some ten feet square, with the post of a screw press in the center rising taller than a man.

Pressing begins at dawn. The grapes are trodden, the *pisadores* wearing boots with hobnail cleats that permit the grape seeds to spurt aside so that they are not crushed. The cloudy juice is caught in barrels, beginning to hiss and seethe almost at once, for the wine of Jerez is known for its *fermentación tumultuosa*. The filled butts are loaded on carts and trucks, and trundled, the wine bubbling and foaming, to the courtyards of the shipping firms, where they are set about, helter-skelter, until the fermentation subsides.

The partially expressed grapes still in the *lagares* are shoveled into a pile around the screw press. A few handfuls of gypsum, heavy in the calcium phosphate which increases the tartaric acidity of the wine, are tossed on the heap. This is called *plastering*. The heap is patted into shape, much the way a child touches up a pile of wet sand, and is bound with a band of woven *esparto*, which is fastened to the screw. A nut, called the *sow* because of the squeaking noise it makes, is set on the screw, handles are inserted, and the men push their way around the heap. As the screw sinks, the juice squirts out between the tightening band of *esparto*.

The men work through the morning, intent on finishing, so that the rising sun will not be able to warm the juice so much that it will begin to ferment while it is still in the *lagar*. It has been done this way for centuries. Scenes on Greek amphorae are no different from those in a *lagar* of today.

Perhaps moonlight as well as sunlight gets into Sherry, because nobody knows why two barrels of *musto* pressed in the same *lagar*, made of grapes from the same vineyard, fermenting side by side in a shipper's courtyard, will produce two entirely distinct types of Sherry.

The wine falls bright in December. In some barrels, a thin white film will have formed on the surface of the clearing wine. There will be none in others. The film is called the *flor*. This flower is produced by a yeast that acts early in the fermentation, a *Saccharomyces*. When it forms, a *Fino* (meaning fine as opposed to stout) Sherry will be made. When it does not form, an *Oloroso*—fragrant—Sherry will be produced. These are the two basic types.

The taster wanders around the courtyard in March, reading the chalked marks on the butts to see which vineyard the wine came from and who made it. North of Jerez is the Carrascal district, whose wines usually produce Olorosos; northwest is Macharnudo, whose wines are usually the special kind of nutty Fino called Amontillado; west and south of town are Anina, Balbaina and Los Tercios, which generally produce Finos.

In the taster's hand is a long wand with what looks like a silver test tube on the end. It is called a *venencia*, and he plunges it deep into a cask, then pulls it out quickly. Raising it in front of him, he directs the stream into tulip-shaped glasses grasped in his fist. Actually, the wine is judged by look and smell at this point, not by tasting. As he smells the wines, in his head is the history of past performances of wines from each vineyard and the characteristics of the wines in each solera. In a morning he will have marked a hundred barrels, tentatively matching each to one of the soleras.

A Fino is marked by a slanting line with a hook on the end of it, called a *Palma*, and an Oloroso is marked by a stroke with a cross-hatch, called a *Cortado*. Wines that are clearly not one thing or the other are called *rayas* if they tend toward the Oloroso, and *entre-finos* if they resemble a Fino. They are usually lighter in alcohol, and often coarser than the more easily classed types, and are set aside to see if they will develop into a type, or are made into cheap wines if they don't. The best wines get a single mark, the lesser ones more, up to as many as four, so the saying goes that a good taster uses much chalk.

The lightest Finos will become a pale golden, pungent wine, extremely dry. The best of them mature in Puerto de Santa Maria, but many mature in Jerez. Over on the seacoast, in Sanlucar, the ocean breezes bring out a special tang in the wine, and the Finos from there are called Manzanillas. These are the driest wines in the world, with a tonic freshness that sets them apart; if casks are moved from Sanlucar to Jerez or Puerto de Santa Maria, they turn into regular Finos, and nobody knows why.

Some of the Finos are quite full and pungent in the beginning, marked by *gordo*, or stoutness, and will take more than ten years to mature, as compared with the classic Fino's seven or eight years. Such wines are matured separately, and become Amontillados. They develop a nutty taste, and retain the fullness they began with. Both Fino and Amontillado have a distinctive taste that comes from the *flor*. They are the perfect drinks before a meal because they make one hungry and because their tonic qualities are refreshing. In Spain, Finos are drunk in the summer, served in the cafés with *tapas*—small plates of olives, or unsalted almonds, slivers of cheese or ham, iced shrimp or crayfish. When the weather's cool, in spring and fall, everybody switches to Amontillado. The *tapas* remain the same.

If the taster finds no *flor* in the wine, or only traces, it will become Oloroso. The fuller Olorosos take a dozen years to mature. The lightest Olorosos—and they are extremely rare, only three or four casks out of a hundred—are classed as Palo Cortados. You can never be sure about a Palo Cortado, for it may begin to veer toward an Oloroso, but if it stays true to type, it will be an incredible combination of lightness and full bouquet and intense taste. One of the greatest of the Jerez firms has a solera of Palo Cortado, painstakingly assembled over the past few decades. Most firms have a butt or two, and the wine is rarely put on the market.

All these Sherries in Spain are dry wines, with no trace of sweetness. The wines are completely fermented out, and all are refreshed with brandy to hold them to the height of taste that they have reached, usually about 17 per cent alcohol for the lighter wines, with a little more added to the Olorosos than to Finos. There is a growing market overseas for the dry Olorosos, but for most markets, the Olorosos are sweetened and darkened to become the cream, or brown or East India Sherries. East India Sherries were so named because it was once thought that the sea voyage helped the wine, and casks were shipped as ballast to East India and back to London. The trip aged the wine quickly, what with the rocking and the heat of the holds, but today most shippers think they can do the job better in Jerez, where the Oloroso soleras are kept. The wines used for color are made of boiled-down must; when boiled down to a third, it is called *sancocho*; when to a fifth, it is called *arrope*. These color wines are carefully made and aged, extremely expensive, and are shipped overseas as Blending Sherry, where they are used to flavor and color whiskey, and to give it the taste of age. *Vino dulce*, the sweetening wine, is made from sun-dried Pedro Ximínez and Muscatel grapes and aged as carefully.

Once the wine is classified the butts are trundled into the storehouses by the *arrumbadores*. The name must come from the sound the casks make on the cobbles. The *arrumbadores* form a *quadrillo*, a quartet of husky men who always work together, handling the casks, caring for the wines, and transferring the Sherries from one solera tier to another. To avoid fire loss, the various tiers of a solera may be widely separated, and it is a common sight to see one of the team trotting along with the big enameled pitcher used for transferring wines. The team will push poles in between the tiers, set a plank across the projecting ends, and one of them will climb up to tap a cask. The wine will come gushing out in a curving stream, but before any falls to the ground the pitcher will be thrust under. The *arrumbadore* will continue his conversation with his fellow, ignoring the quickly filling pitcher, but he can tell by the sound when it is full, and without losing a drop he will twist a second pitcher into the stream, as his partner hustles off with the full one. A team may work together all their lives, and will have a certain disdain for those who work in the vineyards or in the cooperage where the barrels are made.

Each firm has a cooperage, where the staves of American oak are shaped by hand. Spain buys more Louisiana and New York state oak than the United States buys Sherry. The staves are formed and wetted, then fitted together, a fire is built inside, and a group of four men dance around the barrels, rhythmically hammering the hoops in place. Sherry barrels are valuable and are used for aging Scotch, to which they impart color and flavor. They are also highly sought after in other countries that produce wines similar to Sherries, the barrels giving the imitations something of the taste of the real thing.

The storehouses are called *bodegas*, and in Jerez they are like cathedrals: high, stuccoed buildings with tile roofs supported by great columns. They are always cool. High in the walls are open squares that can be covered with *esparto* mats but are usually open, because the air of Jerez is as important to good Sherry as any other element. The light is dim and shadowy, the casks stretch in long rows, piled three and four high, the aisles between of packed dirt. Footsteps are soft pats, voices have no echo. A *bodega* is a silent place.

Sherries never die, becoming more intense and concentrated as the decades pass. Finos have a tendency to change into Amontillados, but there are always a few that will retain the clean, light Fino taste, and when one of these is sixty years old or so, its taste will be almost paralyzing in the mouth. Amontillados and Olorosos are equally intense, a drop or so in a glass of younger Sherry completely transforming the younger wine, rounding and deepening the taste. Great skill is needed to blend the wines, for too much of an old Sherry can throw a young wine out of balance.

Sherries spend their life in the cask. Some firms still follow the ancient practice of leaving the wines on what is called *añadas*, wines of the year, refraining from classifying them for a year or two. Sherries from a particular vineyard will have a tendency toward a type, but vary widely within the type, one month being suited for one style, the next for another. When the decision is finally made, the Sherry will go to a *criadera*, where it becomes "educated" to the other wines of the criadera, and after that it goes to the solera, where its character is fixed. Only the greatest of the nine million gallons of wines generally produced each year go into the soleras. The lesser wines are distilled into a full and excellent brandy.

Sherries do not improve appreciably in the bottle, and many experts feel they become stale if left too long in glass. That is why so many sherries are still bottled from the butt in England, despite the fact that the English generally prefer Sherries with the bottle taste. This staleness does not become noticeable for several months, however, and because of fast transportation, it is becoming the practice to bottle in Jerez. Only one of the major importers in the United States, for instance, continues to bottle Sherries in New York.

Sherry is the sturdiest of wines, a bottle continuing to be good for weeks after it has been opened. But the lightest and driest Sherries are at their best when freshly bottled and promptly drunk. Sherry is the only wine that all experts agree can be drunk while one is smoking, the tobacco seeming to enhance the taste of the Sherry. Perhaps that is why it has been dubbed the wine of welcome and the traveler's wine, suited to moments of relaxation and companionship.

Sherry is a magnificent wine to use for cooking, a teaspoonful or two subtly improving a sauce or soup, a dollop or two bringing out the flavors of well-seasoned or spiced dishes. Sherry is often used as a "finish," put in at the last minute to blend and bring out the flavors of a dish. The effect varies with the type used. It is excellent as a marinade or a baste, and brings out the flavors of fruits and puddings. The English trifle is made by dipping slices of white cake in Sherry, lining a deep dish with the cake, then pouring in a vanilla pudding, which is topped with whipped cream and decorated with candied fruits. One of the classic puddings is the Spanish *flan*, made by cooking in a double boiler equal amounts of Sherry, egg yolk, and sugar, stirring constantly until it begins to thicken. Flan is served as a molded dessert when well-thickened, or as a sauce when not cooked so long.

There used to be a bottle of Sherry in the pantry of every well-managed household, and this came to be called cooking Sherry; the name applies today to cheap imitations that are heavily salted so that they can be sold as a grocery item in spite of their alcoholic content. Good cooks, however, use the best Sherries, and very little of them, a tablespoonful often being enough for a sauce. Sherry flames easily when it is warmed slightly, imparting a rich taste when the flaming wine is spooned over fruits, or over quickly cooked foods like shrimp or scallops or chicken livers. The alcohol evaporates, of course, when Sherry is flamed or when it is used as part of the liquid in a stew.

Some of the Sherries that have the word *dry* on the label are not dry at all, but the word *cocktail* is often used to identify the Finos. Occasionally, you will see the word *Amoroso* on a label; it is not a type, simply being slightly sweetened Oloroso. Still occasionally used is the phrase *Vino de Pasto*, which means table wines in Spanish, and is used to identify sweet, cheap Sherries.

The taste of a Sherry is hard to describe, but one of the most popular accounts is by the writer José de las Cuevas, who insists that one tastes Sherries by successive glasses: the first tastes of almonds, the second of hazelnuts, then comes nutmeg, broth, butter, beef, fowl, apple, and cherries. The tenth glass tastes of Sherry but only for an instant. The Spanish feel that each glass of Sherry is a discovery, so they never say, "Will you have another glass?" but always "Have a glass of sherry." In Spain, one never has a last glass of Sherry. There should be no end to anything so good; it is always the *penultima copa*, the next-to-the-last glass.

Several of the leading firms occasionally send Manzanilla Sherries here, among them González Byass, Pedro Domecq, and Williams & Humbert. La Guita and La Gitana are brand names of firms in Sanlucar that concentrate on shipping this wine.

All the leading firms ship Oloroso Sherries to America, most of them sold as cream Sherries. Some brand names, like Dry Sack of Williams & Humbert, or Brown Bang from Sandeman, or Carlton House from Valdespino, are used to identify certain Oloroso Sherries that are not exceptionally sweet. Most Olorosos and Amontillados, however, are identified primarily with the name of the shipper and the type:

LEADING SHIPPERS

Bobadilla y Cia.	El Marqués del Merito
Diez Hermanos	Martínez Gassiot & Co.
Pedro Domecq S.A.	Manuel Misa
Duff Gordon & Co.	Palomino y Vergara
Garvey S.A.	H. de Marqués de Real Tesoro
González Byass & Co.	J. M. Rivero
Manuel Guerrero y Cia.	A. R. Ruiz y Hermanos
Harvey's of Bristol	Sandeman & Co.
Gutierrez Hermanos	A. de Terry
R. C. Ivison	A. R. Valdespino
Emilio Lustau	Williams & Humbert
Mackenzie & Co.	Wisdom & Warter

Malaga, Rioja, and Others

Wines are made everywhere in Spain, but the best come from the north and Andalusia. Near Jerez is the Montilla district that produces very light, dry wines of the Fino type, which develop a nutty taste when old; Amontillados were named after them, meaning that such wines were like old Montillas. The district of Málaga, on the southern Mediterranean coast and in the hills behind, produces sweet fortified wines, mostly from Pedro Ximínez and Moscatel, the best of which is made like Tokay Escenzia, and is called Lágrima. Then there's the red fortified wine of Catalonia, once called Tarragona Port, the red Priorato, and the wines usually called Malvasia but once called Malmsey, from Sitges and the Canary Islands. These have a good market in Europe.

The best table wines come from the hills of the Rioja district, in the north, near Burgos, from vineyards between Haro and Logroño. When the *phylloxera* struck the French districts in the 1870s, there was a frantic search for vineyard areas, and many *vignerons* brought to the valley of the Ebro their French winemaking techniques. Most of them returned to France, once grafting was developed, but their heritage, and the French wine names, stayed behind. Some excellent red wines are made; many of these take half a dozen years to develop and continue to be remarkable twenty years after the vintage. The quick-maturing reds are often good, but vary widely. The whites are generally soft and slightly sweet, the driest resembling a Graves; many of these also live a decade or more. Vintages are not particularly important, the wines generally being blended, although some go to market under vineyard names, such as Viña Pomal. Well-known producers are the Marqués de Riscal, the Marqués de Murrieta, Bodegas Bilbainas, Bodegas Francos-Españoles, and the Compañia Vinícola del Norte de España, although there are many others.

Districts along the Mediterranean shore include: Valdepeñas, producing stout red and white wines; the white Castell del Remy and Alella; and various pink wines, the best of which is considered to be that of Yecla. All of these are generally drunk young, and are excellent buys when under two dollars a bottle.

Port, Portugal, and Madeira

Port comes from Portugal, but it goes to England. The English, who make no wines, for a thousand years have provided one of wine's most basic elements, customers. British thirst has made Port—as well as Sherry, Hock, and Claret—what it is today. In many ways, London is still the center of the wine world, and after a tour of the miles of wine vaults at the London docks, it is possible to get the feeling that European vineyard regions are mere sources of supply for the British wine trade, which continues to ship bottles and casks all over the world.

The Romans introduced wine to Britons, who were delighted and did not become restive until supplies began to wane with the decline of Roman rule. They morosely nursed mead and metheglin, made from fermented honey, and beer, for a few centuries, seizing on whatever Rhenish and

239

Gallic vintages were brought to them by Frisian traders. William the Conqueror greatly eased the situation, and by 1449 Bordeaux was shipping three million gallons of wine to England. Two years later, their precious claret territory was torn from British hands. Trade ceased.

The English turned to Spain for wines, and the Sherry trade flourished. But conflict culminated in the defeat of the Spanish Armada, and French wines again came to England until heavy taxes were imposed on them in 1689 by Dutch King William. The British turned to northern Portugal for their major supply of cheap table wines. A century later, two thirds of the four million gallons entering England came from Portugal, the rest divided between France and Spain.

In 1678, two sons of a Liverpool wine merchant decided to take a holiday. They had been sent by their father to learn the wine trade in Vianna, the Portuguese port from which some cheap wines were beginning to be shipped. They headed south, and in a monastery they tasted a wine far better than the stuff they had been shipping to England. It was wine from the upper Douro, a precipitous river that rises in the mountain spine dividing Portugal from Spain and flows west to the Atlantic, entering the ocean at Oporto. They bought as much of the wine as they could, dosed it with brandy to keep it stable and healthy, and shipped it to Liverpool. The Port wine trade was established. It was encouraged by a favorable treaty in 1703.

Many of today's firms are English, of course, following the empire-molding principle that he who had the market held the trade. Oporto sprawls on the high bank on the north of the Douro, a city of stone buildings and wide thoroughfares connected by winding, crowded alleys, the town cascading down to the river piers. In the lower town is Factory House, a club of the English firms founded in 1790. Here is held a weekly luncheon, served at a dining table some thirty feet long, attended by members and guests and concluded by the drinking of Port, which is passed clockwise around the table and is supplied in turn by the various members of the Factory. It is marvelous Port, full and tonic, generally better than Partner's Port, the wine reserved for the directors of the company and served by them to guests in their London offices and country homes, and better than the Club Port served at the Wine Trade

Club in the City of London, whose members are those in the English branches of the firms. But there is another Port that is still better; you are sure to hear about it if you go to lunch at the Factory, and you will taste it before the day is out.

A director came out from London to inspect the lodges where the wines were stored, and after lunch the resident manager served him a glass of Vintage Port with the cheese and nuts. The director sipped, savored, and said, "This is better than Partner's Port." The manager nodded. "Of course. It's Manager's Port."

All Port shippers, English and Portuguese, are banded together in a guild called the Gremio, and they work closely together in the interests of the trade. The regulatory body for the government is the Port Wine Institute, the Instituto, which sees that taxes are collected and that wines meet minimum standards for quality and are properly labeled. But it is the Gremio that is basically responsible for Port wine.

The storehouses, or lodges, of the shippers are across the river from Oporto in Vila Nova de Gaia, a vast collection of large buildings in which thousands of pipes are kept. These pipes are long, tapering casks in which the wine is stored; they are made from Memel oak when it can be had from the Baltic forests, and from Portuguese and other oak, when it cannot. The pipes full of purple wine come down from the upper Douro in the spring after the vintage and it is in Vila Nova that they are classified and Port is made. Port is not Port until it is blended.

As the purple wines age in the wood, they pass from Full to Dark Ruby to Medium Tawny and Tawny, which is, finally, a deep amber. Each of the colors has a definite range, and the best wines do not become Tawny until they are thirty years old or more. Such wines are intense and concentrated in taste, too much so to be easily drinkable, and are used for blending. Wines that are less full to begin with may mature in ten years, preserving a certain freshness of taste; these are the basis of most Ports. White Port is made from white grapes, and this can be blended with the more quickly maturing reds to make a Young Tawny, lighter in body and easy to drink. Each wine is kept separate, in marks or *lotes*, according to quality, and each firm's Ruby or Tawny will be blended from different marks. Together, these wines are called Wooded Ports.

Every Port of each company has its own style or character, and the style is kept the same year after year. The styles are shipped to England in casks and bottled there, during a cold snap, when an east wind is blowing, says tradition. The secret of these Ports, young or old, is that they be well made or well balanced, possessing the traditional fruit, character, and style that has been established. Such ports are called "well-shipped wine," high praise to the manager or the younger sons in the business who have gone out to Vila Nova from England.

In exceptional years, a vintage wine will be declared, and most of the shippers will be "together" in agreeing that the wine is exceptional. After two years in the wood, the wine will be bottled or sent to England for bottling. It will remain in bottle for twenty years. Then it will be tasted, and, if ready, it will begin to be drunk. It will continue to be ready, generally improving for another decade or so. When old, a harmless flake of tartar appears in the wine, called *beeswing*, a sign of old Port. The wine develops what is called bottle flavor, and forms a crust, which is why Port is usually decanted. While the crust is forming, the wine is bottle-sick and undrinkable. Frequently a shipper will provide "late-bottled" Vintage Port, leaving it in the wood for five years or so before bottling. This is ready to drink much more quickly than a "regulation bottling," and is the Port for the impatient who can't wait twenty years. The classic vintage is 1896; other declared vintages have been 1900, 1904, and 1908 (now generally past their prime), 1912, 1917, 1920, 1922, 1927, 1934, 1935, 1947, 1948, 1950, 1955. When shipment to London is difficult, vintages are not usually declared, even though the wine warrants it; such years are 1931, 1942, and 1945, this last being magnificent.

Vintage Port will be a dark ruby when it is opened, and will have an amazingly fruity, intense taste, quite different from a Tawny or Ruby. It is illogical, incidentally, to consider Vintage Port "better" than a fine Tawny or Ruby—the wines are different. For a vintage year to be declared there must be a good quantity of exceptional wine. Nearly every year, outstanding vineyards produce some great wines, and shippers may isolate these stocks and make a superior "off vintage." Another classification is Crusted Ports, made when Full or Ruby wines are bottled young. These throw a heavy crust, and taste like a young Vintage Port, if there were such a thing.

Depending on how long they have been in wood, Crusted Ports may take ten years or longer to become ready for drinking.

Books are full of Port, but the story that pleases me most is quoted by Ernest Cockburn in his book, *Port Wine and Oporto*, and is an extract from his great-grandfather's memoirs. The old man was a Scottish judge, and it used to be the custom to have black bottles of Port and biscuits on the bench to sustain the judge if the sessions stretched:

The refreshment was generally allowed to stand untouched, and as if despised, for a short time during which their Lordships seemed to be intent only on their notes. But in a little while, some water was poured into a tumbler and sipped quietly, as if merely to sustain Nature. Then a few drops of wine were ventured upon but only with the water; till at last patience could endure no longer and a full bumper of the pure black element was tossed over; after which the thing went on regularly and there was a comfortable munching and quaffing to the great envy of the parched throats in the gallery.

The Douro valley is a great, wide, winding cleft, the hill wedges rising several hundred feet above the river, their ridges thrusting down into the valley. The road from Oporto curls along the flanks. On the slopes are farms and orchards, pools and rills. Sometimes a footbridge takes a shortcut from the steep side of one hill to the close flank of the next and footpaths angle steeply up and down. On the crests, cypresses are silhouetted here and there against the sky, against the haze of the valley, against the lighter flank of a larger hill beyond. It is a drive through the landscape of a Japanese print.

The vineyards run for thirty miles above Regua, on both sides of the valley, which varies from ten to thirty miles in width. The vineyards on the hills look barren and immense, deeply green, and broken by many terrace walls. Here and there, in a tuck of valley or on a crest, will be a stand of trees and the houses of the growers, some small and others spacious. All growers are members of the Federation of Wine Growers of the Douro, the Casa do Douro, a combination registry, laboratory, and hotel on the main street of Regua. The Casa advises on all matters of grape-growing and wine-making, and helps establish the prices of the wines.

The best vineyards are around Pinhão, these *quintas* being on the Rio Torto and some of the other Douro tributaries which have cut deep, sloping gorges in the soft schistous rock that gives the earth its reddish color and the wine its tonic taste.

Temperatures rise above 100 and fall below freezing, there are torrential rains in the fall and winter, much wind mist; the bend of the hills protects the best vineyards, and with luck, the harvest begins in late September. The grapes are brought by oxcart and truck to the ranch houses and dumped into large stone troughs, the *lagares*. Someone strums a guitar, and men and women climb into the *lagares* and begin treading, stepping high, forward to one end of the trough, then back, for hours.

When fermentation is well under way, and part of the sugar has been converted into alcohol, the juice is run off into *tonels*, large vats, into which year-old brandy has been poured. This stops the fermentation, and the wine stays in the *tonel* during the winter, after which it is run into pipes and sent down to Vila Nova. Today, this transport is done by train, although a few pipes still come down the river on the wide, square-sailed barques that have come to symbolize the Douro.

Some of the wine is bought by stockers, many of whom are in Regua and Pinhão, who buy and mature wines of exceptional quality. A shipper may need a pipe or two in order to complete a style, and these he can get from the stocker. Only the largest companies and oldest firms have large stocks of old wines, and nobody ever has enough. Some of the old wines are almost priceless. They are constantly refreshed with small quantities of brandy and new wines, and they are said to "eat up" the new additions. A few pints of old wine can completely change the character of a younger. The taste of a stocker's old wine, one that was laid down fifty or seventy-five years ago, is almost paralyzing—intense, tonic, and metallic.

When the wines arrive in Vila Nova, they again receive a small dosage of brandy, bringing them up to around 20 per cent alcohol. They are maintained at this strength during their time in cask, and when shipped, they are usually brought to about 21 per cent. Vintage Ports receive an extra degree of alcohol.

Ports are considered to be a sweet wine, but that is not what you notice when you taste the wine, for its fruity, essential quality is what stands out. They are unique wines, and it is ironical that the wine is so frequently and so feebly imitated.

Among the leading shippers are Burmester, Calem, Cockburn Smithes, Croft, Delaforce, González Byass, Graham, Kopke, Mackenzie, Offley Forester, Robertson, Sandeman, de Silva, Smith Woodhouse, Taylor Fladgate & Yeatman, and Warre & Co. There are some eighty recognized shippers, many of whom occasionally send shipments of wine to the United States.

·§ PORTUGUESE TABLE WINES

There's another irony about Port, which is that it is rarely drunk in Portugal. The Portuguese prefer table wines, the green, hard, cloudy *vinho verde*, white wines from north of the Douro, or the rough red Collares, and the soft, sweet Setubal and Bucellas from vineyards around Lisbon. There is a flood of wines, sweet and dry, red and white, from the Estremadura in the area above and below Lisbon. Most of it is *consumo*, table wine to be drunk with meals, and while the sweet, red, fortified wines were once called Lisbon Port, they are no longer shipped under that name. They are finding a market in the United States, however, particularly in the Midwest, where they compete with kosher wines. They are sometimes better than their competitors and appeal to those who like the word *imported* on a label.

·§ MADEIRA

Portugal's island of Madeira, some four hundred miles out in the Atlantic off the African bulge, was discovered by one Zarco in the early years of the fifteenth century. He dubbed it the Wooded Isle because it was covered with a magnificent growth of virgin forest, which he burned down because it was so difficult to clear. The fire is said to have lasted a decade. Colonists planted white wine vines; and the volcanic soil and rich ashes were just what was needed to produce full and fiery white wines—sweet ones from Bual and Malvasia grapes, dry ones from the Sercial and Verdelho. In the course of time, Malvasia became known as *Malmsey*, and Clarence drowned in a butt of it.

Traders carried the wines to the growing colonies of the New World where they became favorites. The wines seemed to improve after the long voyage in the stifling hold of a ship, and it became the practice to store the wines in hot rooms, or *estufas*, for six months or longer. The lesser the wine, the hotter the room and the shorter the time in the hothouse. In small wineries, the wines are stored in glass houses and the sun does the work.

In any event, the wine can live for a century, perhaps even longer than Tokay, and although the solera system is used today, vintage wines were offered before the attack of the *phylloxera* in the 'eighties. The outstanding vintages, some of which are still available today, are 1789 and 1795, 1806, 1808 for Malmsey, 1815 for Bual, 1822, 1836, and 1844. Verdelho was particularly outstanding in 1838 and 1844, all were good in '51, '62, '65, '68, in '70 Sercial excelled, in '80 Malmsey excelled, and all were good again in 1883. But the dates on most Madeiras since then refer to the date when a particular solera was started, and the proportion of really old wines in them is small.

The best vineyards are near the capital, Funchal; to the southwest, at Cama de Lobos; and on the south coast, at São Martinho and Curral. St. Martin and the first two names often appear on labels to identify the district wines, but it is more usual to blend them, those called "Fine Rich Madeira" being based on Malmsey or Bual, those called "Fine Dry" being based on Sercial. "Old Southside" is a name given to pale light blends from the south coast vineyards, and one of the most famous names for a very dry Madeira is "Rainwater," now a proprietary brand of Welsh Brothers. "London Market," "London Particular," and "East India Madeira" were once names used for identifying quality, the last being the best. Each house has its own brand names for its various blends.

The main Madeira types are named after the grapes, however, and come from soleras, no matter what additional names are put on a label. Sercial is the driest and lightest, pale in color, produced from a grape that came originally from the Rhine. It is an excellent apéritif. Verdelho is darker and not so dry, an amber color with a definite bitterness in the aftertaste, and also an excellent apéritif. Bual—the Portuguese spelling is Boal—is medium in sweetness, with a full bouquet, often served with cakes and cookies. Malmsey is dark, full, sweet, and heady, to be served with cakes and other desserts. Sercial and Malmsey are produced from shy bearers, vines that produce few grapes; their wines mature slowly, and good ones are always rare and expensive. Verdelho and Bual are made from vines that bear heavily; the wines develop quickly and are generally inexpensive and good. Like Port, Madeira will keep its freshness only a few days, once opened, and should be drunk promptly. Also like Port, the trade is in English hands. Initial wine-making practice follows the techniques of Jerez, with the exception that distillates of sugar cane, rather than brandy, are used to fortify the wines. The trade was much larger years ago, but the vineyards have suffered from *phylloxera*, mildew, and resulting bad times, while today's wines suffer from poor vinification techniques.

Leading Madeira shippers today are Blandy's, Leacock, and Cossart Gordon, which is the largest. Others are Henriques & Henriques, Kopke, Rutherford & Miles, Welsh Brothers, and Shortridge Lawton.

◆§ SUMMARY

Fino Sherries, particularly the Manzanillas aged in Sanlucar, mature more quickly than other types and are less expensive than Amontillado and Oloroso Sherries. They are also called dry, pale, or cocktail Sherries—and sometimes all three—by the trade. They taste best when chilled.

Amontillado Sherries, really old Finos, should also be quite dry, with a special, nutty taste. They are usually a degree or two higher in alcohol than Finos, and are the dry Sherries most frequently used in or with dishes that have a cream sauce or are full or rich in flavor.

Oloroso Sherries are the oldest Sherries generally available, and the most expensive. They are usually sweetened for export. Dark in color, they are also called brown Sherries, Cream Sherries, or East India Sherries. Lightly sweetened Olorosos are sometimes called Amoroso Sherries on the export market. Excellent dessert wines.

True Sherries come only from Spain, just as true Port comes

from Portugal and Madeira from the island of Madeira. Imitations produced elsewhere, sometimes good, usually bear little resemblance to the genuine wines.

Ports generally available on the American market are the Rubies and Tawnies and are usually the best buys for regular drinking. Crusted and Vintage Ports are imported in small quantities and are usually expensive. Good afternoon and after-dinner wines.

Madeiras, the most popular wines of Colonial America, are unfamiliar to most people today and are generally available in only the best stores. Like Sherry and Port, which are also relatively unfamiliar to Americans, Madeira is apt to be a surprise and pleasure to guests. Good after-dinner wine, or one to serve with dessert.

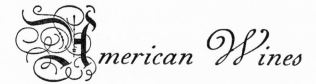

merican Wines

The Vikings called it Vineland. Early explorers told of great tangles of vines sloshing in the tidewater, heavy with grapes. They had a strange taste, these grapes, and made poor wine. But certainly European vines could flourish in the virgin soil. They withered and died. In New England, Maryland, Virginia, the Carolinas, European grapes were set out again and again, and everywhere they died.

In the seventeenth century, Spanish missionaries came up the West Coast from Mexico in the wake of the plunderers, planting missions as well as a grape they called the Mission. This grew in the fertile California valleys, producing a harsh red wine. But it was wine. Then one day, a man named Sutter saw a gleam of yellow in a creek bed, and among the thousands who swarmed westward as a result was a Hungarian who was feverish, not for gold, but for vineyard land. His name was Ágoston Haraszthy, and he finally settled with his three sons, Arpad, Attila, and Gaza, in the Sonoma valley, where Franciscan fathers were supposed to have made the best wines. By 1858 he had planted eighty-five thousand vines collected from all over Europe. He persuaded the state to send him to Europe to get more and returned three years later with two hundred thousand cuttings. In the midst of Civil War nobody cared, but he planted what he could and gave away the rest. The carefully marked identifying tags were lost in the confusion. Even Haraszthy forgot what some of them were, yet many of them grew. When the state refused to repay him for his efforts, he left for South America in disgust. The vineyards survived. Native grapes grown in the East also produced some celebrated wines. By 1877 four million gallons were produced, by 1909 fifty million. Ten years later, Prohibition struck.

In the first scramble, wine grapes were uprooted, and raisin grapes and the prune—that boon to the old and bane of the young —were planted. A loophole in the law permitted people to make things alcoholic for their own consumption, and there was a sudden demand for grapes. Easterners didn't know one variety from another, and bought big, plump table grapes for their winemaking, passing up the small and uninteresting-looking Pinots and Rieslings and Cabernets they found in the markets. Prices reversed, and growers of the noble vines were forced to rip up their shy bearers. Fortunately, a system for making grape concentrate was found, and this saved many of the best vineyards. One could buy a brick of grapes, dump it in water, have a salesman come around to inoculate this with yeast, and a week later there was a tubful of wine. Tasted just fine, it did, and the salesman took care of all the trouble of filtering and bottling.

With repeal, American winemaking started up again, only to be knocked down by the war, when the liquor industry moved into California to buy up all the potential alcohol in the form of vines and vineyards. When distilled at high enough proof, the neutral spirits could be used to make whiskey. After the war, the liquor industry got out of the wine business, and California began building a market for light red and white table wines produced cheaply and in great quantity. If these wines were too coarse and flabby, they were balanced with fruitier and more acid wines. And the wines were pasteurized so that they could not go bad on store shelves.

These are the *standard wines* of California, cheap and easy to drink. The reds are better than the whites, blends made from such common grape varieties as the Mission, Zinfandel, Carignane, Mataro, and Alicante Bouschet. They are grown mostly in the Central valley and in southeastern Ventura County, along with table and raisin grapes, which also get into the wine vats. They are marketed as Claret, Burgundy, or under other European names that have become generic. It is generally agreed that some of these wines are better than much of the *vin ordinaire* produced in France and other parts of Europe.

The *generic wines* range widely in quality, the better the producer the better the blend.

> Burgundy: *Generally full, soft, red wines.*
> Claret: *generally light, red wines.*
> Chianti: *generally full, soft, red wines.*
> Chablis: *generally dry, soft, white wines.*
> Rhine wine: *generally dry, flowery white wines.*
> Sauterne: *somewhat dry, often flowery white wines*
> (*the final* s *is generally omitted*).
> Haut Sauterne: *usually sweet, soft, white wines.*

But table wine is only a small part of wine production. Two thirds of all California wines, over ninety-five million gallons annually, are dessert wines, raised to about 21 per cent alcohol by the addition of brandy, sweetened with sugar, and called port, sherry, or muscatel. They are not at all like the European wines whose names they take. They claim no distinction, they are popular as the cheapest source of alcohol, and are called "smoke" or "Sneaky Pete."

California's best wines are called *varietals*, the names of grape varieties from which they are made appearing on the labels. There are probably not ten thousand acres of fine wine grapes in California, but more are being planted every year. New varieties of grapes, the hybrids, show great promise for more good wines in great quantity. In the East, hybrids are also being used with great success. In both areas, wines from the hybrids are usually identified by number, so their names may never appear on a label. In the East, native grape names appear on the label, identifying the eastern variety.

The varietal wines are generally good in quality, the finest being the red wines. The Cabernets from top producers are at present the best wines of California, often equal in quality to the lesser château-bottlings of Bordeaux. Plantation of Italian grape varieties is small in California, but the best varieties show great promise for the future. There is a feeling that California can produce oceans of good wines, but only small quantities of fine wines from the noble varieties.

GOOD RED WINE VARIETALS

Barbera: This Italian grape of Italy's Piedmont can produce full, fruity red wines.

Cabernet Sauvignon: This Bordeaux grape is usually called simply Cabernet in California, where it produces delicate, balanced red wines that require five or six years to mature. Perhaps a thousand acres are planted. Its cousin, the Cabernet Franc, can also produce superior wines.

Freisa: Often called Fresia in California, this Italian grape from the Piedmont can produce good, fruity young red wines.

Gamay: This red Burgundy grape that excels in Beaujolais can produce excellent young, fruity wines.

Grenache: This pink wine grape of Tavel produces in California *rosé* wines that are generally the equal of any pink wine from Europe.

Pinot Noir: This noble Burgundy grape produces full, red wines of fine quality. With the Cabernet, the best red wines of California. Perhaps six hundred acres are planted.

Zinfandel: The European version of this grape has never been identified. When well made, this full, red wine is excellent. Twenty-five thousand acres.

GOOD WHITE WINE VARIETALS

Chauché Gris: This grape of southern France produces soft, light, flowery wines that are sold as Grey Riesling, California Rhine, or California Chablis.

Chenin Blanc: A Loire grape that produces a soft, full California wine usually sold as White Pinot.

Folle Blanche: This Cognac grape produces a light, dry varietal and is also used to make California Chablis.

Palomino: The great grape of Jerez, occasionally used to improve California sherry blends.

Pinot Blanc: The great white grape of Burgundy produces the best white wines of California, dry and full. Perhaps 750 acres are planted. Used for the best California sparkling wines. Its cousin, the Pinot Chardonnay, is also used to make varietals and sparkling wines. Perhaps 250 acres can be found in California.

Riesling: The great German grape produces excellent dry, flowery wines in California. There are probably less than seven hundred acres planted. California Rieslings are usually identified on the label as Johannisberg Riesling.

Sauvignon Blanc: This Bordeaux grape produces excellent full, soft wines in California. There are perhaps two thousand acres planted. A misnamed Sauvignon Vert is used for California Chablis and Sauterne.

Semillon: The other great Bordeaux grape makes a fine, soft, usually sweet wine in California.

Sylvaner: This good grape of Alsace and Germany produces good, light, flowery wines that are invariably marketed as Riesling. Less than one thousand acres are planted.

Traminer: This Rhine vineyard grape produces good, flowery wines in California. Less than two hundred acres are planted.

Sweetened red wines from a table grape, the Concord, have been made into *kosher wines* for years, and now their market has expanded beyond the descendants of central Europeans living in the cities. Many of these, as well as standard wines made from native grapes, were first made in the East. Their popularity grew, so much so that volume wine producers of southern Europe began to imitate the wines and cash in on the word *Imported* prominently displayed on the label. In strong reaction, Californians took another look at a foreign wine that was growing in popularity, vermouth. The standard wine producers began making pale, dry vermouth at half the price of the imports. Sales rose from a couple of million gallons in 1950 to four and a half million gallons in 1958. And it was at this point that the wine industry saw a new market for still another new group of wines.

This new group of wines would taste good any time, with soda, on the rocks, or right from the bottle. They would be bland in taste, pale or bright in color, and slightly sweet. Some could even be quite dry. Any resemblance to European wines would be a hindrance, if anything. In fact, it might be better not to call them wines at all, because wines were traditionally connected with meals. And they would have brand names, like European apéritifs. These wines would be identified with good times and holiday, with American ideas of leisure, not sidewalk cafés and little bistros. The first such wine was launched in 1956, and now you can buy Thunderbird, Silver Satin, Golden Spur, and others. In a decade, there will be dozens, precisely tailored to American tastes and drinking habits. Ten million gallons were sold in 1960.

California wines can compare with those of Italy, Switzerland, Germany's lesser vineyards, and such French districts as the Rhône, the Loire, Alsace, and southern Burgundy, and the secondary wines of the great districts.

But what is even more interesting is the fact that California will soon be producing good new wines that the world has never known. Zinfandel grapes produce a hearty, full-bodied wine when grown on hillside vineyards, for instance, and many of the lesser varieties surpass themselves in California.

California now produces more varieties of wine than any other wine district on earth. The new grapes will add to the number. And while some growers say there are too many varieties now, the majority get the gambler's glint when new varieties are mentioned. For there is something called wine fever.

Vintners can't be impatient. But they cannot help running a constant fever, either. There are the untried grapes and the untried soils—Everests on every side. There is the quickening of spring every year, the long summer, the ripening fall, and the winter for planning, to think and prepare. Vintners aren't impatient. But there is always something new under the sun, and they are not happy until they've tried it out. Which means more and more good wines.

There are great things afoot in blending varieties. Twenty-two different grapes go into the making of the red wine of Châteauneuf-du-Pâpe. California and the East have never tried such complex blends. But there have been marked successes in blending two or three varieties. The generic wines of all the top vintners are well made and well balanced. And many of them are not blended to traditional types, but are simply blended to bring out the best in the different grapes.

As a result, winemaking in America is heading in two directions. The varietals are more and more expressing what happens to the great grapes when planted in California vineyards. The generics are showing what good winemakers can do when they get good wines to work with; native grapes and hybrids in eastern vineyards produce better wines every year. The growing market is encouraging the winemakers to make more and better wines. It's a good future wherever one looks, with every prospect pleasing.

The Napa Valley

You drive across Golden Gate bridge, rolling along between the round brown hills on the sweeping highway, and across the bay are the white chips of San Francisco. The road cuts off to the right, and after half an hour or so, past the town of Napa, the long valley begins, with low hills on either side. Some are wooded, others are bare knolls with deep green clumps of bushes and evergreens on their flanks. The valley floor is flat, curving up to the hills. A macadam road runs down the center, a spur track beside it. Orchards for a time, then the vineyards begin, a string of houses, a store or two, the bulk of a large stucco building on the right, and a sign: *Beaulieu Vineyards, Rutherford, Napa Valley, California.*

✑ *BEAULIEU VINEYARDS*

Georges de Latour came to the Napa Valley from Bordeaux in the 1880s, and by the turn of the century his vineyards were producing wines from Bordeaux cuttings. For forty years he made his wines in the great tradition, and now his daughter and her husband, the Marquis de Pins, continue to do so. For the past thirty years the cellarmaster has been André Tchelistcheff, a Russian who learned his lore in Burgundy—where they also had trouble pronouncing his name. He is also adviser on winemaking to the Buena Vista winery in the neighboring valley of Sonoma. He, and other winemakers, work closely with the experiment station at the wine college at Davis, part of the University of California where Drs. Amerine and Winkler have worked on many of California's wine-production problems. Two of these have to do with sun days and yeast cultures.

A sun day is one that has the amount of sun needed to ripen grapes. Burgundy needs 150, Bordeaux needs 170, and Dr. Amerine defined California wine districts in these terms, by zones. Zone 1 is high in the hills, too cool for ripening most grapes. Zone 2 is similar to Burgundy; there are several such sections in Napa and Santa Clara. Zone 3, similar to Bordeaux, is also found there, but is much more common in Sonoma and Livermore. Zone 4 includes the central part of the Sacramento valley and the region around Cucamonga near Los Angeles. The most important part of Zone 5 is in the San Joaquin valley south of Merced. These last two produce hot-climate grapes. Noble vines would ripen in such hot zones, but the wines would be ordinary. Each zone is even from year to year, and while no year is apt to produce exceptional wines, neither is there apt to be a bad vintage.

Because various grapes may be planted in adjoining vineyards, wild yeasts cannot be used for fermenting, as can be done in European districts, where yeasts for any particular district are similar. In California, yeast cultures are used. No single yeast causes fermentation, but rather families of them, various strains acting at different points during the fermentation, their actions overlapping and supplementing one another. Some yeasts have a negative effect on proper vinous fermentation, and even where the natural yeasts found in the bloom on the skin of the grapes are used, some yeast cultures are being employed. In California, carefully controlled strains insure a balanced fermentation, suited to the grape varieties planted in the various zones. The result depends less on variations in soil than on details of winemaking.

Beaulieu has some six hundred acres in vine, and across the road are the plantations of Inglenook Vineyards, of about the same size.

⤸ INGLENOOK

Rutherford is a string of a dozen buildings on the right side of the road as one goes up the valley from the town of Napa. Vineyards are on the left, and opposite the one cross-street of the little town is its continuation, a wide, raised, macadam road flanked by almond trees with whitewashed trunks. A neat wooden sign says *Inglenook Vineyards*, and as one drives up to the western foothills, all that can be seen is a small frame ranch house under giant trees. There is a long, low shed; opposite this is a massive masonry front three stories high, a couple of hundred feet long. The great winery suddenly looms in front, white dormers cutting its roof line, a central block of cut, dressed stone, flanked by long, ivy-covered wings. The winery was built in the 1880s by a Finnish sea captain named Gustave Niebaum, who had made a fortune in the Alaskan fur trade. He made some of California's first fine wines, and his descendants continue the tradition.

John Daniel, Niebaum's great-nephew, has run the winery since the 1930s. This is a family business, like the neighboring Beaulieu vineyards. Daniel grew up at Inglenook, fishing for steelhead in the narrow river that cuts through the foothill vineyards, hunting the deer, birds, and small game that live in the hills.

At Inglenook the Pinot Noir is picked first, several days before the Chardonnays. After that comes the Sylvaner, or Franken Riesling, and then the other whites, and finally the Cabernet. Beaulieu and Inglenook constantly vie with each other to see who can produce the best Cabernet Sauvignon, the wines being considered equal to good St. Emilions. Inglenook's light Pinot Noir is always highly praised, as are reds made from the Gamay and the

Charbono. A soft, full white wine from the Chenin grape of the Loire is marketed as White Pinot.

The Inglenook cellars are a model. Originally, a trench was dug into the hill. A stone arch was built in the trench, and the dirt dumped back in around the arch. The front of the arch was flush with the face of the hill, and here was built the façade. The rear of the tunnel was against the solid rock of the hill. It acts as a temperature balance-wheel and keeps the aging vaults almost uniformly cool throughout the year.

Captain Niebaum planted the best vines he could find, European cuttings of fifteen whites and twenty reds, and he followed the best in winemaking tradition. He was insistent on cleanliness. Nothing is more important in winemaking. Actually, wine is sturdy, not delicate, but like milk it is susceptible to bacterial spoilage. It can go bad easily, and that's why cleanliness is so vital. And the less you fool with it, the better it is. In Napa, they like to let the grapes make the wine.

Most of the producers of California's top wines now employ the slow-fermentation process, extending fermentation time by cooling the wine while it is working. Some of them do not put vintage years on the label, contending that there are slight variations in the wine from year to year.

But differences in the wines do reflect differences in the winemaking techniques of the cellarmasters—as to when to pick the grapes and how long the wines should be fermented; what handling should occur in the process, or how long the wines should remain in the storing casks before being drawn off into the aging barrels, or how long they should be aged. The only constant thing about the cellarmasters is that they all try to make wines characteristic of the grapes from which they are made. The arguments about technique are long. And they are critical.

But much handling and long aging removes freshness from the wine. Quick vinification, little handling, and adequate aging to round out the wine result in fresh, firm wines, full of taste. In most wineries, the Cabernet and Pinot Noir are well aged, partly because these wines take a long time to mature, but also because they can achieve a certain delicacy. The top producers are constantly manipulating these values, experimenting to make the best wines from their grapes. Some preserve the young, fresh taste one year and will work the following year to develop the delicacy of a wine.

But all are agreed on one thing: let the grapes make the wine. This means different things in different wineries; one of the pleasures of wine is to taste the differences.

☙ MARTINI, KRUG, AND OTHERS

The vineyard road crooks just at the edge of Rutherford, near the corner of the big building of the Beaulieu winery. It crosses the railroad tracks, then straightens out again for another three miles, running between vineyards and orchards, then ahead appears another big stucco winery, Louis M. Martini & Son.

The Martinis are particularly proud of their mountain vineyards, some six hundred acres in the Mayacamas range between the Napa and Sonoma valleys. Their white wines have a particularly fine reputation.

Almost across the road is the Napa Valley Cooperative Winery, with more than one hundred fifty members, who produce a complete range of wines.

There are several smaller wineries that carry on extensive experimentation with various grape varieties, producing excellent wines in small quantities, some of which find a market outside California. Among these are Frederick McCrea, J. Leland Stewart, Freemark Abbey, and Schramsberg—a vineyard where Robert Louis Stevenson spent part of his honeymoon and which is described in his "Silverado Squatters." Of these small wineries, that of Mayacamas has perhaps the greatest reputation. Its vineyards lie in a great scoop of mountaintop high above the valley.

The main town in the Napa valley is St. Helena, and just beyond the town is the Beringer winery, on the left side of the road. Most of the Beringer wines are sold in California, both reds and whites being marketed under generic names. Grape names are not used on many labels.

Across the road is the Krug winery, run by the Mondavi family, who are vigorously experimenting with white wines. A few of these can now be found outside California, among them Traminer, Johannisberg Riesling, and Pinot Blanc. By prompt vintaging and bottling, and by fermentation at low temperatures, the Mondavis are making wines that do not have the heavy softness of most California whites.

⋙⋘

The Sonoma Valley

Sonoma runs parallel to Napa, and it might be called the Piedmont of California, because many of the vineyards in the south were founded by Italian families and are planted in Italian grapes. Around the town of Ukiah, mostly red wines are made, from the Barbera grape of the Piedmont, the Petit Sirah of the Rhône, and others. The wines are generally fuller than those of Napa. One of the most interesting grapes is the Zinfandel, which has never been traced to its European source, and which can produce excellent full, fruity wines in Sonoma, Napa, and Santa Cruz, when grown in the hill vineyards; elsewhere, Zinfandel wines are less than ordinary.

Farther south is Italian Swiss Colony, one of the giants of the industry, whose post-office address is Asti. Their *Tipo Chianti*, or Chianti type, is one of the most popular of the standard wines, as are those sold under their Gold Medal label. They market wines with grape names under the Asti label, and ship enormous quantities of wine east in tank cars, where it is bottled by the buyers under local brand names. Roma, which owns some vineyards in Sonoma, and other volume producers do much the same thing.

Perhaps the best of the large producers are the Christian Brothers, who own vineyards and buy wines in Sonoma, Napa, and elsewhere, and whose standard wines and brandies have national distribution. Wines from these volume producers are generally light, soft, and without much character, but can often be better than the frequently hard and acid *vin ordinaire* one drinks so happily in Europe.

The smaller wineries of Sonoma, whose production is consumed almost entirely in California at present or whose wines are shipped east for bottling under local brand names, regularly produce good wines. As the market grows, their names as producers will be found on bottles outside of California. Among them are Berti, Black, Cambiaso, Foppiano, Frei, Kornell, Mazzetti, Mazzoni, Nervo, Oneto, Parducci, Pastori, Pedroncelli, Sebastiani, Seghessio, Sink, and Sudini. One of the famous old vineyards was Fountaingrove, which may in the future produce fine wines, as they did in the past. Another formerly famous winery was Valliant, now a whiskey warehouse.

The original Haraszthy vineyards are still in production, part of the Buena Vista Winery, which is owned by Frank Bartholomew, the president of United Press International. A wide variety of wines are produced, many of them available throughout the country.

The most famous sparkling wine of California comes from F. Korbel & Bros., west of Santa Rosa. The sparkling wine is made by traditional Champagne methods.

≈§ ៖≈

The Livermore Valley

The Livermore Valley is in Alameda County, across the bay from San Francisco. It is famous for the white wines from Concannon and Wente, wines made from the same grapes and tasting similar to those from the Bordeaux districts of Graves and Sauternes. Both have begun plantings of Pinot Blanc and Pinot Chardonnay, the white Burgundy grapes, and so have Ruby Hill and Garratti, two smaller producers. Red and rosé wines are made, but those from Napa and Sonoma are generally better. There is a smaller district near the bay, outside Irvington, where the most famous producer is Weibel, noted for its sparkling wines. Los Amigos, now being overrun by suburbs, still makes some good wines, as does Paul Rhodes. The Livermore valley and the Wentes command most attention.

The Livermore valley has a gravelly soil that drains quickly, and it was here in 1883 that Carl Wente decided that he could make good white wines. His sons, Herman and Ernest, have proved him right, for the two brothers have been making white wines from the family vineyards all their lives.

The Wentes have nearly 500 acres in white grapes, and they buy the produce of another 350-odd acres, crushing about two thousand tons a year. Sometimes vinification practice consists in making wine from a blend of Semillon, Sauvignon, and Muscadelle de Bordelais. The Wentes make precisely the same blend. They call it *Château Wente*. It's a generic wine, for there's more than one grape variety in it. All their generics are also labeled *Valle de Oro*, which is what the Spanish called the valley; the only gold from the vale is the color of the wine. The first California wines all carried old-world names, simply because the old names were so famous. To clear up the confusion, the Wentes started varietal labeling, beginning in 1936, the first California vintners to do so. They used the name of their own valley.

But the old-world names are still known. Sauternes is the most interesting, just because it has changed the most. The French spelling has been Americanized a little, dropping the final *s*. And somewhere along the line the belief arose that *Haut Sauterne* was better than just plain *Sauterne*, and it's common practice to see the meaningless phrase on a label. In the same way, somebody got the idea that there was such a thing as a dry Sauternes. There isn't, but people ask for it, and so the phrase is often seen on a label for a California dry wine.

The white grapes from Bordeaux produce a light, fresh, flowery wine in California. They possess a certain natural sweetness that can be preserved by stopping fermentation or by allowing the grapes to ripen very fully. This is particularly true of the Semillon, which produces the sweetest of the table wines. And yet the Wentes make an excellent dry wine from Semillon, by picking the grapes promptly and not allowing them to lose some of their juice by staying on the vines, which is what is done when they want that extra concentration of grape sugar for a sweet table wine.

The Wentes have two concerns, when it comes to white wines, and these illustrate the part man plays in making good wines. One concern is to make varietal wines that are characteristic of the grape. But the Semillon can make a good dry wine and also a good sweet wine; the Wente brothers make both. Another concern is to make good generic wines. These are the result of blending, of balancing the qualities of one grape with those of another; this they can do in making such wine types as Chablis and Château Wente.

ᨏᨏ

Santa Clara

Santa Clara is at the south end of San Francisco Bay, hemmed in by the Santa Cruz Mountains. Leading producers are the Novitiate of Los Gatos, which makes a small quantity of excellent table and sacramental wines, and the Mirassou vineyards, which are planted extensively in fine grape varieties, wines from which are being marketed under the vineyard name. Until recently, many of the best wines were marketed by the most prominent of the Santa Clara producers, Almadén, which makes some of the most popular of the fine California wines.

Up in the mountains, outside the town of Saratoga, are sites for extremely promising vineyards. The first plantings were made there by Paul Masson, a pioneer whose name is now a brand name for wines made from grapes purchased from many small producers.

In the mountains and up the bay are several producers of fine wines, the most outstanding being Martin Ray, who has made perhaps the best of all California wines, but in small quantities. There are legends about some of his Cabernets, said to be equal to some of the greatest wines of Bordeaux. He has made exceptional wines from the Gamay, as have the Digardi vineyards in Contra Costa County, leading many experts to assert that the Gamay, not the noble Pinot or Cabernet, should be made the grape of California, along with the Italian and Rhône varieties. Another famous producer is a San Francisco lawyer, Chaffee Hall, whose Hallcrest wines made from Sauvignon and Riesling are classed as two of the best white wines of California. To the south of his mountain vineyards are those of Valliant and Sons, where fruity white wines are produced. But the wines that are generally available across the country are those from Almadén.

❧ ❧

New York State

The early colonists made wines from grapes they found growing wild, and Captain John Smith reported on twenty gallons he had pressed. The vines might, he said, produce good wines "were they well manured." His optimism was not borne out. The native wines continued to be acid and light in alcohol, with a strange wild taste.

For two centuries the colonists tried to make European vines grow. The European varieties are a single species, *Vitis vinifera*, but the roots of the vine of wine could not resist the burrowing louse, the *phylloxera*, which wasn't identified until the nineteenth century, when it devastated European vineyards. The colonists tried again and again. There seemed no point in domesticating the native vines because of the wild taste. Smith reported on the Messamins, saying the taste did not "so well please"; these came to be called the Muscadine. One of the varieties, the Scuppernong, gained some renown, perhaps not so much for the taste of the wine as for the tang of the name. The native grapes were *Vitis aestivalis*, *Vitis riparia*, and *Vitis labrusca*, and the English translation of the last name pointed to the trouble. Labrusca is the fox grape, and the wines had a musky, foxy smell and taste, pleasant if not too strong, but strange. Not only was this foxiness unusual, it was often overpowering in the wine and was enough to discourage experimentation.

There were accidental crosses between native and European vines, however, and in the first decades of the nineteenth century, the Alexander, the Isabella, and the Catawba were widely planted. Everybody was sure that they were European vines at first, but the

foxy taste developed strongly. Because of their early promise, however, experiments with other native vines were begun, and the wines
were praised. A miserable verse by Longfellow is regularly quoted and
has become a part of wine lore:

> Very good in its way
> Is the Verzenay,
> Or the Sillery soft and creamy;
> But Catawba wine
> Has a taste more divine,
> More dulcet, delicious, and dreamy.

The Catawba has been traced to a vineyard in the District of
Columbia. It made the fortune of Nicholas Longworth, who sold
cuttings to eager growers on the shores of Lake Erie, along the
Ohio and the Hudson, in New Jersey and Missouri. The red Norton
and the misnamed Missouri Riesling appeared, and then from
Delaware (Ohio) and Concord (Massachusetts) came two grapes
that made great names for themselves. The red Concord was handsome and juicy and hardy, an excellent table grape, but the wine
was too foxy and remains so. The white Delaware is generally considered the best of the old vines and is used in present-day sparkling
wine blends along with the Catawba. Vineyards in New York State,
around the Finger Lakes and in Chautauqua County, were established with these grapes; other vineyards were planted in the Middle
Atlantic States and the Midwest.

The art of cross-breeding to develop hybrids had come into its
own, and hundreds were developed on both sides of the Atlantic.
The desire was to find hardy, heavy-bearing vines that would produce good wines in great quantities. Experimentation in the East
was cut short by the establishment of California wines as well as
by Prohibition.

But there was a great need for new varieties in eastern vineyards
after Repeal. Only the most fruitful districts in New York, Ohio,
and along the south shore of Lake Erie remained, but these could
be expanded. A newspaperman, Philip M. Wagner, began experimenting with his own hybrids and those developed in Europe.
From his Boordy Vineyard near Baltimore, he began to sell cuttings
of his hybrids to eastern winemakers and amateur enthusiasts, while
the large eastern producers began to expand their experimental

plantings. These are beginning to flourish, offering a whole new range of American wines.

These hybrids bear the name of the man who first produced them, and are identified by numbers. The names, at least, will become familiar: Baco, Couderc, Burdin, Galibert, Joannes-Seyve, Kuhlmann, Landot, Ravat, Seibel, and Seyve-Villard. The New York State Experiment Station at Geneva is developing some white wine varieties that will someday be widely planted. Wines from hybrids will taste like those from the long-established European vineyards, with secondary characteristics imparted by the locations where they grow. Their use will probably extend the wine-growing areas of the world, and raise the quality of standard wines. And always remains the hope for a miracle, some marriage of soil and vine that will produce a wonder.

There are still some vineyards planted along the Hudson. At High Tor French hybrids are being used; farther up the river, near Highland, are the vineyards of the Bolognesi winery, where American grapes produce pleasing country wines.

In the Niagara District, between Lake Erie and Lake Ontario, Château Gay produces a sparkling Delaware that has won praise. This region is also beginning to make wines from French hybrids. On the Canadian side, an ardent viticulturist named de Chaunac has planted many of the new French hybrids and is now making a few wines from them that are the wonder of eastern growers. He is technical director of Bright's Wines, Ltd., which has extensive acreage in Delaware, Catawba, and Concord grapes, as well as others, from which is produced a range of standard wines. Bright's is the most progressive of the Canadian firms and de Chaunac is becoming something of a legend because of the wines he makes, and because he has successfully grown Burgundy's Pinot Noir. The Niagara peninsula, parts of which extend as far south as Pennsylvania, has become one of the most important vineyard districts in America, its vineyards between the two Great Lakes being capable of producing some of America's most distinguished wines.

The Finger Lakes district, centering around Hammondsport, is the most important wine-producing center in the East. Vineyards are concentrated along the southern shores of Keuka and Canandaigua Lakes—great rolling waves of greenery high on the bluffs above the long, deep lakes. The bluffs rise back of the vineyards to

protect them from the icy winter winds, and the lake waters keep
the temperature from dropping too far below freezing, but this is
probably the coldest vineyard district in the world during the winter.
It may be because of this that there is a general idea that the
Finger Lakes region is the Switzerland of the East, and that the
wines are like Swiss ones. The wines are made from American
grapes, and share with the Swiss wines only a tendency to lightness
and acidity.

The Widmer Wine Cellars are the most important producers of
wines from American grapes. They have specialized for decades in
fine table wines made from the Delaware, Catawba, and Elvira,
among others. The growing season is long enough to permit the
grapes to ripen well, but occasionally Will Widmer and his brother
decide a wine is exceptional and they will denominate it by the
vintage. They also produce a group of well-made generic wines; one
of the best is Widmerheimer, reminiscent of German wines in that
it is white and flowery.

The Finger Lakes are noted for their sparkling wines, well
blended from the American grape varieties, primarily Delaware and
Catawba, with some others, such as Elvira. One of the best winemakers in the country is Charles Fournier, the director of the
Urbana Wine Company. Fournier is an eager experimenter with
hybrids, having perhaps the most varied collection of such grapes.
Two grades of sparkling wines are produced, Gold Seal and a
premium brand called Charles Fournier. Another old firm in the
district is the Pleasant Valley Wine Company, which produces the
excellent Great Western sparkling wine. Both companies produce
a complete line of wines.

By far the largest producer is the Taylor Wine Company, which
has the largest plantation of hybrids, as well as much acreage in
native grapes. They, too, market a complete line of wines, and are
constantly experimenting to improve American winemaking techniques. Grayton Taylor is a leader in the fight against the "tax on
bubbles," which makes sparkling wine high in cost and greatly
limits the market for many of America's most distinguished wines.
There are several smaller producers in the district, but their wines
are rarely as good as the four leaders', and distribution is restricted.

◆§ §◆

Ohio and Elsewhere

Along the south shore of Lake Erie are many vineyards, the industry centering around Sandusky, west of Cleveland. Those in New
York's Chautauqua County are planted mostly in Concord, and are
used for making kosher and sweet wines of slight interest, but as
one goes west, the vineyards are planted in Catawba. The most
celebrated firm is Meier's Wine Cellars, some of whose vineyards
are on islands in the lake. Their sparkling wines have the higher
reputation, but they make several pleasant white table wines. At Sandusky, National Distillers produces the good Bellows sparkling wines
and Lejon vermouth. Several small firms that began making wines
in the early days of the century continue to produce good wines
that have some distribution, among them Dorn, Engels and Krud-
wig, and Lonz. There is considerable acreage of Concord grapes in
Michigan, around Paw Paw; wines from these rarely get out of the
state, which is no loss. There used to be a good many vineyards
around Hermann, on the Missouri, where the American Wine Company once produced Cook's Imperial sparkling wine, but the brand
is now owned by Schenley and the wine is made from the California production. This is true of most of the local brands found
in the cities of the East and the Midwest; bulk wines are brought in
from California for final finishing and bottling, to be sold under
various brand names.

Egg Harbor, New Jersey, and the country around Charlottesville,
Virginia, were once important local wine-producing areas. They
may become so again. Much of the possible vineyard acreage across
the country has never been tested, but here and there, from Texas
to Rhode Island, farmers and amateurs are experimenting with small
plots of hybrids. Most of the cuttings come from that fountain of
hope, Phil Wagner in Baltimore, and while no good wines may
be produced for a decade or so, a good many people are having a
lot of fun serving honest wines they have made themselves.

༻§༺

South America

Wines are made from European vines in many parts of Central and South America. There is great potential in Mexico, for instance, as elsewhere. Much of the wine now produced is good, and almost all of it is consumed in the countries in which it is made. Chile is the exception, with vineyards concentrated just north of Valparaiso and around Talcahuaho, to the south. Wines from the Sylvaner, often called Riesling on the label, are generally bottled in the squat flasks used for Steinwein; so are many of the reds. Sauvignons are grown extensively. The wines are generally fresh and fruity, full in body, and the reds need four or five years to round out. The whites are some of the best buys on the market today, generally being very low in price. The whites should be as young as possible; there are some on the market claiming to be from vintages of a decade ago; if they were genuine, the wine would be completely maderized. They should be light in color, without a tinge of brown, the tell-tale sign of a white wine that has oxidized. The wines are marketed under the name of the vineyard, which is generally named after the proprietor. Names to look for are Undurraga, Santa Rita, Tarapaca, and Vial.

Across the Andes in Argentina, the vineyards parallel those in Chile, extending from Tucumán to Neuquen, a distance of some eight hundred miles. The vineyards were planted by Italians who went there around the turn of the century, and today more than three hundred million gallons are produced each year, twice California's production. Ordinary wine, called *chica*, comes from around Mendoza, and the best wines, rarely exported, come from the fertile area called Río Negro, around Neuquen. Wines from the other producing countries—Brazil, Uruguay, Paraguay, and Peru—have no present distinction and are not exported.

Vermouths and Apéritifs

The world is full of surprises, and one of them is apt to occur on your first day in Italy, when you sit down in a sidewalk café, at last, and order an *amari*. It sounds like the drink of love, perhaps a little sweet and slightly tonic, thirst-quenching and refreshing, tinkling with ice and fizzy with soda. It isn't that at all. Amari is served in tiny glasses, often without ice, sometimes with a melting chip or two, bitter as gall and wormwood. One glass makes you ravenous. Amari are simply bitters, or bitter vermouths, often flavored with quinine, with an intense concentration of taste. They can be used in mixed drinks, with soda, wine, or vermouth itself. A famous one is Carpano's *Punt e Mes*, not to be confused with the equally famous Campari bitters or Fernet Branca. But only the Italians seem to like to drink them straight.

271

Vermouth began to come into its own in the late eighteenth century when Antonio Carpano began selling his tonic wine in Turino. He steeped various herb extracts in sweetened brandy, then added this to white wines. In a few decades, there were dozens of versions, and today Turino is the center of the Italian vermouth industry.

By tradition, Italian vermouth is sweet, red or white, with at least 15.5 per cent alcohol and 13 per cent sugar. Most firms also make a dry white vermouth, at least 18 per cent alcohol and less than 4 per cent sugar. A couple of dozen herbs are used, but the basic taste still comes from wormwood blossoms. White wines of the Piedmont are used, the fermentation being halted so that much of the grape sugar remains in the wine. Any dark color usually comes from aging, or the addition of caramel.

French vermouths, most of which are made in Marseille, are traditionally dry vermouths based on white wines of the Midi, which are made more acid than a table wine. They are often lighter in color than the Italian vermouths, often as pale as a white table wine. A particularly pale and dry vermouth is made in the Savoie, from local wines, especially in Chambéry.

Vermouths are made all over the world, in the traditional manner. In northern Europe, fruit wines are often used in addition to regular ones. A trend toward pale, dry cocktails has led to the bleaching of vermouths so that they are extremely pale, and light in taste. Because these have so little taste and character, one is as good as another. The fashion is changing again, and traditional vermouths are coming back in favor; this is sensible, because so little of a fine vermouth is needed to impart its taste to a drink.

Because vermouths contain so much flavoring material, they often change taste after being opened for a few weeks. Half-bottles which are used up fairly quickly are apt to be sensible buys.

Many apéritifs, which are generally known by proprietary names, are essentially flavored wines with quinine added. Most of them have a red color and are made from red wines, such as Dubonnet or Byrrh, although some are made from white wines, such as St. Raphael. They are generally light in alcohol, usually under 21 per cent. Some are higher in alcohol, like Amér Picon, which is really a liqueur but is drunk as an apéritif. The absinthe variations, also high in alcohol and usually classed as liqueurs, are also drunk generally as apéritifs or after-dinner drinks, most often mixed with water. Lillet is flavored with quinine, with Armagnac as the spirit.

The wines and spirits used in making these aromatic wines are aged well before the flavoring agents are added. The method of providing sweetness varies, but the best qualities of these wines are sweetened with *mistelle*, which is made by adding brandy to unfermented grape juice, in much the way that sweetening wines are made for Spanish Sherries. These are also well aged before they are used. Mistelle is often used by itself as an apéritif base.

Several wines are excellent apéritifs, the best being the dry Spanish Sherries. Some of the fortified wines of Italy, Vernaccia and Muscatel for instance, are fine apéritifs when they are dry. Many of the famous brands of apéritifs are blended in the United States with essences shipped from abroad, and these are sometimes tailored

V E R M O U T H S   A N D   A P É R I T I F S

APÉRITIFS	ITALIAN VERMOUTHS	FRENCH VERMOUTHS
Amér Picon	Carpano	Barton & Guestier
Amourette	Campari	Boissière
Byrhh	Cinzano	Cazalis & Prats
Dubonnet	Cora	Chambéry Dolin
Lillet	Fernet Branca	Cinzano
Pernod	Fratelli Ferrero	Cora
Pikina	Fratelli Folonari	Noilly Prat
Quinquina	Freund Ballor	Nuyens & Co.
Roc	Gancia	Vernat
St. Raphael	Martinazzi	
Suze	Martini & Rossi	
	Mirafiore	
	Ruffino	
	Stock	

to the American taste, being milder than their European counterparts. Several apéritif wines have been introduced on the American market by California producers, generally imitations of European models. They are called specialty wines in this country, and there is probably an enormous market for them when their quality improves.

There's a theory that people like bitterness more and more as they reach maturity, this taste being particularly pleasing before a meal, to contrast with food, most of which has a sweet savor. We are not apt to think of steak or fish or chicken as sweet, yet most meats and vegetables and sauces have this predominating quality. Apéritifs, with their bitterness, and table wines, with their lack of sweetness, whet the appetite and bring out food flavors. Wine buffs are apt to be amused at the French, who like to drink sweet apéritifs before a meal, but the bitterness in the taste is what makes them pleasing, particularly when they are served cold, or with soda and a twist of lemon, as one sits in a sidewalk café watching the world go by.

Ale and Beer

In the old days, the burgomasters of the town tested the beer; in Munich, three were needed, clad in leather breeches. The new beer was called *Salvator*, and the test took place in March. A wooden bench was set in the center of the cellar, the new beer poured over it, and the trio sat down. For an hour they sat immobile, singing thrice a drinking song that was traditional for the occasion, each rendition lasting twenty minutes. Then they stood up. There was great rejoicing if the bench stuck to their breeches, for this was the sign of good beer. Drinking began on April Fool's Day, when the chief burgomaster, decked in robes of state, riding a white charger, raised his glass, then downed it to the shouts of *Prosit!* from the assembled thirsty.

Bavarian beer is dark, although light beer is also made, and both are best known as

Munich beer. *Münchener* is often said to be the finest brew on
earth. But the world capital for beer is the brewers' college in
nearby Weihenstephan, whose graduates are brewmasters all over
the globe. Beer was first made here in the eighth century. The
story goes that a Benedictine monk founded a monastery on the
mountain near the town; meditating one day, he suddenly knelt in
prayer, then rose and thrust his staff into the ground. A spring
welled forth. Beermaking began at once.

Beer is the national drink in northern countries where the vine
is rare and something better than water is needed to keep man
cheerful. All early civilizations made beer. The early Egyptians
called it *hek*, then *bousa*. Beer is made in pretty much the same
way everywhere, not because so many brewmasters are graduates of
Weihenstephan, but because brewing is a matter of boiling malted
grain, called brewing a mash, then adding hops for bitterness, and
yeast to make the liquid ferment. Rice, corn, or wheat is added to
the barley mash to give lightness.

The first boiling governs how much of the mash is converted into
fermentable substances; the longer the boiling the fuller the finished
beer. The resulting liquid, called *wort*, is drawn off into brewing
kettles, through the solid parts of grain that have settled to the
bottom. The solids are then rinsed with water, an action called
sparging, and the liquid is added to the filtered wort. Dried hop
cones are added and the wort is boiled for a couple of hours until
the *hot break*, the point solids are changed to soluble substances
by the heat. The filtered wort is cooled, then passed to the fermenting vats, where special strains of brewer's yeast are added.
Lager is fermented at less than 50° F., and ale is fermented between 50° and 70°, both for about a week.

Ale is made if the yeast works on top of the batch, and is generally stronger in taste and traditionally stronger in alcohol than
lager, which is made when yeast ferments on the bottom of the vat.
Some water is good for making ale, others are best for lager.

Lager means "to store" in German, and storing for about six
months at temperatures just above freezing brings out the character of the beer. The carbonic acid gas given off during fermentation is collected, then put back into the beer when it is ready for
shipment. If cans or bottles are used, the beer is pasteurized so that

the beer will not continue to work and possibly explode. Beer shipped in kegs is not generally pasteurized, and has a more lively, fresher taste, which is why many beer-drinkers prefer draught beer, drawn through clean coils.

Local beers gained worldwide fame, especially European lagers. The Würzburger beers from Franconia are generally fuller and the Berlin beers are often lighter than Bavarian lagers of Munich. A favorite kind of Berlin beer is *kuhle blonde*, or *weissbier*, which is so light and foamy that pints are served in very large mugs. It's supposed to take three days to get drunk on white beer, three weeks to sober up. Such light beers are meant to be drunk in enormous quantities, but the heavy beer of Dortmund that used to be called *adam* is another matter. This beer is supposed to live for a decade or more, a tankard or two making the strongest lose his head.

Pilsener, from the Czechoslovakian town of Pilsen, is one of the light, delicately hoppy beers whose name has gone around the world. The original was made by the Urquell brewery, but now there are many imitators everywhere. The Dutch beers of Amstel and Heineken are easy to find. The Danes are particularly proud of their beers, most of them light, the Tuborg and Carlsberg brews of Copenhagen being generally available. Part of the profits of the Carlsberg brewery are spent each year for sculpture, which is placed about the streets and parks of Copenhagen.

Canadian and Australian beers are particularly good, and it is possible to get good beer in France, Italy, Spain, or anywhere in northern Europe, where there are hundreds of local breweries. Some of the Canadian beers are made in American breweries to Canadian formulas. Mexican beer, the best of which is Carta Blanca, white label, is also brought in. Many of these excellent beers are higher in alcohol than American beers, up to 12 and 14 per cent. Some of the firms make special beer for export, holding them at about 4 per cent alcohol by volume, which is equal to American beers. Many people think this is too light, and that beer so low in alcohol isn't beer at all, but close to near-beer, the name for beer that is less than 1 per cent alcohol, and which the English used to call rotgut.

The English have a way all their own with beer, and most of it is ale. Brown and dark ales are made by heating the malt in the kiln until it turns brown; stout and porter are made by roasting the malt until it turns almost black. *Stout* is black, strong, creamy, and often sweetish. *Porter,* which got its name because London porters used to drink it, is lighter and sweeter, with less taste. Nobody drinks much porter these days, but a lot of stout is drunk, much of it Guinness. The stout from the Dublin brewery is supposed to be better than that from the London brewery, but the water has been matched exactly, and the distinction is slight. The company makes an *Extra Stout,* which is not sweet. Among the best stouts are: Barclay, Perkins' Imperial Russian Stout, which is the strongest; Read's; Simond's; Tollemache; and Whitbread. There's Oyster Stout, from the Isle of Man, and there used to be Milk Stout, which was the name for a particularly creamy version, but the term is no longer legal.

Bitter Ale is the pub favorite, light but hoppy; this is mixed with *Mild Ale,* which has very little taste of hops or anything else, to make half and half. "Half a best bitter" is the thing to ask for. Ten ounces—half an imperial pint—of bitter ale will be served to you. It will be only slightly cool.

X is sometimes used to denote mild ale, *XX* to denote bitter beer, and *XXX* for strong brews, which are also called Double Ale. *Old Ale* is sometimes used to identify strong ale, which may or may not be old, and *Stock Ale* is used to identify an ale that is strong and will keep for a time. *Pale Ale* identifies a lightly bitter ale, and *India Pale Ale* is light but slightly more bitter, the term once having been used for beers that were sent to the tropics.

Burton Ale originally came from Burton-on-Trent, but the name now stands for ale that is fairly heavy, dark, and hoppy. The original brewers of Burton were Bass, Ind Coope & Alsopp, and Worthington, all of whom are still magnificently in business. Burton Ale is supposed to get its distinctive taste from sulphate of lime in the water, which is extremely hard. There's a winter brew made in Burton called *old ale,* usually drunk half and half, with mild or bitter beer. Strong brews, like Bass or Worthington, throw a sediment, so that they should be poured carefully.

London water makes a softer brew because of the calcium in the water, and some of the famous ones are Charrington's, Watney's, and Young's. Other famous brewing towns are Derby, Hull, Manchester, Reading, Stratford-on-Avon, Watford, and Weymouth. The Wrexham Brewery in North Wales, and the William

Younger and J. H. Tennant breweries in Scotland, are equally famous.

Most of these companies make potent fancy brews called *strong ale* or *barley wine*, which have a long secondary fermentation in cask. Most of these are bottled beers, generally served in long-stemmed glasses, and some of the famous ones are Colne Spring Ale, Barclay's Winter Brew, Bass No. 1 Barley Wine, Ind Coope & Alsopp's Arctic Ale, Simonds' Old Berkshire, and Watney's Yorkshire Stingo. These strong, dark beers taste best when they're not too cold.

Women used to make the ale, and a few hundred years ago there was a song that described the general feeling about an alewife abrewing:

> *I'll no more be a nun, nun, nun,*
> *I'll no more be a nun!*
> *But I'll be a wife,*
> *And lead a merry life,*
> *And brew good ale by the tun, tun, tun.*

Men took over when it was realized that money as well as fun, fun, fun could be made by brewing ale for others.

Like all beers, American beers vary with the water that is used, with the brewmaster, and with the general company opinion as to what the public wants in beer, but the trend, as the ads announce, is to lightness. Brooklyn, Newark, Milwaukee, and St. Louis are the production centers for vast quantities of beer, but every major city seems to have its brewery. Americans drink more than two and a half billion gallons of beer each year, and the brew has been the favorite American drink since the Pilgrims stopped at Plymouth Rock because they were running out of beer. A Massachusetts Bay Colony brewery was founded in 1637.

Some seasonal beers are made, of which the most popular is *bock beer*. The name probably is a corruption of the German town of Einbeck, where it was said to have been developed in the Middle Ages. There's a better story about two brewers who agreed to a drinking bout to see which man's beer was better, each drinking the spring beer of the other. Finally, one of them staggered to the door for a breath of air, just as a goat was sauntering by. The buck brushed against the man, who tumbled to the floor, and lay there saying, *"Der Bock, der Bock!"* Although he meant the goat, people decided it was the beer that did it, naming one for the other. Bock beer is made from a mash that consists of two parts barley malt to one of wheat malt, and is drunk only in the spring. It is dark, bitter, and slightly sweet.

Beer is made from malted rye and barley in Russia, where it's called *kvass*, and rice is used in the Orient, although Oriental countries are turning to the European method. *Sam-shee* is the rice beer of China, and *tar-asun* is a Chinese beer made from malted wheat or barley, depending on which grain is most easily available. The best-known rice beer is the *sake* of Japan, which was originally made in China before the beginning of the Christian era. It is usually about 14 per cent in alcohol, and is not carbonated. It is served hot in small porcelain cups, some of which have a hole in them that makes a whistling sound when you take a sip. These are called singing cups.

There are several other mildly alcoholic drinks. *Mead* is a drink made by fermenting honey with water, now being revived in England; the version called *metheglin* made in Wales includes a variety of field and garden herbs. Taste varies with the flowers from which the bees make honey. Honey and apple juice are combined to make *Cyster*, while honey and grape juice are ferments to make *Pyment*, a flavored version of this being called *Hippocras*.

Cider is generally spelled *cyder* in England, where some magnificent ones are made. Fermentation is stopped by adding sweet apple juice when sweet cyder is wanted, but hard cyder, or dry cyder, is allowed to ferment completely. Hard cider is also made in the United States. *Perry* is made by fermenting pears. These are fruit "wines," and they are sometimes made sparkling by the addition of carbon dioxide.

None of these bears much resemblance to beer, but because they are lightly alcoholic, they are drunk as beer is drunk.

The flavor disappears from beer when it is too cold, and a skunky smell develops in beer if it is too warm, or exposed to the air. Cooled or well-chilled beer should be served with some head, so that the bubbles are caught in the foam, the right amount appearing when the beer is poured down the side of the glass.

There is the belief that beer after whiskey is risky. As a matter of fact, it may be a fine idea, a way to reduce the total alcoholic intake, whiskey after whiskey being much more risky. A ridiculous technical paper was presented a few years ago claiming that beer was not intoxicating because it was difficult to drink beer fast enough to send enough alcohol into the blood to make one intoxicated. This is not true.

Beer is a fine drink with fish and sea food, with pork and delicatessen, with cheese and all sorts of cold cuts, with pickled foods and sauerkraut, the last-named being often cooked in beer. Beer is a fine baste for lamb or pork roasts, and is used as a liquid in the Belgian beef stew *carbonnade flamande,* as the poaching liquid for fish, and as a base for a fritter batter and Welsh rarebit. Dried mustard moistened in beer is a fine accompaniment to spicy foods. And there is nothing like a glass of beer when you are in the open or when you've just come back from an outing on a hot day. Beer never tastes better than when it is hauled up dripping after an hour or two in the lake; it's the perfect temperature then, and the perfect thirst-quencher, the essence of holiday.

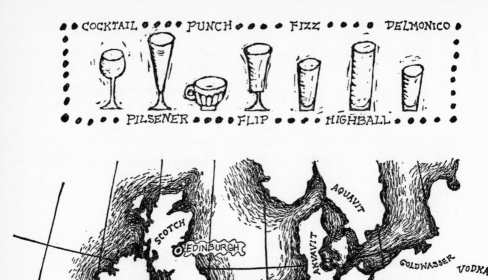

Spirits

One of the pleasantest facts found useful by man during the past few thousand years is that alcohol boils before water does, so that if a fermented liquid is heated and the steam is collected drop by drop, much of the water is left behind. The result is *spirit*. Taste and bouquet come from substances carried over with the vaporizing alcohol, and these secondary constituents are called *congeners*, or congenerics (the latter an adjective become noun), or impurities. Like love, it's a matter of chemistry.

The glorious impurities are mostly esters, acids, and higher alcohols, and there are a dozen or so parts per thousand in any spirit. Esters generally smell sweet and fruity, acids are sharp or sweet, and often weak. Higher alcohols are breakdowns of the basic ones, and can smell yeasty or quite unpleasant. One of these is fusel oil, nauseating and poisonous in large quantities, but adding to the taste of a spirit when only traces are present, in much the way that ambergris enhances a perfume.

Some congeners are undesirable, but these boil off at the beginning and end of a run, which is why the *heads* and *tails* are cut off, and only the *heart* is kept for maturing into spirits. Other congeners come from the oak casks used for aging; these include sugars, tannin, and glycerine. Glycerine adds smoothness, and sweetness, to the spirit and does not vaporize at distilling temperatures. Tannin adds body and firmness, holding the spirit together. Sugars, resins, oils, and other congeners from the cask help round out the spirit, just as do those carried over in the vapors.

The traditional distilling apparatus is the pot still, the ancient *alembic* of the Middle Ages. It is like a teakettle, with the spout on top, extended and coiled. The tapering coil is called the *worm*, and the vapors pass through it to condense and drip into a container. A pot still is inefficient, wasteful of heat, and temperamental, demanding kicks, curses, and constant care to keep it in running order. But the cantankerous copper contraption makes all the great spirits of Europe, and the Highland malt whiskies that are the base of all Scotch blends.

There is a strong belief that too quick and hot a distillation makes poor spirits, so the spirit is usually run through a pot still twice, at low temperatures. The key points in a distillation come when the heads and tails are removed. This is done by tasting the alcohol that drips through the coil. A master distiller can tell exactly when the low-boiling heads, the light fractions, are coming to an end, when the heart is beginning, and when the high-boiling tails, the heavy fractions, are due to appear. Points of cut-off vary with each run, depending on the heat of the fire and the coolness and quality of the liquid being distilled. The distiller has to know the idiosyncrasies of his still, for one may work better on warm days and another work better on cold ones. Distilling is a rare art.

The pot still is slow, finicky, and expensive to operate. In 1815, a Scot named Stein invented a continuous still, later improved by Aeneas Coffey in Dublin in 1830. It is called the patent or column still, and grain spirits are made by pouring a fermented mash, the *wash*, into one pipe and taking alcohol out of another.

The patent still consists of two side-by-side columns, the analyzer and the rectifier. A pipe containing cold wash enters the top of the rectifier, zigzags down through the column, and is warmed by rising vapors. The wash is hot by the time the pipe empties into the top of the analyzer, which consists of a series of compartments into which steam comes at the bottom. The hot wash flows down through the compartments until it is vaporized by the steam.

These vapors are carried over into the bottom of the rectifier, where they rise through a series of perforated plates, to condense on the cold zigzag pipe. The high-boiling vapors, mostly water and fusel oil, condense toward the bottom of the rectifier, drip through the perforated plates, and are run off. The main fraction (the heart) is caught on an unperforated plate. Any desired fraction can be collected, depending on where the solid plate is placed in the rectifier. The higher it is set, the greater the percentage of alcohol the condensed vapor will contain, and the fewer the congeners. The low-boiling light fractions (heads) are caught on another solid plate near the top of the rectifier, or do not condense at all and are run off as vapor. The process is continuous.

Spirits are white when they come from the still, and raw. Those distilled at low proofs are full of taste, and will remain so, even after becoming smooth after years in wood. Those distilled at high proofs have little taste, picking up most of what they do have from years in wood, or, as in the case of gins and some rums, from flavoring agents that are added. Quality depends on the nature of the wash and distillation, primarily, and partly on the development in wood.

Proof was originally determined by pouring spirit on a heap of gunpowder, then setting a light to it. The spirit was under proof if it failed to light, at proof when it burned steadily, and over proof if it exploded. The English still have a particularly ridiculous system for figuring proof, but the American one is simple: proof is twice the percentage of alcohol by volume.

When distilling whiskey, the fractions under 100 proof are called low wines, those from 100 to 159 proof are called whiskey, fractions from 160 to 192 proof are called spirits, and those from 193 to 198 proof are called alcohols. It is impossible to get pure alcohol.

Nobody really knows why one distillation is better than another, or why raw spirits become smooth with age, the chemical and physical changes being complex. What makes a great spirit is a mystery. Like love, one knows it when one finds it.

◆§ SUMMARY

Spirits are difficult to taste because they are high in alcohol, so experts mix an ounce or two of distilled water with each ounce of spirit to be judged, each sample in a large-bowled glass, for comparative judging. Off-tastes, and other characteristics, can then be detected easily.

Full-bodied Scotches, and those with pungency, generally contain a greater proportion of malt whiskies. For light drinks, these call for extra soda or water.

When a straight Bourbon and a blend are available at the same price, the blend is apt to be a better buy because better whiskies are needed to balance the neutral spirits.

Rums from Puerto Rico and the Virgin Islands are generally best buys because they carry lower duties.

An excessive flowery taste is often imparted to gins of low quality, to mask imbalances and hide harshness.

Cognacs, Armagnacs and Spanish brandies vary widely, and like all other spirits, prices in any one line are generally a good criterion of quality.

Because nearly all spirits are blended, comparative tasting is the best basis for judging quality.

Cognac, Armagnac, and Other Brandies

One of life's beautiful moments is the first taste of a great brandy. Even the fumes are heady, and there is a pleasant stinging of eyes and nose. The first sip through stiff lips is cautious, throat tense because it may be too strong, but the taste is light, electrifying, filling the mouth. Senses come to life with the swallow. The brandy is warming, vital, lingering—something felt, not simply tasted. There's no rawness, nothing to make one shudder, nothing displeasing. The lyricists are right. Brandy is an essence, the noblest of spirits, a world of taste concentrated in a mouthful.

Classically, brandy is a distilled wine; the word comes from the Dutch *brandewijn*, burnt wine. In English, the name stands for all spirits from any fruit, not just the grape. In France, all spirits, including those from grain, are called *eaux-de-vie*, from *aqua vitae*, the name medieval alchemists gave to that elixir for which they searched, the precious water of life that would keep men alive for centuries.

◄§ MARC

French brandy made from wine is named by the district from which it comes, Cognac and Armagnac. So is brandy made from *marc*, the *pomace* or cake of pulp left in the press after the juice has been squeezed out. Mixed with water and distilled, it is called *eau-de-vie-de-marc*. It has a strong, grapy, leathery taste, and may take a dozen years to lose its roughness. The best comes from Burgundy, half a million gallons of it. The lees are used to make *eau-de-vie-de-lie*. Very pungent and very rare, some thirty-five thousand gallons are made each year. It is often called *Fine Bourgogne*.

The best *Marc de Bourgogne* will carry the name of the vineyard or town from which it comes. The most expensive is the *Marc des Hospices de Beaune*, a few barrels of which are sold at each year's auction. The *Marc de l'Hermitage* is the best of the Rhônes, and there are several from Bordeaux, the best bearing the name of the châteaux that produce them. A splendid light *Marc de Champagne*, which has great finesse, can occasionally be found.

Every European district produces this brandy. Occasional good ones come from Italy, where it is called *grappa*. In South Africa it is called *dop-brandy*. Marcs demand long maturing. They taste raw and earthy when young, but when they are twenty and thirty years old, they have great power and depth of taste.

◄§ CALVADOS

In Normandy, cider is distilled to make the world's greatest apple brandy, *Calvados*, from the department of the same name. The finest comes from the Vallée d'Auge. The pomace is also distilled to make *eau-de-vie-de-marc-de-cidre*, something we know as apple-jack. Today, applejack made in America is also produced directly from cider. There's a story that cider is often frozen to remove the water, the liquid remaining being called applejack, or distilled into applejack, but if so, it has never been commercially available. Meals are long and large in Normandy, so a custom called the Norman Hole has come to be. The *trou Normand* is a pause between courses when everybody takes a rest and some Calvados before going on to the cheese and dessert. It is not unknown to have such a pause after every course.

ᘓᔓ WHITE ALCOHOLS

Most *eaux-de-vie* mature in oak casks, but there is a large group called *alcools blancs* which are aged in crocks after only a couple of years in wood and which remain clear and undarkened. These are all distilled from fermented fruit juices or a mash of the juice and pulp, and the best French ones come from Alsace. *Framboise* is made from raspberries, *Fraise* is made from strawberries, *Mirabelle* from yellow plums, *Quetsch* and *Prunelle* from purple ones, and *Kirsch* from cherries. Over thirty pounds of raspberries or strawberries are needed to make a bottle of *Framboise* or *Fraise*, and buyers from Europe's top restaurants roam the Alsatian vineyard towns to find a small grower who may sell them a crock or two. When the fruit has pits, some of these are crushed and fermented with the mash to impart a slightly bitter flavor to the *alcool blanc*. *Kirschwasser* is the German name for the cherry distillate from the Black Forest and Switzerland, *Himbeergiest* is the name for the raspberry distillate and *Pflumliwasser* for plum. The white alcohols are penetrating and leathery in taste, something like a *marc*; the taste of the fruit is strongly marked, the bouquet fruity and fine. Many people like to drink them chilled; they are at their best served in small snifters, and if the glass is warmed in the hands after the drink is gone, a series of haunting, lingering perfumes is released, all reminiscent of the fruit from which it is made.

Yugoslavs will tell you that the best of the white alcohols is their *slivovica* from Bosnia, the most famous of the slivovitzes from central Europe, made from pozega plums. The trees must be twenty years old before the plums are ready to be distilled. From Zada in Dalmatia comes *Maraschino*, made from Marasca cherries, which is superior to the Italian version. There's a fiery apricot brandy,

Barat Polinka, from Hungary, and one from blackberries, but these usually require the addition of sugar before distilling.

None of these white alcohols bears much resemblance to such sweetened commercial products as elderberry brandy or blackberry brandy, which have fruit flavoring added to spirit bases. These are more like liqueurs or cordials, which are made by infusing flavors into sweetened spirits. The white alcohols are not sweetened, although the cheap commercial versions may be blended with neutral spirits and flavoring matter to which almond essence is added to give the slightly bitter taste. The process is called *sophistication,* a general term for approximating the real thing in a laboratory, and it is hard to detect. Such brandies are apt to taste synthetic and strong in alcohol, a combination of tastes rather than a single essence of the fruit.

⊷ COGNAC

In France, brandy means Cognac, and you won't be in the prosperous little city on the Charente long before somebody tells you with firm satisfaction that all Cognac is brandy but not all brandy is Cognac. And then somebody else will tell you the story of the Bishop of Angoulême, who, when he introduced himself in Rome, received only blank stares, until he added "I am also the Bishop of Cognac." All the other bishops nodded and smiled, and one said, "Ah, the glorious See of Cognac!" Everybody loves this story in Cognac, and you need the drink to swallow the tale.

Cognac is surrounded by its vineyards, which extend almost to the banks of the Gironde, opposite the Médoc vineyards. A map of Cognac looks something like an egg with a triple yolk, the center just south of town and called *Grande Champagne,* with a semicircle of vineyards below this called *Petite Champagne,* and a group to the northwest called the *Borderies.* These three districts are surrounded by the *Fins Bois,* which is surrounded by *Bons Bois,* and all the rest, called *Bois Ordinaires.* The vineyards were first defined fifty years ago and came under the *Appellation Contrôlée* in 1936, so that from then on all Cognac had to be shipped with a certificate of authenticity, the *Acquit Régional Jaune d'Or.*

The confusing name of Champagne once meant *country* and identified the chalky soil in the midst of woods. The name has stuck, to identify the finest vineyards. Brandies are frequently shipped as *Fine Champagne*, a phrase properly used for blends of Cognacs from both Grande and Petite Champagne, at least half of which must come from Grande Champagne. In a great French restaurant, it is customary to order a *Fine Champagne* to indicate that you want a Cognac of good quality, but the phrase has no weight in a French café, where ordering *une fine* is simply another way of ordering brandy.

There are nearly 140,000 acres in the Cognac district, and almost 65,000 owners. The great shipping firms buy young brandy from the growers, or old brandies from stockers, but several own large vineyard sections as well. The Folle Blanche was once the informing vine, but now the Ugni Blanc is used most, the later-flowering vines not being so subject to spring frosts. The wine of Cognac is terrible, hard and green and usually about 9 per cent alcohol. But it is the perfect wine for distilling.

The grapes are hustled into the presshouses in September and fermented quickly, so that the wine will be acid and free of residual sugar. Many growers have their own stills, but those with few acres use the traveling pot stills that are trundled around the countryside during the winter. About two hundred gallons of wine go into the pot; the alcohol begins to boil off after two or three hours, the heads are taken off, and after eight hours or so the distiller has perhaps eighty gallons of spirit, called *brouillis*, about 25 per cent alcohol. This is combined with two other similar runs, for a second distillation, the *têtes* and *queues* being again removed. These heads and tails are redistilled with the next *brouillis*. The heart of the second distillation is called *la bonne chauffe*. It is about 70 per cent alcohol—140 proof—and in eight years it will begin to be Cognac.

Spirits from the different districts of Cognac vary widely, and blending them is an art. This is done when they have reached some maturity. The Cognac is aged in airy stone storehouses above ground. For a time, the Cognac drops quickly in strength, losing more than a per cent of alcohol a year, and the saying has it that the heavens are Cognac's best customers. After twenty years or so, alcohol evaporation slows down and the Cognacs are apt to increase slightly in alcohol. After thirty years in wood, Cognacs improve only slightly if at all; left too long they will take on a woody taste, as will any spirit. A very rough Cognac may continue to improve for fifty years in cask, while others may get no better after ten years in the wood.

The slowest maturing, most pungent Cognacs come from the district of *Grande Champagne*. They vary widely. Many need to be blended with lighter, more quickly aging spirits from *Petite Champagne* or the Cognac will be too full in body. If they are too austere, they may be blended with soft, supple Cognacs from the *Borderies*, or with those from *Fins Bois*, which have little finesse.

When the Cognacs are blended, they are again put in casks for a few months, so that the brandies can marry. The barrels used for aging Cognac come from the Limousin forests. They, too, have *crus*, like the vineyards, the best oak being in the center of the forests, where the trees grow slowly, producing dense wood. The barrels—and the storehouses themselves—slowly turn black, not entirely from the fumes of the maturing Cognac, but also because the fumes seem to help the growth of a dark green mold, giving the buildings a sooty, gloomy look.

It was once the practice to ship Cognacs in cask, but now the bottling and blending is done by the shippers. The whole operation, from cask to shipping carton, is almost automatic, with guards here and there to attend to controls, and long tables of women who complement the labeling machines by putting on the final glamor of neck label, satin cord, or tissue paper.

Each firm puts out a fairly young Cognac that sells for six or seven dollars a bottle in the U.S.—sturdy, full-tasting spirits that have been aged seven to ten years and then balanced with small quantities of older Cognac. These make some of the world's best highballs and cocktails and are used to make some of the more spectacular dishes that call for brandy. They are generally called *Three Star*.

The custom of putting stars on the bottle is said to have begun in 1811, the Year of the Comet, when sensational wines were made all over Europe. The next year was great, too, so a second star was added to the label, and so was the next, which called for another star. The stars quickly lost any real meaning, and today simply identify the young Cognac in a firm's line. Words sold better than stars in Victoria's day, and because England was the largest market, words like Superior, Old, and Pale came into use. They have no precise meaning today, but strings of letters are used to indicate the older Cognacs, the more the merrier. Very Superior Old Pale is V.S.O.P., often over twenty years old. V.O. means Very Old, usually between ten and twenty years, and so it goes. Some firms insist on calling their brandies after Napoleon, the name being first used to identify Cognacs that he liked, or that dated from his day. Spirits do not improve in bottle, and a thirty-year-old Cognac bottled yesterday will be as good as one bottled a hundred years ago. The increased cost of production and inflation have raised the price of young Cognacs, so that there is not such a wide spread between the young and old brandies today. Old Cognacs are often called *Liqueur Cognacs*, and many of them are excellent values. Price, not stars and letters, is the criterion.

Some of the growers estate-bottle their own Cognacs, and there are many small firms that ship a few cases of magnificent brandies to special customers, but most Cognacs come from the famous firms. Many of them go back two centuries and more, and were founded by Irish and English adventurers who came to the Charente in search of brandies for the British market. The two largest firms are Martell and Hennessey, and others are Hine, Delamain, Bisquit Dubouché, Rémy Martin, and Otard. Monnet, Gautier, Courvoisier, and Calvet are also known.

It is the fashion in some restaurants to serve Cognac from enormous bottles which are always half full. But Cognac is best when it is freshly opened, losing pungency and brilliance after a few weeks of exposure to the air. This is true of all fine bottled spirits, so half-bottles are excellent buys; some people buy large bottles and transfer the brandy to smaller ones that can be tightly corked.

There are some odd preferences in Cognac. Many people associate darkness with age, so young Cognacs are made the color of amber with caramel, which does not change the taste when used in small quantities. Caramel is used to mask the roughness of cheap spirts, but this is not usually necessary with fine Cognacs. Contrarily, old Cognacs are often identified with the word *pale*, the implication being that any coloring is natural. Large snifters, called *ballons*, are doted on by some, and nobody in Cognac objects if people use them, but the best glass is about the size of a long and slender tulip, curving in slightly at the top, so that the bouquet is concentrated. The glass is small enough to be warmed easily in the cupped hand. An ounce or so is a generous serving.

Ten bottles of wine are needed to make one of Cognac, and this *âme ardente*, this ardent soul of wine, has a special ability to give warmth and joy to the drinker. Victor Hugo called it the drink of the gods. Cognac can make the drinker feel like one.

⋘ ARMAGNAC

Gascons look at the Pyrenees, remember the glorious days of d'Artagnan and tell you there are still witches abroad in the land who'll get you if you don't watch out. Armagnac suits this hillbilly country of France, south of Bordeaux, inland from Biarritz and the Basque country.

Big, full-bodied, and pungent, Armagnac seems scarcely related to the light and delicate Cognac from the north. The predominant grape is the Folle Blanche, with some Ugni Blanc and Colombar. Portable stills jounce around the country during the winter, and each grower supervises the long, single distillation of his wines. The brandy comes out at slightly more than 100 proof, and goes into barrels of local black oak. During the course of years, it picks up a great deal of needed tannin, and much of the Armagnac character is said to be imparted by the wood. The best brandies come from *Bas-Armagnac*, the less hilly part of the country, in whose center is *Grand Bas*, where the vineyards are sandy and produce the lightest brandies. *Ténarèze* and *Haut-Armagnac* are also delimited areas. In barn lofts and sheds, the Armagnac matures in the small casks. During the Second World War, many casks were hidden in the hawthorn hedgerows, and some of these casks that suffered through the bitter winters and the broiling summers are particularly prized.

The Armagnac firms are small, and buying is done in the square of the little town of Éauze, in the center of the district. The farmer will have small phials of his golden Armagnacs and darker ones that are older. He will pour a few drops in the buyer's palm. The buyer will rub his palms together, then sniff his cupped hands. The bouquet, and the speed with which it disappears, is the basis of judgment, and a drop on his tongue which is spat onto the cobbles of the square confirms his opinion. If the two agree, the bargain is sealed with a drink at the Café de France, which boasts some excellent Armagnac.

Years ago, Armagnac was considered too powerful for general consumption, so it went to Cognac for blending. But when the control laws were passed in the 1930s, the district began shipping its own brandies in long-necked squat bottles, called *basquaises* after the Basque country where the shape originated. Nobody tried hard to ship fine Armagnacs in the first years of the control laws, largely because there was no tradition and less market for fine quality, but after the war a few shippers began to send out fine brandies, led by a descendant of d'Artagnan, the Marquis de Montesquiou, and the firms of Samalens, and Cave Frères. There is a local legend that Armagnac is an aphrodisiac, but even so, this headiest of brandies is little known outside France.

SPANISH BRANDY

A very full and heavy brandy that often takes twenty years to round out is made in Jerez. It is the most popular brandy of South America, and it can be extremely good, second only to the French brandies of Cognac and Armagnac. Most of the great Sherry houses produce brandies, and probably the most famous are the *Fundador* and the *Carlos Primero* of Pedro Domecq, and the *Soberano* of González Byass.

◄§ GREEK BRANDY

The brandies of Greece have an undeserved reputation, for they rarely come up to those of France and Spain. The best have a distinctive flavor that is sharp and pleasing when the brandies are aged well and not distilled at high temperatures. Much of it goes into the making of *Raki*, which is often sweetened. From Chios comes a resin called mastic that is used to flavor brandy, the product being called *Mastika*. *Ouzo* is generally brandy flavored with wormwood or anise, as well as other aromatics; these are sometimes added before distillation, and the result is a sort of absinthe that turns cloudy when water is added. Both of these are popular in the Balkans and the eastern Mediterranean.

◄§ PISCO BRANDY

One of the early settlers in Peru was the Spaniard Don Gerónimo de Cabrera; in the little town of Ica he began distilling wines, storing them in small earthenware jars made by the Indians. The Indians were of the Pisco tribe, which means bird in their language, and the brandy came to be called *Pisco*, as did the district and the port from which they were shipped. The brandy was well known in Europe even in the seventeenth century, and more than half a million gallons are made each year. The distinctive taste comes from the wild beeswax which is used to line the jars. This ardent water, *aguardiente*, goes to market as Pisco Punch, and its most popular use is in Pisco Sours.

◄§ CALIFORNIA BRANDIES

Most California brandies are distilled for use in making fortified wines, cordials, and flavored fruit brandies. A lot of *grappa* is produced in California and sold as an inexpensive spirit. But some firms work hard to make well-balanced brandies that are not heavy or harsh. The best brandies are aged in white oak casks, carefully blended, and sold at reasonable prices. Many of them are good in mixed drinks.

Scotch, Irish, and Canadian

Usquebaugh, *uisgebeatha*, whisky—the Gaelic water of life—came to Scotland in the days when Columbus was discovering America and the house of Tudor ruled England. Four centuries later, the Scots discovered English thirst and then the rest of the world discovered Scotch, so that today over twenty-one million gallons are wrested each year from the not-too-reluctant distillers. Half of it comes to the United States; the United Kingdom gets a scant six million gallons, which does little to improve Anglo-American relations, except that the money helps.

After centuries of carefree distilling, the pleasant practice was prohibited for a time in the eighteenth because of a bad harvest, and a century later the taxes began in earnest, until the excise duty today is just under twenty-five shillings, nearly $3.50 a bottle. Such wicked actions forced the Scotch to develop the art of illicit distillation and the craft of smuggling.

The trick is to get rid of the smoke. The pot still can be dismantled in a few minutes and quickly buried, but the fires that cause the boil-off attract the exciseman. The smoke from one particularly famous still was once discharged into the flue of a lime-kiln, and one of the arches in an Edinburgh bridge housed a still for years, the smoke being run off through a nearby chimney. The remote highland glens were also popular, the more inaccessible the better. The most famous were those along the river Spey, where a single glen was once said to shelter more than two hundred illicit stills. In the second quarter of the nineteenth century, Glenlivet, the greatest distillery of all, succumbed to a sensible law of temporarily reasonable duties, and the illicit stills began to disappear.

Even the Scots admit that distilling was brought to the Highlands by the Irish; the first distilleries were along the western shores, in Campbeltown and the islands of Islay and perhaps Skye, where Talisker is made. These are the richest and fullest of the malt whiskies and as a consequence are the least popular today. The Highland malts come from distilleries north of an imaginary line drawn from Greenock to Dundee, and these are the ones on which rest the fame of Scotch whisky. There are lighter Lowland malt whiskies, but the Scottish heart hies to the Highlands, to Speyside and Strathspey and Glenlivet.

The best malt whisky, Bruce Lockhart says in summing up the opinion of expert distillers, is "off granite through peat," the malt whiskey thus produced being entirely different from whisky that comes "off peat through granite." If the stream rises in the rocky hills, the clear, soft water makes better whisky than if the water used in its making comes from streams that begin on lower ground.

Scotch comes only from Scotland, not just because of the water, but because of the Highland barley that is used, the Highland peat that malts the barley, and the Highland air in which the whisky matures. There is no other spirit like a Highland malt in all the world. The distilling period runs from October through June. The summer is the "silent period," when the water warms up too much to be used to cool the new spirits. Enormous quantities are needed.

The barley is soaked for a couple of days in cold water and then spread on the malting floors to sprout. After a dozen days, the sprouting has caused enzymes to be formed, together called *diastase*, that can convert the grain's starch to sugar. The sprouted barley, now the green malt, is then taken to the kiln, where it is spread on iron screens through which passes smoke, first from peat fires and then from coke. After three days or so, growth has halted, and the malt is matured for six weeks or more, then cleaned and ground. The grist is then mixed with hot water in the mash tun. Four successive washes remove the starch from the malt, the first two being drawn off into the fermenting backs, or vats, the last two being mixed with the next batch. The sweet liquid drawn off is called the *wort*. The husks remaining are called draff, which is dried to become animal feed.

The worts are cooled, yeast is added, and fermentation is completed within seventy-two hours. The resulting liquid, the *wash*, contains about 10 per cent alcohol and tastes like unbitter beer. The wash is distilled twice, in two different pot stills.

The distillate from the wash, containing about 20 per cent of alcohol, is called the *low wines*. What remains in the still, called *burnt ale* or *pot ale*, is discarded. Many of the wash stills hold ten thousand gallons, about a third of which become low wines.

The low wines are run through small spirit stills, where the first and last part of the run, in Scotland called the *foreshots* and the *feints*, are removed. These go back into the next batch of low wines. The spent lees, left in the spirit still, are discarded.

The whisky fraction collected is usually between 125 and 145 proof. The clear new whisky is brought down to about 125 proof with spring water and stored in oak casks, preferably ones that once contained Sherry. A *first-fill whisky* is the first one to be aged in one of these Sherry butts, from which it picks up a deep amber color. The second fill is lighter. Sherry casks are in short supply these days, and treated oak casks are used, so that the whisky picks up the traditional deep color.

Each distillery makes a distinctive whisky, and part of the uniqueness comes from the still. There's the story of one battered old pot still that made fine whisky but had become so rickety that it threatened to blow up. The owner had a new one built, copying every dent and patch, and the character of the whisky remained the same. The water has much to do with whisky character, and so does the stillman, who decides when to remove the feints and foreshots. But nobody knows precisely why one whisky differs from another.

The whisky ages in unheated storehouses, rounding out at seven or eight years, although some need twelve years to reach their peak. While the legal minimum is only three years, most Scotch coming to the market is usually about eight years or so old.

The most famous Highland malt of all, and by almost universal opinion the greatest, is The Glenlivet. Dozens of distilleries added the famous name to their own, but toward the end of the nineteenth century the courts declared that the name must be restricted to the distillery in the glen of the Livet, and that all others would have to use their own name, and hyphenate the magic syllables. Some thirty do so, among them Balmenach-Glenlivet, Glenfarclas-Glenlivet, and Aberlour-Glenlivet.

The Glenlivet is in every list of great Highland Malt whiskies, but there are many others. In his book on Scotch, Aeneas Macdonald lists a dozen more that are outstanding: Balmenach, Cardow, Clynelish, Glen Burgie, Glen-Grant, Glenlossie, Highland Park, Linkwood, Longmorn, Macallan, Royal Brackla, and Talisker. Of the hundred-odd distilleries now operating, those listed below consistently appear on most lists of outstanding whiskies:

Aberlour-Glenlivet	*Ardbeg* (*Islay*)
Ardmore	*Auchentoshan* (*Lowland*)
Balblair	*Balvenie*
Ben Nevis	*Ben Romach*
Blair Athol	*Bowmore* (*Islay*)
Bruichladdich (*Islay*)	*Bunnahabhain* (*Islay*)
Dalmore	*Dufftown-Glenlivet*
Edradour	*Fettercairn*
Glen Albyn	*Glen Burgie*
Glencadam	*Glenfarclas*
Glenfiddich	*Glengoyne*
Glen-Grant	*The Glenlivet*

Glen Mhor
Glen Scotia (Campbeltown)
Glenugie
Inchgower
Knockando
Laphroaig (Islay)
Longmorn-Glenlivet
Milton-Duff
Scapa
Strathisla-Glenlivet
Tamdhu
Tullibardine

Glen Rothes
Glenspey
Highland Park
Inverleven
Lagavulin (Islay)
Littlemill (Lowland)
Macallan
Pultney
Springbank (Campbeltown)
Strathmill
Tomatin

Even a partial list is tantalizing to the Highlander, not so much because his pet distillery might be left out, as because so little malt whisky trickles into the world unblended.

The Highlander will say any Highland malt is glorious, compared to the blends available, and it is his lament that nearly all malt whisky goes to the Lowlands, to the blenders. Only a few of the still-independent distilleries, like The Glenlivet, Glen-Grant, Glenfiddich, and Balvenie, market at least a portion of their stocks as unblended Highland malt whisky.

A Highlander likes two things naked and one of them is malt whisky, goes the proverb. The wee doch-an-dorris, a farewell drink at the door, is still a tradition in the Highlands, and drams are the drink at a wedding or a wake. But the rest of the world, unmindful of the grand old whiskies, prefers blended Scotch, the lighter the better, mixed with water or soda. What a tale of change it makes.

England was drinking French brandy in the nineteenth century, millions of gallons of it, and the Scottish merchants wondered what they could do about it. Malt whisky was too full in taste for a wide trade. An instrument came to hand in 1830 with the patent still, which makes grain spirits.

Grain spirits are called *silent spirits* because they have little taste and character, even after three or four years in wood. They are made from various grains, and some barley malt is used to convert the grain starch to sugar. The grain whisky is very light in body, imparting this lightness to the malt whiskies with which they are blended, perhaps half and half. The character of the blend depends on the malt whiskies it contains—sometimes a score or more—and each firm guards the secret of its blends. There are over two thousand registered brands.

Dozens of patent-still distilleries were built in the Lowlands, and the distillers banded together to conquer the market. One of the early groups developed into the Distillers Company Limited, formed in 1877, which began buying up malt distilleries to add to their group of grain distilleries.

One of the founders of DCL was John Haig, who continued as an independent distiller and was one of the first to supply blended whiskies to the English market. Haig, along with Mackie & Co. (whose White Horse brand is based on the full, rich Islay malt from Lagavulin distillery), James Buchanan (who made Black and White famous), Johnnie Walker, and Dewar's came to be known as the Big Five and led the invasion of the English market. Together, in the last two decades of Victoria's reign, they revolutionized English drinking habits.

The Scottish blenders were masters of both business and showmanship. It was a sporting age, and Scotch was identified with sport. The whisky barons were patrons of horseracing, dog shows, team sports, and even art. Their delivery wagons and personal carriages were models of display, pulled by the finest teams that could be paired. The men knew how to attract attention.

James Buchanan came to London in 1879 and immediately ordered dinner. He trooped into the best restaurant in town with his party of twelve, all of them dressed to kill, ordered the most expensive dishes on the menu, then sat back and ordered a round of Buchanan's. The headwaiter said he didn't have any. With a roar of outrage, Buchanan swept his party out of the restaurant. The next day he had his order. Born in Canada, he was a great horseman, and famous for his manners. He had a kind of restraint that attracted attention. Not the least of these was the modest label on a bottle of Black and White, so discreet that it was stocked by the House of Commons, where the brand got its start. He was considered one of the greatest tasters of Scotch, and his opinion was desired on every important sale of blending stocks.

Tommy Dewar went to London in 1885 to find a market for the blend his father had developed in Perth. He took a booth at the annual Brewers' Show, where various tradesmen displayed their wares to a genteel crowd. Some of the booths entertained with soft melodies from music boxes. Tommy Dewar used a bagpipe. Tommy hustled around the world making the market while his brother John stayed at home to make the whisky. John became famous for his terse comments, among them "Do right and fear no man, don't write and fear no woman," and "The biggest lies are told on gravestones."

The Highlanders were of several minds about all this. They were selling more malt whisky than ever, even though the crafty Lowlanders were making the lion's share of the profits. And it was amusing to know that the English were drinking a blend and thinking it was the real thing. But generally, the Highlanders hated the blenders, and in 1905 a suit was begun to prevent the blends from being called Scotch. DCL moved in for the defense, and the *What Is Whisky?* case raged for four years until a Royal Commission decided that Scotch whisky was "obtained by distillation in Scotland from a mash of cereal grain saccharified by the diastase of malt." This was a description of grain whisky. There was nothing about double distillation in pot stills, nothing about using all barley malt. In the Highlands, the blow was as bitter as Prohibition.

The blenders gained control of the industry, and their hold was further strengthened during the First World War by the demand for industrial alcohol, a market they also developed. In 1925, DCL was united with the Big Five, mainly as a defense measure against growing government control. Today, DCL controls many of the greatest names in Scotch, and most of the malt distilleries, as well as much of the gin market—and the market for industrial alcohol; they are also deeply involved in the drug and chemical industries. It is one of the most powerful businesses in the world.

The Highlander still holds out for his malt whisky, unblended, which he calls *single whisky* or *self whisky*, and *vatted whisky*, which is made by balancing one malt whisky with another. There is still some demand for single and vatted whiskies in the world. Glenlivet sells a thousand cases of its whisky in the United States each year, and a few others can be found. But most of the world's whisky drinkers agree with the blenders. Malt whisky may be a proper tot after a tramp through the chill, damp wildness of the Highlands, goes the argument, but the man who lives in cities prefers the light, clean taste of blended Scotch whisky. It is refreshing, it is satisfying, and a dram or two doesn't make the drinker want to seize a cudgel and follow the skirling pipes on a raid against the Sassenach.

Blended Scotch whisky still has more taste and character than most spirits, with a lightness that can be gained no other way than by blending. It is famous not just because it was well sold. It is famous because it is good to drink, one of the finest spirits available in the world today.

ᐁ§ ೩ᐁ

Irish

Ireland gave whiskey to the world, everybody pretty well agrees, and *Uisge Beatha* has been made on the Emerald Isle for at least seven centuries. The word is usually spelled with an *e* today, which must certainly stand for Eire. Irish whiskey is made in much the same way that Scotch whisky is made, except that peat smoke is not used to dry the barley malt. Smokeless anthracite is used, so that no fumes pass through the barley, and no smokiness is imparted.

Both malted and unmalted barley are used, along with some oats, wheat, and rye, and the resulting whiskey takes at least seven years to mature, some experts maintaining that Irish must be three or five years older than that before the full taste is developed. The whiskeys are aged in Sherry butts or in uncharred casks made of American oak. The full, distinctive taste of Irish whiskey was popular during the nineteenth century, but lighter Scotch blends stole the market, and recently the Irish, too, have taken to blending their pot-still whiskeys with grain whiskeys in order to offer a lighter whiskey, although pot-still whiskeys are still marketed.

The pot-still whiskeys go through three successive distillations, as do the Scottish Lowland malts. The only Irish whiskeys that use only malted barley in their making are those from the North Ireland distilleries of Bushmill's.

In all, there are five Irish distilleries, each of which puts some pot-still whiskeys on the market. One of them produces a cordial based on heather honey and Irish whiskey, which is of the type of Drambuie and is sold as Irish Mist.

POT — STILL
WHISKEYS

Paddy

John Power

John Jameson

Tullamore Dew

BLENDS

Old Bushmill

Murphy

Dunphy's Original Irish

Crock O'Gold

Tullamore Dew

❧ ☙

Canadian

Canadian whiskies are light blended whiskies, each company using various grains in proportions they think will be most desirable to the greatest number. Canadians traditionally call their whiskies *Rye*, finding this a simple way to distinguish them from Scotch, which they generally call simply *whisky*. The government makes no attempt to dictate to the distillers how their whiskies shall be made, being content with minimum age and quality standards and collecting the taxes. The whiskies are sold through government stores, in standard fifths, in 40-ounce bottles that delight American visitors, and in small pints and half-pints called *mickies*—which delight the Canadians, who good-naturedly suffer all kinds of restrictions on their drinking, imposed by a government which seems to be anxious to stamp out the practice, if only the revenue weren't so great.

In Canada, Canadian whiskies are lowered in proof when prices or taxes are raised, and the proof never appears on the bottle. Today, Canadian whiskies bought in Canada are not much over 70 proof. Canadian whiskies exported to the United States must show their proof on the label, and are usually exported at 86 proof. Three major producers supply most of the Canadian whisky available: Seagram's, Schenley, and Hiram Walker, Gooderham & Worts.

Bourbon, Rye, and Corn

It is said that as soon as the colonists got off the boats, the Scotch and Irish among them took to setting a mash. They had a fine new material at hand, Indian corn. Mix it with a little rye and the distilling kettles produced something that wasn't bad, not bad at all. A year or two in the keg, and they really had something. But it was the Director General of the Colony of New Amsterdam, Wilhelm Kieft, who built the first distillery on Staten Island in 1640, putting Wilhelm Hendricksen in charge as stillman. To make assurance doubly sure, he opened the first tavern on Manhattan Island to guarantee an outlet for his whiskey. He prospered. So did those that followed, making the United States the greatest whiskey-drinking nation on earth. American distilleries today provide the populace with one hundred forty million gallons a year.

309

Pot stills followed the grain into Maryland and Pennsylvania and Kentucky. Plenty of water was needed, the colder the better, and the best was soft water off limestone rocks, for the limestone absorbed impurities. It was a struggle to get the grain back to the seaboard towns, but a jug of whiskey was easy to transport and more desirable. In western Pennsylvania, wherever a score of houses was built, a distillery was set up, to which the farmers brought their rye to be distilled. Secretary of the Treasury Alexander Hamilton levied a tax on the whiskey, and President Washington had to send in troops to protect the excisers and collect the revenue. Some of the distillers retreated to the Carolinas, setting up their stills on tussocks in the swamps; the farmers brought them sorghum cane from which the juice had been pounded, and when the stalks were mixed with swamp water and distilled, the result was *tissick*, white lightning. Other distillers moved to Kentucky, into Bourbon County. But the revenuers followed. Grudgingly, the tax was paid.

Kentucky was deep in whiskey before the Rebellion of 1794. Some say it was Jacob Spears who built the first Bourbon County distillery in 1790, and others say it was Evan Williams or John Hamilton. Over in Scott County, a Baptist preacher named Craig had built a distillery the year before. They were quickly followed by Revolutionary veterans who had set up some fifteen hundred stills by the time of the Rebellion. Kentuckians say their early corn whiskey was preferred to Pennsylvania rye, because Bourbon county whiskey was lighter, with a less grainy taste. Certainly it matured faster and could be drunk younger.

With the coming of the patent still of Aeneas Coffey, Kentucky set to with a will, supplying the frontier as well as the eastern towns. These column stills followed the grain west, into Ohio and Tennessee, Indiana and Illinois. They make whiskies today. But none of it is true Bourbon.

Bourbon comes from Louisville and Lexington, Frankfort and Bardstown, and points between. The law may say that Bourbon must contain 51 per cent corn, no matter where it's made. Kentuckians know different. Bourbon comes from Kentucky.

Taxes continued to raise the price of whiskey, and to encourage moonshining, but the industry grew. A young Scot named Crow arrived in 1815 and brought with him the latest distilling techniques and later helped introduce the patent still. There were other giants on the land: Medleys, Beams, Dants, Wellers, Wathens, and old Isaac Wolfe Bernheim, who made I. W. Harper, taking his own initials and the name of one of his salesmen to name his brand. They were great distillers, men who knew how to nurse the magic out of the grain, how to watch their whiskey in the wood and bottle it when it was at its peak. Then came Prohibition.

Even today, three-fourths of Kentucky's 120 counties are dry, but that is nothing to the drought that lasted until 1933.

Many of the distilleries disappeared, and while a few continued to make "medicinal" whiskey, it was hard times in Kentucky, and worse in Pennsylvania and Maryland and the other states. The art of distilling didn't die, but the market did. Bootleg flooded the country, and Scotch came in by the shipload, getting a piece of the market that got larger every year. When distilling was legal again, the Big Four began buying up the small distilleries and the famous names. Schenley, Seagram's, National Distillers, and Hiram Walker took over the giant's share of the industry.

There are nearly a score of whiskeys that sell a million cases or more a year, including two Canadian whiskies. Here are the leading brands of the Big Four, by millions of cases, roman type indicating blended whiskeys, italics indicating straight or bonded whiskeys:

SEAGRAM
7 Crown, 7 *plus*
Calvert Reserve, 2½
V O, 2 (*Canadian*)
*Four Roses, 1 *plus*
Carstairs, 1 *minus*

SCHENLEY
Reserve, 2
Ancient Age, 1½
J. W. Dant, 1 minus
Echo Springs, 1 minus
Old Stagg, 1 minus

NATIONAL
Old Crow, 2¼
*Old Sunnybrook, 1¼
*P. M., 1 *plus*
Hill & Hill, 1 minus
Old Taylor, 1 minus

WALKER
Imperial, 2½
Canadian Club, 2 *plus*
Corby's, 2
Ten High, ¾

* Blend and straight

Two other straights, Brown-Forman's *Early Times* and Beam Distillery's *Jim Beam*, sell about a million and a half cases each year; *Fleischmann Preferred*, from that blending house, and Publicker's *Old Hickory*, a straight, sell about a million cases a year. The only Scotch in the same league is *Black & White*, which sells about three quarters of a million cases a year.

Rye was the first to disappear in wartime. Rye is full of taste, and before the war it represented 15 per cent of the market. Every important distillery made a Rye. When war came, it was blended with neutral spirits to meet the demand. At first, enough Rye was used so that the blend with neutral spirits had some taste, but as the fighting went on, the percentage of whiskeys in the neutral spirits dropped, sometimes to 20 per cent. When the Rye was gone, still lighter Bourbon was used. There was even whiskey made that had no whiskey in it at all, merely highly rectified spirits with flavoring matter added. Americans became accustomed to the lighter tastes, and when the shooting war was over, a new battle began.

There's a rumor, never substantiated, that one of the Big Four made an exhaustive survey in the mid-1940s and found that people didn't really like the taste of whiskey. But a large segment of the industry, led by Seagram, decided that the American thirst could best be satisfied with a light whiskey, made lighter by blending it with tasteless neutral spirits. One of the best independent producers of such whiskeys is the Barton Distillery. Opposed to them were Schenley and its followers, who felt that straight whiskeys and blends of straight whiskeys were what the public wanted; they could be light, but they should be all whiskey.

Distilling in a patent still is a simple process. For making Bourbon, corn and other grains (called the small grains) are cooked with water. Corn usually amounts to 70 per cent or more, barley malt accounts for another 10 or 12 percent, and rye or wheat usually accounts for the rest. The more corn used the lighter the whiskey.

Fermentation is carried out with yeasts, water, and the residue from the stills, which is called *slop* or *spent beer*. If the fermentation takes less than seventy-two hours, and if some spent stillage is used, the resulting whiskey is entitled to be called *sour mash whiskey*, according to law. This is standard practice. So, legally, all Bourbon is sour mash whiskey. In the old days, spent beer was used exclusively, no water being added; that was sour mash. So, traditionally, no Bourbon today is sour mash whiskey.

The secret of good whiskey lies in details: grains should have low moisture content, less than 14 per cent; the yeast must be of the finest quality, so that fermentation will be even; the temperature of the fermentation must be kept down, so that unwanted acids and bacteria will not form; the small grains must be in the right proportion, so that the whiskey will not be out of balance. When fermentation is ended, the resulting beer is distilled. American whiskeymakers usually distill their whiskeys between 115 and 135 proof. The whiskey is reduced with water to 100 proof and stored in new, charred oak casks.

The casks are placed in bonded warehouses, buildings supervised by the government. Under a whiskey bonding act of 1897, the whiskey could be bottled after four years, taxes were to be paid on it, and a green government seal pasted over the mouth of the bottle, stating the whiskey was *bottled in bond*. The only significance of the phrase is that the whiskey is at least four years old and 100 proof. In any case, the taxes had to be paid on the whiskey after eight years in bond. This was called the force-out. About the same time, other control laws were passed: the coopers' lobby saw to it that Bourbon could only be aged in *new* charred oak casks; the bottlers' lobby saw to it that bottles could not be refilled. None of these laws added anything to the quality of whiskey.

The bonding rule caused no trouble until 1950, when the distillers made tremendous quantities of whiskey in expectation of a shortage due to the Korean War. The shortage never developed, but the large distilleries, particularly Schenley, which believed in straight whiskeys, were faced with the problem of taking whiskeys forced out of bond and flooding the market with them. It was cheaper to pour the whiskey down the drain than to pay the tax. Until the summer of 1958, old straight whiskeys were on the market at lower prices than younger whiskeys blended with neutral spirits, the whiskeys being taken out of bond and marketed under unknown brand names. But a new law extended the time in bond to twenty years, so that taxes need not be paid during that time unless the whiskey is withdrawn from bond. But another change in taste had occurred. The public took to the light, straight whiskeys, passing up the blends. Today, it's anybody's guess what will happen.

In Kentucky, there's no question as to the best whiskey. It's Bourbon. Various Bourbons may be blended, the result being called a *Blend of Straight Whiskeys*. But no neutral spirits are added. *Bottled in bond* is preferred, the Kentuckian feeling that he is perfectly capable of adding his own water, if he wants to. And age doesn't matter so much, for the distillate can be managed so that it will reach bottle ripeness at four, eight, or twelve years. The best Bourbon probably needs six to eight years in wood, and all of them decline after twenty years in cask. A well-matured Bourbon is called sippin' whiskey, and there's talk about fightin' whiskey, cryin' whiskey, and fallin'-down whiskey, although nobody knows what happens to a batch to produce one of these. Bourbon and branch water is the classic drink, with or without ice, and the water should come from a small stream that bubbles out of the rocks.

There's a saying that a Kentuckian drinks whiskeys nobody ever heard of, from small, independent distilleries that have not been taken over by the Big Four. It is true that many of the famous old brands have been standardized to a type, or have been made into blends, actions called "corrupting a brand," by the trade. A favorite brand is a matter of choice. On any list of great straight Bourbons you are apt to find such names as those listed below, and there are others:

Cabin Still and Old Fitzgerald
Fairfax County and Virginia Gentleman
Glenmore and Yellowstone

Heaven Hill	*Hoffman*
I. W. Harper	*J. W. Dant*
Jim Beam	*Maker's Mark*
Michter's *	*Thompson Willets*
Waterfill & Frazier	*Wild Turkey*

* Michter's is a pot-still whiskey, the only one made in this country. Its grain proportions are unknown.

∾§ RYE

Rye is out of favor these days, the lighter Bourbons having taken the market, but at one time full-bodied Ryes were the favorite drink in Pennsylvania, Maryland, and the cities of the Atlantic seaboard. Rye whiskey must be composed of 51 per cent rye grains, the small grains usually being composed of barley, with some corn or wheat. There are four leading brands on the market.

A pot-still Rye of high quality is now being made by old-fashioned methods in Sheridan, Lebanon County, Pennsylvania. The stillman, Everett Beam, is a descendant of Jacob Beam, who came to this country before the Revolution and settled in western Pennsylvania only to pick up and move to Kentucky after the Whiskey Rebellion. He became dissatisfied with the yeasts available, and, about 1800, sent back to Germany for a strain he had heard about. It arrived in a copper jug and cost five hundred dollars. He began paying off the debt in monthly installments, and after his death his eldest son finished the payments. The German jug yeast is still in the family, and if you want to make whiskey with it, you hire a Beam.

The best rye grain is Rosen rye from Michigan's northeast peninsula. The grain must be hard, sweet, clean, and plump, and it cannot come from fields near which onion or garlic is planted because it will pick up the flavor. A new hybrid rye is being developed, *Tetrapectus*, which may prove best in the future. The rye is ground and mixed with boiling water and spent beer from the previous day's distillation, the temperature is lowered, barley malt and corn are added, and then yeast. The fermented beer is distilled in a patent still, then a pot still. Special care is taken to vent off unwanted vapors, there being a feeling that they impart what is called hog-track odor to new whiskeys. Careful venting avoids the odor.

The new whiskey is put in cask for six years. From the wood, it picks up tannin, sugars, and other traces that round out its flavor. A poor whiskey seems to draw too much from the wood, and the storehouse smells of whiskey. A good whiskey draws less from the wood, and the storehouse smells of oak. The storehouse is ventilated so that plenty of fresh air can get at the casks. The air, too, seems to help develop the whiskeys.

It is a fine American whiskey. But it is also Rye, full of taste, and the fashion is for light spirits. Rye may disappear completely before the wheel turns. But there are some distilleries in the country that don't believe so. For a few years, anyway, Americans will still be able to find good Rye.

◅§ CORN

Corn whiskey is made from a mash that is at least 80 per cent corn. When it is distilled at a proof that is not too high and aged well, it is a light and pleasant whiskey with a pronounced taste. It has never become universally popular because Bourbon, using slightly less corn and more small grains, has a rounder, better-balanced flavor when well-made. Corn likker also suffers because of all the denigrating nicknames stuck to it: squeezin's, mule juice, white lightning, jug whiskey, kickapoo joy juice, and what have you.

Whiskey can be made from any grain, and is. Wheat would make fine whiskey, and is used as part of the small grains in some of the best Bourbons, but some stillmen think it sticks in the still, gumming the works. Sticking actually has nothing to do with it. If the price of wheat were lower, we would be drinking Old Thresher wheat whiskey, distilled beside cool mountain springs in nature's old way, to give us goodness at the lowest gash per gulp.

Grain and all kinds of industrial alcohol, sugars, starches, and other fermentables are distilled in the illicit stills that abound in the cities and in country areas all across the land. A few small pot stills in the South can make glorious whiskey, but this seldom gets a chance to age, any more than did the magnificent and illicit applejack once made in Virginia, New Jersey, New York's Westchester County, and other apple-growing areas. Today, illegal whiskey is almost entirely rotgut, sold in blind pigs, or over the counter in crossroads general stores and slum tobacco shops, wherever there is a gathering of thirsty poor. The stuff is always dangerous, and sometimes fatal. Only the desperate, the foolish, or the stupid drink it. This bootleg accounts for one out of every four bottles sold in this country, something in the neighborhood of fifty million gallons a year. The high tax on legal whiskey helps bootleggers thrive. But there's a growing demand for good whiskey, both straight and blended, and the industry offers a tremendous range to choose from.

Gin—Mother's Ruin— and Other Spirits

One day in the middle of the seventeenth century, a Dutch apothecary in Leyden, who called himself Sylvius, put juniper berries into spirits to find out how it would taste. Juniper wine tasted fine and was good for the kidneys; maybe juniper in spirits would be better. It was.

He began selling the medicine to his customers, calling it *genièvre*, the French name sounding fancier than the Dutch. It seemed to be just the thing for what ailed the Dutch. Anyway, they felt better after a dram or two. If the feeling didn't last, there was more where that came from, and it was cheap. The seventeenth was a troubled century; so was the eighteenth, and poverty called for some relief from the misery. Queen Anne provided this shortly after she came to the throne in 1703 by raising the duty on French wines and spirits. Geneva

317

was the answer, and Holland's gin caught on in England. It sold for pennies, and gin palaces sprang up everywhere. All you needed to be in business was a sign and a few gallons of the stuff. Here was one of the signs: "Drunk for a penny, dead drunk for two pence, clean straw for nothing."

Gin hasn't changed much in the last three centuries. It is still neutral spirits, flavored mostly with juniper, but other flavoring agents include orange peel, angelica root, coriander, and several more. Quality has improved. Neutral spirits are made when any mash is distilled at a proof above 160, so that practically no congeners are carried over in the distillation. American gin is made with neutral spirits that are over 190 proof, almost pure alcohol, and English gins are made from neutral spirits between 180 and 190 proof. Plymouth gin has a full taste because the mash is specially treated before distillation.

The spirits are reduced to 120 proof with water and distilled a second time in a column still that has what is called a gin head. This is the container in which the vapors pass through the flavoring agents, picking up from the botanicals the highly aromatic volatiles. The result is rectified spirits, rectification being the act of changing the character of a spirit by blending or additions. In the legal sense, cordials are rectified spirits. When bonded whiskeys are blended, this does not constitute rectifying but is called commingling. The reduction of proof with water is not considered to be rectifying.

Dutch gin is still known as Holland gin, Geneva, or Schiedam gin (Schiedam once had two hundred distilleries). Today, these gins are made by grinding up the flavoring agents with a barley malt and distilling at low proof, just under 100, so that it is high in congeners and full in taste. In northern Europe, gins are called *Schnapps*, and some of them are quite spicy. *Kümmel* is similar, cumin being the principal flavoring agent in the finest types, coriander in the others. Because many Kümmels are sweetened, they are generally considered to be liqueurs.

Old Tom gin was once popular in England. This is a gin which has been sweetened with sugar syrup and is a good gin to use for making cocktails that call for sugar. A whole group of gins are made by adding flavorings—mint, orange, lemon, and others—but these are really cordials with a gin base because most of them are sweetened. They are sold as mint gin, orange gin, and so forth. Gin is seldom aged, the flavor coming from what has been added to the neutral spirits, not from the action of wood on spirits. Standard brands generally maintain a high quality. Some are more flowery than others.

Golden gin is simply gin that has been stored in wood for a time, picking up some color from the wood, but it is difficult to detect much change in taste. The Dutch gins also have a yellow tinge, but this is added to make them look more appealing. Cheap gins, made by adding flavoring essences to neutral spirits, are called compound gins; they have a raw and unpleasing taste of alcohol.

ৰ্জ AKVAVIT, AQUAVIT

This is the national drink of Scandinavia, drunk neat and chilled, often with *smörgåsbord* and other food. It is distilled from grain or potatoes at a very high proof, then diluted. Caraway seeds are added, it is distilled again, filtered, and bottled at 90 proof. Often, other seeds are infused, as are lemon and orange peel. It is not usually sweet. Danish *Akvavit*, particularly *Aälborg*, is considered best; but Norwegian *Aquavit* from *Löiten, Lysholm* and *Linie Aquavit*, which is sent to Australia and back to reap the benefits of the sea voyage, as well as Swedish *Andersson*, and *Oeverste-Brannvin*, are popular.

ৰ্জ VODKA

Vodka is neutral spirits filtered through charcoal. It tastes of alcohol. It can be distilled from anything, but rye malt is generally used. After vodka is filtered it is bottled at 100 proof, 86 proof, or 80 proof, cut by the addition of water. It is not aged. It is neutral.

Vodka is supposed to have come from Russia, but it is made all over northern Europe, and elsewhere. In the satellite countries today and in Russia itself, vodka serves the same function that gin did in England in the eighteenth century. Vodka is very expensive in eastern Europe, but shoes and clothes cost more, and a man might just as well spend what money he has for escape. Vodka has a great advantage over other spirits; it will make intoxicating anything liquid without much effecting the taste of what it's put into.

Zubrowka is vodka with some Zubrowka grass steeped in it, giving it a slight bitterness and some aroma. Various other herbs and flavorings can be added to vodka to give it some taste. When you start doing that, you begin to make *Schnapps*.

⊷§ PULQUE AND TEQUILA

The maguey cactus takes eight years to mature. Just before it does, its crown of leaves is cut off, the pulp is scooped out, and the hole fills with sap which ferments. This is *pulque*. It is thirst-quenching and much prized by the Indians of Mexico, who make various versions from the other varieties of the agave cactus. Pulque is distilled to make *Tequila*. The approved way of drinking Tequila is to sprinkle some salt on your thumb or in the web between the thumb and first finger, then squirt a wedge of lime in your mouth, toss in the salt, and then the Tequila. The drink is fiery. Tequila is generally distilled twice in pot stills, and the best is aged for a time in wood. It is usually bottled at 90 proof.

Mescal is made much the same way from a different variety of agave. Some of the cactus pulp is included in the fermentation, as with Tequila. A single pot-still distillation is customary. Mescal is not aged and is bottled at about 90 proof. It has a weedy taste. It contains small quantities of mescaline, the alkaloid that causes hallucinations, and the drink is used in various Indian ceremonies.

⊷§ ET CETERA

Tiquira is made in Brazil from tapioca roots, which are malted and fermented, distilled at high proof, then watered down to 90 proof for drinking.

Okolehao is distilled in Hawaii from a mash of molasses, rice, and juice from baked ti-root, aged in charred oak casks, and bottled at 80 or 90 proof. It is dark brown and tastes of ti-root. White Okolehao is made by using cocoanut milk instead of ti-root juice.

Rice is fermented and distilled in the Orient, the Tartars of Central Asia drink fermented mare's milk and call it *koumiss*, then distill it in earthenware pots and call it *Araka*, and the Germans distill corn to make *Kornbranntwein*. There are others, for man is a distilling animal. Give him starch or sugar, and he's sure to try to find out what it will taste like when it comes out of a still.

 *um*

We owe it all to Columbus. He brought
sugar cane to the West Indies and by 1520
the colonists and the natives were busily
making rum. The name probably comes
from the last syllable of the Latin word for
sugar, *saccharum*, but that seems much too
logical. It may have come from sailor slang,
a word made up from the grunt a sailor
makes when he pulls an oar, each stroke
bringing him that much closer to shore and
his tot. The rum in those days lacked something—according to an old manuscript describing Barbados, written in 1651 and now
in Trinity College, Dublin: "The chief fuddling they make in the island is rum-bullion
alias kill-divil and this is made from sugar
canes distilled, a hot, hellish, and terrible
liquor."

The fuddling was the important thing,
and rum was the all-American drink for three

hundred years. The custom was to mix it with something, anything. A punch was one of sour, two of sweet, three of strong and four of weak—lime juice, sugar, rum and water—but the proportion varied to match the mood. *Bogus* was rum and beer in equal parts, *Stonewall* was rum and cider. *Bombo* was rum, sugar, water and nutmeg; if you left out the nutmeg, it was *Nimbo*, which was heated with a loggerhead, a knob of iron with a handle that was originally used to heat calking pitch.

And there were others. *Swizzle* was first made on St. Kitts and spread to all the islands: one part rum and six water, with flavoring, made foamy with a swizzle stick. This was cut from an odd bush that had several branching roots. You rolled it between your palms, the many twigs frothing the drink. *Grog* was rum and water, first issued to his sailors by Admiral Vernon in 1740. He had holed up in Jamaica after a raid and needed to give his crews something to keep them from running wild. The sailors called him "Old Grog" because he wore a grogram coat, and switched the name to the drink. The daily tot continues in the British navy to this day, but some choose money instead of rum, to the disgust of older tars.

Rum was rough in those days, even when mixed with other things. A drink made with brandy, wine, porter, lime-peel, nutmeg, and rum was called *rattle-skull*. It was not at all unfair to blame the rum. But rum had something, even then. One colonial comment was: "A very baneful, heady, bilious drink in great request."

After a time, the fuddlers got production far enough ahead of consumption to be able to let the rum age a little, and at least some of the nineteenth-century rums were magnificent. "Good rum cools the heat and heats the cold, wets the dry and dries the wet," wrote a New Englander. Rum finally came to mean all good things, particularly anything good to drink.

But the custom of abusing it seemed to increase as rum improved. As the inhibiting spirit of the nineteenth century began to take its toll of joy and pleasure, drink became Demon Rum, a drunk became a rummy, and bootleggers and their boats became rum-runners. Latter-day rum-makers didn't do much for their product, either, sending to this country during the Second World War stuff called "rum" that was as revolting as the worst ever swallowed by a buccaneer or dubbed firewater by an Indian.

A bad taste lingers in the memory, and a dozen years passed

before people began drinking rum again. The great brands had not been corrupted, but even these suffered until the shudders had faded. A tax advantage for Puerto Rican rum, and a Mature Spirits Act, instituting quality controls, put on the American market a range of rums at low prices. The world's greatest mixer is here again, a little lighter than formerly in some cases, better than ever in others.

Rum is usually classed as light or dark, but this is mostly a matter of added coloring, because rum comes white from the still and is slow to pick up color from wood. Typing by color began in Cuba, where *Ron Carta* and *Ron Oro* came to be known as Silver Label and Gold Label. Rum is sometimes classed as light-bodied, full-flavored, or aromatic. Cuban and Puerto Rican rums are light-bodied, Jamaican and Haitian rums are full in flavor, as are those from Barbados and Martinique, while aromatic rum comes from Java via Holland and is called *Batavia Arrack*. This is distinctive because some rice, and even palm wine, is used in the fermentation.

There is really no way to class rums, however, because each island runs the gamut from white to dark, from light to full. Generally, those from the British and French islands have more taste than the light rums of Cuba and Puerto Rico. The rums of the Virgin Islands, Mexico, and New England rum made from West Indies molasses, are generally pungent.

Rums are ready to drink after three years in the wood and continue to improve for about twenty years. The kind of taste varies with the type of distillation and the way the rum is flavored, so that the rum of each island is distinctive. Less of the full-bodied rums are needed for making drinks. Rum is the perfect hot-weather drink because it sends hot blood to the surface, says the theory, and most people who live in the tropics agree. They will also say the same about practically anything else alcoholic. The real argument for drinking rum in warm weather is simple. Nothing tastes better with fruit juices. In winter, nothing is so warming. White or dark, light or full, good rum tastes good, and every island has its treasure. Not all of it is pirate gold, buried in the sand.

☙ CUBA

Cuban rum was the lightest of the Caribbean until a few years ago; the traditional white rum, the color of tarnished silver, can be magnificent. Molasses is poured into gigantic wooden vats, a special yeast culture is added, and the ferment lasts about three days. The fermentation is quick so that excessive flavoring is not picked up. For the same reason, distillation is at a high proof, nearly 180, in column stills. The new alcohol is then filtered through sand and charcoal to remove still more of the flavoring, something that is also done with vodka and some whiskeys. The rum is colored with caramel or prune juice, again something that is done in all distilling countries. It is then flavored with various mixtures of brandy, Sherry, raisins, prunes, or bay leaves and other ingredients. These are called flavoring agents, and their addition is a common practice in the making of many spirits, such as gin and liqueurs. Each firm's formula for flavoring agents is a guarded secret. Rums distilled at high proof, then flavored, are also made in Barbados, some of the other islands, and Demerara, but such rums are fuller and quite different in taste. On all the islands, new rum is put in barrel at the distilling proof and reduced to market proof when it is bottled. The most famous of the Cuban rums is Bacardi.

☙ JAMAICA

The finest of the highly flavored rums come from Jamaica, where pot stills are used, and where British laws of quality control are followed. The sugar cane is crushed, then the cane juice is heated almost to boiling, so that the sludge will settle as it cools. It is reheated, treated, and skimmed; the liquid is evaporated and the sugar crystallizes, leaving molasses behind. The molasses and the skimmings are mixed with what is left from the previous distillation. This residue is called *dunder* and looks like pea soup. It is allowed to ferment, sometimes for two weeks or longer. If no yeast is added, some of the crushed cane, called *begasse*, is sometimes tossed in. The trend now is toward using yeast cultures, which allow for quicker and more even fermentation. Double distillation in the pot stills is never higher than 176 proof, and only caramel is added, for coloring. This is considered the best way to make rum.

Much Jamaica rum, and also Demerara rum, is sent to London for aging, the English climate being considered particularly good for developing the taste. These are called London Dock rums, and are often ten or more years old. In all the islands, and in London, blending is a standard practice, rums of various ages being balanced to bring out the taste. Perhaps the best known of Jamaica rums is Myers, but there are many others, among them Dagger and Lemon Hart.

◄§ HAITI

Haitian rums are not so full as those from Jamaica, although production methods are similar. Distillation to a high proof is customary on all the islands, the only desired congeners being the esters; the more acid the mash, the more esters. These minor elements, perhaps two parts in a thousand in Jamaica rum, are what impart the rummy flavor. The slightly lighter, slightly less pungent Haitian rums are sometimes called brandy rums, as are those of Barbados. The most famous rum of Haiti is Barbancourt, which is made by an old family on the island. Rhum Sarthe also has a good reputation.

◄§ PUERTO RICO

Puerto Rican rums are today the lightest that are made, preserving a fresh, clean taste in both the light and dark types. Distilling is particularly meticulous, the rum coming from the column stills at less than 160 proof. Molasses is used for the mash, as are yeast cultures, and fermentation is usually less than a week. No flavoring agents are added, it is reported, and the legal minimum for aging is three years. This is often enough for such light rums, although many of them age longer, continuing to improve in the wood, but picking up fullness. Because they enter duty-free, they are lower in price than on the mainland market. Federal tax must nevertheless be paid by the buyer before he brings his stock back home.

⋅§ VIRGIN ISLANDS

Cruzan rum from the island of St. Croix is the best known of those from the little cluster of islands east of Puerto Rico. Production follows the Puerto Rican practices, but the rums are fuller. As on all the other islands both light and dark rums are made, but the taste is about the same, the dark rum being somewhat sweeter. Rum is traditionally dark, because in the old days of careless distilling, some of the molasses color came over with the alcohol. People have the idea that such spirits should be dark, and distillers in all countries cheerfully oblige. Virgin Island rums enter the U.S. free of duty. Perhaps the most famous of the Cruzan rums is Bellows.

⋅§ MARTINIQUE

The rums of Martinique and the other islands of the Leeward and Windward groups are, like those of Jamaica, full-bodied and highly flavored. Most of those from the French islands go to France. All of them have distinctive tastes, depending on the molasses used, the distillation, and the time they spend in the white oak casks. Martinique rums are generally the fullest of all. Rhum Negrita is the best known.

⋅§ BARBADOS

These are lighter than Jamaica or Martinique rums, and a weird collection of flavoring agents is used, including coconuts, added during fermentation. Still others are added after fermentation, including Sherry and Madeira. Some of them are magnificent.

⋅§ MEXICO

Mexican rums are generally light-bodied, with a distinctive taste because they are aged in Sherry casks. Few flavoring agents are added.

◦§ DEMERARA

These are the fullest of the British rums, made on the South American mainland in British Guiana. They are particularly fruity, and many of them are aged at the London docks. Fruits and spices are the main flavoring agents, and a lot of caramel is added to darken the rum and flavor it as well. The wines are filtered before shipping because so much has been added to them.

◦§ NEW ENGLAND RUM

Made from West Indian molasses, these rums are usually distilled at 160 proof, and are pungent, but not particularly heavy in body or taste. This was an enormous industry in colonial days, and the most famous was Medford rum. The rum picks up a certain character, considered similar to London Dock rums. One of the few New England rums still available is that of S. S. Pierce.

◦§ OTHER RUMS

The Philippines produce light rums, with a distinctive taste reminiscent of vanilla, but the most famous rum outside the Caribbean is *Batavia Arrack*, from Java. The Dutch built up this trade and drink quantities of the light, somewhat sweet rum. Rums, generally called *raki*, are made wherever sugar cane grows, including Russia, in the oases around Tashkent. Most rum, though, is produced in the West Indies.

In various parts of the Caribbean, rums with special flavors, such as banana and pineapple, are produced. These are rarely available off the home islands, and are really better classified as rum-based cordials than as rums.

To get some idea of the different rum drinks, take a trip to one of the tropical bars that are flourishing in the big cities. The various punches, bowls, and long drinks are exotic and presented with cheerful showmanship. It's difficult to choose a bad drink, and the long list will show why rum is called the greatest mixer in the world.

Liqueurs and Cordials

The ancients spiced and sweetened wines to make them taste good, and when medieval monks began distilling they did the same thing with the raw alcohols they made. Elixirs for longer life, cure alls, love potions, and aphrodisiacs called for roots and herbs, seeds and spices, that were distilled with the wines, or steeped with, or percolated into the ardent waters. With most of them, the effect was imaginary but intoxicating, and anything that tasted unpleasant was masked by sweetness. A man wooing a maid would offer her a potion and wait for the magic ingredients to work; the expectant damsel might only think she was feeling amorous, but that might well be enough.

The French and Dutch cordialize with chortling zeal, but every country has produced a few that are distinctive. By the nineteenth century, every great event was hon-

331

ored with a new cordial or two. An English Christmas was hardly complete without the Christmas cordial made by the master or his lady—usually fruits soaked in gin, which was cheap. The cordials that have come down to us have delighted generations, and some of them are miracles of taste.

Liqueurs are spirits that have been sweetened and flavored, according to the law. Cordials are the same thing, although the word is sometimes limited to those flavored with fruits. Both must contain 2.5 per cent of sugar by weight. Some are often miscalled fruit brandies, a term legally reserved for distillations from a fermented mash of fruit containing less than 2.5 per cent sugar. Synthetic or imitation flavorings cannot be used, but vegetable colorings are all right to use.

Cordials are generally served as they come from the bottle, in ridiculous little pony glasses. Brandy glasses or small snifters offer enough room for the air to release the pleasing aromas. Many cordials taste better chilled—this cuts the sweetness. The taste and aroma change as the cordial warms in the glass, warming you.

There's no sensible way to classify cordials. Grouping by taste seems logical, but the range is immense. Each cordial tastes sweet and strange and different. *Triple secs* are Cointreau, Curaçao, Grand Marnier, and the like. These taste of orange. The *creams* have a generally smooth texture in the mouth. Cordials based on brandy form a family, as do those flavored with herbs, or those flavored with fruits. Those with complex flavorings are generally called *Monastery liqueurs:* Bénédictine, Chartreuse, Claristine, Elixir d'Anvers, Raspail, Trappistine, Vieille Cure, and so on. Those that imitate green or yellow Chartreuse are called *liqueurs vertes* or *liqueurs jaunes*. The best classification is a list.

Cordials vary widely in proof, ranging down from 110 of Green Chartreuse to the 60 or 70 of some of the *crèmes*. Still lower are the flavoring syrups and essences, which often are confused with cordials. Like bitters, they are rarely drunk by themselves.

⋖§ SYRUPS AND BITTERS

Syrups are usually used in mixing drinks. Some contain alcohol and are classed as cordials. *Cassis* is a famous syrup from Dijon, deep red in color and made from black currants. *Falernum* is a syrup from the West Indies that tastes of almonds and limes. *Maraschino*, sometimes a cordial, is also a flavoring syrup made from Marasca cherries. *Orgeat* and *Noyau* both taste of almonds.

Some of the syrups contain no alcohol: *Grenadine* tastes of pomegranates and is used to color drinks pink; *Gomme* is primarily a sugar syrup, mostly sugar and water, with a neutral taste.

Bitters are used to add tang to a drink. Medicinal bitters are sometimes drunk alone, as stomachics for what is politely called tourist complaint and gastric disturbances. Nonmedicinal bitters, such as *Orange Bitters*, are used strictly for flavoring, and are usually low in alcohol content. Both generally have the taste of quinine, or some other bitter bark, and each proprietary brand has its own formula. Some run as high as 80 proof. Angostura from Trinidad, Peychaud from France, and Fernet Branca from Italy are among the best known, but others are Abbott's, Amara, Bonnekamp, Calysia, Campari, Apricot Bitters, Khoosh, Orange Bitters, Peach Bitters, Secrestat, and Tangerine Bitters. Medicinal or not, they can do wonders for certain drinks.

ᴥᔓ ABSINTHE

Legally, all cordials are sweet, but the most famous liqueur of all is absinthe, which isn't sweet at all. It isn't legal, either. Absinthe contains wormwood, which drives men mad when taken in excess, the way one takes absinthe. It tastes of licorice. It turns milky when water is added, and should really be classed as an apéritif. Many like it as an after-dinner drink. Absinthe used to be bottled at 136 proof, but modern versions are about 86.

Devised in Switzerland, its licorice taste and green color come from artemisia, although many other herbs are added. A French expatriate named Ordinaire made the original formula in the late eighteenth century, then sold it to the firm of Pernod. Production was moved to Tarragona, Spain, when absinthe was outlawed in France and Switzerland. The ban spread, and now most available absinthe contains little wormwood. There are dozens of versions: Pec and Pernod are the most popular ones in France; the dry Chinchon, and the sweet or dry Ojen and El Mono, are the Spanish favorites. Ouzo is the Greek version and Anisette is made by many firms. Others include Abisante, Anesone, Anis, Anisado del Mono, Burger, Oxygenée, and some raki. On the Riviera, the favorite café drink is *pastis*, a slang word for an absinthe substitute and water, perhaps with ice, made like a short highball. The Absinthe Drip was the pet of the international set in the Twenties. It called for a special glass and spoon, but the idea was to drip water through a sugar cube before you began sipping. The various imitations are generally good, and in spite of the often dour stories about absinthe, the various drinks are exhilarating, and perhaps responsible for the phrase *giggle water*. They are fine thirst-quenchers.

~§ ADVOCAAT

Really a sort of eggnog, made in Holland by adding fresh eggs to brandy. Various imitations are made all over the world; an Italian one of eggs and Marsala is sold under the proprietary name *Marvo*.

~§ ANANAS

A smooth, sweet, syrupy cordial with little color that derives its taste from pineapples. It is one of the creams, generally called *Crème d'Ananas*, so called because the flavor comes primarily from a single fruit. Creams are generally very sweet, and can be made by adding fruit essence to spirits, rather than by steeping or infusion, which is better, or by distillation, which is generally considered the best way to make cordials.

~§ ANISETTE, ANIS, ANESONE

A mild, clear liqueur that derives its flavor from aniseed. Like absinthe in taste, it also turns cloudy when water is added. The licorice flavor is popular around the Mediterranean, where it is considered a *digestif*, the French word for after-dinner drinks that counteract what the English call post-prandial languor. Often drunk with soda water or water, and ice. *Anis* is the Spanish version; *Anesone* is Italian, less sweet and stronger, drunk straight or in coffee. One of the best is by Marie Brizard.

◄§ APRICOT LIQUEUR, ABRICOT

Apricots are infused in high-proof brandy in a cask for several months. The brandy is poured off, the fruit is then distilled, and this is added to the original brandy. The whole is sweetened, reduced to 60 to 80 proof, and bottled. Production methods vary, but this is the traditional way. If the crushed fruit were made into a mash, then fermented and aged, the result would be called apricot brandy.

◄§ ARRACK PUNSCH

This is the national liqueur of Scandinavia, made by adding sweetening and flavoring agents to *Batavia Arrak*, the Java rum. It is also called *Caloric Punsch*. *Arrak* becomes *raki* in the eastern Mediterranean and Asia, where it originally referred to various palm-tree distillates or to the *koumiss* of central Asia, which is made by fermenting mare's milk. In Asia Minor today, *raki* generally means a brandy flavored with aniseed and coriander, turning milky when water is added.

◄§ BANANE

A cream that derives its taste from bananas. A native Haitian version is called *Balsam*.

◄§ BÉNÉDICTINE

One of the oldest liqueurs, said to date from the first days of the sixteenth century, when Benedictine monks in Normandy produced the elixir. The order has nothing to do with the commercial company in Fécamp that now produces it from a formula that contains some three dozen herbs steeped in brandy. This is redistilled with Cognac and still more flavoring agents and aged for four years in casks. Like the formula for Angostura bitters, only three people are supposed to know the secret, and these three are never supposed to travel together. *B & B* was made because the firm discovered that people were mixing Bénédictine half and half with brandy to get a less-sweet drink, and the company decided to do the mixing themselves, to save their customers the trouble. *D.O.M.* appears as a slogan on the bottle, and means *Deo Optimo Maximo,* "To God, most good, most great." It is one of the most famous of the Monastery Liqueurs.

BLACKBERRY LIQUEUR

Made by steeping blackberries in sweetened brandy for several days. Blackberry brandy is made by fermenting a blackberry mash, then distilling.

CALISAY

A liqueur flavored with cinchona and other barks, popular in Spain.

CENTHERB

A French liqueur that contains a hundred herbs.

CHARTREUSE

The most famous of all liqueurs, Chartreuse is still made by the Carthusian monks at the monastery of Grand Chartreuse, near Grenoble. The formula was given to the order in 1607 by a grateful Marshal of France. This was improved on, a century and a half later, by one of the monks. The monks were expelled from France for a time around the turn of the nineteenth century, but returned to make their liqueur again until 1903, when they were once more expelled. A commercial firm tried to imitate the formula, but the result was horrible. The monks set up shop in Tarragona, Spain, but they could not find there the more than 120 herbs, roots, and seeds needed for the formula. The French government allowed them to return in 1938, anxious for the income from a market that was almost destroyed. A few bottles of yellow pre-expulsion Chartreuse are still around; the taste is more delicate than the Chartreuse of today. One of the old bottles costs $125. The *Liqueur des Pères Chartreux* is now made in the original distillery from the ancient formula, which is based on fine old brandy. The green Chartreuse is bottled at 110 proof, and is generally preferred to the *Chartreuse Jaune*, bottled at 86 proof; the *Verte* has a few more herbs and spices. The French are amused to call it a lady's drink. The idea is that women pretend not to like extremely potent drinks, yet somehow manage to order the most powerful available. There are many imitations, none of which compares to *La Grande Chartreuse*.

◢§ CHERRY LIQUEUR

Cherry Heering from Denmark is the most famous of the cherry liqueurs, made by steeping cherries in sweetened brandy. The stones impart a slight and pleasing bitterness to the liqueur. A French version is *Cherry-Rocher*.

⊌§ CHINA-CHINA

A proprietary name for a liqueur made in Voiron, France, with a spicy flavor derived from cloves, mace, cinnamon, and other flavorings.

⊌§ CLARISTINE

A spicy liqueur from a formula that was originated in the nunnery of Clarisses in Dinant, Belgium, now a proprietary name of Leroux & Company.

⊌§ COINTREAU

One of the Triple Secs, *Cointreau* was first made at Angers from a brandy base, but now the same formula is used to produce the clear liqueur in this country. Many liqueurs are now made in the United States from the original European formulas, and it is difficult to detect any differences between the American and European versions.

⊌§ CORDIAL MÉDOC

Very similar to a Triple Sec, this cordial is made in Bordeaux and flavored with oranges, cacao, and Cognac.

⊌§ CRÈME DE CACAO

A cream of cocoa that tastes of chocolate, and some vanilla, it is often called *crème de* cocoa, which makes purists wince. The best is said to be made from cocoa beans grown in the Chaow district of Venezuela.

✒ CRÈME DE MENTHE AND OTHER CREAMS

Cream of mint, whether white or green or red, derives its flavor from peppermint, the color added merely to make some drinks look better. The Pippermint of Get Frères is the best. Many of the creams are clear and colorless, and all are characterized by a syrupy smoothness. Most of them taste best chilled, or served over cracked or crushed ice. *Crème de Fraise,* or *Sirop de Fraise,* is not the same as the white alcohol distilled from strawberries and called simply *Fraise.* The confusion extends to other fruit creams and brandies. *Crème de Noyaux* is made with fruit stones and other flavorings, for instance, and its almond taste is pleasantly bitter, while *Noyau* is a syrup tasting of almonds. The French names are usually used to identify the other fruit cordials:

CRÈME	FRUIT
Ananas	*Pineapple*
Cerise	*Cherry*
Citron	*Lemon*
Limon	*Lime*
Mandarine	*Orange*
Orgeat	*Almond*
Rose	*Oil of rose and vanilla*
Vanille	*Vanilla*
Violette	*(best from Mexican vanilla)*
	Oil of violets and vanilla

✒ CURAÇAO

First made in Holland from the green, bitter peels of oranges from the Dutch island of Curaçao, off Venezuela. A kind of Triple Sec, famous ones are produced by the Dutch firms of Bols and Wynand Focking.

◆§ DRAMBUIE

This famous Scottish liqueur, developed by a French retainer of Prince Charles Edward in 1745, derives its flavor from Scotch herbs, heather honey and Highland malt.

◆§ EAU–DE–VIE DE HENDAYE

A proprietary liqueur, originally from the French port, containing a great many herbs.

◆§ ELIXIR D'ANVERS

A proprietary now used by the Antwerp firm of Beukelaer to identify a liqueur with a cinnamon taste.

◆§ FIOR DI ALPI, FIORI ALPINI

The flowers of the Alps are yellow liqueurs shipped in tall thin bottles that contain trees of rock crystal. They are spicy and vaguely reminiscent of yellow Chartreuse.

◆§ GOLDWASSER

A Kümmel, flavored with caraway and cumin and with a strong taste of coriander, in which tiny flakes of gold are suspended. In ancient days, precious metals and jewels were often ground and dissolved or suspended in drinks in the belief that they were a boon to health. The flakes in Goldwasser are harmless. The taste comes from orange peel and spices and was originally supposed to have been made in Danzig. The group is called *Liqueurs d'Or*.

⋖ GRAND MARNIER

One of the most distinguished of the Triple Secs, an orange flavor with a Cognac base. The *Cordon Jaune* is more expensive and higher in quality than the *Cordon Rouge*. It is now made in the United States from the original formula.

⋖ IRISH MIST

Made from herbs, honey, and Irish whisky. A proprietary.

⋖ KAHLÚA

A coffee liqueur.

⋖ KÜMMEL

Kümmel is generally not too sweet, and most of its flavor comes from caraway seeds. The French Kümmels are sweeter than Berlin or Munich Kümmels, and generally are drunk after dinner. They call it *Aquavit* in Norway and Sweden, *Akvavit* in Denmark. Scandinavian varieties are produced by state monopolies. Other Kümmels come from Danzig, Breslau, Magdeburg, and even Siberia. Goldwasser is Kümmel with coriander and gold flakes. Allasch Kümmel is sweet, flavored with bitter almonds and other herbs.

⋖ MARASCHINO

Best known as a red and sweet flavoring, the cordials are clear in color. The best come from Zada, Yugoslavia, but good ones are also made in Italy.

⋖ OUZO

An absinthe substitute flavored with anise, from Greece.

◄§ PARFAIT AMOUR

An American cordial, purple in color, with a lemon-and-citron flavor.

◄§ PEACH LIQUEUR

Made by steeping fresh and dried peaches in spirits.

◄§ PIMIENTO DRAM

A base of Jamaica rum, with red pepper, spicy and sometimes hot.

◄§ PRUNELLE

Made from plums of the same sort that go into the flavoring of sloe gin, plus other flavorings.

◄§ RASPAIL

Named after the originator of this Monastery Liqueur, who believed in the value of camphor as a protection against plague, and so flavored it.

◄§ RATAFIA

Also called *liqueurs de ménage*, these homemade liqueurs are made by macerating fruits or infusing flowers or other flavorings into brandy or alcohol. Acacia flowers, quince (*coings* in French), even nuts, fennel, and angelica are used to make assorted ratafias, recipes for which are found in French cookbooks.

◆§ ROCK AND RYE

An American cordial made by steeping citrus fruits and others in Rye whiskey. The original version consisted simply of adding rock candy to Rye whiskey; this is still available without the fruits.

◆§ ROSOLIO

A pink liqueur flavored with rose petals and spices, popular in Italy and the Near East.

◆§ SLOE GIN

An American cordial made from the sloe berry, similar to prunelle but with a more pronounced sloe flavor.

◆§ STREGA

The most famous of the Italian liqueurs, of the monastery type, and similar to yellow Chartreuse.

◆§ SWEDISH PUNSCH

A version of Arrack Punsch, with similar flavorings.

◆§ TÍA MARÍA

A coffee liqueur.

✑ TRAPPISTINE

A proprietary of the Monastery type, similar to Bénédictine, and named after Trappist monks.

✑ TRIPLE SEC

The first of the orange-flavored cordials, generally white. The name has come to mean all orange-flavored cordials, such as Curaçao and Cointreau.

✑ VAN DER HUM

Mandarin oranges are the predominant flavor of this South African cordial that has a spicy taste because of the many other flavoring agents used. It is often drunk half and half, with brandy, as Bénédictine sometimes is. *Van der Hum* means "What's his name" in Afrikaans, so named to make it easy to remember.

✑ VIEILLE CURE

A proprietary name for a liqueur that contains some fifty herbs in a base of Armagnac and Cognac. The name means "the old cure," not "the old priest" (*curé*).

✑ WISHNIAK

A cordial flavored with cherries and spices, from Poland.

Bowls, Punches, and Cups

"*Waes Hael*," said the lovely Saxon maiden, as she handed the flowing bowl to good King Vortigern in the year of our Lord 450. When his courtiers explained that she was wishing him luck in the old Saxon tradition, he kissed her pale lips, sipped, seated her beside himself, and personally looked after her health. Thus, the wassail bowl became part of the Christmas tradition in England. The first English drinking pledge was a drink to health at a feast of peace.

Wassail used to be served in shallow wooden bowls bound with silver bands. They were called *mazers*, and it became the custom for carolers to carry the bowl with them on their rounds, offering draughts to those they serenaded; the listener took a sip, then tossed a coin into the bowl. It used to be made of hot spiced ale, with toast floating in it, but the wine of Jerez came to be

345

used. Always there were roasted crabapples bobbing in the wine.
Robert Herrick's verse contains the classic recipe:

> Next crowne the bowl full
> With gentle Lamb's Wool;
> Adde sugar, nutmeg and ginger,
> With store of ale too;
> And thus ye must doe
> To make the Wassaile a swinger.

But he forgot the apples.

The bowl was decked with ribbons and got to be called Lamb's
Wool because of the toast, which ingredient also came to be the
name of the pledge made over a drink. The best modern version
substitutes beaten egg whites for the toast.

Dissolve a cup of sugar in half a cup of water, adding half a
teaspoonful of freshly ground nutmeg and a teaspoon of ginger.
You can also add a half-teaspoonful each of allspice and ground
mace, three cloves, and a small cinnamon stick, if you wish. Bring
this to a simmer, add two bottles of Fino or Amontillado, and bring
this to the simmer. If you use Oloroso, the wassail will be sweeter
and you may want to reduce the amount of sugar. In a punchbowl,
beat the yolks of six eggs until lemony, then fold into them the
stiffly beaten whites. Add the hot wine slowly, stirring steadily, and
drop in six freshly roasted crabapples or love apples. This will serve
a score of people. You can add a cup of brandy if you wish, but
the punch is authoritative enough without it, and is not overly
sweet or rich. Wassail is traditional all through the Christmas season and for Twelfth Night, when the greens come down. *Waes Hael*
means "be hale," and the proper response is *Trink Hael*. The
wassail is traditionally accompanied by songs and revelry and is for
times when joy reigns unrestrained.

Hebe, the daughter of Zeus, was cupbearer to the gods, until she
was replaced by the boy earthling Ganymede, but both of them
served spiced wines, not so different from the punches and bowls
made today. A cup is a punch made in a pitcher, and a bowl has
come to be just another name for a punch. The last word comes
from the Hindustani one meaning "five," because the traditional

punch is supposed to have five ingredients: a base, or diluent, usually of wine, fruit juice, tea, or water; a spirit; sweetening; herbs or spices; and something sour to contrast with the sweetening or another spirit to make it stronger.

Bowls used to be quite distinctive, and one of them is *May Wine*, made by steeping *Waldmeister* (the herb woodruff) in a bowl of new wine, then adding fresh wild strawberries; brandy is also often added. The English went in for other versions, many of them based on milk, like the *syllabub*. Anne Boleyn called it sillybubbles; the way it was made for her was this: whip a quart of heavy cream, adding half a pound of sugar, setting apart some of the froth to serve on top, then add to the remainder a pint of red wine and half a pint of ale; fill the glass halfway with the mixture and top with the whipped cream. But this was a lazy lady's way. The syllabub was originally a posset, made by milking a cow into sweetened beer until the beer frothed. An eighteenth-century recipe gives the principle and the purpose, in rhyme, for the sack posset of a later day:

> From famed Barbados on the western main
> Fetch sugar half a pound; fetch Sack from Spain
> A pint, and from the Eastern coast
> Nutmeg, the glory of our Northern Toast.
> O'er flaming coals together let them heat,
> Till the all-conquering Sack dissolves the sweet.
> O'er such another fire set eggs twice ten,
> New born from foot of cock and rump of hen;
> Stir them with steady hand and conscience pricking
> To see th'untimely end of twenty chicken.
> From shining shelf take down your brazen skillet,
> A quart from gentle cow will fill it.
> When boil'd and cool'd put gentle Sack to Egg,
> Unite them firmly like the Triple League;
> Then covered close together let them dwell
> Till Miss twice sings—"You must not kiss and tell!"
> Each lad and lass snatch up their murdering spoon
> And fall on fiercely like a starved dragoon.

One of the old traditions for the holidays that still continues here and there is *Snapdragon*. A metal dish is bordered with holly, and a stalk of muscatel raisins is set in the center. Brandy is poured over the raisins until they are covered, then set alight, and the revelers take turns snatching the brandied raisins from the burning.

Snapdragon and the *eggnog* carry on the memories of olden days. Eggnog is the modern version of the syllabub. It is supposed to be sweet and rich, but here's a not-so-sweet version: Beat the yolks of six eggs until lemony, adding half a cup of sugar during the beating, then fold in the stiffly beaten whites, into which a quarter-cup of sugar has been beaten. Stir in a pint of heavy cream and one of milk, or a quart of light cream, then add a pint of good Bourbon and half a cup of Jamaica rum. Pour the creamy mass into a punch-bowl and let it chill in the refrigerator for at least an hour. Grate nutmeg over the bowl just before serving. The nog should be very cold, and the colder it is the less sweet it tastes. This batch is nearly three quarts, the average serving is two cups apiece, the average cup holds four ounces, so this should serve a dozen people—twenty if you are offering other drinks. Some people use Rye or Brandy in place of the Bourbon, others add vanilla to the milk, or substitute a pint of vanilla ice cream for the cream, which makes the nog much sweeter. In that case, use only half a cup of sugar in all; you might make the less-sweet version, setting out a sugar bowl beside the punchbowl. Some people reserve a portion of the whites to float on top of the nog. It is important to taste while making, to be sure there is enough whiskey and enough rum.

Mulled wine is usually made to serve a crowd. In two cups of boiling water, simmer the long peels from a lemon and an orange, four or five lumps of sugar, a teaspoonful of allspice and two tea-spoonfuls each of cloves and cinnamon. Add two bottles of young red wine (a Beaujolais would be fine) and bring again to the sim-mer, serving with grated nutmeg on top. If you leave out the herbs, using ice and soda instead of hot water, and the juice of the orange and the lemon, you make a cup that the Spanish call *Sangria*, which is really a pitcher full of Sangarees; this may call for the addition of two or three shots of brandy.

Queen Victoria's recipe for mulled wine was simple; to mull wine, "boil some spice in a little water till the flavor is gained. Then add an equal quantity of good port wine, some sugar and nutmeg. Boil, and serve with crisp unsweetened biscuits."

Vin chaud is still easier to make. Put a spoon in a glass, set a small lump of sugar on the bowl of the spoon, fill with hot red wine, add a twist of lemon, and use a cinnamon stick to stir with.

Glög is the Scandinavian version. Simmer pints of red Bordeaux and Fino or Amontillado Sherry with a cup of Cognac or Armagnac, along with a quarter-cup of sugar and an ounce of bitters—although you can use the mulled wine seasonings instead of the bitters. Almonds and raisins can be added to the pot while the wine comes to a simmer, or can be placed in the Old-Fashioned glasses in which *glög* is usually served. An accompaniment to this is walnuts soaked in Oloroso for a few hours; these can be served hot by bringing the nuts and wine to a boil for a few seconds.

Port Negus was invented by an English colonel in the days of Queen Anne. He came home grouchy one afternoon shortly after the turn of the eighteenth century, having had a miserable afternoon hunting rabbits. His name was Francis Negus, and he loved Port. He dumped a couple of tablespoonfuls of sugar into a pitcher, dissolving it in the same amount of hot water. Then he peeled a lemon, dropped in the peel, then squeezed it, and poured in the juice. He heated a bottle of Tawny Port in a saucepan, poured in the wine, then poured in a cup of boiling water. He served the wine in goblets to his shivering hunting party, grating nutmeg into each glass, and as the quartet of sportsmen began to thaw, spring must have seemed a little nearer.

A single drink of this can be made by rubbing a small cube of sugar on a slice of lemon, dropping this into a goblet with a splash of hot water, then adding two jiggers of Port and filling the goblet with boiling water; a twist of lemon and some grated nutmeg add the needed spiciness. There's a summer version, not invented by the colonel, which calls for cracked ice instead of water and an orange slice for the nutmeg; it's called a *Cobbler*.

Bishop comes from Dutch sailors, who taught it to English tars, who spread it around the Empire. Sailors and soldiers have always been the inventors or discoverers of drinks, warriors in every age bringing home fabulous concoctions that astonish those who stayed behind. The Dutch were great shippers of wines and spirits, and when William and Mary took the throne of England, the sailors' *bisschopp* helped relations to become warmer. An orange is stuck with a dozen cloves and roasted, preferably on the end of a long fork over an open fire, although an oven does as good, if not as cheerful, a job. When the orange is browned, it is quartered and simmered with a bottle of Port for a quarter of an hour. It's served in mugs, with a grating of nutmeg, and some people like to add cinnamon, too. For more sharpness, the juice of half a lemon and its peel can be added at the last minute, with a little sugar if that makes the drink too tart. If it's a gala moment, float a spoonful of brandy on the mug of bishop, and set aflame. Very good with apple pastries or candied apples, a festive Dutch treat. Some people use red Bordeaux instead of Port, but this is not as good, and there's an American version called the Farmer's Bishop, which is made by pouring a pint of brandy into a punchbowl along with the roasted orange, which is sprinkled with sugar. You light the brandy, then douse the blaze with a quart of cider, preferably hard, grating nutmeg and cinnamon on top. Three Bishops, Farmer's or otherwise, are enough for anybody. The first drink makes six servings, the second makes a dozen, and the variations are as wide as your thirst, your stocks, and your imagination.

Hot Toddy is the answer when the weather is chilly or wet and you think you may be coming down with something. It can be made in a bowl or a pitcher, but all that's really needed is hot water and a bottle. Brandy, rum, or whiskey will do. The supply of hot water can be on the stove, on the hob, or in a chafing dish, and to make a drink, you can put a small lump or a sprinkle of sugar in an Old-Fashioned glass, add a slice of lemon stuck with a clove, pour in a jigger of spirits, put in a spoon, and fill with hot water. If you have a cold coming on, add some lemon juice but leave out most or all of the sugar and the cinnamon. If you use half a lemon and rum as your spirit, the result is *grog*.

Fish House Punch is perhaps the most famous punch of all, dating from Ben Franklin's day. Dissolve half a pound of brown sugar in a pint of water or cider, add a fifth or a quart of lemon juice, a fifth of Cognac or Armagnac, and two fifths of Jamaica rum. Half a cup of a cordial (peach brandy or framboise are good) adds that something extra. The punch should be chilled before serving, then poured into the punchbowl with a block of ice; a bottle of soda water can be added. This will serve a score of people twice.

Rum punch is a classic. Here is one of the best versions, which will serve a dozen. Grate the rinds of two lemons into a bowl, add a third of a cup of brown (or white) sugar and a teaspoonful of ginger, and muddle well. Add the juice of the lemons, then pour this into a saucepan, along with a bottle of dark rum and a quart of boiling water. Let this simmer for five minutes or so, then serve in mugs with grated nutmeg. Three limes can substitute for the lemons, a spoonful of allspice or a clove or two can be added, and the drink can be stirred with a cinnamon stick. Some people use coffee or tea instead of water. Ice and soda makes the cold punch. A version that's a single serving, for a nightcap, is made by adding a shot of rum to a cup of coffee, with a little brown sugar and a twist of lemon, plus a cinnamon stick to stir with.

White Wine Punch is made by spiking a couple of bottles of German wine with a quarter-cup of brandy, then adding a quart of soda water just before serving. Frozen fruits, or fresh ones, can be added, and a jigger of a liqueur—cream of mint, for instance—adds the extra something.

Gin Punches are endless, but perhaps the classic is made by adding half a cup to a bottle of sparkling wine, using a jigger of some such cordial as Crème de Menthe or a Triple Sec to bring out the flavors, balancing the whole with the juice of half a lemon or a lime and a little sugar or honey. Gin or rum are the best spirits for bringing out the flavors of fruits and their juices in a punch, each producing distinctive tastes; brandy brings out the taste of wine punches well, and applejack develops the taste of peaches, pears, and apples. The liqueurs add their own special tastes to a punch, projecting their character amazingly. Too much spirit will throw the taste of the punch out of balance; tasting is the only way to judge the right amounts.

A *cup* is a punch in a pitcher. One of the best is made by pouring two jiggers each of brandy, peach brandy, and rum into a pitcher, adding the juice of a lemon and a tablespoonful of sugar, then filling the pitcher with a bottle of sparkling wine. A three-quart pitcher will hold this as well as a slab of ice made by freezing an ice tray without its dividers. This is a version of *Military* Punch, which becomes *Navy Punch* if you add pineapple sticks. By replacing the rum and peach brandy with Chartreuse and Maraschino, you get something entirely different, which is called *Champagne Punch*. If you serve it in a pitcher, though, remember it's called a cup.

Artillery Punch is almost as famous as Fish House Punch. To serve a dozen people, combine in a punchbowl containing a block of ice these chilled ingredients: a quart of strong black tea and one of Rye whiskey, a fifth of dry red wine, a pint of Jamaica rum, half-pints of gin and brandy, a jigger of Bénédictine, a pint of orange juice, and half a pint of lemon juice. Some sugar can be added for sweetening, and lemon peels can be used for decoration. This punch is popular because it is strong but doesn't seem so, the taste of one spirit masking another.

Bombay Punch is also famous, and much better. Combine in a bowl set in crushed ice a fifth of brandy, a fifth of Amontillado, a quarter-cup of Maraschino, a cup of Curaçao, and two quarts of chilled soda water. Garnish with fruits, and just before serving add four bottles of sparkling wine. This will serve thirty or forty people.

The Bar and Its Glitter

Mixed drinks developed in bars, and have become a sort of folk art in the world of drinking, as measured and controlled as the dance. The bartender's movements follow a set pattern, as do his conversation and public personality. The drinks themselves are completely formal. A cocktail is served in a three-ounce stemmed glass, a highball is served in a six-ounce tumbler with two ice cubes and a swizzle stick. There are some twenty kinds of mixed drinks, each made according to a formula, many of them served in special glasses. The formality of the drinks, the mystery and the glitter of the bar combine to give a man a great sense of freedom, alone, apart from the crowd and a part of it. A bar is the perfect atmosphere for a drink. And what a choice there is!

A *Cobbler* is usually served in a footed goblet almost full of pieces of ice and contains a wine or spirit, some flavoring, and fruit. It is traditionally served with a straw and a spoon. For a brandy cobbler, sprinkle the ice with sugar, add a teaspoon of Curaçao and two ounces of brandy, decorating this with a slice of orange or lemon, or fruit of the season.

A *Cocktail* is the result of a mixture of a spirit with a fortified or aromatic wine, or fruit juice, stirred or shaken with ice, then strained into a glass. Nobody knows where the name comes from. James Fenimore Cooper says an Irish barmaid named Betsy Flanagan used to finagle chickens from a Tory farmer during the Revolution, serving them to Washington's officers, and decorating the special drinks she made with a feather from a cock's tail. An unlikely story, but, however it started, there are hundreds of drinks now called cocktails.

The most famous is the Martini—three, four or five parts of gin to one of dry vermouth, stirred in a shaker with ice, and strained into cocktail glasses. Some people make them stronger, others use pale, bleached vermouths, and in Florida and the tropics the liquid ingredients are chilled before mixing so the drink won't be diluted. Stirring is what makes the difference, and many say that a good Martini should be at least a quarter water, so that the two alcoholic ingredients are well married. There seems to be some chemical reaction between gin and vermouth, because one's not enough and two's too many. Authorities say the power of a Martini is psychological; drinkers disagree. A very smooth Martini, without the shudder, can be made with a Fino Sherry, preferably a Manzanilla, mixed six parts gin to one part Sherry. Vodka has now become fashionable for making Martinis, but the taste is somewhat insipid. For a change, people rinse the glass with absinthe or add a drop of bitters. An olive adds to the intensity of the drink, but many people prefer a lemon peel rubbed around the rim of the glass then twisted over the poured drink, so that the lemon oil adds its freshness; some people like the peel in the cocktail. A *Gibson* is a Martini with an onion in it.

A good bartender will chill cocktail glasses, making each round separately; a rule of thumb is to use two or three ice cubes for each drink in the shaker. At home, people often use the cocktail glasses for measures—making a Martini, for instance, by pouring half a glass of vermouth and two of gin into the pitcher, thus making two cocktails plus dividends.

The *Manhattan* calls for one part sweet vermouth and two parts rye or bourbon, although many like more whiskey. A *dry Manhattan* contains dry vermouth in place of sweet and the drink is usually mixed with Martini proportions. Fino Sherries for dry Manhattans and Olorosos for sweet ones make excellent variations.

A *Collins* is served in a tall highball glass that is sometimes frosted and is decorated with orange or lemon slices and a Maraschino cherry. Ice is put into the glass and sprinkled with sugar, then the juice of half a lemon or lime is added, and two ounces of gin or other liquor. This can all be shaken in a shaker, although the traditional way is simply to stir, then fill the glass with soda. The liquor is always added to a drink just before the soda or other mixer.

A *Crusta* is a drink served in a large wine glass the rim of which has been rubbed with lemon, then dipped in sugar. A long and curling peel of lemon or lime is fitted into the glass, with a cube of ice. Into a shaker of cracked ice, put a dash of Angostura bitters, a teaspoonful of Maraschino, the juice of half a lemon, and two ounces of liquor. Shake, then strain into the glass.

Daisies are served in large cocktail glasses or goblets. Grenadine is generally used for sweetening, although cordials may be substituted. Pernod is sometimes used, a dash or two adding sharpness. A teaspoonful of grenadine and the juice of half a lemon are put in a shaker of ice; two ounces of liquor are added. After shaking and straining into the goblet, the drink is topped with soda water.

A *Fix* is a small cobbler, strong and sweet, served in a small tumbler with shaved ice. In the glass, moisten a sprinkle of sugar or a small cube with a teaspoonful of water, add the juice of half a lemon and two jiggers of gin or other liquor, fill with shaved or finely cracked ice, stir gently, decorate with a slice or twist of lemon, and serve with a straw.

A *Fizz* is served in a small highball glass, a jigger of liquor being shaken with a teaspoonful of sugar and the juice of half a lemon. Strain into the glass and top with soda water. Orange or lime is often used for the juice, frequently two of the juices are combined, grenadine is used instead of sugar, and the white or yolk of an egg (or both) often included to make Silver, Golden, or Royal fizzes.

A *Flip* is made with an egg, sugar, and wine or liquor, is usually served in a whiskey-sour glass or a wine glass and dusted with nutmeg. A sprinkle of sugar and an egg are put in a shaker full of ice, three ounces of brandy, or Amontillado or Oloroso Sherry are added, and the drink is shaken and strained into a glass.

A *Float* is made by floating a spoonful of cream on the surface of a liqueur or by filling an Old-Fashioned glass with two cubes of ice and soda, then floating brandy or other liquor on top, by resting a spoon on the surface of the soda and gently pouring the liquor into the spoon.

Frappés are made by filling a cocktail glass with finely cracked or shaved ice, then pouring in the liquor. A perfect after-dinner drink is made by mixing a jigger of gin with a jigger of green crème-de-menthe, then pouring this into the ice-filled glass. Served with a straw.

A *Julep* is made by crushing or bruising fresh mint with sugar in a tall glass, then filling the glass with finely crushed ice and then filling with liquor, working a long spoon up and down in the glass so that it will frost. Any liquor can be used, except in Kentucky, where Bourbon is traditional.

The *Highball* usually consists of two ice cubes, two ounces of whiskey, and two ounces of water or soda, although whiskey tradition originally omitted the ice, calling simply for a splash of water, or perhaps a splash of soda. Even this was a concession, for the only classic way to drink fine whiskey, or whisky, is straight, with perhaps a sip of water now and then from another glass. A recent American version is to pour the whiskey or whisky into an Old-Fashioned glass containing a couple of ice cubes or cracked ice; a twist of lemon is sometimes added to whiskey or whisky served *on the rocks*. If the glass is filled with shaved ice, and then whiskied, the drink is called a *mist*.

A *Puff* is served in a small tumbler and is made by putting two ice cubes in the glass, adding two ounces of liquor and the same amount of milk, filling with soda water, and then stirring gently.

A *Rickey* is made by squeezing half a lime or a lemon quarter into a small highball glass and dropping in the shell, then one or two ice cubes and a shot of liquor, and filling with soda or other mix. Grenadine or sugar is sometimes used, along with other sweet-enings.

Sangaree is the name for two distinct drinks. One is served in a tumbler, with nutmeg on top. A sprinkle or small cube of sugar is muddled in the bottom of the glass with a teaspoonful of water, then ice and a jigger of liquor are added. Any wine can be sub-stituted for the liquor, but all call for a grating of nutmeg.

Another *Sangaree* is made with two shots of Port, or Amontillado or Oloroso Sherry, placed in a tall glass with a sprinkle of sugar and some cracked ice, then filled with water or soda. A pony of brandy and the juice of half a lemon or half an orange can be added to this drink, several of which are usually made in a pitcher and decorated with long peels of an orange and a lemon along with the juice.

Scaffas are potent drinks made by combining liquor and liqueur in a cocktail glass, adding a few drops of Angostura, stirring gently, then serving. A pony of brandy is often combined with Mara-schino, but Bénédictine is generally used with gin, rum, or whiskeys.

Shrubs are served hot or cold from a large pitcher, and are made by soaking fruits in spirits for a few days. Hot water can be added to a mug containing one or two jiggers of the Shrub, or soda water can be added to a highball glass containing ice. A Brandy Shrub is made by adding the juice of six lemons and the peel of two to two bottles of brandy. This is allowed to stand for three or four days, then a bottle of Fino or Amontillado Sherry is added, along with two pounds of sugar. Stir until the sugar has dissolved, then strain through sieve or cloth and bottle tightly. Fruit garnishes are often served in glasses of Shrub. Currant Shrub is made by boiling a quart of currant juice with a pound of sugar for ten minutes and, after this has cooled, adding a quart of brandy. Shrubs made by boiling other fruits generally call for less sugar. Quarts of rum and orange juice, combined with half a pound of sugar, also make a good Shrub.

A *Sling* is a sweetened spirit with bitters, served in a highball glass. A Singapore Sling is made by putting a sprinkle of sugar and a dash of bitters in a shaker full of ice, adding the juice of half a lemon, two ounces of gin and one of cherry brandy, then straining into a tall glass, adding ice, soda, and a twist of lemon or a slice of cucumber; Bénédictine can be added. Pimm's Cup #1 is a Gin

Sling base to which a mixer is added, #2 is a Whisky Sling, #3 is brandy, and #4 is rum and brandy. Southern Comfort can be served the same way.

A *Smash*, or a *Mojito*, is a small julep served in a mug or a small tumbler. A Brandy Smash is made by putting a sprinkle of sugar and a little water in the bottom of a tumbler with some mint, then filling the glass with cracked ice and brandy, the glass being made to frost by working a spoon up and down in the drink. A *Mojito* calls for rum, and the juice of half a lemon or a lime is used in addition to the sugar, mint, and rum.

A *Sour* is made by putting a small sprinkle of sugar and the juice of half a lemon in a shaker full of ice, adding a shot of whiskey and, after the drink is shaken, straining it into a stemmed glass designed for sours; this is decorated with half a slice of orange and a maraschino cherry. The decoration is not necessary, and other liquors can be used. Freshly squeezed lemon juice and some sugar are essential. This drink betrays the use of poor ingredients, and its making is a measure of a good bartender. If the bartender pours prepared lemon juice from a bottle instead of squeezing the lemon as he makes the drink, he has no pride in his craft or is too rushed to make a good drink.

A *Swizzle* is made by twirling a swizzle stick in a glass or pitcher: squeeze half a lime, drop the shell into a highball glass, sprinkle with sugar, add a shot of rum and a dash of bitters, fill the glass with shaved ice, and then swizzle until the drink froths.

A *Toddy* is made by putting a small cube or sprinkle of sugar into a small tumbler, moistening this with water or bitters, then adding two cubes of ice and two ounces of liquor, garnishing with a slice of orange and a maraschino cherry, and serving with a muddler or a spoon, which is used to stir the drink to the desired sweetness. Soda water can be added to fill the glass, or liquor can be used. Some people like to fill the glass with cracked ice. The most popular cold toddy is the Old-Fashioned. Hot toddies usually substitute a clove or a grating of cinnamon or allspice for the bitters, and a twist of lemon for the orange. Maple syrup, brown sugar, honey, or molasses can be used for sweetening. Hot water or cider can be used to fill the glass.

Zooms are made by putting a teaspoonful of honey and a tablespoonful of cream in a shaker full of ice, adding a jigger or two of spirits, then shaking and straining into a wine glass or cocktail glass.

ppendix

359

Buying Wines

It is quite easy to buy wines. No product is better labeled. Almost every liquor store in the country, including the one in the neighborhood, has at least a few standard brands of wines and spirits. But this knowledge is no help when confronted by the hodge-podge on the shelves. Confusion is compounded when the clerk comes up and asks if he can help; odds are that he can't. The bottles are arranged so that the ones you see are the ones you buy, and these may be ones that return the store the largest profit rather than those that offer the most satisfaction.

But the confusion is superficial. The way out of the bewilderment is to buy in the best store in the area, which may very well also be the biggest, with the widest range of choice. The chances are that such a store may have a few representative bottles from at least the great wine districts, and a fair range of spirits. Scouting the shelves is easier when you decide what you are looking for before you go into the shop— Burgundy or Bordeaux, say, or Italian wines or Rhine wines. Even the labels in a single section can be confusing when they are unfamiliar. The easiest way is to shop by mailing piece or advertisement; every store of any standing in the wine and spirit trade will make regular offerings of its stock; by checking these listings, you will have something definite to look for.

You can judge a store quickly by its wine stocks. A poor store will jumble all the wines together, a few cheap regionals and some of the more expensive wines from the most famous regions, but very few wines at reasonable prices in the two- to three-dollar group; the bottles will more than likely be standing up on the shelves; bargain wines and fancy bottles will be prominently displayed. A good store may not have a wide selection but it will be logically arranged; there will be good stocks of table wines costing around two dollars a bottle. An exceptional store will have several two- to three-dollar wines from all the great regions, and a few selections of table wines from the Loire, the Rhône and Alsace, from the Moselle and the Rheinhessen, and from Italy, Austria, Switzerland, and California. A good store will also offer storage facilities, special prices for purchases of two bottles or more, and mixed cases of wines or spirits.

A good test of a store is to see if it is possible to buy a mixed case made up of three to six different wines, at a cost of about twenty dollars for the twelve bottles. If there is a bewildering selection of wines to choose from, you're in a fine store. The way out of the dilemma is to buy a mixed case of white wines, and a couple of mixed cases of red wines, which will delight the merchant. If the wines then delight you your buying problems are over.

If the store is unfamiliar, but the stocks look promising, you might start by buying a mixed case of white wines; perhaps two different Pouilly-Fuissés or whites from the Beaune Slope, two different whites from the Loire or from the Moselle, or a couple from Switzerland, Alsace, or Italy. If you want to try the merchant's red wines, choose pairs from the Beaune Slope, Beaujolais, the Rhône, Italy's Piedmont, or the minor château-bottlings from Bordeaux. There's a way to avoid confusion and doubt—follow the suggestions of the shop owner for some of the wines.

There are fewer white wines in the world than red, so it should be a fairly simple matter to spot a couple of different white wines you want. When a clerk approaches, tell him that you want to buy a few bottles of white wine, and would like to talk to the wine buyer. He is usually the owner or the manager, and you are most apt to catch him in the store in the middle of the morning or the afternoon, at a time when he will have a few moments to talk. Tell him you want to buy a mixed case of whites, indicate the two or three you want, tell him you want to spend less than twenty dollars a case, and ask him what he recommends; if he makes good choices, follow his advice; if he makes poor selections, buy a couple of the wines you have picked out and let it go at that. The transaction should take ten minutes. A few days later, buy a mixed case of reds. Pay by check, so that you can get on the mailing list; mailing pieces from good shops always offer excellent buys.

One of the dangers of wine buying is finding a few you like; the tendency is to stick with these. But the world is full of wines. New York has the best selections of wines in the world, and people from all over the country send their orders to New York; if only to check on local merchants, it's a wise move to get on the mailing list of the top New York stores, such as Sherry Wine & Spirits, 679 Madison Avenue; M. Lehmann, Inc., 40 East 66th Street; Bloomingdale's, Macy's, and Gimbel's. In most states, you can order direct from these stores, or have your local merchant get the wines for you. In addition, watch for wines from this country's two best wine buyers, Frank Schoonmaker and Alexis Lichine. Châteaux-bottlings from Bordeaux are available from many different importers, the quality of the wines depending entirely on how they have been handled and cared for during shipment.

❧ ❧

Stocking Wines and Spirits

The man who has a cellar has a treasure of delight. But few of us have room for large stocks of wine, and the shops must store wines for us. Most of the good ones do, without charge, or a charge of a dollar a case after the first year. As a consequence, a cellar isn't needed for the enjoyment of wines, and all of us can find space for a case or two, on a shelf or in a closet.

The number of wines to keep on hand can be measured by the number of wines drunk in the course of a month. If we have a bottle of wine once or twice a week, and perhaps have guests for dinner every other week, we need a dozen bottles on hand, with perhaps another dozen as a reserve and for variety. It's pleasant to have three or four bottles of a wine on hand, so that we can pull a cork whenever we feel like it and still have a bottle or two left when company comes. A stock of two cases would mean having five or six different wines in the house. People generally like to have two bottles of red wine on hand for every one of white.

Wines are most reasonable when bought by the case, because a case is generally sold at a 5- or 10-per-cent reduction. Most good stores will sell a mixed case, charging the average case price, so that three or four different wines, or even more, can be selected. They will generally do the same thing with spirits. These are wines for current drinking, but if there is some cellar space, most people like to buy some wines to lay away for drinking in the years ahead, when the wines have matured. These *vins de garde* are relatively inexpensive when they come on the market, and increase in price as the years pass. A small cellar of such wines might consist of half a dozen cases, or twenty, depending on your future plans and the availability of wines. Because great vintages come along only two or three times a decade, and the wines may take several years to mature, people usually maintain fairly large stocks. These stored wines are generally what is thought of as a wine cellar, not so much the wines for current drinking. Even with a fairly large stock of laid-away wines, it is a good idea to buy at least a portion of the wines in mixed cases, because some will mature faster than others, and some will never rise to expectations, while others will far exceed them. A large assortment of such wines is generally called a *library*, partly because browsing can be so rewarding.

For current drinking, most of the wines should be young, if only because old bottles are so expensive. The best wines of Bordeaux may take a decade to mature, and top Burgundies may take as long; bought off the shelves of a wine shop, such mature wines will cost five or six dollars a bottle, the high cost taking some of the joy out of the drinking. This consideration affects the choices in the cellar of six cases listed below, the average case price being kept at thirty dollars or less. The ideal way to start a wine cellar would be to buy six cases like these, adding a case or two every month or so, depending on the amount consumed.

This is an excellent way of keeping track of how much you spend on drinkables. Many people don't want to know, of course. Buying by the case may not save a great deal of money, but it saves last-minute trips to the store. Actually, having a stock on hand doesn't seem to increase the amount of drinking in the long run. With wines on hand, however, there's a tendency to drink less hard liquor.

Wines, particularly ones that have been in bottle five or six years, get out of balance when transported. Young wines stand up better to moving. Both can be drunk at once, on the day of delivery, but if there is a delay, the older wines may need a week or so to settle down.

Vibration and temperature change are bad for wines. They should be stored away from light, on their sides so that the corks will stay wet and not shrink. Wines will stay in good condition for six months or longer, if stored on a closet shelf that is 70°, or even warmer, but a cooler temperature is more desirable. The perfect temperature is 55° or cooler, but a wine will keep well if the storeroom is ten degrees above that.

Most people like to keep a record of the wines they drink, something more than an itemized bill, and one of the best records is a collection of the labels themselves, with notes about the wine on the back of the label; some people paste the labels in a book or on a file card.

CASE OF RED BURGUNDIES: One or two wines from the Côte de Nuits, two or three from the Côte de Beaune, these last being ready to drink first, and generally lower in price. In a mixed case, you might buy three or four bottles of one or two wines, the rest in pairs. 2–5 years old.

CASE OF WHITE BURGUNDIES: A Chablis, a Meursault or a Chassagne-Montrachet, a Corton or a Puligny-Montrachet, two Pouilly-Fuissés. 2–3 years old.

CASE OF RED BORDEAUX: One or two wines from the Médoc, Graves, and St. Émilion or Pomerol; château-bottlings, but not from the Grands Crus. 3–5 years old.

CASE OF WHITE WINES: Two or three bottles from Germany, the Loire, Alsace, Graves, Italy, Switzerland. 2–3 years old.

CASE OF RED WINES: Two or three bottles from Beaujolais, Hermitage, or Châteauneuf du Pape, from the Piedmont or Chianti, from the inexpensive châteaux-bottlings of Bordeaux. Young as possible, except for Hermitage (4–6 years old).

CASE OF AMERICAN WINES: Two or three varietals from California, a New York State wine from native grapes, a Chilean white wine, some *rosés* from California. Young, or nonvintage.

When first stocking a cellar, it is desirable to lay in a mixed case of two or three bottles of dry Spanish Sherry, two Ports, and a Madeira, one or two bottles of French and Italian Vermouth, and at least a bottle or two of Champagne or sparkling wine. For more extensive stocks, buy Burgundies and Bordeaux by the case, laying down a case of *vin de garde* for every two cases of wine in your current cellar.

Most people stick to whiskey and gin or vodka, and rarely have a store of other spirits for those moments when a change is called for. Cognac, rum, and cordials are good to have on hand. A young three-star Cognac for mixed drinks; an older Cognac or Armagnac for sipping; both light and dark rum; a marc or calvados or an *alcool blanc*; a bottle of crème de menthe and one or two other cordials might also well be on hand. The cordials might be bought in half-bottles, because they are apt to last for a long time. A bottle of grenadine, or some of the other flavorings, greatly increases the variety of drinks that can be made.

The spirits can be stored on a shelf or in a cabinet, standing, because they do not improve with age or in the bottle, remaining as they were when they were bottled. Racks or bins for the wines are easily made or bought, although a compartmented whiskey case turned on its side serves very well for wines. The white wines should be kept in the coolest spot you can find because they age faster than the red wines.

❦

Glasses

The best glasses are the simplest, with large bowls the size of an apple. Glasses are properly held by the stem, but cupping the bowl is pleasant, because the tulip shape neatly fits the fingers. A wine taster holds a glass by the base, with his thumb on top. It's hard to set down a glass held this way; you have to slide it onto the edge of the table, or transfer it to the other hand.

A highball glass is preferable to the cocktail-sized glasses so often used in restaurants. Often, the best choice is a stemmed water goblet, and ask the waiter to exchange small wine glasses for these. I also often ask the waiter to remove the water glasses when the wine is served, particularly when the table is crowded. Room in the glass, and on the table, is needed to enjoy wine. I like wine glasses that have a flat or curving bottom, except for Champagne glasses, which should be narrow, with the bowl coming to a point so that the bubbles have a source from which to rise. I like tall highball glasses, not too fat, and squat but slim glasses for toddies. For cocktails, the glass I prefer is like a German wine glass with a shorter stem. The whiskey-sour glass is wonderful for drinks that are shaken.

I like the long-stemmed, short-bowl glasses made for German wines because it is pleasing to drink wines from a long-stemmed glass. They're not necessary, though. One style of glass, if it is large—at least six ounces—will do for all wines. The classic shapes all taper in at the top.

But the important thing is glasses that are large enough. They don't have to be filled, but they should have plenty of room, and even a cocktail glass should be part chimney; at least half of a wine glass should be chimney. An attenuated wine glass with a flat bottom to its bowl, one that looks something like a whiskey-sour glass, is the most pleasant shape for brandies and cordials; a larger version is fine for sherries and ports.

 familyولا

Reading Wine Labels

Wines are well identified on the labels, in spite of the trade's urge to present the smallest wines in the grandest style, and explanations are more confusing than the markings that reveal so much of what's inside the bottles. Misleading phrases like "Grand vin," and "Mis en bouteille dans nos caves," are made to sound like legally sanctioned phrases such as "Grand Cru Classé," and "Mis en bouteille au domaine," or "à la Propriété," or "au Château," which indicate estate or château bottlings. But the fake phrases are a give-away, so that the fraudulent wines are easy to identify.

Any confusion arises because table wines are known by the places from which they come or the grapes from which they are made, so that the American concept of brand names does not apply. The names are foreign, but logical, and the systems of marking, rather than the names themselves, serve as guides.

Beaujolais, for instance, is a red-wine-producing district of Southern Burgundy; a wine so marked will be a blend from lesser vineyards. "Beaujolais Supérieur" is a wine that by law must contain an extra half per cent of alcohol, and is a superior blend. Still better wines include the township name, such as "Beaujolais Fleurie," and these are blends from vineyards in the township. The next step up in quality would logically be wine from an actual vineyard, but in Beaujolais this specification is apt to be a pretension because the wines are not so distinctive that a vineyard name is needed to get good bottles. Vineyard names need to be looked for only on great wines from the townships of Bordeaux, Burgundy's Côte d'Or, and Germany's Rhine and Moselle districts, where the more specific labels identify the best wines. Here's what to look for on the labels of wines in the various groupings:

REGIONAL WINES: The name of the region—Bordeaux, Burgundy— identifies the least expensive wines from the region, good blends for everyday drinking. The phrase, "Appellation Contrôlée," is used on all French wines to indicate that the wines meets legal standards set for each region, district, town, and vineyard, and is always an assurance that the wine is authentic. A round, red neck seal similarly identifies regional Italian wines.

DISTRICT WINES: Wines bearing district names—Haut Médoc, Graves, St. Émilion, Pomerol, and Sauternes in Bordeaux; Côte de Nuits or Côte de Beaune in Burgundy; Mosel, Rheingau, Rheinhessen, Rheinpfalz are German examples—are blends from district vineyards and are superior to wines that merely bear the regional names. These are usually well-made wines, suited for regular drinking.

TOWNSHIP WINES: The presence of a town name on a label indicates that the wine is considered better than one bearing only a district name. A wine is marketed with the most specific name to which it is entitled. In many cases, however, the distinction between a district and a township wine is one of price, not quality. Wise buyers often jump from district to vineyard wines, unless they happen upon a particularly good shipper's blend. Town names like Beaune, Pommard, and Volnay, along with the others in Burgundy, are examples of names that may identify a superior wine. The district name is enough on all wines not from the great districts.

VINEYARD WINES: All the great table wines go to market with vineyard names on the label. Vineyard names are important in Bordeaux, Burgundy, and the German districts, but are not usually significant elsewhere. The presence of a vineyard name on a wine from one of the great districts is generally a mark of a superior wine. The best of these vineyard wines are estate or château bottled by the vineyard owner, and his name as "Propriétaire," or "Récoltant," or the name of the actual winemaker as "Viticulteur," "Éleveur," or "Vigneron," will appear on the label. The German phrases will be found in that chapter. Often, the grower sells the wine to a shipper, whose name as "Négociant" will appear on the label, which is not assurance of estate-bottling. To get around this, a "négociant" may often add "propriétaire" to his label, but he then must indicate where his vineyards are; it is of no significance if the word "propriétaire" does not apply specifically to the vineyard in question.

WINES MARKETED BY TYPE: All fortified wines, aromatic wines, and sparkling wines are marketed by type and by brand names, because such wines are normally blended and vineyard names do not apply. The type names indicate degree of dryness, usually, and quality depends on cost and reputation of the brand.

VARIETAL WINES: Alsatian wines, California wines, and others, are marketed under grape names, and such wines are usually superior to those that use only a regional name. The wines are invariably blends, generally of good quality, from districts whose vineyards do not warrant vineyard identification.

GENERIC WINES: Certain wine names from famous European regions and districts have become so famous that they are used all over the world to identify wines that are patterned after the European wines. Such names include Sauterne (without the e in California), Chablis, Burgundy, Rhine Wine, Sherry, Port, and others. These wines are rarely more than ordinary, on a par with French wines that would be labeled "Burgundy," for instance. They are generally low in price, and often better than merely drinkable. The labeling is confusing, and is gradually disappearing.

⋘ ⋙

Ordering Restaurant Wines

Ordering wines in restaurants is an easy matter because the choice is so limited and mark-ups are so high. The restaurateur frequently makes his selection from what is available on the local market, where pickings may be slim, concentrating on a few familiar wines from the important regions because his distrustful customers shy away from wines they have never heard of. Current restaurant practice is to offer wines at two or three times the retail prices, so that even a two-dollar Côtes du Rhône may cost four to six when plunked down on a checkered tablecloth, often even more if the napery is white. Consequently, except for the odd bottle of a famous and high-priced wine to dress his list, impress the pretentious, and coerce the prodigal, the restaurateur further limits his selection to low- and medium-priced bottles, to overcome the prudence of his warier customers. Most of his selections must come from the rarely better-than-ordinary wines from shippers whose distribution is wide and whose blending vats are large. On most lists, one such wine is about on a par with another, all are overpriced, and all are worth little more than a shrug.

A few good restaurateurs are now adopting the enlightened policy of charging the retail price of a wine, plus corkage, which should be no more than a dollar or two a bottle for the extra service and glasses. Such benefactors also search the markets for the good wines of small shippers and make a point of bringing such wines to the attention of their guests. They also make a point of describing a wine accurately in their lists, including the vintage and the producer and the place from which the wine comes, some even going so far as to paste sample labels into the list so that the customer can see beforehand what he is getting. An adequate description of the wines in a list is generally a sign of a well-chosen cellar.

The best test of a good restaurant winecellar is a glance around the dining room. If there is a bottle on one table out of ten, the wines are almost certain to be good and sensible in price. If there is wine on one table out of five, only the most parsimonious, impecunious, or stingy would forgo the joys of the cellar. A second glance should give some idea of which wines are being drunk. This can be gauged according to the shape of the bottles—slope-shouldered ones from Burgundy, the high shoulders from Bordeaux, the slim taper for Rhine wines, or squat Chianti flasks.

If no wine is on the other tables, this *may* be a reflection on the taste of the diners, not the excellence of the cellar. A glance at the wine list will show whether the discerning restaurateur has found some of the several good wines that are in every market; if such wines are there, suggestions as to other and unfamiliar wines deserve to be accepted. This encourages the restaurateur to keep trying to find good bottles in the market, and gives him a chance to build his wine business so that he can buy larger quantities at lower prices, get special shipments from other markets, and widen his selections. Such restaurants deserve to be patronized and recommended, and are invariably willing to stock wines their customers discover, this aid to procurement being considered a duty of wine-drinking diners.

On many wine lists, there are only three or four bottles worth considering. Most of them consist of shippers' wines from the various regions and a few well-known Bordeaux châteaux; Germany is represented by a Liebfraumilch, Italy by Chianti or Valpolicella, Burgundy by Beaujolais. Any of these might do, but if the list also includes a Côtes du Rhône or a Châteauneuf du Pape, a St. Émilion, Loire, or Moselle, a Swiss wine or a California varietal, the list is worth looking over, and the captain's suggestions are most likely worth considering.

In many cases, however, choice is so limited as to be almost nonexistent. The list may look long and imposing. Customarily, there is a page devoted to Champagnes, followed by a list of other sparkling wines. There are lists of Spanish Sherries, of Vermouths, lists of apéritifs, and sometimes a few Ports and Madeiras, the presence of these last two being a good sign. But none of these wines is customarily drunk with main courses, so that for a wine with a meal the place to look is among the listings for table wines—red, white, or *rosé*—which should properly be listed by region or country, the red wines being mostly under headings of Bordeaux, Burgundy, Rhône, and Italy, the whites under the same headings plus Alsace, Germany, and Switzerland. All these are generally concentrated in the middle of the list or book, with California, New York, and other regionals immediately following. A good list is kept up to date, with wines no longer in stock being struck out and wines not ready to drink being left off the list, but as neither of these practices is generally followed, the list of available wines is further reduced. Young wines of Bordeaux and Burgundy's Côte d'Or can be ignored, and anticipation of a chosen wine must be restrained until the bottle is actually brought to the table and the vintage is verified.

It is not unknown to have a young vintage passed off as an older one; winemanship calls for rejection of any substitutions.

Restaurant winemanship also calls for quick and casual reading of a wine list, delay having come to be considered a sign of confusion or even doubt. If the list is badly organized, time taken to find the proper listings is not counted as delay. A common ploy is to leaf rapidly through the lists of sparkling and fortified wines and Bordeaux, to check first the Burgundies, estate-bottlings of which are hard to obtain outside the big cities. This gives the proper picture of speed and decisiveness, at the same time causing a sinking sensation in the breast of the restaurateur, who knows he isn't offering much to choose from, beyond the shippers' regionals, some Beaujolais, and perhaps an ordinary Pommard, Volnay, or Beaune. Anything beyond this deserves attention.

In order to read a wine list quickly, it is customary to order the food first, then decide whether you want a red or white wine. Most people order fowl, fish, or beef in restaurants, so a party of four is apt to select food that goes with either. In such a case, half-bottles of both are called for; ordering a *rosé* is considered to be ducking the problem. For this reason, strong-minded wine drinkers are apt first to select a wine they like, then depend on the captain to suggest the food, thus neatly tossing the burden of decision to him, yet reserving the right to question the choice when later asked if everything has been satisfactory.

Wines are meant to be enjoyed, not analyzed, but there is a need to be able to recognize what it is in a wine that gives pleasure, or detracts from it. This is quite simple when two wines are tasted, a sip of one followed by a sip of the other; one of the wines is likely to be fuller in taste or aroma, fresher or less acid, than the other, and a preference is easy to decide upon. But judging a single wine is another matter, and for comparison one must go to memory. A good wine, of course, should taste good, and anything unpleasant in the taste—a mustiness, excessive flatness or harshness, a taste of grapes and not of wine—indicates that the wine is poor. If any wine tastes or smells of cork, or if a white wine has a strawlike, brackish tang, the wine has gone bad, and can be sent back to the store or the winecellar for replacement. When ordering a wine in a restaurant, it is customary to be presented with the first pouring, in order to judge whether the wine is sound, not so that it can be criticized or praised. And just as you would send back a tough steak or a poorly cooked one, so you should send back a wine that does not taste good. This is quite beyond a matter of personal preference. Nobody has any trouble recognizing a bad steak. It is as easy to recognize a bad wine.

Winemanship aside, the purpose of a wine list is to present the full contents of the cellar to a diner, just as the menu presents the kitchen. As noted, most restaurant wine lists are pretentious and badly organized, while the cellar is constantly being replenished with stocks not yet listed. It is always good sense to ask for suggestions from the captain or wine steward after first checking the general price range in the list. If the unlisted suggestion is average in price it warrants consideration; if it is high in price, or an obvious suggestion like a Great Growth of Bordeaux or Burgundy, the suggestion can be ignored.

Some knowledge of wines locally available is needed in order to enjoy wines simply and casually when ordered in restaurants. When there is doubt, a good but widely distributed wine is often the best choice: a Beaujolais, a good château-bottling from Bordeaux, a Chianti, a California varietal, for the reds; a Loire, a Swiss or Alsatian, an Italian Soave or Orvieto, an estate-bottling from the Rheingau or the Moselle, for the whites. If on the list, a Côtes du Rhône or a Châteauneuf du Pape is invariably a good, inexpensive red-wine choice, a white Burgundy or German wine is a good white wine choice.

Wine-list prices can be checked against the menu, and table wines should not cost more than twice the price of the main dishes. This is not a tight rule, however, because many restaurants feature stews and grillades, cooked foods that call for young wines that are simply hearty in taste and should never cost more than five dollars a bottle. Subtle dishes with sauces are ones that more normally call for the great wines of Bordeaux, Burgundy, and Germany, which may currently cost six dollars and more.

Drinking wines in restaurants adds to the festivity of the occasion, and it is often more of a pleasure to drink two half-bottles of different wines than to drink a single bottle. Since cocktails customarily precede an American dinner, a single half-bottle is often as much as one ought to drink. Still, it's a fine thing to have a white wine with the fish or a light red with the pâté or the first few mouthfuls of the main course, then continue through the cheese with a fuller red wine. Table wines do not taste good with salads containing vinegar, or with desserts, so the wine should be finished before these courses are eaten. A dry Spanish sherry is the perfect drink to precede a meal or to accompany a soup or fish course, so good that it is worth forgoing an extra cocktail—or dispensing with them completely.

It is the Continental custom not to smoke between courses, the practice being modified in the United States so that people generally do not smoke during a course, but this has nothing to do with wine. For smokers, smoking seems to add to the pleasure of drinking wines, and if this isn't annoying to others, there is no reason concerned with wine for refraining.

Wines are listed by number on most wine lists. The number generally refers to the bin in the winecellar, and it is quite proper to order by number and not by name. This is, in fact, considered an acceptable wineman ploy, with the further advantage that the sometimes unfamiliar pronunciation of the wine name can be avoided. It is important to note the vintage, however, because new shipments are often placed in the old bins.

Dry white wines, always drunk before red wines, taste best with fish, sea food, and spiced meats like sausages and delicatessen. They are the wines most commonly drunk with *pasta* in Italy.

Red wines usually taste best with meat and fowl of all sorts.

Rosé wines are drunk in place of white wines, or follow them when a light main course is served, and it has become common to drink them with casseroles and in place of red wines, although they are usually too light for most meats.

Champagnes may be drunk with anything, although they taste best by themselves or with white-wine foods.

Spanish Sherries are most commonly served before meals, with bits of ham and sausage, nuts and olives, cheese and shrimp. The Finos are often served with fish and sea food, with Chinese and other Oriental dishes; the Amontillados are served with soup, lobster, and creamy or spicy dishes. The sweet Oloroso or cream Sherries are served with desserts, particularly cakes and puddings.

Ports and Madeiras are served with desserts, or to finish a meal with nuts, cheese, and fruits.

Sweet white wines—like Sauternes, Tokay, the German Auslesen, and Vouvrays or Saumurs—are served by themselves during the day, with fish and sea food that have sweetish sauces, and with desserts.

These are not inflexible rules, however, but matters of practice, simply indicating the sort of foods with which the wines taste good. An even simpler rule of thumb is to drink wines of the country with national dishes, suiting your own fancy. White and *rosé* wines are always chilled, only light reds like Beaujolais or Bardolino are served cool or at cellar temperatures, other reds being better served at room temperature.

When the wine is excellent in a restaurant, it is customary to mention this to the captain or wine steward in much the way you would express satisfaction to the waiter about food or service.

✍§ *TIPPING*

In a restaurant, it is customary to tip the wine steward or captain who serves the wine; your table waiter is automatically taken care of by the regular tip. In some places, a captain who serves wine does not expect anything extra for that particular duty, the service being part of the attention he pays to you; in a good restaurant, it is proper to give him a dollar for each bottle he serves, but the amount depends on what you customarily give him. If he has been especially attentive for a dinner party, a dollar per person is about right, no matter how much wine he has served. If the wine is handled by a wine steward, he should be given fifty cents or a dollar for each bottle he serves; if he has chosen the wine for you, a dollar is about right if the wine bill is less than ten, two dollars is about right if he has served four people, or two bottles, and five dollars is about right if it has been a large dinner party. Overtipping, particularly in a place where one is a regular customer, is bad form. It is customary to tip wine stewards and captains on the spot, not by adding it to the bill.

ᥱᥤ ᥱᤰ

Wine Etiquette

Although there is great concern about the correct service of wine, there are few rules. The host always opens and pours the wine, never the hostess. It is customary for the host to pour the first few drops into his own glass, the original idea being that any bits of cork would go into that glass, not those of the guests. If a waiter or butler pours the wine, he also pours the first few drops into the host's glass, at which time it is customary for the host to smell, and even taste, the wine to make sure it is sound; he then nods so that the servant can pour wine for the others, first the ladies and then the men. This procedure can be followed with each bottle, but it should always be done as quickly and unobtrusively as possible. After the first service, the host may do the pouring, or may ask one of the other men at the table to replenish the glasses, if that is convenient and formality is not necessary. In a restaurant, the captain or steward generally does the pouring, although the host may do so. When everybody has been served, the host takes the first sip to signify that the wine is ready for drinking, usually giving some salutation or a toast; today, the host may ask the hostess to make the toast, or even the guest of honor, although this is not proper in the old tradition, which required that the host first salute his guests before any other toasts. Even at a buffet dinner, the host pours the first glass of wine, although the bottles can then be left on the sideboard and the guests can help themselves; it is customary for the man to pour the wine for his dinner partner, never the reverse, even when there are individual carafes at each setting. In public, a woman never pours the wine if a man is present; this is the major rule in modern wine etiquette. If there is no host, the hostess will ask a male guest to pour the wine.

A minor rule of etiquette is that the wine is poured after the food has been served. A wine glass is never filled more than half way, and it is customary to have a separate glass for each wine served.

ᥱᤰ DECANTING

Young wines develop in the presence of air, seeming to lose any tendency to hardness, which is one reason why so many fruity wines seem to taste better as the meal progresses. But this is not so true of old wines, those ten years and over, although a few minutes of exposure to the air may rid the wine of any mustiness or other slightly undesirable qualities that may result from being so long in bottle. It is the current opinion that aldehydes, rather than esters, contribute most to a wine's bouquet, and these do not develop appreciably in contact with the air. Consequently, old wines probably should not be decanted, but be poured carefully from the bottle, not more than a couple of hours after opening. Such wines should still be swirled in the glass, though, so that the evaporating alcohol will release the bouquet.

꯴ ꯶

Winemanship

The long history of wine, with its intimations of regality and splendor, is frightening to the uninitiated, and this apprehensiveness has created an aura about the whole business of drinking. The natural and easy act of sipping is impressive, if only because what's sipped is considered to be rare and expensive. But to preserve the enjoyment of wine drinking, it is necessary to separate from it as much pretension as possible, and this calls for winemanship, and calls for restraint.

There is really nothing one can do when a portly, smirking sommelier bends low before you, hissing ingratiatingly, and sweeps open an oversized ornate book containing lists of wines contained in the cellar. This behavior is an insult to the human condition and to the simple nature of wines. But he is a product of that segment of the restaurant world where servility is considered service, and he is not easily to be avoided. Winemanship calls for doing nothing but ordering as quickly as possible, with the instruction that you will personally handle the pouring, and the information that you will tip him accordingly if he will leave you alone. Winemanship calls for ridding the surroundings of irritations as quickly as possible.

Many waiters and captains are a servile lot because they are serving, not being served. Winemanship calls for accepting the service as a business, a profession, or an art, depending on which level it is being offered. In each case, quickness is desirable, but not haste, and a wineman will recognize the caliber of the waiter and suit his ordering to that level. A businesslike waiter may attempt to take control by saying, "I'll take your order now." If you are ready, all is well; if you are not, the only answer is, "I'll give my order later." A truly professional waiter might say, "We are ready to serve you," and an artful waiter might say, "Are you ready to be served?" The wineman understands that the decision rests with him, and he will try to take advantage of the service when it is offered by getting the orders promptly from his guests. But the guests are the important thing, and the waiter waits, unless the wineman feels that the waiter can be told to get orders from each guest; a wineman never lets the waiter do this without permission.

The greater the wine, the more flurry is connected with its serving, so the wineman has a tendency to avoid ordering great wines. If the wine steward suggests such a wine, in an effort to jack the check, the wineman promptly says he would like something else. If the steward holds back the wine list, or makes unsolicited suggestions, the wine-man simply asks to see the list, even though he is then put in a position to choose promptly. In any event, the more flurry from the steward, the simpler the wine that is chosen, and the smaller the tip. A Beaujolais is preferable to pomp.

The worst restaurant pretension is the use of baskets, which are rarely necessary, even for ten-year-old wines. A basket, with its broad base, is somewhat more stable than an upright bottle on the usual small restaurant table. But if there is room, the wineman always asks that the basket be removed, if only because he wants to watch the level of the wine in the bottle in order to see any sediment as he pours. He usually prefers to pour his own wine, because waiters do it too rapidly, and rarely watch for sediment, which doesn't hurt the wine at all, but which is not good to drink.

If the wine is corky, maderized, or otherwise bad, the wineman says to the waiter, "This wine is bad." The waiter usually calls the captain or the steward, and the wineman repeats the simple remark. If the bottle is not removed at once and replaced with another, the wineman asks that it be taken away. If the bad wine appears on the bill, the wineman asks for the steward or the captain, and says, "You have charged me for the bad wine." If any question is raised, the wineman pays the bill, showing no concern and never arguing, and scratches the restaurant off his list.

If a wineman can't find a wine he wants on the wine list, he orders beer or another round of drinks.

The wine should be served first to the man who has ordered it. If the waiter does not know this, and starts pouring first for one of the ladies, the wineman tells the waiter to let him taste the wine. When it is poured in his glass, he tells by a sniff if the wine is sound. There is rarely the need to taste the wine, unless there is a corky smell, or a white wine is too brown in color, or unless the wine is clouded; even so, he might avoid tasting the wine because it would taste bad. He simply says, "The wine is bad," then asks for another bottle.

Winemanship is not a matter of establishing one's own position, of showing off, or of making the restaurant personnel uncomfortable. It is simply a matter of getting the wines you want with a minimum of attention and fuss. Winemanship also involves the responsibility of rejecting bad wines, and seeing to it that the service is done simply and well. In many cases, this is a matter of telling the waiter what to do, with as few words as possible, or showing by example how simply wine can be ordered, tasted, and drunk. Sometimes this can be uncomfortable. But usually the mistakes and pretensions are slight, and more amusing than irritating, calling for a laugh rather than a scowl.

꡴꠹ꢀ

Bibliography

Wines have been written about for a couple of thousand years, and while many of the books are fascinating, only the modern ones contain practical information for the wine buyer today. One of the best general books, with excellent material on the recent history of wine and its chemical properties, is L. W. Marrison's *Wines and Spirits* (Penguin). For further material in English on French wines, I must express a preference for *Wines of France* (Knopf), which I wrote with Alexis Lichine. For German wines, my preference is Frank Schoonmaker's *Wines of Germany* (Hastings House), although I have also enjoyed perusing *Rhineland Vineland* by S. F. Hallgarten, published in England by Paul Elek, and Langenbach's *Wines of Germany*, also first published in London. For Italian wines, see a government publication called *Italian Wines and Liqueurs*, by R. G. Dettori, and for Ports there is the excellent but privately printed *Port Wine and Oporto*, by Ernest Cockburn. André Simon, P. Morton Shand, and H. Warner Allen have all written extensively on wines and spirits, particularly the individual books in the Constable Wine Library series, while R. Postgate and T. E. Carling have written popular short guides, the first for the consumer, the second for the London trade. The best book on American wines is Philip M. Wagner's *American Wines and Wine-Making* (Knopf). And there is Roger's book on *Bordeaux* (Scribners).

If language is no barrier, the most complete works on French wines are the separate atlases published for each major district by Lamart, complete with maps and photographs, for the Appellation d'Origine, the out-of-date compendium on Bordeaux wines by Cocks and Feret, and the still more outdated *Le vin de Bourgogne* by Camille Rodier. Two classic texts are Basserman-Jordan's massive work on German wines and M. M. Gonzalez Gordon's book on Sherry.

As for spirits, my favorite book about Scotch is Sir Robert Bruce Lockhart's *Scotch* (Putnam), although I've also enjoyed J. M. Robb's and the one called *Whisky* by Aeneas MacDonald. The classic text on Cognac is *Histoire du Cognac* by Delamain. I know of no good book on Bourbon, or other spirits.

Of the older books, I still use Frank Schoonmaker's *Wine Dictionary* (Hastings House) and I also like to look over *The Complete Wine*

Book by Schoonmaker and Marvel (Simon and Schuster). *Grossman's Guide to Wines, Spirits and Beers* (Scribner) contains information on bar management and other retailing matters. For detail about wine production in California, Amerine and Joslyn's *Table Wines* (University of California) contains many scientific facts, an excellent listing of recent papers, and a scientific description of fermentation which delights me: ". . . a process of a series of reversible inter- and intra-molecular oxidation-reductions, phosphorylations, and an irreversible decarboxylation." The definition continues from there; if this is the sort of specific thing you want, here is the book for it.

Nobody can get the feeling of wine literature, however, without reading George Saintsbury's *Notes on a Cellar Book* and *In Search of Wine* by Charles Walter Berry. These are the two classics of the post-Edwardian era, their American predecessor being Emerson's two-volume work, *Beverages Past and Present*, which is a sort of golden bough of drinking lore. Of the Victorians, the most interesting are Redding and the books by the Vizetelly family.

Other interesting writers on wines include Maurice Healy (*Stay Me with Flagons*) and G. B. Stern (*Bouquet*), as well as Julian Street, Ernest Peixoto, and Berton Roueche, whose *New Yorker* series on alcohol, *The Neutral Spirit*, was later published as a book by Little, Brown. English literature, of course, is full of wines, among books worth noting being Meredith's *The Egoist* and Belloc's *The Path to Rome*.

Books on food and cookery that contain references to wines, particularly the unknown country wines of France that never leave the district, are Austin de Croze's *What to Eat and Drink in France* (Warne), written during the Depression, and the recent *Food of France* by Waverley Root (Knopf). *Italian Bouquet* by Samuel Chamberlain (Gourmet) has good notes on Italian wines. In addition, the books of James Beard contain excellent wine material, as do the classic French cookbooks.

Generally, wine is meant to be drunk, not read about, but there is a certain pleasure in being familiar with the literature, particularly Saintsbury and Charles Berry, Emerson and Redding, the Constable Wine Library, and the still-untranslated foreign classics. Reading them is something like raising a glass with another generation and makes one part of the long history that reaches beyond Rabelais and Chaucer, Herodotus and Noah, giving the feeling that wine will gladden the heart of man until the end of time.

⋙⋘

Trade Abbreviations

A—Amontillado
a.—are, 100 square meters
A.B.C.—Alcoholic Beverage Control (Board)
abf.—abfüllung
A.B.I. Permit—Alcoholic Beverage Import Permit
A.D.E.B.—Association pour le développement de l'exportation des vins de Bordeaux
alc.—alcohol
Amont.—Amontillado
A°—anno
a/R.—am Rhein
Artis.—Artisans
A.T.U.—Alcohol Tax Unit
B & B—Bénédictine and Brandy
B & S—Brandy and soda
B/B—Bottled in Bond
Bbn.—Bourbon
B.E.B.—Best Ever Bottled
Belles—Bouteilles
B.I.B.—Bottled in Bond
Bord., Bordx.—Bordeaux
B.P.S.—British plain spirits
bot.—bottle, bottled
bbl.—barrel
Burg.—Burgundy
B.W.—Bonded Winery, Bonded Warehouse
C.E.—Cuvée Extra
Ch.—Château
Champ.—Champagne
Chât.—Château
Châtau—Château
Cia.—Compañia

Cie.—Compagnie
C.I.F.—cost, insurance, and freight
Cr.—Croix
Cresc.—Crescenz
D.—dash, distillery
D. & R.—Distiller and Rectifier
D.C.L.—Distillers Company Limited
décl—$\frac{1}{10}$ liter, 3.38 ounces
Dist.—Distiller, distilled, distillery, district
Disty.—Distillery
dkl.—decaliter
dl.—deciliter
Dom.—domestic
D.O.M.—*Deo Optimo Maximo* (To God, most good, most great)
D.P.—Duty Paid
dy.—duty (tariff)
E-B.—Estate-bottling
E.M.—English market
Et.—Établissement
Ex.—Extra
F.A.S.—Free alongside steamer
F.C.—Fine Champagne (Cognac)
fgn.—foreign
F.O.—Fine Old
F.O.B.—Fine Old Blend
F.O.E.S.—Fine Old Extra Special
frs.—francs
gal.—gallon, 3.78 liters
g.n.s.—grain neutral spirits (alcohol)
ha.—hectare, 10,000 square meters, 2.47 acres

hecto.—hectoliter, 26.42 gallons

hhd.—hogshead

H^{nos.}—Hermanos (brothers)

I.B.—In Bond

imp.—imported

I.N.E.—Instituto Nazionale per L'Esportazione (National Export Institute of Italy)

I.R.—Internal revenue

kg.—kilogram, 2.2 pounds

l.—liter, 33.81 fluid ounces

Lda.—Limitada

Ltd.—Limited

m.—meter, 39.37 inches

M. d Ch.—Mis du Château (Château-bottled)

mm.—millimeter

n.g.s.—neutral grain spirits

N.P.U.—*Ne plus ultra*

N.V.—Nonvintage

o.p.—over proof

orig.—original

pf.—proof

p.g.—proof gallon

puns.—puncheons

putt.—puttonyo

P.X.—Pedro Ximénez (blending Sherry)

P.X.V.—Pedro Ximénez Viejo (blending Sherry)

R. & R.—Rock and Rye

R. C. Bordx.—Registre du commerce, Bordeaux

Rect.—Rectifier

rep. pt.—reputed pint (1/12 imperial gallon)

rep. qt.—reputed quart (1/6 imperial gallon)

R.L.—Restaurant Liquor License

R.L.D.—Retail liquor dealer

R.W.—Restaurant Wine License

S.A.—*Société Anonyme* (French)

S/A.—*Società Anonima* (Italy)

Saut.—Sauternes

Sawfa.—South African Wine Farmers Association

S. en C.—Sociedad en Comandita (limited partnership company)

S.F.C.—Superior Fine Cognac

S.L.A.—State Liquor Authority

S.O.—Superior Old

S^{te.}—Société

Ste. A^{me}—*Société Anonyme* (French)

str.—straight

Sucrs.—Sucesores

sup.—supérieur

u.p.—under proof

U.S.P.—United States Pharmacopoeia

U.S.S.G.—U.S. Storekeeper-Gauger

V. de P.—Vino de Pasto

V.F.C.—Very Fine Cognac

vint.—vintage

V.O.—Very Old

V.O.P.—Very Old Pale

V.O.T.—Very Old Tawny

V.O.X.—Very Old Xerez

V.S.—Very Superior

V.S.O.—Very Superior Old; Very Special Old

V.S.O.P.—Very Superior Old Pale

Vve.—veuve (widow)

V.V.O.—Very Very Old

V.V.S.—Very Very Superior

W.—Retail Wine License

W.D.W.—Wholesale dealer in wines

w.g.—wine gallon

W.W.—Wholesale Wine License

W^{we.}—Witwe (widow)

❦ ❧

Metric System of Weights and Measures

MEASURE OF LENGTH

Kilometer	= 1,000 m.	= 0.62137 mile, or 3280 ft. 10 in.
Meter		= 39.37 in.
Decimeter	= 0.1 m.	= 3.937 in.
Centimeter	= 0.01 m.	= 0.3937 in.
Millimeter	= 0.001 m.	= 0.03937 in.

MEASURE OF SURFACE

Hectare	= 10,000 m²	= 2.471 acres
Are	= 100 m²	= 119.6 sq. yds.
Centare	= 1 m²	= 10.7639 sq. ft.

LIQUID MEASURE

Hectoliter	= 100 liters	= 26.4178 gals.
Liter		= 33.81 fl. oz., or 1.0567 qts.
Deciliter	= 0.1 liter	= 3.381 fl. oz.
Centiliter	= 0.01 liter	= .3381 fl. oz.
Milliliter	= 0.001 liter	= .03381 fl. oz.

WEIGHT

Kilogram or Kilo	= 1,000 grams	= 2.2046 lbs.
Gram		= 0.0353 oz.

৺ CONVERSIONS

CHANGE FROM	TO	MULTIPLY BY
acres	hectares	.4047
feet	meters	.3048
gallons	liters	3.7853
inches	centimeters	2.54
miles	kilometers	1.6093
ounces avdp.	grams	28.3495
pounds avdp.	kilograms	.4536
quarts	liters	.9463
yards	meters	.9144
Fahrenheit	Centigrade	minus 32 times 5/9
Centigrade	Fahrenheit	times 9/5 plus 32

~§ ह~

Pronunciation

Pronunciations aren't to be worried about, nonchalance being the most satisfactory attitude, but here are a few wine names that one might choose to be particular about.

Aloxe-Corton   ah-lohss cor-tawn
Amontillado   ah-mawn-tee-*yah*-do
Anisette   ah-nee-set
Armagnac   ahr-mahn-yack
Barolo   bah-*ro*-lo
Barsac   bar-sahck
Beaujolais   bo-zho-lay
Beaune   bone
Boal   bo-*wahl*
Bonnes Mares   bon mar
Bourgogne Blanc   boor-go-nyuh blahn
Calvados   cahl-vah-dose
Capri   *cah*-pree
Chablis   shah-blee
Chambertin   shahm-behr-tan
Chartreuse   shahr-truhz
Châteauneuf-du-Pape   shah-to-nuhf dew pap
Chianti   *kyahn*-tee
Clos de Bèze   klo duh behz
Clos de Vougeot   klo duh voo-zho
Cognac   cone-yack
Corton   cor-tawn
Côte Rôtie   coat-ro-tee
Crème de Cacao   crem duh cah-cah-oh (or cah-cow)
Crème de Cassis   crem duh cahs-seess
Crème de menthe   crem duh mahnth

Curaçao   cue-rah-so
Dubonnet   dew-bawn-nay
Eau de vie de Marc   oh dvee duh mar
Échezeaux   eh-sheh-zo
Fino   *fee*-no
Gevrey-Chambertin   zhuh-vray shahm-behr-tan
Gewürz-Traminer   guh-*veertz* trah-*mee*-ner
Graves   grahv
Haut Sauternes   oh so-tairn
Hermitage   air-mee-tahz
Hochheim   *hock*-hime
Hospices de Beaune   ahs-pees duh bone
Johannisberg   yo-*hahn*-nees-bairg
Juliénas   jool-yay-nah
Kirsch   keersh
Kümmel   *Kim*-muhl
Lacryma Christi   *lah*-cree-mah *crees*-tee
Liebfraumilch   *leeb*-frow-meelsh
Mâcon   ma-cawn
Madeira   mah-*day*-rah
Malaga   *mah*-lah-gah
Manzanilla   mahn-tsah-*nee*-yah (or mahn-thah-*nee*-yah)
Marsala   mar-*sah*-lah
Médoc   may-dawk
Mercurey   Mare-cue-ray
Meursault   mure-so

Montilla mawn-*tee*-yah
Montrachet mawn-rah-shay
Moselblümchen mo-zuhl-*blim*-chen
Moulin-à-Vent moo-lan ah vawn
Musigny moo-zeen-yee
Nebbiolo nehb-*byo*-lo
Neuchâtel nuh-sha-tell
Nierstein *neer*-shtine
Nuits-St. Georges nwee san zhorzh
Oeil de perdrix uhl duh pare-dree
Oloroso oh-lo-*ro*-so
Orvieto or-*vyeh*-to
Pomerol pom-roll
Pommard po-mar
Puligny-Montrachet poo-leen-yee mawn-rah-shay
Pouilly-Fuissé pwee-yee fwee-say
Pouilly-Fumé pwee-yee foo-may
Quetsch ketsh
Quinquina can-kee-nah
Richebourg reesh-boorg
Riesling *rees*-ling
Rioja ree-*oh*-hah
Romanée ro-mah-nay
Rosé ro-zay
St. Émilion san-tay-mee-yawn
Sangiovese san-jo-*vay*-zay

Saumur so-muhr
Sauternes so-tairn
Sercial *sehr*-see-ahl
Slivovitz *shlee*-vo-veets
Soave so-*ah*-veh
Steinwein *shtine*-vine
Sylvaner sil-*vah*-ner
Tavel tah-vell
Tequila teh-*kee*-yah
Tokay Aszu to-*ki* ahs-*tzoo*
Tokay Szamorodni to-*ki* sha-muh-*rud*-nee
Traminer trah-*mee*-nur (or trah-mee-nair in Fr.)
Valpolicella val-po-lee-*chehl*-lah
Verdicchio vehr-*deek*-kyo
Vernaccia vehr-*nach*-chyah
Vin Santo veen *sahn*-to
Vino de Pasto *vee*-no deh *pahs*-to
Volnay vawl-nay
Vöslau *fuss*-lah-oo
Vosne-Romanée vone ro-mah-nay
Vouvray voo-vray
Würzburg *veerts*-boorg
Zeltingen *zell*-ting-en
Zinfandel zin-fan-dell
Zubrovka tsoo-*broff*-kah

꧁ ꧂

Index

About the Author

William E. Massee was in Paris writing documentary films a dozen years ago when he was asked by an importer to collaborate on a book on French wines. The result was a five-month trip through the great wine regions, tasting as many as fifty wines a day, and *Wines of France*, written with Alexis Lichine. Since then, he has written a *Wine Handbook* for the novice, hundreds of articles for magazines and newspapers, and an advertising column on wines and spirits. Today he is a consultant on public relations and advertising to the wine and spirit trade, and is now completing a book on regional and classic dishes and the wines that go with them. Mr. Massee is married to the artist Dorothy Ivens, who contributed the jacket design and drawings for this book.